Badfellas

Paul Williams is Ireland's most respected crime writer and journalist. Williams has been on the frontline of crime journalism in Ireland for almost twenty-five years exposing the crime lords and their rackets. A qualified criminologist, he has won a string of major awards for his courageous journalistic work, including Print Journalist of the year, Campaigning Journalist of the year, the Humbert Summer School International Media Award and the Irish Security Industry Association's Premier Award. His previous best-sellers include *The General*, *Gangland*, *Evil Empire*, *Crime Lords*, *The Untouchables* and *Crime Wars*. Williams has researched, written and presented a number of major TV crime series, including award-winning *Dirty Money* (TV3) and *Bad Fellas* (RTÉ). He is a member of the internationally respected International Consortium of Investigative Journalists (ICIJ) based in Washington DC.

Badfellas

PAUL WILLIAMS

PENGUIN

IRELAND

PENGUIN IRELAND

Published by the Penguin Group
Penguin Ireland, 25 St Stephen's Green, Dublin 2, Ireland
(a division of Penguin Books Ltd)
Penguin Books Ltd, 80 Strand, London WC2R ORL, England
Penguin Group (USA) Inc., 375 Hudson Street, New York, New York 10014, USA
Penguin Group (Australia), 250 Camberwell Road,
Camberwell, Victoria 3124, Australia (a division of Pearson Australia Group Pty Ltd)
Penguin Group (Canada), 90 Eglinton Avenue East, Suite 700, Toronto, Ontario, Canada M4P 2Y3
(a division of Pearson Penguin Canada Inc.)
Penguin Books India Pvt Ltd, 11 Community Centre,
Panchsheel Park, New Delhi – 110 017, India
Penguin Group (NZ), 67 Apollo Drive, Rosedale, Auckland 0632, New Zealand
(a division of Pearson New Zealand Ltd)
Penguin Books (South Africa) (Pty) Ltd, 24 Sturdee Avenue,
Rosebank, Johannesburg 2196, South Africa

Penguin Books Ltd, Registered Offices: 80 Strand, London WC2R ORL, England

www.penguin.com

First published 2011
2

Copyright © Paul Williams, 2011

The moral right of the author has been asserted

Set in 12/14.75 pt Bembo Book MT Std
Typeset by Jouve (UK), Milton Keynes
Printed in Great Britain by Clays Ltd, St Ives plc

A CIP catalogue record for this book is available from the British Library

ISBN: 978-1-844-88271-7

www.greenpenguin.co.uk

Dedicated to the memory of innocent businessman Roy Collins,
who was murdered because his family stood up to evil.
And to his courageous father, Steve, who has become a voice
for the silent majority whose lives have been blighted
by organized crime.

Also to the memories of all the innocent people whose
lives have been cut short by Gangland killers.

Contents

Contents

Introduction

Since the late 1960s a nasty, brutal and violent parallel universe called Gangland has evolved in Ireland. Over the past four decades this dark underworld has destroyed countless lives, demoralized whole communities, and even threatened to undermine the commercial and social cohesion of an entire city. This is the world of organized crime, where life is cheap and the wages of sin are irresistibly tempting. Here power is seized by force, maintained through fear, and lost by the assassin's bullet.

Badfellas is the story of how organized crime has gained a foothold in Irish society over the past forty years. It reveals how a generation of young petty thieves, delinquents and so-called revolutionaries emerged in the 1960s to bring an end to an era of superficial innocence. These new criminals were the founding fathers of Gangland. Together they ushered in a culture of guns and narcotics, murder and mayhem – and an alternative economy which today is worth over €1 billion a year.

This book tells the story of how organized crime evolved in each of the four decades, illustrating how the foundations were laid for the violent gang culture we have today. *Badfellas* tells the stories of the major players and events which have moulded the criminal underworld. It also examines how crime levels on the streets of the Republic were influenced by the fallout from the Northern Troubles and charts how the Godfathers and paramilitaries became indistinguishable from each other – and collectively tried to intimidate and undermine the wider society.

Badfellas provides a chilling insight into the phenomenon of the gangland murder, which first appeared in 1982 and which has escalated dramatically ever since. It traces the genesis of the gang wars in the Noughties, which were fuelled by the excesses of the Celtic Tiger, and claimed 200 lives in the process.

As Ireland continues to struggle under crippling debt and economic meltdown, the one group that will not accept redundancy are the citizens of Gangland. *Badfellas* tries to give an understanding of how we got to this stage in our social history – and how the story is far from over.

Welcome to *Badfellas*.

Paul Williams
October 2011

PART ONE

The Late 1960s and 1970s

1. The Beginning

Easter Sunday, 10 April 1966

Soldiers, airmen and sailors paraded in step down Dublin's O'Connell Street, to the rousing drums of army bands. As they trooped past the reviewing stand in front of the GPO, the rumble of a 21-gun salute, coming from the grounds of Trinity College, could be heard in the background. Fighter jets and helicopters performed a flyover and then, as the Tricolour was raised, soldiers manning the ramparts on the roof fired a volley of shots in unison. Over 200,000 people were crammed into Dublin city centre, craning to catch a glimpse of the pomp and ceremony. Ireland was commemorating the Golden Jubilee of the 1916 Easter Rising – and celebrating it as the catalyst of the hard-won Independence which followed. The ceremony was a hugely symbolic milestone in the history of the young Irish Republic. It was an opportunity to display the new State's pride in the past and hopes for the future. Ireland was showing the world it had become a modern, peaceful, independent nation.

President Eamon De Valera, one of the original leaders of the Rising, took the salute. He stood on the steps of the historically iconic building, where fifty years earlier his comrade Padraig Pearse had read out the Proclamation of the Irish Republic to the bewildered Dubliners who were taking the air on the sunny, spring holiday. Within a week, the city centre was in ruins and Pearse and most of his fellow leaders were awaiting execution. The aftermath fuelled a new quest for freedom and was followed by the War of Independence and a treaty with Britain that led to civil war. Out of the blood and ashes emerged the Irish Free State. The Golden Jubilee remembering the Rebellion, and those who gave their lives for freedom, was an opportunity to consign the deeply divisive wounds of the Irish Civil War to the history books. The Republic was looking to the future with a new optimism.

In his address to the crowds De Valera declared: 'Thanks be to God the dissensions and differences we have had down here [the South], they are now past, we are all on the straight road, marching again, side by side.'

But the 84-year-old President, the 900 medal-wearing veterans and the politicians who shared the reviewing stand could not have imagined where that 'straight road' was leading. Within a few short years the decades of peace the country had enjoyed since the Civil War would be shattered and forgotten, as terrorists and criminals brought the gun and the bomb back to the streets of Irish cities and towns.

The 1966 commemoration was a watershed in the history of organized crime in Ireland. It marked the twilight years of what many would come to regard as an Irish age of innocence. Behind the peaceful façade, a generation of juvenile delinquents were already cutting their criminal teeth.

Former Detective Superintendent Mick Finn spent thirty years as a cop in Store Street Station, in Dublin's 'Charlie' or C District HQ. The police of C District covered the commercial heart of the city around O'Connell Street, as well as some of its most deprived residential areas. It holds the record of being the busiest police station in the country since the foundation of the State. Finn remembers the 1960s as an era of innocence: 'When you went out on the beat you had a baton, a whistle and perhaps a torch. There were very few patrol cars; there was one uniformed patrol car and a car for detectives. The crimes were innocent by comparison with today – mainly break-ins to shops, warehouses and stores and there was some pickpocketing and bicycle thefts. You also had break-ins into public houses or post offices, where professional safe crackers blew the safes and stole cash and insurance stamps. Within a decade or so that was all to change very dramatically.'

Despite its violent origins, Ireland had been an extraordinarily peaceful and law-abiding society since the establishment of the Free State. In fact the crime rate was so low that the Garda Síochána was allowed to decline in strength and there were discussions in Government about the viability of keeping some prisons open. In 1951 there were 6,904 Gardaí, but by 1963 that had fallen to 6,401. But behind the scenes a whole series of events and social factors were conspiring to create a period of unprecedented turmoil and crisis in Ireland. As the military forces marched in step down Dublin's main boulevard, the leaders of the Republic strained to avoid mentioning the elephant in the room – Northern Ireland. Its partition as a separate State from the rest of the country in the Treaty that ended the War of Independence was the reason for the Civil War. It had remained a ticking time bomb since then – and an explosion was imminent.

Sectarian apartheid against the minority Catholic/Nationalist population by the Protestant/Unionist majority, and the denial of their basic civil rights, had turned the six counties into a tinder box. Both communities feared and loathed each other in equal measure. The 1916 Jubilee commemoration gave Loyalists an opportunity to intensify their persecution of Catholics. The terror group the Ulster Volunteer Force would officially declare war on the IRA, which was largely dormant at this point. Their only military act in years had been blowing up Nelson's Pillar, in the middle of O'Connell Street, a few months before the celebrations. The commemorations also gave a political platform to the Rev. Ian Paisley, an implacable enemy of nationalists, the Republic and the Roman Church. He marked the occasion with a thanksgiving ceremony to thank the Lord that the Rebellion had been defeated. Over the next few years, the Northern Government feared it was losing its stranglehold over the Catholic population and literally tried to beat the civil rights movement into submission. The authorities' violent rejection of a peaceful plea for equality lit the fuse. It finally exploded in the summer of 1969 when the North erupted with the Battle of the Bogside in Derry and anti-Catholic pogroms in Belfast. The IRA then went through an acrimonious split in December 1969 that produced Provisional Sinn Féin and its so-called army, the Provisional IRA ('Provos'), on one side and Official Sinn Féin and Official IRA ('Stickies') on the other. Two equally violent factions, the Ulster Defence Association (UDA) and the Ulster Volunteer Force (UVF) emerged from the Loyalist side. The fallout ignited almost three decades of butchery, which became known as the Troubles.

Inevitably the bushfire spread to the South. In the early 1970s it threatened the very existence of the State. The Provos and their political wing, Sinn Féin, would do everything they could to destabilize the Republic and warp the institutions of the young State. Most significantly the Provos would also bring a new level of organization to crime as they robbed banks and payrolls throughout Ireland to raise funds for the 'struggle'. They organized kidnappings, bombings and assassinations and insidiously agitated social unrest. The terrorists made crime look easy, as the Gardaí and legislature were ill-equipped and unprepared for the era of the gun. The number of illegal firearms on the streets increased and so did the willingness to use them.

Added to this highly volatile situation was the emergence of a cohort of angry young men who were attracted by the lucrative opportunities available in the new business of crime. By the time De Valera spoke at the 1966 Easter Parade, these new Irish rebels were well on their way down a different road to the straight one he had envisaged. Many of the young miscreants appearing in the juvenile courts at the time would become household names over the next four decades, for all the wrong reasons. Some were destined to become major players on the international crime scene and even feature in Hollywood movies. Names such as Dunne, Cahill, Cunningham, Hutch, Mitchell and Gilligan were already appearing on charge sheets in stations across Dublin. They were also listed as inmates in the notorious industrial and reformatory schools around the country. When they reached maturity these law-breakers would create a Republic of their own – an elusive brutal world called Gangland. They would be the leaders of this parallel society, but unlike the men of 1916, these rebels would become synonymous with fear and intimidation.

By 1966, the social factors which would contribute to the explosion in serious crime had lurked, like a festering sore, behind the façade of normality that had prevailed since the foundation of the State. The crippling deprivation of a marginalized underclass had been carefully ignored by the new rulers of the fledgling Republic, even though they'd promised to relieve the harshness of colonial oppression.

The Democratic Programme of the first Dáil in 1919 outlined the social vision for a free Ireland as the War of Independence from British rule began. It basically promised that things were about to get a lot better – just as soon as freedom was achieved. They declared that there would be prosperity and equality for all. The leaders were particularly unambiguous about their plans for the care of the nation's children: 'It shall be the first duty of the Government of the Republic to make provision for the physical, mental and spiritual well-being of the children, to secure that no child shall suffer hunger or cold from lack of food, clothing, or shelter, but that all shall be provided with the means and facilities requisite for their proper education and training as Citizens of a Free and Gaelic Ireland.'

But the founding fathers soon forgot their revolutionary rhetoric and reneged on their side of the deal.

In the first years of the new nation, industrial unrest among workers, looking for their share of the Independence dividend, was put down with the full force of the Government's boot. All that had changed, it appeared, was the nationality of the hand holding the whip. The respected historian Professor Diarmaid Ferriter noted in his acclaimed 2010 TV documentary series, *The Limits of Liberty*, that despite the high-minded aspirations, life was to get a lot worse under the Tricolour and the Free State. While much was promised, little was delivered. He observed that the Government was preoccupied only by power and was controlled by small elites.

The State and the Church formed a powerful, conservative alliance. They demanded unquestioning acceptance and blind obedience from their subjects. The relationship was later given expression through the close association between the Archbishop of Dublin, John Charles McQuaid, and Eamon De Valera. Between them they would dominate Irish life for forty years. McQuaid, who reigned from 1940 to 1972, was an admirer of FBI Director J. Edgar Hoover. In his role as custodian of Irish morality, McQuaid zealously used Hoover's methods to keep tabs on people from all walks of life. According to his biographer, the writer John Cooney, McQuaid 'imposed his iron will on politics and society by instilling fear among his clergy and people'.

The partnership ensured that an undemocratic Church, with a mandate only from God and the Pope, would play a pivotal role in maintaining the steadfastly conservative State. There was no room for new ideas or social progress, for fear that they might undermine the morality of the nation – and challenge the power of those in charge. The Establishment ensured that dissent was excluded and controversy was buried.

After Independence in 1922, Ireland slid into a stultifying rut that led to the stagnation of the socio-economic life of the country. Any semblance of the life and romantic ideals which the socialists and poets who led the 1916 Rebellion had fought for were obliterated during the grim 1930s, 1940s and 1950s. It became clear that some of the State's founding fathers held the lower classes, the people they claimed to represent, in barely disguised contempt. And nowhere did this harsh attitude become more evident than in the treatment of children.

By 1930, the problems of rape, sexual abuse of minors and infanticide were prevalent in Irish society. A judge in Clare even called his court the 'dirty assizes' such was the volume of sex-related cases coming before him. In response the Government established a commission, chaired by barrister William Carrigan, in June 1930. Its mandate was to investigate the disturbing level of sexual crimes throughout the country and to compile a report which would provide the basis for changes in legislation and social policy. The Commission examined illegitimacy, the age of consent, homosexuality (a crime until 1993), child sexual abuse, rape and prostitution.

The Garda Commissioner of the day, Eoin O'Duffy, told the Commission that the sexual abuse of girls under 13 was 'alarming'. In his submission O'Duffy reported on what he viewed as the general immorality of the country: 'An alarming aspect is the number of cases with interference with girls under 15, and even under 13 and under 11, which come before the courts. These are in most cases heard of accidentally by the Garda, and are very rarely the result of a direct complaint. It is generally agreed that reported cases do not exceed 15 per cent of those actually happening.' The Commissioner also noted: 'Offences on children between the ages of 9 and 16 are, unfortunately, increasing in the country.'

The Carrigan Commission reported in August 1931 and made 21 recommendations for legislative change, including increasing the age of consent to 18 years. But the report was considered so sensitive it was decided that it should not be discussed in the Dáil. Instead, it was buried and forgotten.

This unwillingness to tackle social issues was central to the ethos of governments at the time. Kevin O'Higgins, the first Minister for Home Affairs (later to be the Department of Justice), quickly dismissed the intent of the 1919 Democratic Programme as 'largely poetry'. In *The Limits of Liberty*, Professor Diarmaid Ferriter uncovered long-buried documents that betrayed the true feelings of some of the people in power. The evidence was contained in a memo from William T. Cosgrave to his colleague Austin Stack, and concerned the children reared in the hated workhouses. In May 1921, while both were ministers in that first government, Cosgrave wrote: 'People reared in Workhouses are no great acquisition to the community and they have no idea whatever of civic responsibility. Their highest aim is to live at the expense of the rate payers. Consequently, it would be a decided gain if they were to take it into their heads to emigrate. When they go abroad they are thrown on their own responsibilities and have to work, whether they like it or not.'

Two years later Cosgrave became the first Taoiseach of the Irish Free State.

A hugely controversial 1960s documentary had also exposed the unpalatable truth about post-revolutionary Irish society. A year after the Jubilee commemoration, a Dublin-born journalist, Peter Lennon, returned from his new home in France to make the powerfully iconoclastic film *The Rocky Road to Dublin*. Lennon posed uncomfortable questions about the type of society that had evolved since the foundation of the State in 1922. He argued that the revolution that achieved Independence had failed to live up to its idealistic origins and had been hijacked by vested interests. In the opening sequence he put the question, 'What do you do with your revolution once you've got it?' He painted a bleak picture of a country which had 'nearly sank underneath the weight of its heroes and clergy'. Lennon argued that the country of his birth had been stultified by a combination of religious oppression and cultural isolation. He described the Republic as 'a country with its future in the hands of people who think in terms of the past'.

In the documentary the writer Sean O'Faolain, whose acclaimed short stories had charted the development of modern Ireland over forty years, gave his own brutally honest view of the Republic. 'The society that actually grew up [since Independence] was a society of urbanized peasants; a society that was without moral courage, constantly observing a self-interested silence; never speaking in moments of crisis; a constant alliance with a completely obdurantist, repressive, regressive, and uncultivated church. The result of all this was that '32, like '22, simply spawned a society utterly alien to the Republic. It went on and has gone on, a society in which there are blatant inequalities and in which the whole spirit of 1916 has been lost. If those 16 men of '16, before the bullet crashed into them and before the rope tightened on their neck, if they had seen the kind of Ireland that would come out of their sacrifice, they would have felt their efforts had been betrayed and their sacrifice in vain.'

The film, which won international acclaim, outraged the Church/State alliance and an equally conservative Irish media, who rubbished both the film and its maker. Although the documentary could not be banned by the censor, as it had no sexual content, the Government still managed to have it barred from cinemas and national television. The people of Ireland would not get to view *The Rocky Road to Dublin* until almost forty years later.

Further evidence of this political indifference in 1966 was the lack of reform in the system. In the case of children, The Children Act of 1908 had been intended to begin the process of humanizing reformatory and industrial schools and to reduce physical punishment. But the 1908 regulations were not changed in Ireland until the 1970s – even though more progressive regimes had been developed decades earlier in Britain and Europe. The 1941 Children Act even allowed for the reduction of the minimum age at which a child could be incarcerated to under six.

The Catholic Church, which had control of the education system in the new State, had also inherited the dreaded industrial and reformatory schools – a challenge they accepted with great enthusiasm. Industrial schools were established in 1868 for orphaned, neglected and abandoned children. In theory the industrial schools were intended as a training ground to turn out the well-rounded, productive, Catholic citizens that their families were unable to do, often due to poverty and death. In a repressive society, where contraception was a venial sin and there was a chronic lack of education among the poorer classes, large families were inevitable. When a mother had too many mouths to feed and could no longer adequately care for her offspring, the only alternative was these schools. Children as young as five and six were committed to these institutions, and they often remained there until the age of 16. Paying the Church to deal with the problem was an easier option for the Government than tackling the reasons why children needed care in the first place. Reformatory schools were established by Act of Parliament in 1858. They were essentially prisons for children found guilty of criminal offences, such as burglary and vandalism. The reformatories were intended to reform errant children and put them back on the right road. It was in places like Daingean and Letterfrack that many of the criminal Godfathers who would emerge from the 1970s onwards got their first taste of incarceration. There were at one time a total of sixty reformatory and industrial schools in the country.

In reality, the two institutions were veritable Gulags, asylums of appalling misery and suffering, run by sadistic, religious orders. With the full support of the law, they were dumping grounds for the orphaned, the deprived and the wrongdoers. Youngsters deemed 'troubled' or beyond parental control also qualified for forced admission to both institutions. Rape, gross sexual abuse, torture, psychological abuse and starvation were constant features of life in this barbarous regime. Childhood innocence ended as soon as an inmate walked through the front doors. Systematic abuse and violence replaced the child's basic needs of love, affection and nurturing. The regime turned out generations of dysfunctional, traumatized and damaged people. In May 2009, the Ryan Report on the Commission to Inquire into Child Abuse (CICA) at state institutions since the 1930s found that the entire industrial/reform school system 'treated children more like prison inmates and slaves than people with legal rights and human potential'. It also concluded that the sadists and paedophiles were protected by their religious superiors and that their crimes were covered up.

The industrial and reformatory school system was a major contributory factor in producing a generation of young criminals. They shared the life-changing experience of enforced imprisonment at the hands of the religious orders. Many of the gangsters who emerged in the late 1960s, 1970s and 1980s had also been brutalized while they were inmates in these institutions. But when victims began to reveal the terrible truth of what had happened to them there, former inmates who had become hardened criminals remained silent. In their world, admitting that they had been abused would be considered a sign of weakness. One notorious armed robber, interviewed by this writer, only spoke about his horrendous experiences in the reformatory school thirty years after he'd begun a successful career holding up banks and shooting at cops. 'I was put away for two years for stealing from a shop. Even though these people claimed to be religious, there was no mercy or compassion. The beatings and the sex abuse were just part of life in the place. After a while you almost began to think of it as normal. Those fucking monks and priests destroyed a lot of lives.'

The future gangsters also developed strong bonds of loyalty and friendship, forged in reformatory schools such as Daingean and Letterfrack. These bonds would become an important factor in the organization of crime in later years. Reform school brothers-in-arms would eventually provide the nucleus of the country's first organized crime gangs. One of them was Martin Cahill, who would earn infamy as the notorious gang boss 'the General'. The two years he spent in St Conleth's Reformatory School in Daingean, County Offaly, helped to mould the development of a sociopath. He would later recall bitterly: 'If anyone corrupted me it was those mad monks down in the bog.'

These former inmates were released with a deep-seated hatred for the rest of society. They were poorly educated but they had learned one important lesson from the religious orders – that violence was the most effective tool in life. They would spend a lifetime fighting back and getting even.

The addresses on the rap sheets of the new generation of villains illustrate another contributory factor in the evolution of organized crime in Ireland. It is no coincidence that the vast majority of the gangland pioneers came from so-called working-class areas, plagued by high unemployment and deprivation. In 1922, the Free State had inherited a huge slum problem in Dublin city centre, where over 80,000 people lived in rundown tenements. The situation was similar in every other city in the country. Death and disease stalked the dangerously dilapidated tenements and by the mid-1920s Ireland's infant mortality was the highest in Europe. By the 1930s, 112,000 people were crammed together, living in 6,300 tenements in Central Dublin. In 1936, the capital was deemed to have the worst slums in Europe. Some tenement areas had 800 people living in a single acre. As many as 100 people shared a house, with individual families of up to 15 and 20 members wedged into a single room. A primitive toilet and water tap in the rear yard were shared by all the inhabitants. Unemployment rates were high and those lucky enough to have jobs were poorly paid and could barely support their large families. Alcoholism and domestic violence were commonplace, as was prostitution.

Attempts to clear the slums were seriously restricted, due to the huge economic difficulties with which the fledgling Free State had to contend. The financial burden of the cost of structural damage in the two wars – put at £30 million – absorbed a large proportion of government expenditure. The country's fragile economy also suffered severely as a result of the worldwide Depression in the 1930s. De Valera's isolationist economic policies and his neutrality stance during the Second World War contributed to maintaining the crippling levels of poverty. Inevitably 'slum clearance' slipped down the political agenda. It was no coincidence either that many of the rack-rent landlords who lived off the earnings from the overcrowded ghettos were 'pillars of society', and generous benefactors to political parties.

In the slums, most crime came in the form of the notorious street gangs. They were made up of idle young men, organized along street lines, with nothing else to do but fight and drink. On 21 September 1934, the *Cork Examiner* reported the upsurge in street violence: 'A new trouble has broken out in Dublin. It is giving considerable anxiety to the Garda Siochana, for it is no less than a gang warfare.'

The most notorious of these groups was the Animal Gang. It was regularly involved in bloody street battles with gangs from other tenement neighbourhoods. Knives, potatoes laced with razor blades, knuckledusters and lead-filled batons were their weapons of choice. A Garda report at the time noted: 'There is no political significance attached to the formation or activities of the Animal Gang – the members of which are hooligans, pure and simple.'

The street gangs never became organized enough to establish criminal empires like the ones developing in American cities such as Chicago and New York. In the hungry, jobless Ireland of the 1930s, 1940s and 1950s there wasn't very much to rob, and anyone who did commit that type of crime was quickly caught and jailed. Gardaí enjoyed an almost 100 per cent detection rate for many decades. At that time, serious crimes were so rare that a safe cracker was seen as a criminal mastermind. The Animal Gang eventually faded away, and now the first Irish criminal gang is barely even mentioned as a footnote in the history books.

In the 1950s the Government finally launched a series of building programmes to ease the centuries-old problem of the tenement slums. Over

time, thousands of houses were built on greenfield sites on the edges of
Dublin city, in places like Ballyfermot, Crumlin, Inchicore, Cabra,
Donnycarney, Glasnevin and Marino. There were also major housing
projects in Limerick and Cork. In the move to better living conditions,
however, whole communities were uprooted and separated. The sprawling new estates were lonely places for many of the inhabitants. Lifelong
neighbours, who had been crammed together in the slums, found themselves living miles apart. The overall effect was a breakdown in social
cohesion and an unravelling of the ties that had bonded communities
together. The new working-class suburbs had little to offer, apart from
improved accommodation. They quickly became unemployment black
spots and did not solve the poverty problem.

In 1968 an RTÉ documentary, *The Flower Pot Society*, examined the
movement of the slum generation. An unidentified interviewee predicted the problems of the future: 'Dublin Corporation are dealing
with people all of whom are the same class. It's much easier to treat
them like an army and to transplant them from A to B. They have very
little choice in the matter. If a child is to improve it will be in spite of
their environment – and not because of it.'

The migration from the tenements continued throughout the 1960s
and 1970s. More houses were built, pushing the boundaries of the city
out even further, to gobble up fields in Finglas, Blanchardstown,
Coolock and Clondalkin. New flat complexes were also being built in
Central Dublin. In 1966, the Government marked the Jubilee of the
Rebellion by commencing construction on its most ambitious housing
project ever – a huge complex of tower blocks in Ballymun, a stretch of
countryside near Dublin Airport. Completed in 1969, the complex
comprised 7 15-storey tower blocks, and several long 8-storey spine
blocks, which 30,000 residents soon called home. Each tower block was
named after a leader of the 1916 Rising. The flats quickly became a
dreary eyesore, and by 1979 they had become a monument to a well-
intentioned but deeply flawed social housing policy. The complex was
bereft of even the most basic amenities for its army of children and the
50 per cent of adults who were unemployed. For many it became a no-
hope, desolate ghetto, with the highest rate of transfer applications
anywhere in the country. Ballymun became a dumping ground for
problem tenants and unmarried mothers.

While the vast majority of decent people who lived in the gloomy estates and new flat complexes struggled through life without involving themselves in crime, it is an escapable fact that they were criminogenic environments, in which the underworld thrived. Families such as the Dunnes, Cahills, Gilligans, Mitchells and Cunninghams had all been moved from the inner-city slums to places like Crumlin, Drimnagh, Finglas and Ballyfermot – areas which would eventually be claimed as gangland territory. It was from these new ghettos, using the links forged in the reformatory schools, that the ruthless young hoods would embark on their journey of mayhem. This was where the story of organized crime in Ireland would begin.

As De Valera watched the Jubilee celebrations in 1966, it was obvious that there was a lot more wealth in Ireland than ever before. Irish society was changing at a faster pace than at any stage since Independence. The country had begun to enjoy unprecedented levels of economic growth and prosperity, thanks mainly to Sean Lemass who had taken over as Taoiseach from De Valera in 1959. Under De Valera, the 1950s had been one of the worst decades in the nation's short history. It became known as the time of the disappearing Irish. Between 1951 and 1961 an estimated 500,000 people had emigrated; it was accepted as a cultural necessity. It made life somewhat more bearable for those left at home, as it eased demand on scarce resources. The money emigrants in Britain and the USA sent home to their families became a major source of income for the country's foundering economy. But Lemass's Programme for Economic Expansion was the first glimmer of hope, and it finally dragged Ireland out of the dark ages.

It sparked a boom period in which the Irish economy enjoyed the fastest growth in Europe. The number of cars on Irish roads trebled between 1951 and 1968. In 1962, the marvels of the outside world, with its different values and cultures, were beamed into homes across the country with the launch of the new national TV channel, RTÉ. In the year of the launch there were 93,000 licensed televisions in the Republic; six years later, as wealth grew, there were almost 400,000.

Ireland was also becoming an urbanized society, as the population moved from the land to the cities, particularly Dublin, securing jobs in the growing industrial and public service sectors. Between 1950 and

1969 the numbers living on the land dropped from half the population to less than a third. The dramatic increase in demand for houses among the burgeoning middle classes created the country's first building boom. As living standards improved there was more money and disposable wealth than ever before.

The new age of consumerism provided many lucrative opportunities for the emerging criminal gangs. Unlike their predecessors, in the likes of the Animal Gang, there was plenty for the new mobs to steal, as the gulf between the haves and the have-nots widened. However, despite an underlying and steady increase in offences such as burglary and larceny, Irish crime was still not a source of major concern in 1966. In fact the Government was giving serious consideration to closing down prisons, where the daily average population was 300 inmates. (Four decades later it would be over 4,000.) In the Garda crime report for that year there were six murders and seven cases of manslaughter recorded nationally. Most murders and violent deaths were the result of so-called crimes of passion, domestic disputes or rows over land. There were no armed robberies.

The Gardaí enjoyed an almost 100 per cent success rate when it came to solving murders and an average of 80 per cent in all other crimes. The numbers of Gardaí were more than adequate to police a law-abiding population of less than three million people. The report on crime by the Garda Commissioner of the day noted that 'no organised crimes of violence' had been recorded.

Officially, at that time, there was no drug problem in the country either. But the seeds of the crisis were already germinating. Throughout Dublin, there were small groups of drug abusers and addicts, whose habits were fed mainly by the medical profession. Drugs were considered to be a health problem and some doctors were incredibly lax and irresponsible when it came to dispensing prescription drugs. In 1966, the Commission of Inquiry into Mental Illness warned the Minister for Health: 'Drug addiction in this country could reach serious proportions unless a constant effort is maintained to prevent the abuse of habit-forming drugs.' The authorities ignored the Commission's early warning.

In the early 1960s a young Limerick man called Des O'Malley began practising as a solicitor in the family firm. Just ten years later, in 1970, he would be given the job of Minister for Justice and find himself on the frontline of an unprecedented crisis that seemed to come out of nowhere. He recently recalled a much more innocent time: 'I practised law in Limerick between '61 and '69 and I used to spend at least one day every week on criminal law. But there was really very little crime at all in Limerick, it was petty crime all the time and it was nearly all disposed of in the District Court. I used to appear in the Circuit Court and I can recall at the start of sittings, the county registrar presenting the judge with a pair of white gloves to signify that there were no indictable crimes in the city or county of Limerick, returned for trial in that term. And that used to go on, term after term, all over the country. I don't think there'd have been white gloves given to the judges in Limerick in the '80s, '90s, the 2000s or that there ever will be again.'

Around the same time as O'Malley was starting to work as a lawyer, former Detective Superintendent Mick Finn had just graduated from the Garda training depot, which was then based at HQ in the Phoenix Park, Dublin. After a brief stint in Fitzgibbon Street Station, in the north inner-city, he transferred down the road to the C District HQ at Store Street Station. Over those first few years as a cop in Store Street, Finn witnessed, at first hand, the social factors that led to the area's steady decline into serious organized crime: 'People who initially got involved in crime did so out of need, running into shops and stealing bits and pieces, sometimes out of hunger. As they grew up they became a part of different gangs and some were fortunate enough to be weaned away from it. One of the main factors for young people falling into crime was their family conditions. In a lot of cases circumstances were not good, families were dysfunctional and they had nobody to show them the way. It is an accepted fact that deprived areas will produce criminals. And it is always those areas that the police will concentrate on because criminals live there. Crime is a consequence of how they were reared, where they were reared and what was available to them during their early times.'

As an organization, the Garda Síochána had fallen into a state of complacency in 1966. It reflected the demeanour of the State since Independence – it was inward-looking and insular. If senior management had looked across the water to Britain, where armed robberies had become commonplace since the early 1960s, they might have made some preparations for what was coming. But the Garda authorities were notoriously reluctant to keep in step with a dramatically changing world. A stiflingly conservative ethos also frowned on innovation. As a result the Gardaí didn't have the planning, equipment or numbers to confront the well-armed and organized criminal gangs when they arrived on the scene.

On the afternoon of 27 February 1967, crime moved to another level when three masked raiders burst through the front doors of the Royal Bank of Ireland in Drumcondra, North Dublin. They ordered everyone to put their hands up. Two of the raiders, armed with revolvers, covered staff and customers, while the third jumped the counter and emptied the tills. The hoods sped off in a stolen getaway car less than four minutes later. They had taken £3,265 in cash – worth over €50,000 in today's values. The gang had just pulled the first armed robbery in Ireland since the Second World War. It was a professional, well-planned heist and it sent shockwaves through the Establishment.

Nothing would ever be the same again.

2.   Saor Eire

The armed robbery in Drumcondra, Dublin, on 27 February 1967 was an inaugural event – and was greeted with public shock throughout Ireland. This was the first time that guns had been used on Irish streets for many decades. For their part the Gardaí had no experience in investigating such well-planned crimes. The country's first professional armed gang had also set an example for scores of other would-be blaggers. They'd shown them how easy it was to rob banks and not get caught. No one realized it at the time, but the mob involved in the robbery had heralded the arrival of organized crime in Ireland.

But the robbery crew was no ordinary criminal gang. It was a well-organized, heavily armed, highly motivated and dangerously volatile group. Their 'jobs' were meticulously planned and executed with a ruthless efficiency and military precision. Over time the heists grew more audacious – and reckless. This mob saw themselves more as rebels with a cause than mere thieves. They were a motley collection of dissident republicans, socialists, anarchists and criminals who gathered together under a flag of convenience to justify their actions. The gang were the self-appointed vanguard of working-class resistance, and the Drumcondra job was the first military action in a new 'socialist revolution'. But the quasi-political misfits were too busy robbing the capitalist system to find time to choose a name for their small army of idealists, desperados and chancers. They styled themselves on the iconic South American rebel leader Che Guevara. It took two years (and several robberies) before they came up with a name they could agree on – Saor Eire.

Although largely forgotten now, Saor Eire, or 'Free Ireland', played a pivotal role in the evolution of organized crime and terrorism in modern Ireland, even though they preferred to describe their motives as purely political. Saor Eire claimed the proceeds of the robberies would be used to finance a movement that would encourage workers and small farmers to rise up against the State. Together they would overthrow the capitalist system and replace it with a workers' republic. The maverick group claimed it was fighting a war in the name of the working classes and downtrodden in society. But the group never stood on the steps of the GPO and declared their objectives to the people they planned to save. Instead, in February 1967, they armed themselves and got on with the job of emptying bank tills, supposedly on the people's behalf.

Three years after that first job, however, Saor Eire had become 'Public Enemy Number One' in the eyes of all classes of Irish society. In the end the only group they encouraged to rise up was a generation of dangerous young villains.

The names of the men who formed the nucleus of Saor Eire have also been largely forgotten through the gun-smoked mists of gangland history. The emerging crime families and the IRA, who came after them, took all the prominent spots in the Badfellas' hall of infamy. Several of Saor Eire's leaders, young men such as Joe Dillon, Frank Keane, Martin Casey and Liam Walsh, had deserted the ranks of the IRA during the early 1960s. They left in protest over its political direction and a lack of military action. The four young leaders had been influenced by the left-wing ferment which swept across the Western world during the 1960s – the decade of free love and radical thinking.

The seeds of Saor Eire can be traced to a disaffected former young IRA member called Joe Dillon from Portmarnock, County Dublin. In December 1965, the 19-year-old was charged with an attempted armed robbery. Described as a casual waiter, Dillon was also charged with stealing a car and possession of a handgun when he'd tried to hold up the Dublin Corporation rent office in Coolock, North Dublin. The young republican's associates and supporters began a campaign to stop his prosecution, claiming that he was being framed by the police because of his politics. Many of the people involved in the protest would form the nucleus of the new revolutionary army.

In May 1967, three months after the Drumcondra robbery, Dillon was convicted on all charges for the 1965 robbery attempt and sentenced to five years in prison. At the time such a sentence was considered unusually harsh – armed crime was practically non-existent so the sanctions were light in comparison to more recent history. The sentence was reduced to three years by the Court of Criminal Appeal that July. Joe

Dillon then went back to the High Court in August 1967 to challenge an order transferring him from Mountjoy Prison to Portlaoise Prison. During a break in the proceedings, and a mix-up between prison officers over who should be watching him, Dillon strolled out of the Four Courts and went on the run. He had been in custody for less than three months.

In the meantime the ex-IRA men had joined forces with Trotskyites Peter Graham and Maureen Keegan of the Labour Party's Young Socialists. Graham and Keegan were also members of the Trotskyite United Secretariat of the Fourth International. The new Saor Eire 'army' also recruited members of the Irish Workers Group, a small Marxist group made up of Irish expats living in London. It was headed by Gerry Lawless, who later worked as a journalist with the *Sunday World*. In addition, Saor Eire enlisted several young Dublin criminals, who were attracted by the anarchic rhetoric and the chance of making some easy money. The group provided funds to Peter Graham, who was chairman of the Young Socialists, with the intention of pushing more radical policies in that organization. At its full strength Saor Eire was said to have had a total of about sixty members scattered between Dublin, Cork and Derry. Its hardcore membership consisted of no more than twenty dissidents.

At 34, Frank Keane was the oldest member of the group. Born in Mayo, his family had moved to live in Finglas in Dublin when he was in his late teens. The TV serviceman joined the IRA in the 1950s and had been the OC (Officer Commanding) of the organization's Dublin Brigade. Keane was jailed for 18 months for his first overt action on behalf of Saor Eire, a few months after the Drumcondra robbery, when he tried to burn down the Fianna Fáil party HQ in August 1967. He was released after four months. Martin Casey and Liam Walsh, both of whom were from Dublin, had also been members of the IRA who left because of a lack of military action. Together the four young men would be a dangerous mix.

On 19 April 1968, Joe Dillon turned up again. This time he was with three other members of Saor Eire on a return visit to the Royal Bank of Ireland in Drumcondra – the scene of their first job. The robbery was carried out using the same modus operandi that would define all their jobs: staff and customers were threatened at gunpoint, shots were fired in the air to prevent heroics and the robbery was over in less than four minutes. In the second raid they got away with a similar amount of cash – £3,186.

Most of Saor Eire's robberies were 'half and half operations' – half the proceeds went to fund the war and the other half went into the pockets of the patriots. No one asked any questions about this dual motivation.

On 20 June, the gang hit the Hibernian Bank in Newbridge, County Kildare and left with £3,474. Frank Keane and 23-year-old Simon O'Donnell from Dublin were arrested by Gardaí two days after the Newbridge raid, when they were stopped in a van containing combat jackets and cash. Although there wasn't a compelling case against them they were both charged with the robbery. They got bail and went back to work.

Four months later, the organization was again in need of funds for the cause and themselves. On 3 October 1968, four members of the gang, Thomas O'Neill, Padraig Dwyer, Sean Doyle and Simon O'Donnell, targeted the Munster and Leinster Bank in Ballyfermot, West Dublin. The members of Saor Eire were about to show their propensity for reckless violence. This time their stolen car had been spotted near the bank before the raid and the Gardaí were alerted. A young cop called Martin Donnellan was in the first patrol car that responded to the call. He had only been in the force for four months and he was about to receive a baptism of fire. As the Garda car approached, the revolutionaries abandoned their plans to rob the bank and drove off at speed.

Donnellan, who retired at the rank of Assistant Commissioner in 2007, recalls what happened next: 'As we arrived outside the bank we spotted the four men and it was obvious they were about to rob it. There was a high speed chase and, as we followed them up Kylemore Road, Padraig Dwyer put his head and shoulders out the back window of the car and fired several shots directly at us. We dived down in the car, as the driver swerved left and right to avoid the gunfire. We continued after them until the getaway car crashed on Cooley Road in Drimnagh and the raiders ran through gardens. They were still armed and shouting at us: "This is political." We shouted that we were also armed, which we weren't, and they ran out onto another road, where they encountered two more uniformed guards who managed to disarm and arrest them. One of my colleagues, Kevin Duffin, grabbed Simon O'Donnell around the neck as he raised a rifle to take aim. The weapon was ready to fire. It was pure luck that no one was killed or injured and it was obvious that they had no compunction about shooting a policeman. This was the first time that I ever witnessed such violence. For me that was the end of an age of innocence. There were no armed robberies until the day when Saor Eire appeared and claimed it was political. My career started at the same time as organized crime took off – it became an integral part of my life for over forty years.'

When the crashed getaway car was searched, Gardaí uncovered a cache of four rifles, six automatic pistols, two revolvers and 500 rounds of ammunition. Saor Eire believed in making sure they were well armed. O'Neill, O'Donnell, Doyle and Dwyer were arrested and charged. All four got bail, including O'Donnell, even though he was already out on bail for the Newbridge bank job back in June. O'Donnell and Dwyer promptly went on the run.

'The four men we arrested that day were seasoned members of what became known as Saor Eire. They figured that robbing banks was political; at least that's what they were trying to say. They went to trial and they were eventually convicted of attempted murder and attempted bank robbery but most of them got very short sentences which reflected the attitude of the judiciary at the time. They were supposed to be political. Now I'd put that in inverted commas, like lots of robberies that were carried out after that, a member of the gang would speak with a Northern accent and claim it was for the cause.'

In March 1969, after a lull in their activities, Saor Eire went back to work and pulled off their most audacious heist to date. Eight gang members, dressed in combat fatigues and armed with machine-guns, invaded the Northern Irish town of Newry, County Down, situated a few miles across the Border. They took over the centre of the town and fired shots into the air. Three raiders first hit the Bank of Ireland, and then the Northern Bank minutes later. They were chased back to the Border by the Royal Ulster Constabulary (RUC), with both sides exchanging gunfire. Once they reached the South, they vanished into a maze of back roads. The so-called Republican Trotskyites had got away with Stg£22,000 – the biggest cash robbery in Irish history, on either side of the Border.

The bandits were so elated by their stunning success that this is when they met to decide on a name for their organization – they wanted the world to know who they were. The members of Saor Eire were beginning to believe in their own invincibility. At that meeting they also decided that the Dublin Government and its agencies would be regarded as legitimate targets. They vowed not to surrender their weapons if challenged and began releasing statements to the media, proclaiming their objectives.

On 14 August 1969, four members of the gang robbed the National Bank in Baltinglass, County Wicklow. During the robbery, shots were fired and the staff were threatened. Two of the raiders forced the manager to open the safe while sticking a gun in his eye; another gun was pressed against his head.

A month later, on 25 September, the gang struck again. This time they took over the town of Kells, County Meath, by cutting the phone lines and blocking approach roads. Then they robbed the National Bank at their leisure, before leaving town £3,000 richer. The revolutionaries also hit the Northern Bank on the South Circular Road, Dublin, in the same month.

In a statement issued to the *Irish Times* shortly afterwards, the gang claimed responsibility for the Kells job. Describing themselves as the Saor Eire Action Group, they claimed that the proceeds of the robbery would be 'used to finance a movement which will strive for a workers' Republic'.

On 3 October, the Garda Commissioner, Michael Wymes, sent a confidential directive to all Garda stations in the country. It left no doubt that putting Saor Eire out of business was now the number one priority of the force. After listing the string of armed robberies attributed to the gang, the document stated: 'Information to hand is that these raids are the work of a group styling itself "Saor Eire" who cannot be regarded as having any political motives and are nothing more than a gang of armed bandits whose unlawful activities must be opposed by all the resources available to the Force.' The document included photographs and descriptions of 13 of the most prominent figures within the organization. Officers were instructed to familiarize themselves with the faces of the country's most dangerous criminals.

In the meantime the gang began recruiting new members. They

rented a cottage and lands on a quiet country lane near Lacken in the Wicklow Mountains, and used it as a training camp and hideout. Saor Eire bought military equipment, including combat uniforms, boots, flak jackets, two-way radios, detonators and explosives. They also had a firing range and acquired a large stockpile of arms and ammunition.

In late 1969, Saor Eire took delivery of a number of small consignments of 9mm and .22 Star pistols which had been stolen from Parker-Hale Ltd, a munitions factory in Birmingham. A Dublin criminal, Christy 'Bronco' Dunne, who was closely associated with Saor Eire's Liam Walsh and Martin Casey, had developed a lucrative little business selling firearms stolen from the plant. The colourful crook had extensive underworld contacts in England. Using a factory employee, he organized the theft of at least 35 weapons and acted as a go-between in arranging their sale to Saor Eire. The weapons were separately packaged and shipped to Dublin over a number of weeks, with their arrival specifically timed to coincide with the duty rosters of certain Customs officers. They ensured that the parcels got through unchecked.

The arms theft was uncovered soon afterwards by UK police. When intelligence about the gun-smuggling operation eventually filtered back to the Gardaí it confirmed their suspicions that Saor Eire was being assisted by people with a lot more power than Christy Dunne – people at the heart of the Republic's government.

In the summer of 1969 the cauldron that was Northern Ireland finally boiled over with the Battle of the Bogside in Derry and sectarian attacks on Catholics in Belfast. Refugees fled to the Republic as the violence intensified and hundreds of families were burned out of their homes. At that point the IRA was also in a state of internal turmoil over the political direction it should pursue. It led to a bitter split which created two factions. Official Sinn Féin and Official IRA ('Stickies') emerged on one side. They broke with the traditional republican goal of a 32-county Irish Republic and opted for a united working-class revolution by workers on both sides of the sectarian divide. On the other side of the split, Provisional Sinn Féin and the Provisional IRA ('Provos') wanted to pursue an armed struggle to get the British out of Ireland. The developments were deeply worrying for the Jack Lynch-led Fianna Fáil Government in the South.

Cabinet papers from April of that year, released under the thirty-year rule, reveal that a collective decision had been made by the Cabinet to foment a split in the IRA. The Machiavellian plot was to try to weaken its militant leadership in Dublin while creating an organization that would be amenable to Fianna Fáil control in the North. The Department of Justice had recommended a policy of deliberately dividing the IRA's rural conservatives from the urban radicals, who were seen as the greater threat. An account in the name 'George Dixon' was opened in a bank on Baggot Street with £100,000. Charles Haughey, who was Minister for Finance, had control of this special account. The Government provided the money ostensibly to relieve the plight of nationalists in the North, but the real purpose of the George Dixon account was to fund one section of the movement and supply it with arms. It was left to Haughey and his Donegal colleague Neil Blaney, the Minister for Agriculture, to implement the plan. Neil Blaney was a friend of Liam Walsh, who provided the channel into Saor Eire.

A report in the *Irish Times* in March 1970, focusing on the growing problem of the Saor Eire robberies, first revealed the uneasiness among senior Gardaí that there was 'more than a little political tolerance of the elements involved'. The source of the story was referring to collusion between members of the Fianna Fáil Government and the gang. A memo found buried in files in the Department of Justice over thirty years later seems to corroborate those suspicions. The document was written by Peter Berry, the Secretary of the Department at the time. In it, Berry noted he had received reliable information that Jock Haughey, Charles Haughey's brother, had travelled to London with Martin Casey, in November 1969, for the purpose of buying the arms from the Parker-Hale armoury. It named both Saor Eire's Martin Casey and Christy Dunne as being centrally involved in the operation. During the trip, Haughey and Casey signed into the Irish Club, on London's Eaton Square, with false names. Jock Haughey gave the name George Dixon. The department memo went on to claim that Charles Haughey and Neil Blaney had full knowledge of the Saor Eire gun-running expedition.

As Ireland prepared to cross the threshold of a new decade, the Official and Provisional IRAs began following the lead of their former comrades. Like the Saor Eire gangs, the two IRA groups started organizing their own 'expropriations' for the cause, by robbing banks, post offices and payrolls. Following a further spate of hold-ups in November 1969 and early December, the Justice Minister, Michael O'Morain, announced to the Dáil that the Garda authorities had to allocate men to stand guard outside banks in Dublin. This was in a bid to stem the sudden upsurge in robberies. Flying squads, drawn from the small group of armed, plainclothes officers in the force, had also begun patrolling the city. But they couldn't cover everywhere.

Between 1970 and 1971, Ireland experienced the fastest-growing crime rate in Europe. On 20 February 1970, Saor Eire carried out another audacious commando-style heist, similar to their operations in Newry and Kells. This time, eight armed men took over the sleepy village of Rathdrum, County Wicklow – not far from the gang's training camp in Lacken. The job was well planned in advance. Just before the robbery the main telephone lines to the village were cut. Then the team stormed into the village with military precision. Wearing combat fatigues and armed with pistols and machine-guns, the revolutionaries terrified the peaceful inhabitants of Rathdrum, who had previously only seen drama like it on TV. The raiders marched into the Hibernian Bank and fired shots in the air to show the staff they meant business. 'Open up or I'll shoot,' one of them shouted. The manager handed over the contents of the safe, £1,900. Outside other raiders fired two shots over the head of local Garda Frank Arrigan and held him at gunpoint. Garda Arrigan would later claim the gunman was Frank Keane. As they made their getaway in two stolen cars, the raiders stopped at the local gunsmiths and grabbed five shotguns, three rifles and a revolver to augment their arsenal. They drove off and vanished into the countryside before the alarm could be raised.

The escapades of the workers' champions were causing intense embarrassment and anger in the Gardaí. The gang usually managed to get away and were generally running rings around them. And when cornered, as they were in the Ballyfermot incident, they showed that they had no reluctance about using lethal force to resist arrest. Saor Eire was the first criminal mob to take full advantage of a malaise which had set in over decades of law-abiding peace in the Republic. An Garda Síochána was firmly rooted in a halcyon age, where a handful of burglaries were considered a crime wave. Detection rates in all categories of crime were favourably high. But solving petty crime was child's play compared to dealing with well-organized, criminal enterprises. Decades of poor pay and working conditions had also eroded morale to breaking point. Gardaí, who then lived in their stations, were being accommodated in conditions described in a government report as 'sub-standard and not fit to live in'. Members worked for as many hours as were required, for no extra pay. In 1968, the rank and file membership finally took industrial action. Throughout the country large numbers of Gardaí refused to turn up for work or called in sick. As a result, the Government established the Conroy Commission to investigate grievances over pay and work conditions. In January 1970, it made over fifty separate recommendations, including the introduction of a basic 42-hour week and a shift system. Pay was also to be increased through overtime allocations. Implementing the new regime, however, created more problems.

Critics argued that a lack of adequate planning about how to apply the new working conditions threw the Garda organization into further disarray and seriously hampered its ability to investigate crime. Local superintendents found themselves trying to juggle between the limited man-hours laid down by the Department of Justice and limited overtime budgets. It meant that whole districts were often left without police cover and squad cars were grounded simply because the money to pay the crew had run out. Cordons, which were intended to be set up after major crimes, such as the Rathdrum robbery, could not be activated if local commanders had spent their overtime allocation for the month. The situation caused morale to plummet even further. In the definitive history of the Force, *The Garda Síochána: Policing Independent Ireland 1922–82*, the author Greg Allen summarized the state of policing in the first few years of the 1970s. He wrote: 'A measure of the demoralisation that set in was the virtual eclipse of the Garda Síochána as a preventive force, as patrols disappeared off the streets. Apart from the occasional sighting of a patrol car, citizens could travel the length of the country without encountering a uniformed guard.'

There was also serious concern about the lack of investment in basic equipment. Officers had good reason to complain that the criminals were going to work better equipped than they were. Saor Eire members were using two-way radios to co-ordinate their raids and stealing high-powered getaway cars which easily outran the cars in the Garda fleet. Any attempt to mount a co-ordinated manhunt for the raiders was virtually impossible because there were huge black spots in the Garda national radio network, and no aerial support available. By 1970, the group probably had as many guns as were in the entire Force.

The Garda Síochána was not the only organization ill-equipped for the new challenges. The justice system was also languishing in a different age. In the 1970s, the waiting list for the growing number of criminal trials began to clog up the whole system. The result was that the time lapse between someone being charged and then coming to trial stretched into years.

In 1966, the Supreme Court had ruled that people could not be kept in custody while awaiting trial unless there was clear evidence they intended to abscond or interfere with witnesses. It meant that it was virtually impossible to keep a suspect in custody, even if that person was facing a number of charges. Gardaí argued that there would be a reduction in the number of robberies if the bail laws were tightened up and suspects were held in custody until trial – but the law remained unchanged.

In the early stages of the Troubles there was also a degree of ambivalence among the judiciary – and indeed the wider society – towards the paramilitary groups. This is borne out by a perusal of newspaper reports on armed robbery trials at the time. In a more naïve era, a 'political' motive for a crime was treated as a mitigating factor. As a result, every hoodlum caught coming out of a bank with a gun in his hand had a cause. The gangsters and the terrorists couldn't have picked a more favourable environment in which to launch their new business.

An unidentified Garda source, quoted in the *Irish Times* after the Rathdrum heist, summarized the situation: 'It is taking the public a long time to realise what is involved in these situations. The political people may not mean to shoot, but there may be accidents and somebody may have a go, or – and I feel this may be happening already – this bank robbing has been shown to be a "good thing" and there's no reason why it should be confined to politically-minded, young men. There may be bloody-minded, young men at it too, and then the public may not be so complacent about it.'

After the Rathdrum raid the Central Detective Unit (CDU), which was based in Dublin Castle, was tasked with launching a co-ordinated counter-offensive against Saor Eire. All available intelligence on the members and their associates was collated. Surveillance, such as it was in a time when there were no specialist units, was placed on known sympathizers and suspects; informants were squeezed for what they knew.

Within weeks of the Rathdrum job a plan was put in place to round up all known members of the organization, in a massive search and arrest operation. At the last moment, however, the operation was called off by someone in higher authority. No explanation was given and it further fuelled rumours of an unholy alliance between the men in the combat fatigues and those in suits.

The decision to cancel the operation would have devastating consequences.

Dick Fallon spent most of his 23 years in the Gardaí as a beat-cop on the streets of Dublin's north inner-city. Originally from Lanesboro in County Roscommon, he was one of four brothers in his family to join the Gardaí. The 44-year-old was married with five young children. Fallon had a reputation as a tough but fair cop, who was on first-name terms with every criminal in the city. By April 1970, he was well acquainted with the members of Saor Eire, many of whom were living in his district.

The veteran cop mentored the young, fresh-faced recruits, many of them from the country, whose first glimpse of the big city was the alien world of Mountjoy Station – next door to the country's main committal prison. One of his brightest protégés was a young Kerry man called Tony Hickey, who joined up in 1965.

The now retired Assistant Commissioner recalls: 'When I arrived from Templemore I was stationed in Mountjoy Station where Dick Fallon would have been one of the senior Gardaí and he mentored us younger people. At the time Ireland was a pretty stable, conservative society and serious crime was virtually unheard of. There was a certain amount of burglaries, larcenies; a certain amount of violence such as bad rows outside pubs. Some people carried knives and guns were most unusual. But that changed with the arrival of Saor Eire.'

Hickey never forgot the last time Dick Fallon offered him advice:

'Dick Fallon was very concerned about the activities of Saor Eire and how their robberies were becoming more violent. In his wisdom he probably knew it was only a matter of time before they killed someone, especially a Guard. I remember the day he stood in the front office in Mountjoy Station at parade time and addressed our unit before we went out on the beat. He told us to be extra vigilant and careful on the street. In his case, he said, a Scott Medal awarded posthumously wouldn't be any good to his widow. His words turned out to be very prophetic.'

On 3 April, six weeks after the dramatic assault on Rathdrum, funds for 'the cause' were already running low. Five members of Saor Eire parked a stolen getaway car on Lincoln Lane and waited for a few minutes to scan the area. The lane was situated at the rear of the Royal Bank of Ireland branch on Arran Quay, on the northern quay of the River Liffey. The gang had earlier planned to hit a bank on Dorset Street but abandoned the idea when they spotted a truckload of soldiers parked outside. The revolutionaries were not yet ready to take on the army. The bank on Arran Quay was their second choice. The robbers were armed with a machine-gun and pistols from the consignment stolen in Birmingham. They cut the phone and alarm wires at the rear of the building and ran down a side passageway. When the wires were cut a flashing, yellow light was set off on a console in the Chubb security company's monitoring office in Leinster Street. It indicated that the alarms had been tampered with. As the light flashed, a Chubb employee phoned the main switchboard at the Garda Command and Control room in Dublin Castle to report that a possible incident was occurring.

At 10.45 a.m., the three Saor Eire members pulled masks over their faces and burst through the doors of the bank, shouting: 'This is a stick up.' Customers and staff were ordered to face the wall and were covered by a raider carrying the machine-gun. 'Stay where you are or you'll get this,' he shouted, as his two comrades jumped over the counter. They began filling two bags with cash.

When Garda Command and Control relayed the call to go to Arran Quay, Dick Fallon was sitting in the back seat of the nearest patrol car, Delta One. Although still in uniform, he was officially off-duty. The patrol car crew, Paul Firth and Patrick Hunter, were giving him a lift to collect his car from a local garage. They were on North King Street when the call came through and they raced to Arran Quay. One of the officers asked Fallon if he wanted to get out but he said he would go with them.

In the few minutes since the yellow light had started flashing, the raiders had filled their bags with £3,270. As they were heading for the doors one of them warned: 'Don't follow us or you'll have it.' It was their thirteenth major robbery in three years.

Fallon and Firth had got out of the patrol car and were walking towards the entrance of the bank as the raiders were leaving. When the raiders saw the uniformed Guards they made a dash for their getaway car. Garda Fallon sprinted after them, followed by Firth, while Hunter called for more back-up. One of the raiders shot Dick Fallon in the arm but he kept going. As they rounded the corner on to a side passageway, he grappled with one of the raiders and another shot rang out. A second gang member doubled back and shot the officer in the head at close range. Dick Fallon fell face down on the concrete pavement as the raiders ran to the waiting getaway car. He died as his colleague whispered a prayer in his ear.

Dick Fallon was the first Garda to be murdered in the line of duty since 1942 – and the first to become a victim of Ireland's new culture of violent crime. Over the next 15 years another 11 Gardaí and a soldier would also be gunned down as they tackled bank robbers, kidnappers and terrorists. Like Deirdre Fallon, their widows would be left to collect their posthumous Scott Medals for bravery. Retired Assistant Commissioner Tony Hickey was one of the officers who raced to the bank when the call went out that a colleague was down. 'It was hard to believe what had happened,' he remembers. 'We were at the scene very quickly and there was shock, there was horror, it was unprecedented. It certainly was a watershed as far as policing in this country was concerned. It would be fair to say that nothing would be the same again. Armed crime and murder and shootings would become so commonplace.' Five years later Hickey, who would become one of the country's top investigators, also received a Scott Medal for bravery. He and three colleagues, all of them unarmed, disarmed two armed robbers in a post office hold-up.

The investigation into the Fallon murder provided evidence of how hopelessly ill-prepared and disorganized the Force was to deal with violent crime. The initial shock at the news that a Garda had been gunned down was followed by utter confusion. The Gardaí had no experience of investigating crimes like this. No one seemed to know whose job it was to cordon off the scene and to search for evidence. The technical skills necessary to lift vital forensic clues were sadly lacking. A special report in the *Irish Times*, by security correspondent Conor Brady, noted how journalists, cameramen and nosey members of the public were allowed to tread all over the crime scene. Most damning of all, a few days later a child found spent bullet casings near the spot where Garda Fallon was shot. It was a hugely embarrassing episode in the history of An Garda Síochána and an indictment of the pervasive ineptitude.

Despite the fact that the modus operandi of the robbery immediately pointed to Saor Eire, the homes of known suspects were not searched until several days later. By then any evidence linked to the murder was long gone. The task should have been made easier because of the similar operation that had been planned in February but the delay was never explained. Another link with Saor Eire was established when the bullets found in Dick Fallon's body were tested. The results showed that they came from the weapons stolen in Birmingham.

The Government joined the public chorus of condemnation and hurriedly announced a £5,000 reward for information leading to the capture of the culprits. In response Garda management took the unprecedented step of issuing the photographs, names and addresses of the seven Saor Eire members they wanted to interview in relation to the murder. They were published in the national newspapers the following morning. The names on the list were Simon O'Donnell, Joe Dillon, Patrick Dillon, Frank Keane, Thomas O'Neill, Sean Doyle and John Morrissey, all of whom were already on the run. But somehow that exercise was also bungled. Two of the addresses given for the men were wrong – one was the home of Brendan Behan's mother, and the news editor of the *Irish Times* lived at the other.

The following day an open letter from Frank Keane was published in the morning newspapers. In it, he accused the police of making scapegoats of him and the other men on the list, who were 'in all possibility quite innocent of this unfortunate crime'. Keane then fled the country to England.

The Fallon murder caused bitter internal recriminations in a Force already riven by low morale. The uniformed and 'crime ordinary' branches, both of which were unarmed, wondered why armed Special Branch officers hadn't responded to the call sooner. It also inevitably sparked the ubiquitous debate about arming the police. This would become a recurring theme over the years when other members of the Force were murdered.

On 29 April, the Special Branch discovered the training camp at Lacken, County Wicklow. They recovered firearms, detonators, combat uniforms and other military equipment. Questions were asked as to why it had not been found earlier. Informants had already revealed that Saor Eire was operating a camp somewhere in the Wicklow Mountains.

The murder of Garda Fallon caused an unprecedented public display of grief and anger. The Government hadn't organized a State funeral but on Monday, 6 April Dublin came to a standstill as people turned out to honour the fallen policeman. Thousands left their homes, schools and workplaces to pay their respects along the route, as the funeral cortège slowly made its way across the city. It passed from the policeman's church of St Paul of the Cross in Mount Argus, Harold's Cross, through O'Connell Street and onwards to Balgriffin Cemetery in the north of the city. Up to 2,000 Gardaí marched in step behind the hearse for the entire journey. The Garda Band, which had been dissolved on cost-cutting grounds five years earlier, voluntarily reformed to lead the funeral of their slain colleague. A solemn silence fell over the city as the hearse passed the GPO. The sound of the Gardaí's marching feet in step behind it signalled the death knell of peace in Ireland.

The treatment of Dick Fallon's widow and children by the Government and the Garda authorities in the months and years that followed was nothing short of shameful. Despite the expressions of support at the time, they were effectively forgotten about. Deirdre Fallon was left to rear her children with little financial support and even had to pay for the funeral herself. The gunmen destroyed more than one life when they opened fire that morning in April 1970.

In the corridors of power Dick Fallon's murder caused panic behind closed doors. Rumours of collusion between government figures and Saor Eire were no longer being whispered around Leinster House as deputies spoke openly of an unholy alliance. Within weeks of the murder the Taoiseach, Jack Lynch, was informed that ministers Charles

Haughey and Neil Blaney were involved in a plot to import arms from the Continent for nationalist defence committees in Belfast. The plan had been hatched as the Six Counties descended towards all-out civil war; Northern republicans had asked the ministers for weapons to protect their communities. An Irish army intelligence officer, Captain James Kelly, had been sent to the Continent with a big shopping list: 200 machine-guns, 84 light machine-guns, 50 general-purpose machine-guns, 50 assault rifles, 200 pistols, grenades and a large amount of ammunition. The arsenal was enough to equip an army battalion. Blaney had recruited an interpreter, an Irishman of Belgian origin called Albert Luykx, to help organize the deal. Haughey, as Minister for Finance, with overall control of Customs and Excise and the George Dixon bank account, would ensure that the arms were paid for and smuggled into the country without being stopped.

Although the arms deal was never finalized, Jack Lynch, who claimed no knowledge of the plot, sacked both ministers on 6 May 1970 in a bid to salvage the integrity of the Government. The Minister for Justice, Michael O'Morain, was also sacked from the Cabinet. Other prominent members of Fianna Fáil resigned in support of the dismissed ministers.

The suspicions of collusion between Saor Eire and the government ministers had also been confirmed. But in the Dáil, Neil Blaney went to great lengths to distance himself from the charges of arms smuggling and from Saor Eire. He described the rumours that he'd had anything to do with subversives as 'sinister, subtle and blackguardly'. He declared: 'I have no guns; I have procured no guns; I have paid for no guns and I have provided money to pay for no guns.' Blaney referred directly to Saor Eire, now the most hated group in the country: 'They are a lousy outfit. I have nothing but the utmost contempt for them.' In the aftermath of Dick Fallon's murder, it was clear there would be no more government-sponsored plots to arm republican groups. The days of Saor Eire were numbered.

Haughey, Blaney and Captain Kelly were subsequently charged with conspiracy to illegally import arms into the country. The charges against Blaney were dropped in the District Court and both Haughey and Kelly were acquitted after trials by jury. Less than a decade later, Charles Haughey became Taoiseach, at a time when the Provos were at the height of their murderous, criminal war. Captain Kelly claimed for the rest of his life that he'd been working with the secret approval of the Government.

Des O'Malley, who was appointed as Minister for Justice to take over from O'Morain, believes that the 'Arms Crisis' posed a sinister threat: 'It became clear when the attempts to import arms came to light, that there was a very serious threat indeed to the very integrity of the State because in 1969 and 1970 there was subversion within the State, within the very Government that was there to represent and protect the State and its citizens, and that made it so much more sinister. And it was perhaps the most serious threat to the State internally since the civil war and in many respects I suppose it could be compared to the potential threat from outside during the Second World War.'

A week after the sensational ministerial sackings in Dublin, Saor Eire leader Frank Keane was arrested. Police in London captured him on behalf of the Irish authorities, who had issued warrants for his arrest. The Gardaí had moved quickly to assemble their case against Keane and two other members of the gang, Joe Dillon and John Morrissey. But evidence against the men was weak. It was mostly dependent on Garda Paul Firth, who claimed he could identify them.

The State applied to the British courts to have Keane extradited to face trial for the murder of Dick Fallon and the Rathdrum escapade. Frank Keane challenged his extradition in the Old Bailey on the grounds that his was a political crime. He admitted being a former member of the IRA and a leader of Saor Eire. Cathal Goulding, Chief of Staff of the Official IRA, sent a sworn affidavit to the hearing. He said Keane had been a member but had been dismissed from the organization over 'policy disagreements'. Keane also produced testimony from witnesses who claimed that money from the armed robberies had been used for political purposes in Northern Ireland.

Meanwhile, on 17 June 1970, a jury in the Central Criminal Court found Padraig Dwyer guilty of shooting at the four unarmed Gardaí during the failed Ballyfermot robbery in October 1968 and of possession of firearms with intent to endanger life. The plumber had been recaptured in England and, like Frank Keane, fought extradition on the grounds it was a political crime. Incredibly, Dwyer only received a two-year suspended jail sentence in what could be seen as an indictment of the ambivalence of the times. Sean Doyle later got two years for his part in the same incident but was released after three months. This was after he gave a strict undertaking that he would not get involved in any more causes. Thomas O'Neill was also eventually convicted for the Ballyfermot incident and received two concurrent sentences of 18 months each. Simon O'Donnell was still on the run.

In July 1970, Saor Eire showed that it hadn't gone away when an explosion ripped through the offices of Dalton Supplies in Bray, County Wicklow. No one was hurt in the blast. The social revolutionaries issued a statement claiming responsibility for the attack. In a declaration sent to the national newspapers they claimed the bomb was intended to force the company to accept recommendations made by the Labour Court on behalf of the workers. The unions didn't appreciate the unsolicited 'help' from cop killers.

Then, on 13 October, 30-year-old Liam Walsh was blown to pieces. He was carrying a bomb along a rail track at the rear of McKee Army Barracks on Blackhorse Avenue in north Dublin. Martin Casey, who was with Walsh, was critically injured in the blast but survived. When their bodies were searched, the two men were carrying Star pistols from the consignment stolen in Birmingham. The Saor Eire leader was given a paramilitary-style funeral on 17 October which was attended by over 1,000 mourners. In what was seen as an attempt to add insult to the memory of Dick Fallon, Walsh's funeral procession was diverted down O'Connell Street as it made its way from Inchicore to Mount Jerome Cemetery in Harold's Cross. It stopped outside the GPO where speeches were made and a volley of shots was fired by Christy 'Bronco' Dunne.

Frank Keane fought his extradition case all the way to the House of Lords but eventually lost. The Saor Eire founder was sent back to Dublin and his trial began in June 1971. On 25 June a jury acquitted him of the murder of Garda Fallon, after witnesses failed to identify him as one of the raiders. The only positive identification of Keane at the scene was by Garda Firth. The other 38 witnesses testified that the raiders were wearing masks.

Keane was re-arrested the same day and this time charged with the Rathdrum heist. He was granted bail and a year later was again acquitted. Keane could only be identified by one witness, Garda Arrigan, the officer who had been held at gunpoint during the robbery. The court ruled that the Garda's testimony could not be relied upon in the absence of other eye-witness testimony.

The former Saor Eire leader never featured in the courts again. Both Frank Keane and his pet political project seemed set to fade into obscurity but then, on 31 August, a four-man gang robbed the Ulster Bank in Kilcock, County Kildare. Shots were fired and the gang leader, Frank Ward, told the terrified customers and staff that they were from Saor Eire. Ward was typical of the hoods attracted to the gang. He was a violent and highly dangerous criminal who would go on to make his mark in gangland history.

On 16 October 1971, the Gardaí finally caught up with Joe Dillon and John Morrissey. They had been lying low in a safe house, in Bayside on Dublin's north-side, and were captured after a high-speed chase. It ended when Special Branch detectives opened fire on their getaway car with a Thompson machine-gun. Both men were armed with handguns when they were arrested. Joe Dillon had been on the run since he'd walked out of the Four Courts in August 1967. The two terrorists were charged with the murder of Dick Fallon and remanded in custody.

Nine days later, on 25 October, the Trotskyite Peter Graham was murdered by Saor Eire members in what is believed to have been a row over money. The infamous 'Guevarists' had begun to implode. The chairman of the Young Socialists was first tortured and beaten with a hammer, before being shot in the neck and left to choke on his own blood. He was 26 years old. Graham's funeral was attended by many well-known republicans and left-wing radicals. Among the mourners was RTÉ reporter Charlie Bird, who was pictured giving a clenched-fist salute at the graveside. Graham's Young Socialist comrade Maureen Keegan died from cancer in 1972.

A month after the murder, in November 1971, Joe Dillon was jailed for six years for the Drumcondra robbery in 1968. His fingerprints had been found in a glove left behind in the gang's getaway car. Two days later his comrade, 29-year-old Martin Casey, was jailed for four years for possession of firearms in connection with the bomb blast near McKee Barracks. He was subsequently acquitted of the 1969 Baltinglass robbery in the Special Criminal Court. Casey made no public issue of his trip to London with Jock Haughey.

In January 1972, Joe Dillon and John Morrissey stood trial for the murder of Dick Fallon. They were also acquitted because of the unreliable visual identification by Garda Paul Firth and other inconsistencies in his evidence. A month later the two hoods received 18 months each for possession of firearms at the time of their arrest. On the same day, two RUC policemen were shot dead when their car was sprayed with machine-gun fire in Derry. The Provos had already seized Saor Eire's revolutionary limelight.

As the trial of Dillon and Morrissey commenced, Gardaí also caught up with Simon O'Donnell. He hadn't been seen since he'd gone on the run in 1968 but he was one of the men sought following the Fallon murder. Despite the heat now coming down on what was left of Saor Eire, O'Donnell was still busy raising money for his cause. He was captured after a hold-up at the Ulster Bank branch in Ranelagh, Dublin, on 6 January 1972. O'Donnell and his Saor Eire criminal associate, Tommy Savage, had got away with £1,827. Savage, a 22-year-old chemical processor from Swords, had only recently joined the 'cause' and this was his first time coming to the attention of the Gardaí. The two blaggers had been arrested after they were found hiding in a house near the bank they had just robbed. The remnants of Saor Eire were nabbed after a bank employee followed them to the house and called the police. The house was surrounded and O'Donnell and Savage surrendered. When Savage came out with his hands up, he made an impromptu speech on the pavement. He said: 'I only want a fair trial. I have nothing whatsoever to do with the bank robbery in Ranelagh.' The money was never recovered.

In March, O'Donnell was tried for the 1968 Newbridge robbery. He was acquitted by a jury, again because of the weak evidence against him. Immediately afterwards he was remanded in custody for the robbery in Ranelagh. A month later he was convicted for that offence and jailed for seven years. In his defence, his counsel told the court that he had been stealing the money for a political cause. He was never charged with the Fallon murder.

Tommy Savage was convicted a few weeks later on the same charges and also got seven years. Gardaí said that Savage came from a good family and implied that he had been adversely influenced by Simon O'Donnell. Mr Justice Butler told Savage that if, after serving three years, he had complied with normal prison regulations, the remainder of the sentence would be suspended. The judge said he 'objected strongly to people taking advantage of the present political state of the country to give cheap, petty crime a political connotation'. But Tommy Savage had no intention of ever going straight and this was the only time the police ever said anything good about him. In the years to come he would continue to straddle the worlds of organized crime and dissident republicanism. For Savage, the Ranelagh job was the start of a long and violent criminal career.

Simon O'Donnell was back before Mr Justice Butler two months later for the Ballyfermot shooting in 1968. This time he pleaded guilty and received another ten years, the longest sentence yet handed down to any of the Saor Eire mavericks. During the hearing, Mr Justice Butler asked if O'Donnell could give an undertaking that he would no longer involve himself in political organizations. He refused. In passing sentence, Judge Butler commented on what the rest of the Establishment were beginning to finally realize: 'Far too many petty criminals are masquerading under the banner of patriotism and committing crimes for their own selfish ends.'

Within two years of Dick Fallon's murder in April 1970, Saor Eire had faded into obscurity and most of its leaders were never heard of again. In May 1973, its members in Portlaoise Prison announced that they were resigning from the organization because it had been taken over by 'undesirable elements and gangsters'. Members of the group in Cork and Dublin had joined emerging criminal gangs or the Official IRA, which was also heavily involved in organized crime. Other former Saor Eire members joined the Provos. Some of the most ruthless armed robbers and drug-dealers who emerged during the following decades came from the ranks of the socialist revolutionary mob. Almost thirty years later Joe Dillon, who had continued to be an active republican, joined the dissident 32-County Sovereignty Movement and acted as its official spokesman. Dillon and his comrades totally opposed the Peace Process in the North. They accused the Sinn Féin and IRA leadership of selling out on their old ideals of achieving a united Ireland through force of arms. The veteran Saor Eire member soon found himself in trouble with the law again. On 5 January 1998, he was arrested with two other men and charged with possession of an explosive substance with intent to endanger life. They eventually stood trial before the Special Criminal Court in June 2001. On the eighth day of the hearing, counsel for the State dramatically announced that it would not be proceeding any further. The decision to enter a *nolle prosequi* on all the charges came after the court ruled that coded numbers, referring to members of the Garda National Surveillance Unit, should be disclosed to the defence. The Gardaí argued that by making the numbers public it would remove cover from the specialist unit and inhibit future investigations. Joe Dillon walked out of the court a free man.

In 1974, a group of former Saor Eire members, including Tommy Savage, helped spawn a new Marxist terror gang, the Irish National Liberation Army (INLA), following an acrimonious split from the Official IRA. The INLA and its political wing, the Irish Republican Socialist Party (IRSP), officially came into existence at a meeting in a Dublin hotel on 19 December 1974. Its leader was Seamus Costelloe, a former Official IRA man from Bray, County Wicklow. He styled the organization on terror groups such as the Red Brigade and the Baader-Meinhof gang. The INLA's purported aim was the establishment of a socialist united Ireland. It took over where Saor Eire had left off.

The organization became a magnet for criminals and the lowlife dregs of republicanism. In essence their cause of an 'Irish socialist republic' was a flag of convenience for psychopaths, mass murderers, drug-dealers and thugs. Among the INLA's leaders were cold-blooded killers Dominic McGlinchey and Dessie O'Hare, who, between them, were responsible for some of the worst atrocities of the Troubles. Their more 'celebrated' acts of war included an attempted massacre at a Pentecostal prayer meeting. Three church elders died during the attack and seven more were seriously injured when gunmen sprayed the congregation with machine-gun fire.

The INLA's inglorious, disreputable history is dominated by a string of internecine blood feuds. Members of the organization have murdered more of their own comrades than British soldiers. Like Saor Eire, the new organization's selective interpretation of Marxist doctrine also meant that they had no qualms immersing themselves in organized crime, drug-trafficking and gangland murder.

A year later, in June 1975, Liam White, a leading Saor Eire member in Cork, who also had links to the INLA, was murdered. He was shot 14 times by two men with machine-guns. White was given a paramilitary-style funeral and his brother told reporters: 'Saor Eire will revenge his death.' The Official IRA was suspected of carrying out the attack.

Shortly afterwards Saor Eire was officially disbanded, but by then it had already started to fade into history. In its short, violent existence it had failed to wrench power from the capitalists and create a workers' republic. It had, however, succeeded in making armed robbery an attractive proposition for the up and coming gangsters.

Saor Eire's revolution had won independence for a place called Gangland – and one of its former associates was destined to become Ireland's first undisputed Godfather. His family-based criminal empire would have a profound influence on the future direction of Irish organized crime. That man was gun-smuggler Christy 'Bronco' Dunne.

3. The Godfather

Christy 'Bronco' Dunne always wanted to be the Godfather of a Mafia-style crime syndicate, and he craved the notoriety and status enjoyed by underworld celebrities like the Krays in London. Bronco fancied himself as a real-life version of Michael Corleone, the central character in the powerful *Godfather* movies of the early 1970s. Tall and handsome, with a glib tongue and a good command of the English language, Bronco exuded charm, bravado and menace in equal amounts. He relished his image as the neighbourhood bad boy and working-class hero. He already had the nucleus of a 'family business' around him – seven fiercely loyal younger brothers, whom he'd taught to steal when they were still children. Saor Eire gave him his first big break on the road to gangland stardom.

Although not a formal member of the group, the accomplished chancer managed to place himself prominently among the leaders of the Che Guevara wannabes. Running with gangland's first real hard cases satisfied Bronco's hunger for recognition and street cred. In his eyes, it made him a major player. Dunne was introduced to the socialist revolutionary 'family' by Liam Walsh and Martin Casey. When his Saor Eire pals then blew themselves up while transporting a bomb, Bronco seized the opportunity to make a name for himself.

With most of Saor Eire's leadership wanted for the Dick Fallon murder and a string of heists, Christy Dunne was given the task of organizing a hero's send-off for Walsh. An old friend and mentor of Christy's, Father Michael Sweetman, officiated at the funeral Mass, which was attended by over 1,000 mourners. Afterwards a lone piper and a paramilitary colour party led the funeral procession through the streets of Dublin. The procession stopped outside the GPO, the spiritual home of Irish resistance, to eulogize their fallen comrade.

Father Sweetman gave a homily on the replenishing powers of the Resurrection, while Christy Dunne spoke about the 'Insurrection' Walsh had supposedly died for. Not content with enthralling the mourners with his passionate oratory, attention-seeking Dunne produced a handgun.

He fired a number of shots into the air to prove his dedication to 'the cause'. He was subsequently charged with the incident and the case was heard in the Dublin District Court in February 1971. Justice Robert O'hUadaigh threw out the charge on a legal technicality and told Dunne he was free to go. But Bronco had other plans. He expressed his gratitude by jumping up and punching the judge. When Gardaí finally dragged Bronco off the bench, Justice O'hUadaigh gave him six months to calm him down. As a result the opportunistic rebel became a folk hero on both sides of the prison walls. By the time he was released, he'd parted with radical politics but he quickly put to use what he had learned from Saor Eire.

Within a few years, Christy Dunne had achieved his life's ambition. He and his brothers Shamie, Henry, Larry, Mickey, Robert, Vianney ('Boyo') and Charlie had become the first family-based gang in Ireland. Under Christy's leadership, they were a highly efficient team of armed robbers – bound together by blood ties. The name Dunne became synonymous with Irish organized crime and earned its infamous place in Gangland's history books. The Dunnes began to spread their operation, inducting other young hoods, such as Martin Cahill and Paddy Shanahan, into the Mafia-style family.

The Dunne brothers were men of 'respect' in the Dublin underworld, which meant everyone was afraid of them. Christy nurtured his image as the untouchable gang boss. He would brag that the Dunnes were skilled craftsmen at the 'job' and the cleverest villains in town. The colourful crook was a popular addition to Dublin's thriving social scene and he befriended a number of well-known journalists and celebrities. In the less enlightened, more innocent 1970s it was considered chic to hang out with 'bad boy' gangsters and republicans in the city's fashionable bars and clubs. But despite his best efforts, Bronco was no Don Corleone.

In November 1983, media-friendly Bronco agreed to take part in an interview on RTÉ radio to discuss his family's reputation as the Irish equivalent of the Mafia. 'I would have to take responsibility for introducing serious crime into the family only because I felt that with my brothers, that if we ever would do anything together, which we have done, that it was a closely kept secret between us. We worked together, we could depend on each other for our lives and we knew that whatever we did no one else would ever know about it,' he candidly revealed.

Then he reverted to his favourite role of 'the victim' – a part he performed with aplomb whenever the necessity arose: 'I think it was convenient for the authorities, and the police in particular, to have a family like the Dunnes who I regard as just scapegoats, to have their names bandied about by the people who knew that we could not come back to them and argue these points with them and say: "Look you are wrong accusing us of this – why don't you come forward and we will meet you."'

Bronco went public because his family had indeed become famous and most of his brothers were household names – but it wasn't for the type of hype he had intended. A few years earlier most of the Dunnes had moved on from armed robberies into the much more profitable business of hard drugs – despite the disapproval of their big brother. They'd introduced the scourge of heroin to Dublin's working-class neighbourhoods, with catastrophic consequences. The family name was dirt and the brothers were despised. Christy had been forced to mount a damage-limitation exercise on their behalf: 'A lot of my family live in sub-standard accommodation that has been given to them by the Corporation. Dublin Corporation has made it quite clear that under no circumstances will the Dunnes ever be housed in anything other than sub-standard accommodation. I feel that my family, like most other unfortunate people living in these areas, became victims.'

When asked about his own reputation as a Godfather he was unusually coy: 'I am not a Godfather, I am a *good* father.'

Christy Dunne was born on 10 October 1938, the first child of Christy Senior and Ellen Dunne. The couple, both born and raised in inner-city slums, had married two years earlier. Christy Junior's father, nicknamed 'Bronco' after the cowboy Bronco Bill, was 22 years old and Ellen was 15. After their wedding the couple first rented a rundown tenement flat in Kildare Street, before moving to another one-roomed hovel in New Street. Over the next two decades or so, Ellen Dunne endured 22 pregnancies, of which 16 children survived after birth – 11 boys and 5 girls. When she wasn't expecting, Ellen Dunne tried to feed her large family with the meagre income she made running her small second-hand clothes stall. It was in the Iveagh Market, off Francis Street in the Liberties area of south inner-city Dublin.

Christy Senior was a violent alcoholic who stumbled from one job to another. His own father, Christy Junior's grandfather, had abandoned his family in the 1930s and gone to live in Liverpool. Christy's grandfather claimed he was forced to leave because of his republicanism – he had been on the anti-Treaty side during the Irish Civil War. As a youngster Bronco Senior had been in and out of trouble with the law. When Christy Junior was two, his father was convicted of manslaughter. He had killed a drinking buddy who was paying too much attention to his mother (Christy Junior's grandmother). Christy Senior punched his victim so hard that the man fell down and cracked his skull on the floor. He went into a coma and died a week later in hospital. Bronco was sentenced to 18 months in Portlaoise Prison, where, over thirty years later, his sons would also take up residence – for much longer periods. By the time he was sent down, Ellen had had another baby and a third was on the way.

The killing consolidated Christy Senior's reputation as a hard man. He told his young sons that he was proud of what he had done – he was defending the honour of the family. After his release from prison he went to work in wartime Britain, but was deported twice for not having a proper permit. Christy Senior, like his father before him, also claimed to be a republican and was pro-German during the War. When he came home for good there was no work in poverty-stricken Dublin. The lack of work and the inevitable hardship it brought on his family, however, did not interfere with his drinking habits. During a boozing session one night, the republican rebel produced a revolver and fired off a shot in the pub. As a result he was arrested and given six months in Mountjoy Prison to help him sober up.

It was in this atmosphere that Christy Dunne and his siblings were reared. In 1951, the ever-increasing Dunne family – Ellen Dunne endured her twenty-second pregnancy four years later – were moved to a new Corporation house at Rutland Avenue in Crumlin. It was part of the Government's slum clearance programme but the new house changed little. The problems of poverty and deprivation had just changed address with the Dunnes. Their mother simply couldn't cope and their father was rarely there. When he was at home violence was a way of life. The children would watch their father beat their mother when he fell in from the pub. Bronco Senior would also beat manners into his children, and when he wasn't around Ellen, who was a hard drinker too, beat them in a vain attempt to control them. The children were often left to fend for themselves for long periods without either parent. They began running wild, stealing or begging for food to eat. Many of them were reared by their grandmother, Nellie O'Brien, including Christy Junior. His brothers Larry, Henry, Robert and Boyo once spent several weeks hiding out in the Glencree Caves in the Wicklow Hills, sleeping rough and stealing food from farms. At the time, they ranged in ages between seven and ten. The children were found after their family got concerned and Gardaí launched a full-scale search.

Bronco Junior looked after the neglected youngsters as best he could – when he wasn't in custody or on the run from the police. Inevitably Christy Junior was the first of the brothers to get involved in crime – and he soon showed his younger siblings how it was done. With typical bravado, he once claimed that at the age of ten he was robbing more than some men earned in a week. He stole food from the shops and coal from the dockyard to bring home to his deprived family. Christy would allow his brothers to bunk off school and took them on mini-crime sprees. After a while they quit school altogether. In the Dunne household, a hunger for food far surpassed any appetite for education and their parents didn't care. An old family friend once recalled visiting the house and finding Christy Junior standing in the middle of a room, with no furniture, dishing out stew from a pot to eight of his hungry siblings.

One by one, the other brothers began to get involved in petty crime. Christy, Shamie, Larry, Robert, Henry, Boyo, Mickey, Hubert and Charlie had all started their criminal careers by the age of ten. All the Dunne brothers, with the exception of Shamie, would spend most of their teenage years in and out of Ireland's notorious industrial and reformatory schools. They were convicted on a variety of offences, from truancy to theft. Despite being wild they never, however, bothered any of their neighbours. Christy Junior and his siblings adhered to the few family precepts which had been beaten into them. They were to be courteous, take pride in their appearance and, above all, never steal from their own people. Neighbours who remember the family said that the Dunnes kept very much to themselves and did not share their problems with anyone.

In 2011, at the age of 73, Christy Junior gave his first interview in almost thirty years. It was for a documentary on gangland in Dublin shown on the National Geographic channel. Unlike the majority of his contemporaries, the years had been good to Ireland's longest-living gangster. Wearing his long silver hair tied back in a neat pony-tail, he looked like an ageing hippie. The gangland grandfather recalled what life was like growing up in his family: 'When we were kids we robbed. My father was in prison and my mother found it hard and we just took it upon ourselves that she should have the comforts around her. I had to cook for them [his siblings], get them ready for school and advise them to do the right things in life – especially, don't get caught!'

Christy got his first taste of incarceration at the age of 12 when he was sent to the Carriglea Industrial School in Dun Laoghaire for truancy. He later described the place as like something from a Dickens novel – a miserable existence of constant beatings and hard, physical work. One of the sadistic brothers told him that the punishment was to make them better individuals, better Irishmen. Bronco didn't agree and ran away. He hid out with his grandmother Nellie O'Brien. He later recalled of his first stint in custody: 'That made things worse for me. The brutality and deprivation was unbearable.'

While on the run Christy spent time in England, where he worked in a coal mine and laboured on building sites. He was a big lad for his age and no one seemed to notice that he was only in his early teens. Christy was also a tough kid who could stand up to people twice his age. In 1955, he returned home after his 14-year-old brother Hubert drowned. He'd been swimming near Upton Industrial School in County Cork and his death was witnessed by his brother John, who was also an inmate. Christy Junior decided to stay at home and mind his brothers and sisters, while his father took off to England looking for work. Shortly after Hubert's death, Ellen Dunne gave birth to her youngest child, Gerard. She then had 15 children, ranging from 17-year-old Christy Junior down.

Bronco Junior quickly got back to doing what he did best – thieving. Shortly afterwards he was sent to Marlborough House, a remand home in Dublin, after he was convicted of burglary. The judge in the juvenile court told him he was a rogue and a pest. Dunne was rather flattered. He wanted to be Public Enemy Number One and have his mugshot displayed on the wall of every police station in the country.

The young criminal was soon achieving his dubious goal in life. Bronco Junior was regularly before the courts and served a number of short sentences in Saint Patrick's Institution for young offenders, where he was respected by the other juveniles as a serious criminal. When he got out at the age of 17, he teamed up with two other associates and they specialized in robbing country shops and pubs. By the time he was 18, he claimed he had done more than 200 burglaries.

Soon afterwards, Bronco wrote an unpublished autobiography called 'Wildfire'. It would have been the first book exposing the inhumanity of the industrial school system. A crime journalist with the *Irish Press*, Sean Flynn, who read the unpublished manuscript, described it as 'sometimes cruel and harsh, sometimes fragile and sensitive, reflecting the contradictory instincts of its author'. Bronco tried to have it published and, he claimed, a number of publishers agreed to bring it out but each one withdrew for fear of libel. In the manuscript he summed up his attitude to crime: 'I never thought of reforming, I just wanted to rob and achieve a sense of importance.'

By the time he was 22 years old, Christy 'Bronco' Dunne was satisfying his craving for recognition. One day he was identified by a Garda who spotted him behind the wheel of a judge's car he had just stolen. Bronco was arrested and ended up in Mountjoy Prison for a few months. He was applauded by the older lags for his derring-do – and used his time there to finish his criminal education. He liked to do something unusual during the commission of a crime and then read about it in the newspapers. But despite Christy's efforts, it was other members of his family who first made it on to the front page of a national newspaper.

In May 1960, a large picture of his eight-year-old brother Henry adorned the front page of the *Daily Mirror* in London under the heading 'ANY-ONE LOST A SON?' Henry had been found by police sheltering under London Bridge. He and 12-year-old Larry had decided to go to England in search of their father. They had saved the money for the boat fare to Holyhead and the train to London. When they arrived, the two resourceful kids went to the home of a great-grand-aunt with whom they had once spent a holiday. They didn't know the woman had died and her home had since been sold. For five days they roamed the streets asking strangers if they knew a 'Mr Dunne'. At night they slept under bridges and bushes. Henry was identified after the newspaper report and a relative found Larry on the streets looking for him. The police reunited them with their father and the happy occasion made more headline news. Bronco Senior then sent them home to their mother.

Henry was sent to Upton Industrial School, County Cork, when he was convicted of larceny and receiving stolen goods later that year. He was subsequently transferred to Artane Industrial School in Dublin, where he remained until he was 14. Larry also spent time in Daingean and Letterfrack Reformatories before he decided he had had enough and absconded to England. Boyo, Robert, Mickey, John and Gerard also spent time in Upton and Artane. Mickey and Boyo received particularly savage beatings and Boyo was hospitalized as a result. When Mickey and his brothers were allowed home for the summer of 1955 his father saw the extent of his injuries and decided that he wasn't going back. The 11-year-old was sent to Birmingham to live with his older sister. He remained there until 1968, when he came home after serving a short prison sentence for burglary.

In 1990, this writer interviewed Henry Dunne shortly after he was released from prison for firearms' offences. He blamed the industrial/reform school system for brutalizing him and his brothers. Dunne believed the institutions had a damaging influence on youngsters who later turned to crime: 'They beat and abused us so much, they made animals of us. When we came out of there all we wanted to do was hit back at society. We were angry and warped, with no loyalty to anyone except our own. They savaged us even when we played by the rules. After that we felt what's the fucking point? The Brothers made us the way we became and crime was the obvious choice. When we came out we just wanted to fuck up society.'

Sceptics would say that this was an easy cop-out, considering that the vast majority of inmates who endured the barbaric system did not become criminals. Through the years the Dunne family's well-worn defence was that they were more victims than villains. It originated with their older brother Christy, who worked it out while he was languishing in his cell in Mountjoy Prison. He developed a deep-rooted resentment and blamed society for making him a criminal. He rationalized that his crimes were committed out of economic necessity, in order to feed and clothe his family. In a corrupt, capitalist society working-class people were left without jobs, education or self-esteem, and forced to live in squalor. Crime, Christy decided, was the only way of fighting back against the system. He blamed the police, the politicians, the judges and everyone else in authority for his predicament. As far as he was concerned, the Dunnes were as much victims as the people they robbed.

After he finished his stretch in Mountjoy in 1960, Christy Dunne was soon on the run again, this time on a robbery charge. Bronco sought shelter from the law with Father Michael Sweetman when he escaped from two detectives who tried to arrest him. The priest harboured Dunne for six months in the Jesuit Retreat House in Clontarf. Father Sweetman was a well-known campaigner on behalf of the underprivileged and deprived in society. He had a genuine interest in trying to help young offenders like Bronco Dunne to reform. The Jesuit first befriended the aspiring gangster while he was being held in Marlborough House. Sweetman was one of the first people to listen sympathetically to the confused young Bronco and to treat him like a man. The pair formed a strong bond of friendship and Father Sweetman became a close family friend. Over two decades, the kind-hearted cleric regularly appeared as a character witness for the Dunne brothers in court. Each time he would explain the family circumstances to the judge and plead for a chance to help them reform. Bronco wrote of Fr Sweetman: 'He was a priest, a father, a friend and a teacher. I always felt I really wanted to keep out of crime after talking with him. He was the only one to make me keep from crime. He took time and great patience to help and teach me. He showed me the way of God.'

In the retreat house Dunne attended daily Mass with the priests and worked hard. He convinced his mentor that he had changed and wrote about his salvation from crime: 'I knew I had passed the stage of being drawn back to my old environment. How I wish men could see how stupid a life of crime is. I always knew I would have to answer to God for the wrong I had committed, but still I could not lead a decent life. I felt I was owed something from somebody.'

Father Sweetman believed him and made approaches to Charles Haughey, who was the Justice Minister at the time, the Attorney General, Aindrias Ó Caoimh, and Assistant Garda Commissioner William Quinn, to ask them to give Christy a chance. It was agreed with Fr Sweetman that Christy Dunne had made a serious decision to go straight. Haughey remarked at the time that six months' lying low in a Jesuit retreat house was 'as good as any jail sentence'. But Commissioner Quinn had a better knowledge of the Dunnes than Haughey and warned: 'You'll never be able to reform any of that family.'

After leaving the Jesuits, Dunne did attempt to go straight. He married Jeanette Bermingham, an attractive young woman from Dublin's south-side, with whom he had four children. Bronco worked as a taxi driver and then started a building firm with his brother John – the only brother who went straight, following his stint in Upton Industrial School.

In 1966, Bronco's aspirations towards respectability got him involved in the presidential election campaign of Fine Gael candidate Tom O'Higgins. Dunne was attracted by the liberal wing of the party. It espoused a vision of a more egalitarian society, where the working class got a bigger slice of the cake. Dunne canvassed for votes and even supplied a lorry for a mobile platform during the Dublin campaign, but Eamon De Valera won. He was re-elected for a second term with a narrow majority.

Bronco soon got bored with conformity and he felt that the middle-class party membership was sneering at his social pretensions. At the same time the brothers' building business foundered. Bronco inevitably blamed the police and not the quality of the workmanship. Some years later, his brother Shamie used a similar excuse to explain his failure as a legitimate businessman. When he returned to Dublin from London in 1970, Shamie set up a mobile hamburger business. He blamed the Gardaí, and not the burgers, for the fact that the enterprise soon failed. Henry Dunne at one stage made the same claim. The Dunnes didn't believe in accepting personal responsibility.

Inevitably Bronco's changing politics attracted him to the rhetoric of hard-line, republican ideology – and Saor Eire. He befriended Martin Casey and Liam Walsh, who were pleased to discover that he and his brothers had extensive underworld contacts in England. Through Bronco's connections in Birmingham, they started smuggling 9mm and .22 Star pistols into Ireland from the Parker-Hale armoury. Christy was running with the heavy-hitters at last – and making money out of it.

In his interview for the National Geographic channel in 2011, Dunne was still coy when asked about the smuggling operation: 'I was named in a court trial in England that I was supplying guns to people in Ireland. If I did do it, I would be proud to do it at the time because of the situation in the North of Ireland. I was never charged with it.' But Ireland's longest-living arch villain was anxious to maintain his image as a republican rebel. He claimed he 'collected' weapons with the help of other criminals, which he then 'handed over to people who needed them'. When he was asked about the weapon used to murder Garda Dick Fallon in 1970, he replied: 'They said the gun that shot him [Fallon] I brought into the country . . . but sure I mean I cannot say anything about that. It was all just speculation. I was never charged with it.'

In 1972, Dunne was jailed for two years for receiving stolen goods. He claimed later that the goods were a truckload of food, destined for people in the North.

After Dunne's release from prison his marriage to Jeanette broke down; she left with their four children. Like his father before him, Christy Junior had neglected his wife and children. He was too busy pursuing his dream of gangland infamy. He was also fond of drink and had a serious gambling problem which often left him penniless and his family wanting. Bronco, an incorrigible womanizer, soon met and fell in love with Mary Noonan, an attractive 17-year-old girl from Coolock, North Dublin, who was at least half his age. The couple went on to have three children together.

With his growing responsibilities Christy needed a steady supply of money, and began organizing robberies with some of his brothers. Gradually the other brothers came home to join the well-organized family 'business'. They had been in and out of UK prisons and had made contacts in London, Birmingham and Liverpool that would stand the family well in the future.

Christy, Henry, Shamie and Larry were the nucleus of the mob. Although they never killed anyone, the Dunne brothers had no reservations about using violence on a job. Henry was considered to be the brother with the most 'bottle' who revelled in the excitement of a heist. Henry once explained that the guns were brought to 'control the situation' and ensure that the victims allowed them to get on with the job. If anyone decided to 'have a go' and they got hurt in the process, that wasn't the Dunnes' fault because they had been warned. It wasn't personal, just business. But not all the brothers were natural-born blaggers;

some of them had to work at perfecting their 'skills'. Shamie had a lucky escape during his first job with the family, a security van hold-up. He was accidentally shot in the arm by Larry who wasn't accustomed to handling a firearm.

The Dunne brothers soon became a highly effective team of blaggers. While banks were their main targets, everything was up for grabs – post offices, payrolls, supermarkets, pubs, jewellers, petrol stations and book-ies. The loot was divided up equally among the brothers and other members of the family were also looked after. Christy kept a fund off-side to 'finance' the logistical side of the operation.

The family brought a new level of sophistication to the business. Christy had learned a lot from Saor Eire. They were among the first criminals to realize that the day of the ad hoc heist was over. Careful planning was crucial to success – and a big cash reward. As a result Garda detection rates plummeted throughout the 1970s as armed robberies became a major industry. Other hoods branched out to provide logisti-cal support to the gangs. Some underworld entrepreneurs provided getaway cars and either sold or rented weapons for jobs; others pro-vided information, safe houses and alibis. Hairdressers did a profitable sideline in making wigs and false beards. One Dublin hairdresser, Billy Wright, was shot dead after one of his customers suspected he had acted as a police informer. Business was booming and Christy Dunne, head of the 'family', was ideally placed to play a pivotal role. He became a bro-ker for various gangs – setting up jobs and providing inside information on cash movements – for a percentage of the take.

There were so many heists taking place that it became something of a national joke. Popular comedian Niall Tobin even used it for a sketch on a TV show, when his newsreader character presented a robbery report in the form of the weather forecast: 'Today there were robberies in Carlow, Athlone, Navan and Dublin. Tomorrow they will be in Kil-dare, Tipperary, Cork and Monaghan and next week . . .'

On the street, uniformed and plainclothes officers were literally being outgunned by the robbers – the majority of detectives were still unarmed until the early 1980s. Cops could only stand by and watch helplessly when they arrived on the scene or else possibly suffer the same fate as Garda Dick Fallon. Many brave officers tried to intervene and were held at gunpoint, pistol-whipped and shot at.

The best of the robbers could do a hit in less than three minutes, but the cream of the profession could be in and out in 90 seconds. The Dunnes were the leaders of an underworld elite and, as the number of robberies continued to rise, well-armed criminals were becoming dangerously reckless. In September 1975, Ireland was reminded again of the dangers posed by the crime gangs. An unarmed off-duty officer, Garda Michael Reynolds, was shot dead when he chased a gang, following a hold-up at the Bank of Ireland in Killester, North Dublin. A married couple, Noel and Marie Murray, both former members of the Official IRA who described themselves as anarchists, were subsequently charged with Garda Reynolds's murder. During the trial Noel Murray declared that the couple's 'whole purpose in this State is to destroy it'. They were convicted by the non-jury Special Criminal Court and sentenced to death by hanging for the capital murder of a Garda. The execution orders were overturned by the Supreme Court, on the grounds that neither of them knew their victim was a Garda, and they both got life in prison.

The Garda Reynolds murder caused massive public anger but it made little difference to the crime mobs. The Garda authorities were being overwhelmed by the high levels of serious crime and appeared powerless to take on the blaggers. Christy and his siblings openly bragged that they were running rings around the police – and this was not idle bravado. If a robber wasn't actually caught doing the crime, the chances of them being convicted were practically non-existent. At the time, the laws were such that the Gardaí could not arrest and question a suspect while an investigation was ongoing. Instead a criminal was 'invited' to the station to help the police with their enquiries. Many cases invariably foundered on legal loopholes that were not closed until the 1980s.

While the strength of the Garda Síochána was increased dramatically, the structures and practices in the organization remained the same. In the five years between 1970 and 1975 the number of Gardaí grew from 6,500 to 8,500. By the early 1980s, the strength of the force had risen to 11,500 but the Troubles, and the spill over into the South, was the primary security concern of the State. The bulk of the extra personnel were diverted to the Border and anti-terrorist duties. From 1970, the Provos had unleashed mayhem, robbing banks throughout the country to fund their war. They also carried out murders, kidnappings and bombings. The ordinary blaggers took full advantage of the confusion;

they would muddy the waters of police investigations by using Northern accents and telling their victims the money was for 'the cause'. Christy Dunne claimed authorship of that novel idea. In September 1977, following a spate of robberies in which a publican was shot dead, the Provos were finally forced to issue a statement denying any involvement in 'recent appropriations'. By the end of the decade, Garda chiefs estimated that non-political criminals were responsible for 70 per cent of all robberies.

In Garda HQ there was just one officer assigned to collate intelligence on 'crime-ordinary' activity, using an antiquated index card system. An ad hoc robbery squad was eventually set up in the Central Detective Unit (CDU) in the mid-1970s to investigate heists. But only 20 men were assigned to the squad and the manpower was divided up as they worked on a three-shift system. The squad knew that the only way to win was to catch the robbers in the act and that meant planting informants in their midst. The Dunnes soon learned to organize themselves into 'cell' structures, similar to those used by the Provos. Only those involved in the small, select group would know where and when a job was to take place.

Christy looked down his nose at the cops who tried to keep him and his family under surveillance. A gangland snob, he called them poorly paid 'culchies'. In the clubs he would often send an expensive bottle of champagne over to his Garda watchers, to show them that crime paid.

While other criminals kept a low profile, the Dunne brothers were never shy about flaunting their new-found wealth after a big heist. They wined and dined in the best clubs and restaurants in Dublin. One of their favourite haunts was a club on Nassau Street called Vile Bodies. The Dunnes would turn up with their wives, girlfriends and associates and take the place over, ordering the most expensive champagne in the house and buying drinks for everyone. They wore designer suits, expensive jewellery and drove flash cars. Their wives and girlfriends also had all the latest designer fashions. Mickey Dunne was such a natty dresser that his associates called him 'Dazzler Dunne'.

Life looked like it couldn't get any better. The brothers were the princes of the city and Christy was king.

4.   The Dunne Academy

The Dunne 'Academy' was Gangland's equivalent of a premier, third-level educational institution. The industrial/reformatory schools and young offenders' prisons had provided their students with a first- and second-level education, but it was the Dunnes who showed them how to excel at a life of crime. Christy Dunne and his brothers helped pickpockets and burglars make the transformation into well-organized, armed robbers.

By the mid-1970s the era of the armed robber had been firmly established. During Saor Eire's three-year reign there had been 18 robberies in Ireland. Between 1972 and 1978 that figure rocketed to over 200 a year and the amount of money stolen increased fifteen-fold to £2.3 million. Older criminals remember these as the halcyon years of organized crime – a time when a hoodlum could drive a Jaguar and live in a mansion, despite having no visible means of income. Each week he could pop down to the local Labour Exchange to collect his unemployment assistance; then later he could return with a sawn-off shotgun and help himself to a much more generous pay out. Every Thursday and Friday businesses, banks and the Gardaí braced themselves for another wave of hold-ups. The terrorist and 'crime-ordinary' gangs committed robberies all over the country. Their activities created a boom in the security industry. The physical face of towns and cities were changed for ever, with the installation of reinforced steel shutters, metal grilles and alarm systems, as banks and businesses tried to keep the robbers out.

As the Dunnes' 'Academy' grew throughout the 1970s, the brothers often divided into different teams to do robberies because the pickings were so easy. Any 'outsiders' brought in to take part in heists were carefully screened by Bronco before being accepted into the gang. Only criminals with whom solid bonds of loyalty had been established in the reform schools and prisons were fully integrated into the organization.

Among the Dunnes' closest friends and associates were criminals Joey Skerrit, Martin Kenny and Joe Roe. They had grown up with the Dunnes and were considered loyal 'soldiers'. It was a badge of honour in the underworld to be classified as a member of the 'family'. There was also a close friendship between the Dunnes and another up-and-coming crime family, the Cahills. Martin Cahill and his brother Eddie had done time in Daingean Reformatory School with Larry Dunne. Soon other gangs were being formed by 'graduates' of the 'Dunne Academy'.

Behind the façade of the charming rogue, the head of the 'Academy', Christy Dunne Junior, was a ruthless hood. He didn't want to confine himself to armed robberies and soon discovered he had a flair for an even nastier type of crime – 'Tiger kidnapping'.

On 10 February 1975, six armed men burst into the Dun Laoghaire home of Robert Halpin. He was the manager of West's jewellers in Grafton Street in Dublin, one of the longest-established jewellers in the capital. The gang, which included Martin Cahill, held his terrified wife and three children hostage while they waited for Halpin to return home at midnight. When he walked through the front door he was surrounded and manhandled by the raiders. They demanded that he take them to West's immediately. The jeweller told them that the safes could not be opened until 8 a.m., so the gang held him and his family overnight.

The following morning, three members of the gang brought the manager to the store, while the others stayed with his family, to ensure that nothing went wrong. They forced him to hand over £170,000 worth of gems. Before they left the jewellers, they tied Halpin up and took his car. At the same time, the other members of the gang released Halpin's family.

Christy Dunne had pulled off another record – the biggest jewellery robbery in the State's history. Shamie had arranged to sell the loot to a London fence called Les Beavis after the robbery. Beavis was due to pick the jewels up a few days later but Bronco disagreed. As head of the 'family', he insisted that he would dispose of the jewels himself. It was to be a big mistake.

A few weeks after the robbery, word reached the Central Detective Unit (CDU) in Dublin Castle that a man, high on their 'most wanted' list, was trying to offload the proceeds of the West's robbery. Bronco had put the word out through the gangland grapevine that he had some very hot merchandise for sale. Detective Superintendent Mick Sullivan had suspected Christy Dunne was behind the job, but he'd had nothing to go on until informants tipped him off.

Det. Supt Sullivan used his limited resources to set up a sting operation to trap Dunne. The detective contacted a dodgy businessman who owed the police a favour. The businessman agreed to set up a meeting with Bronco, after he'd established that he was interested in buying the stolen jewellery. The first meeting took place on 13 March. Dunne offered the businessman the jewellery for a bargain price of £45,000, cash. The businessman said that he'd try to set up a deal with an American buyer but he needed to see some of the merchandise first and value it for himself.

Bronco agreed and the next day he brought the businessman to a field outside the city. Two members of the 'firm' produced bags containing jewels from the West's heist. Keeping his Garda handler in the loop throughout, the informer continued to negotiate with Dunne over a number of days, until a figure of £37,000 was agreed.

The following day the businessman and Bronco went to the Dunne family home on Rutland Avenue, Crumlin. Security was tight – two gang members guarded the front of the house and there were two more at the back. The loot was hidden upstairs. It took the bogus buyer a few hours to sort through and itemize the jewels. Later that night, he reported back to Det. Supt Sullivan and his team. Christy was taking the bait.

When the informant returned home he got a surprise – Bronco was waiting for him. He was worried that the cops were on to him. The mob boss insisted that the businessman store the loot overnight in his house. The informant had no option but to agree and Dunne left. The businessman immediately called his police handlers and his house was placed under surveillance. When he returned for the jewels Bronco would be walking into a trap.

The following afternoon, Dunne arrived at the businessman's house. He thought he was coming to collect £37,000 in cash. Det. Supt Sullivan and his squad swooped as Dunne placed the jewels in the boot of the businessman's car. The Godfather had finally been caught red-handed. He was even wearing one of the solid gold bracelets that had been stolen from West's. The police reckoned they had a cast-iron case against him. He was arrested and charged with the West's robbery and receiving the stolen jewellery. Despite Garda objections, Bronco was released on bail.

Christy Dunne might have had serious charges hanging over him but it was still business as usual. Bronco continued to direct the family's operations and oversee his academy of crooks. He was determined to fight the system and win his case. Like most career villains, he had a good working knowledge of the law – or thought he had. Bronco said he learned the law when he was in Mountjoy Prison, under the tutorship of an older criminal who had a library of law books in his cell. And whenever he or any of his brothers were in a tight spot with the law they invariably cried 'stitch-up'. Years later, standing in front of the Four Courts building, he portrayed himself as a victim in his war with the law. 'At one stage [in the 1970s] I had fourteen trials pending in this court and was acquitted of all of them except one. Every crime in the book I was charged with. It was a continuous battle and I remember I was in the law courts for years. I don't think I gave them [the police] the run around. It's just that they were anxious to put me away because they obviously considered me to be a threat,' the ageing hippie said, without the faintest hint of irony.

The 'firm's' next major target was Brereton's jewellers and pawnshop on Capel Street in Dublin city centre. On 19 June 1976, members of staff were getting ready to close the shop. The last customers of the day were three ladies from Belfast who'd come down for a day's shopping in Dublin. They were chatting about how much they were enjoying the break from the tensions of the Troubles when a priest walked into the shop, and produced a handgun. As the 'priest', Bronco's brother Robert, pulled a mask up to cover his face, three other masked men ran in behind him. They were Joey Skerrit, Shamie Dunne and Londoner Patrick O'Sullivan. O'Sullivan, who had Irish parents, had done time in prison with Shamie. He had recently joined the Dunne 'family' firm.

The Brereton's heist was a particularly violent crime as the four hoods showed no mercy to their victims. The owner of the store, John Brereton, made a run for the door but was grabbed and pistol-whipped by two of the raiders. He fell to the ground and one of them continued beating him. When his son, John Junior, came to his rescue he was also set upon and severely beaten. The shop owner was dragged into the basement where he was hooded and tied up. His injured son, the other staff members, and the three women who had been enjoying a stress-free day in the South, were also brought to the basement. The gang rifled through the drawers upstairs. When they couldn't open one of the safes they dragged John Brereton up to unlock it. When he said he didn't have the key his son, who was bleeding heavily, was dragged upstairs and a gun was held to his head. 'Give me the fucking money,' the 'priest' demanded. When Brereton refused, Robert Dunne told the raider holding the gun to count to ten and then 'blow it off'. One of the shop assistants produced the key when the raider reached 'six'.

As the gang emptied the contents of the safe, John Brereton pleaded with them to leave the pawn stock because it included important family heirlooms belonging to local people. The working-class hoods didn't care and took it all. One of them threatened him: 'If you don't shut up your head will be blown off and your body brought to the Wicklow Mountains and you will never be found.'

In all the raiders took £60,000 worth of assorted jewellery and £5,000 in cash. None of the haul was ever recovered. As they were leaving, O'Sullivan told them in his cockney accent: 'It's for the cause; the insurance will look after it.'

John Brereton and his son were hospitalized after the savage attack. The father received 30 stitches and his son 65. In a series of searches in the homes of Joey Skerrit, Robert, Shamie, and their father, Bronco Senior, the Gardaí found items which linked them all to the robbery and the theft of the getaway car. In a line up, two of the victims pointed out Robert Dunne as the man who'd pretended to be the priest.

The four hoods, including Bronco Senior, were charged with the violent robbery. Christy Junior, Henry, Gerard and Larry later claimed that they were drinking with the three men when the crime took place. Three years later Robert Dunne was the only member of the gang who stood trial for the robbery. He was acquitted. Robert's accomplice, Joey Skerrit, was accidentally shot dead six years later by a fellow gang member during a robbery in Limerick.

Bronco Senior was interviewed eight years later by the journalist Tom McGurk, for a special Channel Four documentary on Dublin's drug scene. McGurk asked him about his sons' criminal activity. The old man sat next to his wife, in front of a fire, drinking whiskey. She was on a bottle of stout.

McGurk asked old Dunne, 'Were you aware that your sons were robbing banks?'

'I was yes. Yes and I quite admired them for it.'

'Why?'

'As long as nobody was hurt.'

'Why?'

'They were getting money the handy way; there was no loss of life; no malicious damage or injuries to anybody.'

'But they are taking someone else's money?'

'Yes, but how do you know whose money it is in the banks. How did they get it?'

It was obvious that old Bronco had passed on his selective memory to his sons.

After the Brereton robbery, Patrick O'Sullivan and Christy Junior hatched a plan to cash in stolen drafts and cheques from a bank in Dublin city centre. The cockney was getting the precious documents, together with authorized signatures, from a crooked porter at the bank. They decided to cash several of them, one after the other, in Allied Irish Bank branches in London. Unfortunately the lackey they sent to cash them in screwed up. When he handed in the first draft, which Dunne had filled out for £15,000, the gang member misread it and asked for £1,500 instead. Staff got suspicious and asked him to come back later. The henchman's survival instincts kicked in and he headed back to Dublin. A second runner was sent to try again, but he was immediately caught and ended up getting a 12-month jail sentence.

As Christy Junior's trial for the West's heist was approaching, he needed funds. Shortly after 8 p.m. on 11 January 1978, just a month before the trial, a post office van carrying a consignment of cash and jewellery from the Munster mail train was stopped by a uniformed Garda. The van was en route to the Central Sorting Office, which was located in Sheriff Street, in Dublin's north inner-city. When the van came to a halt, the 'cop' pulled out a gun and pointed it at the driver. At the same moment Christy Dunne, who was also armed and masked, appeared at the other window. The 'cop' and the gangster ordered the driver and his helper to get into the back and to keep their mouths shut. The 'Garda' was Paddy Shanahan, a recent recruit to the Dunne 'firm' and one of the most unlikely armed robbers in the history of Irish Badfellas.

Unlike his partners-in-crime, 32-year-old Shanahan from Kill, County

Kildare, couldn't blame society for ending up on the Dunnes' side of the tracks. Shanahan came from a respectable middle-class family who lived in the heart of horse-breeding country. As a young man he was an excellent student and sportsman and was never in trouble with the law. The teachers at the Christian Brothers secondary school he'd attended in Naas had high hopes for young Shanahan. He left with a good Leaving Certificate and spent a year studying English and History at University College Dublin, before dropping out. He then ran an auctioneering and tarmacadam business for a while. But the Christian Brothers' star pupil soon discovered that he had a natural aptitude for another form of business – crime – and he began operating with another aspiring gangster, John 'the Coach' Traynor. Through Traynor, Shanahan met other Dublin-based villains. Considered an 'outsider' at first, he gradually won the trust of Joey Skerrit and did some robberies with him. Skerrit introduced the well-spoken 'culchie' to Christy and Henry, who regarded him as a very strange character. The brothers accepted him into the 'family' more out of curiosity than anything else. Many years later, Henry Dunne described Shanahan's motivation: 'He loved crime; he was fascinated by the whole thing. He wasn't like the rest of us. We did it for a living; he did it for the buzz. He loved dressing up [for a job] and handling guns.'

Shanahan and Dunne jumped into the front of the post van and drove it to a disused storage yard on a side street near the derelict docklands. Other members of the gang, including Larry and Shamie Dunne, were in another car covering the action in case they were needed. The hijackers ordered the postal workers to get out of the van and lie on the ground. Shanahan, who had robbed mail trains with Traynor, knew what he was looking for. He grabbed seven, specially coloured bags carrying registered mail, which often contained cash and cheques. The two raiders then jumped into a waiting getaway car and drove to a house on Dublin's north-side to empty the bags.

Christy and Shamie took the cash and selected packages away to sort through them. They had a strict rule that associates did not get to count the proceeds from a heist. The robbery hadn't been very worthwhile, as most of the cash in the haul was worthless. The notes had been perforated before being returned to the Central Bank for incineration. Shamie dumped a large batch of small, brown envelopes into a skip, thinking they were of no value. But a few days later the newspapers reported that over £100,000 worth of industrial diamonds, stolen in the post office van robbery, had been found in a skip in North Dublin. Shamie, who was illiterate, couldn't read the words 'Industrial Diamonds' on the envelopes and hadn't bothered to ask one of his brothers what they said. He went back to the skip in the forlorn hope that the cops might have missed some of the haul. When he found nothing, he vented his anger by beating up an innocent man who just happened to be walking past.

Despite his indefatigable bravado, Bronco decided to go into hiding before his trial for the West's robbery, which was due to start on 23 February 1978. Not only was he avoiding a possible conviction but he had also run foul of another criminal family. Christy Junior had been caught having an affair with a daughter of the family, who was much younger than him. A bench warrant was issued for Bronco's arrest when he failed to appear. Dunne had achieved his youthful ambition – whether he liked it or not. As he was about to reach his fortieth birthday, his name and photograph were circulated to every police station in the country.

The following day, 24 February, West's jewellers was robbed for a second time. Detectives uncovered leads which pointed in the direction of one of Bronco's pals, Eamon Saurin. The two blaggers were sharing the same safe house in Sundrive Road, Crumlin. Saurin was an armed robber, originally from Liberty House, off Sean McDermott Street in Dublin's north inner-city, who was wanted by English police for the robbery and murder of a pensioner in 1972. He had been arrested in Dublin on an extradition warrant in 1974 but jumped bail during the proceedings.

Almost a month later, on 19 March 1978, Saurin and a criminal associate, Laurence 'Clicky' Maguire, met another armed robber called Christy McAuley from Donnycarney, North Dublin. After a booze-fuelled night, Saurin accused McAuley of 'riding' his girlfriend while he had been on the run. McAuley, who was gay, told him he was wrong. Later that night McAuley gave Saurin and his friend Clicky Maguire a lift home. On the way Saurin asked McAuley to pull in on Killester Avenue. When McAuley stopped the car, Saurin, who was sitting in the passenger seat, pulled a pistol and shot him twice in the head. The injured man managed to get out of the car but collapsed on the pavement. Saurin put two more rounds into him for good measure. 'He won't shag my chick again,' Saurin told Maguire, who was stunned by what had happened. Maguire made a full statement to Gardaí the next day. Saurin was quickly identified and a manhunt ordered. Christy Dunne's associate was now wanted for murder in two jurisdictions.

Two days later, the Bank of Ireland branch in Finglas was held up by an armed gang and relieved of almost £19,000 in cash. This time Henry Dunne was charged with the heist, after a witness picked him out on an identity parade. By now the courts, like the police, were becoming familiar with the ways of major villains. As usual, Henry applied for bail and it was granted – but for the ground-breaking sum of £20,000. This was an astronomical amount of money for the time and is equivalent to approximately €120,000 in today's values. Despite the fact that he had no visible means of income and was officially unemployed, Henry Dunne had no problem stumping up the cash for the court and he was released. It would be another 18 years before the State would finally have the powers to investigate the source of a criminal's wealth. Six months later the charge against Dunne was dropped, on the instructions of the Director of Public Prosecutions (DPP).

Meanwhile Christy had decided to give himself up. Before he handed himself in he wrote to several journalists in Dublin, to ensure he got the maximum publicity for himself. One letter he wrote to *Sunday World* journalist Sean Boyne was headed: 'Christy Dunne on the run, 9th April, 1978.' In the letter Bronco made wild allegations that he was the victim of Garda corruption. He claimed that a detective had tried to shoot him and that he was only saved because bystanders got in the way. He never offered any proof to back up his claims.

When Bronco stood trial for the West's heist in the Central Criminal Court in June 1978, Mr Justice Finlay directed that the robbery charge be dropped due to a lack of evidence. Dunne now only faced a charge of receiving the stolen jewellery. The DPP decided not to call the businessman who had acted for the Gardaí, for fear that his life might be in danger. Intimidation had worked in Bronco's favour again. His defence team argued a convincing case that he could not be accused of receiving the stolen jewellery because the bags were in the informant's car when the Gardaí swooped. A jeweller also gave evidence on behalf of the defence. He said that the bracelet Dunne was wearing at the time of his arrest could have been bought in ten other jewellery shops around Dublin. The jury found Dunne not guilty. Bronco was ecstatic.

Dunne's acquittal, however, aroused suspicions among other criminal outfits. They believed that it had been a quid pro quo arrangement for information Christy had provided on their activities. But it wasn't an issue that the other criminals were prepared to take up with the family – they were still too powerful. The West's debacle also created a rift among the brothers, with several of them blaming Bronco for losing the jewels. Some of them stopped speaking to each other but they still ensured that the rows were kept 'en famille'. The split widened, however, when certain members argued that some of the brothers were not contributing enough to those who needed support.

Bronco's days as the head of the crime family were coming to an end. The brothers formed sub-groups within the overall gang structure, with Larry and Shamie on one side and Christy and Henry on the other. Joe Roe, who had been ferociously loyal to his mentor Christy, also cut his ties. Their relationship had soured after they'd planned an armed robbery at a post office in Pearse Street while Bronco was on the run in the spring of 1978. Roe, who was responsible for organizing transport for the gang's operations, claimed that Bronco had 'bottled' it at the last minute and he was left to do the job with others. Despite his grievance, Roe still showed his 'respect' for the self-styled Godfather and gave him a share of the takings. After that he would only work on jobs with Henry.

It was also the beginning of the end of the Dunne 'Academy'. It fell apart when the family discovered a new, much more lucrative business, with a lot less risk – the Dunnes were about to start dabbling in the drug trade.

By the latter half of the 1970s there was an increasing demand for drugs in Ireland. The evidence was there, but no one in authority appeared to be bothered about dealing with it. Between 1977 and 1979 there were a total of 581 burglaries in pharmacy wholesalers and drug manufacturers in the Irish Republic. In 1976 alone there were 141 such robberies, of which 115 had taken place in Dublin.

On the last weekend of July 1978, Christy, Henry, Shamie and Joe

Roe broke into the Antigen pharmaceutical factory in Roscrea, County Tipperary, and stole £300,000 worth of the powerful painkiller Palfium. Henry was the only one who realized the true value of the little pills on the black market. He had developed an addiction problem while being treated for serious burns (see Chapter 5). Henry's habit had taught him the value of the drugs and he bought the haul from his accomplices. At the time a Palfium tablet was worth £3 on the streets and Henry turned a tidy profit from the deal. It was to be the turning point for the Dunnes.

By the latter half of the 1970s, cannabis had been established as the drug of choice for a young generation. Unlike LSD, people who smoked dope didn't tend to jump off buildings in the hope of flying. Cannabis or hashish was considered a harmless, soft drug and people from all walks of life enjoyed a few joints. Criminals in the UK had first realized the potential of hashish in the 1960s when it was smuggled into prisons. Inmates doing long stretches found that enjoying a quiet joint was preferable to the dubious attractions of knocking back 'hooch' fermented in piss-pots. The prison authorities tolerated it because it kept the lags calm. English villains had also been introduced to the charms – and potential – of hash while on holidays or on the run in the south of Spain and Morocco. Throughout the 1960s they had gradually decommissioned their sawn-off shotguns and balaclavas for an easier, and much more profitable, way of life. It wasn't long before the UK drug lords showed their Irish contemporaries the ropes. Among the first to sign up were Eamon Saurin and Pat O'Sullivan, two close associates of the Dunnes.

Saurin had been running with a number of English crime gangs until pensioner Kenneth Michael Adams was murdered in November 1972. When police in Birmingham nominated Saurin as their prime suspect, he returned to Dublin to avoid arrest. Saurin loved his dope-smoking so much that he supplemented his income from armed crime by selling hash. He bought it from his contacts in the UK and Amsterdam. He is one of the first criminals credited with smuggling commercial shipments of cannabis and heroin from Amsterdam into Ireland in the late 1970s. He soon began supplying hash, and later heroin, to the Dunne brothers.

In between pulling strokes with his old pal Shamie Dunne, cockney

Patrick O'Sullivan was also a significant drug-trafficker, operating between Europe and the US. O'Sullivan had invested some of his profits in US businesses, including a carpet factory in California, but he also regularly found himself doing heists to get cash to fund his investment in drug deals. He often brought a few kilos of heroin back from the US to sell in London. He tried to convince the Dunnes that heroin was the future but, like most villains, they were reluctant to get into 'smack' because it was still an unknown quantity. Cannabis, however, had a ready and expanding market so the Dunnes decided to focus on that.

In the summer of 1978, Christy and Shamie Dunne took delivery of 13 kilos of hash from a Turkish crime gang based in London. The gang was introduced to the Dunnes by an enigmatic Irish businessman known by the pseudonym 'the Prince'. He acted as a broker for international drug deals and fraud rackets. Originally from County Clare, the Prince first got involved with the Dunnes when he fenced stolen jewels, bank bonds and travellers cheques for them. He spent several years in the UK before returning to Ireland. He was a sophisticated, polished global player who easily juggled his business interests, on both sides of the law. The Prince's list of international contacts included the American and Sicilian Mafias, and drug producers in the Middle East.

To the outside world he was a successful businessman, who lived with his wife and family in a luxurious mansion in Wicklow and drove a top-of-the-range BMW. But the truth is that the Prince is one of the most important faceless players who has lurked in the shadows of organized crime for the past forty years. The underworld would not operate as efficiently if it wasn't for clean-cut crooks like him. The Prince has been linked to the money-laundering activities of several crime syndicates, at home and abroad. Despite the fact that he has featured in several international criminal investigations, the Prince has never been caught. He has only one minor conviction, for possession of hashish. His legitimate business interests today include investments in a huge hotel and apartment complex on the Continent. The Dunnes' associate is still classified as a major international crime figure by law enforcement agencies on both sides of the Atlantic.

The Prince was one of the sources for the seminal 1985 book *Smack*, which was the first book to expose Ireland's developing crime crisis. Co-author Padraig Yeates summed up the significance of the partnership between the Dunnes and the Prince: 'He was a very accomplished criminal who cut his teeth in England. He met the Dunnes and realised there was a marriage of convenience here. He basically introduced them to contacts in the Middle East and they began smuggling heroin and cannabis into Ireland. The Dunnes quickly realised that this was much safer and more profitable than trying to rob banks.'

The London-based Turks wanted to set up a cannabis-smuggling route between Cyprus and the rest of Europe, using Ireland as a transit point. The Prince invited them to Ireland to meet what he told them was the biggest Irish crime family. The Turks were also introduced to the family by a relation of Saor Eire man Liam Walsh, Christy's former republican ally whose funeral he'd organized eight years earlier. The Dunnes came highly recommended and the Turks were anxious to meet them in person. A group of four Turks, including the leader of the gang, arrived in Dublin in a Rolls-Royce – with the 13 kilos of hash. The car had been specially adapted to carry drug shipments and the trip to Dublin was a trial run. Shamie and Christy agreed to buy the drugs for £15,000.

Despite their hefty reputations, Shamie and Christy had problems getting the money together to pay for the haul – it would be a recurring problem for the brothers. They paid some of the money in cash and the rest in stolen travellers' cheques. The Dunnes also provided an Irish passport for the leader of the Turkish delegation. Christy Dunne and the Prince ran a successful sideline providing genuine Irish passports to international crime gangs. Ireland's policy of neutrality has ensured that Irish passports have traditionally been popular, not only with criminals but with international spy rings, hit squads and arms-dealers. Passports from a batch of 100 which had been stolen from the printers in Artane for Bronco and the Prince later turned up in drug busts in New York, Karachi and Amsterdam. The Turks accepted the mixed pay off and didn't get a chance to suss that their new friends in Dublin were not exactly the Mafia as, a short time later, the gang were arrested on drug-smuggling charges in the UK and ended up behind bars.

The Prince also introduced Shamie Dunne to contacts in North Africa so that he could buy large quantities of Moroccan hash direct from the producers. A number of shipments were successfully trans-ported into Ireland. The family then sold the hash wholesale to the increasing number of cannabis dealers who had sprung up to supply the expanding market. The Moroccan connection was cut off when the Dunnes inevitably fell behind in their payments. There was a serious shortage of the drug in Dublin as they tried to source new contacts. While they were still having problems finding a new hash supplier, a flood of high-quality, cheap heroin suddenly hit the international market. The Dunne brothers were about to move into heroin.

Between 1979 and 1980 two world events had a dramatic effect on organized crime in Ireland. In Iran, the pro-Western Shah was overthrown by fundamentalist Muslims, led by the Ayatollah Khomeini. The country's aristocracy and business elite converted their mountains of gold and diamonds into heroin, which was much easier to transport. When they fled to the West they sold the drugs for dollars and various European currencies. Around the same time, the Russians invaded Afghanistan to prop up the Communist administration which was under threat of being overthrown by rebel forces. By the late 1970s the tribal areas of the country – and neighbouring Pakistan – had replaced the Golden Triangle of South-east Asia as the world's largest heroin producer. It was in these areas that resistance against the Soviets was strongest. The tribesmen, who were traditional opium poppy farmers, dramatically increased their production of heroin. It was sold on the world market and with the proceeds they bought weapons for their war with the Russians.

As a result of these two events, there was a sudden glut of heroin in the Western markets and organized crime began to invest in the wholesale drug trade. Heroin presented a huge opportunity for making money, as supply created a rapid and escalating demand. The international crime syndicates began to expand their markets. As they did so, drug treatment clinics throughout Europe and the US recorded a dramatic increase in the number of people with heroin addictions. The Prince was one of the brokers entrusted with finding new markets and he contacted the Dunnes. Author Padraig Yeates described the significance of their partnership: 'When The Prince met the Dunnes the rules changed, drugs were suddenly part of the life of Dublin and they have been ever since.'

In 1979, there was an increasing demand for synthetic opiates in Ireland – and a ready-made market for heroin. As it was still not widely available, drug addicts were getting their hits elsewhere with drugs stolen from pharmacies and factories. Larry and Shamie, who were occasional users of heroin and cocaine, decided to set up separate heroin-dealing operations and began testing the market. A dealer could treble, and even quadruple, his original profit in a short period. It made the proceeds of a good armed heist look paltry by comparison. Eamon Saurin and Pat O'Sullivan supplied the first shipments of heroin, which arrived in Dublin that autumn.

One by one the brothers got involved in the deadly new trade, while Christy stayed away from it. Larry and Shamie supplied other members of the family, who, in turn, ran their own local patches. They already had a network of contacts and 'graduates' from their crime academy. Henry wasn't the only family member with a drug problem either. Mickey, Robert, Gerard and their wives, as well as their sister Collette, all ended up as addicts.

Shamie and Larry first targeted the rundown, impoverished inner-city Corporation flat complexes of Dolphin House, Fatima Mansions and St Theresa's Gardens, on the south-side of the city. The bleak, barrack-style complexes were to be used as the testing ground for the Dunnes' market research. At first the heroin was harder to sell than hash but Larry had a cunning plan to deal with that. He instructed his pushers to give out free samples in the area, particularly to young teenagers and adults who would try anything for kicks. They even gave the heroin to children in local inner-city schools. At first people smoked or 'popped' it. Then they progressed to injecting it into their veins with syringes.

Larry's marketing strategy was a success and demand soon started to rise. Within weeks, heroin addiction had spread like an inferno across the south inner-city. The flat complexes were turned into squalid shooting galleries for the army of emerging drug addicts. Heroin brought chaos to an already hopeless situation. Over a year later it hit the north side of the River Liffey, destroying areas of Sean McDermott Street, Sheriff Street and Liberty House. Larry Dunne employed the same successful marketing template as before. In a matter of weeks, the area was in the grip of a monstrous heroin plague.

Although Shamie had the largest operation, it was Larry who emerged as the main player in the new family business. He was one of the last members of the clan to get involved in armed robberies and the drug trade brought out his real criminal talents. Unlike his other brothers, Larry kept his head down and took a long-term view.

The Dunnes were forced to find alternative suppliers when Patrick O'Sullivan was jailed for cocaine dealing in Los Angeles and Eamon Saurin ended up in prison. The drug-dealing fugitive was finally arrested on 16 July 1981, in a flat at Raglan Road, Ballsbridge, Dublin, for the Christy McAuley murder he'd been charged with in 1978. The trial went ahead on 10 December, but the chief prosecution witness, Clicky Maguire, refused to give evidence. 'I am the person who has been running from people on both sides of this situation,' he told the judge. Maguire was jailed for contempt for a month and Saurin's trial was rescheduled for June 1982. This time Maguire didn't turn up and the State was forced to enter a *nolle prosequi*. Saurin was promptly extradited back to England where he was jailed for life for the Kenneth Adams murder.

While Shamie scoured the markets looking for cheaper deals from new suppliers, Larry decided to pay over the odds to an American mob for continuity of supply. The man at the head of the well-organized drugs network was involved in moving heroin from Pakistan to the US via Copenhagen. He ran an international operation from leafy South Dublin, after he'd quietly moved to Ireland to escape the attentions of police forces all over Europe.

The Dunnes' heroin was brought in by couriers from Amsterdam, Paris, Malaga and London, usually through Irish airports where there were few checks. The drug was brought to safe houses where it was diluted or cut with a variety of bulking agents, including talcum powder, glucose, milk powder, chalk, Bisto and curry powder. It was then repacked and sold to mid-level dealers, who in turn sold it down the chain. On its way through the supply chain it was diluted down several times more to maximize profit. By the time it hit the streets it was sold in £10 and £20 deals to pushers and addicts, with an average purity of around 10 per cent.

When Larry Dunne's drug operation was at full tilt, it was estimated that he was making an average of £12,000 per week, or €60,000 in today's values. By then Christy Dunne was no longer the pivotal player in the family business – and the Dunne 'Academy' was no more. But

Bronco did continue to deal in the hash trade and organize bank robberies with former 'students'.

One observer eloquently described the Dunnes' new business enterprise: 'The Dunnes did for smack what Henry Ford did for the motor car: made it available to the working man and woman, even the kids on the dole, even the kids at school.'

The heroin plague was here to stay.

5. The General

If the Dunne 'Academy' had kept records of their brightest students, the one whose name would have been at the top of the 'Roll of Honour' was a strange, complex and menacing character named Martin Cahill. Of all their alumni, he would go on to become the most legendary criminal mastermind in the history of the Irish underworld. He became the ultimate anti-hero, whose 'talent' for organizing major robberies led his underworld associates to nickname him 'the General'. With his gang he was responsible for some of the most brutal and outrageous crimes ever seen in Ireland. His name was synonymous with violence, fear and intimidation.

No criminal over the past forty years has had such a formidable reputation in the eyes of the Irish public as the General. Cahill's crimes and extraordinary antics, as he played what he called the 'game', made him a household name. His willingness to drop his trousers and show off his Mickey Mouse® underwear, while at the same time hiding his face behind sinister balaclavas, made him the subject of intense curiosity. Everyone wanted to see the face of the underworld's hooded bogeyman. Psychologists would describe him as an anarchist, suffering from acute paranoia, with multiple personalities. In fact there was enough material in Cahill for a PhD on the criminal mind – and for a book and no fewer than three movies. By comparison, Christy Dunne only ever got 15 minutes of fame.

But unlike his one-time mentor, Cahill never set out to court the limelight, it was just that his 'strokes' and acts of violence made it impossible for him to avoid it. Over two decades, he organized the theft of art, jewels and cash, worth well in excess of €60 million. His meticulously planned robberies included one of the biggest art heists in the world. Cahill preserved his position as an untouchable gang boss by instilling fear in other criminals. When people got out of line they were punished by being shot, beaten or, in one case, nailed to the floor. But when it came to his choice of victim he was egalitarian – they came from both sides of gangland's razor-wire fence. Unlike any other criminal, the General took his war to the State and especially the Gardaí, for whom he harboured a pathological hatred that became more and more irrational over time. While other villains did everything to avoid the cops, Cahill spared no effort trying to humiliate them. He equipped his extensive arsenal of firearms by robbing the Garda depot where confiscated weapons were stored, and he stole the country's most sensitive crime files from the office of the Director of Public Prosecutions. Getting one over on the police was sometimes the sole motivation for his more mischievous strokes.

When the law got too close for comfort the General resorted to acts of chilling savagery, similar to those employed by the Sicilian Mafia. He bombed the country's top forensic scientist, and shot a social welfare inspector just because his dole payments had been cut. Cahill also burned down two Dublin criminal courts in a bid to stop an armed robbery case being heard against him. He even dug up the greens on the Garda golf club and later openly taunted them about getting a 'hole-in-one in Stackstown'. In his latter years, his arrests were accompanied by tyre-slashing sprees which were carried out by his henchmen in Dublin's middle-class neighbourhoods. It was his way of demonstrating his annoyance to the public – and embarrassing the police in the process.

In appearance too, Cahill was somewhat unusual. Short, portly and bald, dressed in worn jeans and stained T-shirts he looked more like a down-at-heel bag-snatcher than a criminal mastermind. The General was a man of many contradictions. He was obsessive, conniving and clever; sometimes compassionate and often cruel. He was also different to other hoods because he didn't drink, smoke or take drugs. His main orientation in life was towards crime – plotting it, committing it and talking about it. Cahill's other passions were pigeons, motorbikes, cakes and curries. Cahill's love life was like every other aspect of his anarchic character – bizarre, complex and different.

While he no more resembled the popular concept of an ardent lover than he did a swaggering gang boss, he shared the love of two women in his life – his wife Frances and her sister Tina. The sisters were happy to share the man they both loved, and between them they gave birth to the General's nine children. In his anarchic world there was nothing strange about the arrangement. To him social morals were dictated by a hypocritical Establishment, ruled by corrupt politicians and a perverted church.

Cahill had created his own parallel universe, with its own set of rules and standards. The world beyond the borders of Gangland was there to be robbed and its inhabitants were seen as the enemy. Rejecting society's codes of behaviour was integral to Cahill's philosophy in life, which was best summed up by his favourite song – 'Que Sera Sera!'

Like the Dunnes, and most of his fellow mobsters, Martin Cahill was born into abject poverty, on 23 May 1949, the second child of Agnes and Patrick. His mother endured 21 pregnancies, from which 15 children survived – 8 boys and 7 girls. One child, a toddler, was killed when she was hit by an ice-cream van. Cahill spent the first 11 years of his life in an overcrowded slum at No. 6 Grenville Street, in Dublin's north inner-city. Grenville Street had changed little since 1898, when it was described as 'Hell Street' where 'drunken brawls, stone throwing and filthy practices' were its main characteristics. The large family often went hungry as Patrick Cahill's meagre wages as a lighthouse keeper could not support them. He also drank heavily at the expense of his wife and children. Martin Cahill, who never drank, later bitterly recalled that his father had little to show for a life as an honest man.

In 1960, the Cahill family was moved to Captain's Road, Crumlin. They settled into one of the thousands of houses built on the edge of the city to clear the slums and give people a decent place to live. But poverty followed the slum refugees and the estates became a breeding ground for young criminals. Most of the members of Cahill's gang came from Crumlin, which became the de facto spiritual homeland of organized crime in Ireland. He attended school in Kimmage but dropped out because, he claimed, the teachers beat and humiliated him. This experience added to his detestation of normal society.

Even before he reached his teens, Martin Cahill was becoming a prolific burglar, as were his brothers John, Eddie, Anthony, Paddy and Michael or 'Styky'. Like the Dunnes, the young Cahills were making a name for themselves as very good 'house-breakers'. He was 12 when he received his first criminal conviction on 15 September 1961, on a charge of larceny. At the time he was given the Probation of Offenders Act. It was meant to act as a caution to encourage him to mend his ways but he had no intention of doing that. Two years later he was back before the Metropolitan Children's Court on more larceny charges and was fined £1 – it didn't deter the young burglar. He was up again two months later, this time for two counts of larceny and was given a one-year suspended sentence. On 20 September 1963, he was given one month's detention in Marlborough House detention centre in Glasnevin, on two charges of burglary. Cahill was building up an impressive CV as a young delinquent.

At 15, Cahill made his first journey outside Dublin when he travelled to Belfast for an interview to join the Royal Navy. He later recalled how applicants were given a list of trades and asked to chose which one would suit them best. Cahill picked bugler. Unfortunately, he'd misread the word and thought it was 'burglar'. He reckoned that breaking into houses on behalf of the Royal Navy, and being paid for it, was just the job for him. The stuffy officers on the interview panel were stunned when the young Dublin lad explained his choice of trade. He didn't get to join up.

A year later, Cahill was arrested in connection with a string of burglaries. A young cop called Dick Murphy convinced Cahill to confess to the crimes and make a full statement. It was the last time the General ever admitted to anything. As a result, he developed an intense hatred for Murphy, who became one of the city's leading detectives. On 9 July 1965, he was convicted and sentenced to two years in St Conleth's Reformatory School in Daingean, County Offaly.

The General's first taste of incarceration would have major repercussions for Irish society. In Daingean, Martin Cahill formed strong bonds of friendship with several other juvenile delinquents, who would usher in a new era of organized crime. Two of Martin's brothers, Anthony and John, were incarcerated in various reformatory/industrial schools at the same time. They also established important alliances with other young hoodlums. This was where Gangland's brat pack set up their networks and began their journey together.

St Conleth's Reformatory School was run like a brutal prison camp by the Oblate religious order, who subjected the teenagers in their care to systematic, savage beatings and sexual abuse. Martin and his younger brother, 13-year-old Eddie Cahill, were both in the hellhole at the same time. Martin was seen as a strong, silent character, who sized up every situation and made the best of a bad lot. He never made eye contact with his captors because to do so would be to acknowledge their authority. If he saw a piece of paper on the ground he picked it up rather than suffer the indignity of being told to do so. By contrast his brother Eddie was a hothead who openly fought against authority – and gave the sadistic brothers an excuse to beat him. Eddie would become one of the most violent members of the General's gang.

Martin Cahill made two very important contacts in Daingean. He struck up a strong friendship with Larry Dunne, which brought their two families together, and he also befriended 14-year-old John Cunningham, who would later become known as the General's 'Colonel'. Cunningham was sent to Daingean for two years in 1966 when he was convicted of house-breaking and larceny. The two hoods became close friends and partners-in-crime. John Cunningham's family had also been part of the mass exodus from the slums. They'd been moved from a tenement on Blessington Street, around the corner from Grenville Street, to a new house in Le Fanu Road in Ballyfermot, West Dublin.

John's brother Michael would also become a career criminal, and they went on to do armed robberies with both the Cahill and Dunne clans. Other young crooks came into the fledgling criminal network, including two notorious fraudsters and chancers, John Traynor and Sean 'the Fixer' Fitzgerald, who in turn became members of the Dunne/Cahill crime network. Another young gun who became allied to the Badfellas' brat pack was a diminutive little thief called John Gilligan, whose family was moved from slums in Grangegorman, in the north inner-city, to Loch Con Road, close to the Cunninghams' home in 'Ballyer'. Gilligan, whose criminal career started with a conviction for stealing chickens at the age of 15, managed to avoid being sent to the reform schools. He would go a long way in his criminal career.

Brothers from two other families also became important members of Gangland's first generation: George and Paddy Mitchell from Benbulbin Road in Drimnagh and Michael 'Jo Jo' Kavanagh and his brother Paddy from Crumlin. They all started off as burglars but were soon in the thick of the action. Many of them had also cut their teeth as inmates in the asylums run by the religious orders. George Mitchell, nicknamed 'the Penguin', started working as a truck driver for the Jacobs biscuit company in Tallaght, Dublin, as a 16-year-old. It was an ideal job for a gangster who would specialize in organizing major warehouse robberies with his pals Martin Cahill and John Gilligan. The Mitchells and the Kavanaghs were soon classified as dangerous criminals who were involved in armed robbery, fraud and, later, drugs.

The brat pack included the extended families of the main players and some individual associates, such as Martin 'the Viper' Foley and his best friend Seamus 'Shavo' Hogan, both of whom were also from Crumlin. Together, these families and individuals would form the complex network at the centre of organized crime. They were the driving force that made the underworld what it is today. The fact that the vast majority of them came from Crumlin, Drimnagh and Ballyfermot is one of the reasons these suburbs are known as the birthplace of Gangland. Everyone involved in the emerging, underworld syndicate worked with Martin Cahill at various stages in their criminal careers. All of them considered him to be their General.

By the time 18-year-old Cahill finished his sentence in Daingean in 1967, the Corporation had moved his family to a dilapidated flat complex in Rathmines, called Hollyfield Buildings. His parents had fallen hopelessly into arrears on their rent payments in Crumlin. The semi-derelict flat complex was a dumping ground for tenants who couldn't pay the rent or were too troublesome elsewhere. The inhabitants were treated as social outcasts. Built in 1911, the dwellings consisted of 120 one/two-bedroom flats. They stood in two-storey blocks and resembled a military barracks. Some of the buildings were considered to be perilously close to collapsing and sewage ran from broken drains. One former resident commented: 'It was the worst, poorest, smelliest, rat-ridden scum-pit in Dublin.' But Martin Cahill loved the place because it symbolized his world. Out of this imposed isolation grew a deep-rooted sense of loyalty and contempt for authority — factors which moulded Cahill's complex personality. 'What [the authorities] never counted on was that we'd like it. Everyone knew everyone else and we all looked out for one another,' he fondly recalled.

Hollyfield was a breeding ground for outlaws. For most families crime was the principal source of income for food and clothes. The Cahill brothers became professional burglars and plagued the large houses in the neighbouring areas. The General was considered to be one

of the best 'creepers' in the city and 'worked' every night of the week –
he was rarely seen out during the day. Even when he graduated to
organizing big cash heists, he still went 'mooching' at night. He once
commented: 'If you think that you can see everyone but they can't see
you, then you will be invisible.' Cahill's passion in life was rummaging
through people's homes while they slept in their beds. He was also a
sleazy voyeur who liked to watch the goings on in the bedrooms of the
big houses. Cahill revelled in his anti-social existence and once compared his beloved Hollyfield to an anthill: 'If you were looking down at
Hollyfield from above at night you would see the ants moving out in all
directions in search of the honey-pot.'

Cahill and his brothers took part in large-scale burglaries from warehouses around the country with members of the gangland brat pack,
including John Gilligan and George Mitchell. The Penguin selected targets as he delivered Jacobs' biscuits all over Ireland. But on 19 March
1970, Cahill ran out of luck when he received a four-year jail sentence.
He had been caught red-handed in a lock-up garage in Rathmines with
a haul of cigarettes which had been stolen earlier in Portlaoise. While
inside Cahill shared a landing with Christy Dunne, who was doing a
two-year stretch for receiving stolen goods. Their friendship solidified
the alliance between the two families.

By the time Cahill was released from Mountjoy Prison on 25 January
1973, Gangland had transformed. The Dunnes, and many of his associates, had become armed robbers. Christy and his brothers offered to
show Martin the ropes. The house-breaker from Hollyfield joined their
'Academy' and soon discovered he was a natural-born blagger.

Henry Dunne was considered to the most 'talented' and dangerous
robber in the family. He loved the frenzied excitement of pulling off a
job. The more difficult it was the better. It was his idea to first start hitting cash-in-transit security vans. In an interview in 1990 he proudly
explained the logic for the initiative: 'Why should we be hitting individual banks when we could hit the money from ten of them in the
back of a van? We just watched it collecting the cash and then hit it . . .
simple. We never went out with the intention of hurting anyone but
when we came through the door we were going to get what we came
for.' In an interview with this author in 1994, for the book *The General*,
Dunne explained how Cahill first became involved with his family

business: 'Martin and Eddie first met Larry in Daingean and they decided that they would work together when they got out. When Martin came out [in 1973] we teamed up with him, Eddie and John and started doing strokes. We were pulling off jobs that were being blamed on Saor Eire which suited us fine at the time.' Martin Cahill's first armed robbery was planned by Henry Dunne.

For weeks Henry, Martin and Eddie Cahill watched one particular security van as it did its regular collections, across the south of the city on Monday afternoons. It wasn't a difficult job because the van never changed its route or schedule. Henry Dunne recalled the General's inaugural blag. 'Martin wanted to hold up a supermarket in Rathfarnham but I said let's do the security van collecting the money instead. I told him that you could get the money from eight banks in the back of the van. So he sussed out the security van that collected the cash and we watched it for two weeks. It was our first job together.'

On Monday, 18 November 1974, the gang watched as the van left the Securicor Depot in Herberton Road, Rialto at 3.30 p.m., to begin its rounds. Over the next two and a half hours it collected cash from seven branches of the Allied Irish Bank in Ballyfermot, Bluebell, Kimmage, Dundrum and Rathfarnham. Its final collection of the day was from the Quinnsworth supermarket on Marian Road in Rathfarnham. Darkness had fallen as security man John Tennyson collected a canvas bag containing £900, just before the shop closed at 6 p.m. As Tennyson returned to the van a 'woman' pushing a buggy walked towards him. His partner John Moraghan, who was sitting with the cash in the van's vault, released the bolt locking the door, so Tennyson could get in quickly.

Dunne remembered: 'There was me, Larry and Shamie, as well as Martin, Eddie and John Cahill on the job. Martin's brother-in-law from Hollyfield, Hughie Delaney, was given the job of hiding the money afterwards. Everyone had a part to play and we had to pounce on the security man just as he was getting back into the van. Then we had to get in at the guy in the back who was in the vault with the money and the radio.'

As soon as the door opened, the 'woman', Henry Dunne, dumped the buggy and pulled out a sawn-off shotgun. At the same time Eddie Cahill, wearing a cap and wig, appeared behind the security man and hit him hard on the back of his helmet. Tennyson was turned around and hit in the face and forehead with a revolver, breaking his teeth and leaving a gash in his forehead. The security man then got a boot in the chest, as the cash bag was torn away from him and he was pushed face down on the pavement. Tennyson was warned that he would be shot if he moved. At the same time, Martin Cahill got into the van, just as Moraghan was about to radio for assistance. He grabbed the security man and pulled him out, shouting: 'That means you too.' Two other members of the gang ran into the supermarket and the newsagent's next door. They ordered everyone to lie down and warned them they would be shot if they tried to call the cops. A few minutes later, the robbers sped off in two getaway cars. They got away with £92,600 in cash – the equivalent of around €1 million today.

Henry Dunne recalled: 'We [Dunnes] were used to the buzz from a good job but Martin was all excited and said he loved it. He was a natural and after that he was doing at least one decent job, every week or so. But the day after a big robbery he still went out breaking into people's houses after pulling a big one. He was strange like that.'

Within an hour of the robbery, the Gardaí began to make progress in their investigation of what was now one of the biggest cash robberies in the history of the State. Shortly after the heist, garage owner John McKenna spotted a number of men acting suspiciously. They were standing around a yellow Volkswagen car at the end of the cul-de-sac beside his premises on Garville Lane in Rathgar. When he approached them they said the car had broken down. McKenna gave them a push to start it. When the men left he checked the area and found some of the empty cash bags from the Securicor van. He had also taken the registration number of the VW. Gardaí later located the car abandoned in the area, and when they searched it they found a sawn-off shotgun. Detectives then checked the registration and discovered the car belonged to 22-year-old Martin Foley, a petty thief and a known associate of the Cahills, from Cashel Avenue in Crumlin.

When Foley was approached he told detectives he had loaned the car to Hughie Delaney earlier that day and hadn't seen it since. Foley told them that Delaney had given him the log book for his own car, a Triumph Toledo, as security against the Volkswagen. The truth was that Delaney's car had indeed broken down and Foley had loaned him his VW to take away the money after the gang dumped the getaway cars.

The hood, who would be a central member of the General's mob for the next 16 years, wasn't about to take the rap for his pals.

At the same time an off-duty Garda revealed that he had spotted Martin and Eddie Cahill, with Delaney, two hours before the robbery. They were trying to start Delaney's broken-down Triumph on Effra Road in Rathmines – just before Hughie had borrowed Foley's VW. It was also the same area where one of the getaway cars had been dumped. The focus of the investigation turned to Hollyfield Buildings and three of its residents, who were well known to the Gardaí.

The flats of Martin and Eddie Cahill and Hughie Delaney were searched the next morning by a team of officers led by Detective Inspector Ned Ryan. Nicknamed 'the Buffalo' by colleagues, Det. Insp. Ryan was a tough, uncompromising country cop who had been appointed to the Rathmines 'P' district a year earlier. He was determined to stamp out the crime epidemic emanating from Hollyfield Buildings and was well aware of Martin Cahill's potential for mayhem. Ryan had encountered Cahill some time previously while investigating a payroll snatch that the Dunnes had pulled. The pair took an instant dislike to each other. Det. Insp. Ryan told Cahill that his days as an up-and-coming criminal were over and Martin would be 'reduced to robbing grannies' handbags' by the time he was finished with him.

When questioned, Delaney made a number of verbal admissions about being involved in the crime. The three men were arrested and charged with the robbery two days later. They were also charged with the burglary in which the sawn-off shotgun found in Foley's car had been stolen and with the theft of the two getaway cars. The charges against the General and his brother, however, were dropped before trial, due to a lack of evidence, but the State had more against Delaney. They had Foley's evidence about loaning his car to the General's brother-in-law. Gardaí also had the garage owner John McKenna, who could place Foley's car at the scene where the cash bags were found.

On the first day of Hughie Delaney's trial in July 1976, Martin Foley failed to turn up in the Central Criminal Court and a bench warrant was issued for his arrest. In the absence of the main prosecution witness, the evidence of John McKenna was not enough to prove the case and Delaney was acquitted. Immediately after the trial the gang decided to exact revenge on John McKenna for doing his civic duty. Cahill, Henry

Dunne and other gang members broke into his garage at Garville Lane and set it ablaze. It was a routine operation that went badly wrong. Dunne was trapped inside when the fire prematurely ignited. He was severely burned by the time Cahill and the other henchmen dragged him away from the flames. Christy arranged for him to be brought to a safe house in Dun Laoghaire where a crooked doctor treated his wounds. It took months for Henry's burn wounds to heal and the medic helped ease his pain by administering large doses of morphine. By the time the wounds had healed Henry Dunne had developed a drug habit.

With the trial out of the way and Delaney free, Foley re-emerged two weeks later and handed himself in. When he was brought before the court, Foley claimed that the Provisional IRA had kidnapped him. He said that he knew the identity of his 'abductor' but insisted: 'If I give his name, my life is not worth living.' He denied, under oath, that he had been paid to 'get offside'. Mr Justice Gannon released Foley, remarking, in reference to the kidnap yarn: 'Something should be done about it. I cannot direct what should be done, it is not my function.'

Not everyone who was associated with Cahill and the Dunnes was operating in gangs. Between 1974 and 1975 a mysterious 'lone raider' began holding up banks around Dublin. In less than a year he had done at least a dozen jobs. The mystery character attracted intense curiosity from both the underworld and the Gardaí. His modus operandi was distinctive. Before each heist a Mini car was stolen and the robber was always described as being a tall and plump male figure. Following one incident, when a member of the public grappled with the robber and was left holding three jumpers, the police got a vital clue – the lone raider was a master of disguise. They subsequently discovered that it was not unusual for the unknown robber to dress up as a woman when he was on a 'job'.

The Central Detective Unit (CDU) eventually caught up with the lone raider in 1975. He was caught after a robbery at the Mater Hospital in Dublin. He was charged with that robbery and a second one from a bank on Merrion Row, on the south side of the city. The raider was identified as Patrick Eugene Holland and he would become one of gangland's most infamous hit men, known simply as 'Dutchie'.

The gangster Dutchie Holland was very different to the rest of the underworld population. It was hard to find a reason why someone like him had become a professional criminal in the first place. Dutchie was born on 12 March 1939, and grew up in the countryside, at St Lawrence's Road in Chapelizod, West Dublin. He came from a world completely alien to the likes of the Dunnes or the Cahills. The family was middle class and well-off. Dutchie once described how he'd had an idyllic, privileged childhood. On his seventeenth birthday his parents had given him a car – a luxury far from the reaches of the majority of the impoverished Irish population in 1956. In his younger years he was a dedicated athlete and played professional soccer for a time. When he was in his late teens he went to America and joined the United States Marine Corps. He returned to Ireland in the early 1960s. Through his teenage years and early twenties he was never in trouble with the law. He claimed that the turning point in his life came in 1965, when he got his first criminal conviction for receiving stolen fur coats. Holland claimed he had been set up and the experience left him with an abiding hatred for the authorities.

With two armed robbery charges pending against him, Holland became something of a celebrity in gangland after his capture. Other hoods wanted to work with him. Dutchie broke with his own rule of working alone and teamed up with Michael and John Cunningham, who were also running with both the Dunnes and the Cahills. In 1976, John Cunningham was jailed for 18 months for an armed hold-up at his local post office, but he was out by Christmas. On 29 December 1976, Holland and the Cunninghams robbed the takings from the Carlton Cinema on Dublin's O'Connell Street, during the main feature of the night. The Cunninghams were later arrested at a New Year's party. In a search of Michael Cunningham's house in Rathfarnham the police recovered the guns and the cash stolen in the job. On 3 January, Holland, Michael Cunningham and two other men were charged with armed robbery. With three armed robbery charges against him, Holland skipped bail a month later and went to Chicago, Illinois with his wife. On 7 February a warrant was issued for his arrest. Years later Dutchie claimed to Gardaí that he had made ends meet in Chicago by working as a hit man for the Mafia.

In 1981 Dutchie was caught after he slipped back into the country for a wedding and decided to stay for a few months. The lone raider financed his extended holiday at home with a string of armed robberies and pay-roll snatches. Gardaí had identified Dutchie as the likely culprit and had issued a nationwide alert. He was arrested as he was about to take a ferry to France, en route back to the US. He was subsequently jailed for a total of seven years. When he was released from prison, Dutchie went to work with the Cahills.

The General had learned one important lesson from his first major heist – the need for meticulous planning. Henry Dunne had described him as a 'natural' but the relationship between Martin Cahill and the Dunnes turned sour a year later when he and his brothers took part in the West's jewellery robbery. It had been agreed that the Cahills would get a share of the loot but Christy lost it following a Garda sting operation (see Chapter 4). Cahill, however, later spotted Larry's wife, Lilly, wearing jewellery that he suspected had come from West's. After that Martin always referred to Lilly Dunne as 'diamond Lil' and swore that he would never work with Christy Dunne again. The West's job had also led to a rift between Christy and his siblings. Shamie and Larry later invited the Cahills to get involved in the drug trade with them but the General declined. Cahill would later claim that he had no time for drugs. Several of his friends and family members were junkies. He once commented: 'Never trust a drug fella . . . they're like a helpless thing, not a human being at all.'

In 2011, Christy Dunne tried to rewrite history and claimed that he and Cahill had worked together for years. He said that the General had 'collected' weapons for him, on behalf of Northern Catholics. In an interview for a documentary, Dunne said: 'At the beginning of the Troubles I remember telling Martin that any weapons he came across would be welcome. No one made the connection between me and him because I was older. He was close to my younger brothers. He went out all over the country and he brought me back hundreds of weapons and I turned them over to the people who needed them.' But the General wasn't around to comment on the allegation. Most people believed that Dunne hadn't lost his penchant for bluffing.

In any event, by 1975 the General had learned enough from the Dunne Academy and he set up his own armed robbery gang. The Cahills and their associates soon began to attract the attentions of the authorities. They were robbing banks, security vans and factory bank rolls so often that they were soon averaging one 'stroke' each week. The General's gang were also pulling off aggravated burglaries, which involved breaking into people's homes and holding them hostage at gunpoint while they robbed the place. The ruthless new kids on the block were becoming an embarrassment to the Gardaí.

A month after the West's robbery a burglary by Cahill's siblings Michael 'Styky' and Anthony ended in murder. John Copeland, an economist with the Central Bank, was stabbed to death in his home in Rathmines on 24 March 1975. The Cahill brothers had burgled the apartment earlier that night and had returned when 22-year-old Anthony discovered that he had left a torch at the scene. It was one of the cardinal rules their brother had drilled into them – never leave any evidence behind. When the victim returned from a rugby training session, he found Anthony Cahill in his home. During a scuffle, John Copeland was stabbed once in the chest with a kitchen knife. When the brothers were questioned about the murder, Styky made a statement implicating Anthony. He was charged a month later with the murder and burglary. Martin was furious that his brother had broken the family code of *omertà* and co-operated with the enemy. He taught Styky a lesson by giving him a severe beating.

Despite the serious charges pending against Anthony, the robberies continued. In 1975 Det. Insp. Ned Ryan was transferred to the CDU to head the 'Flying Squad'. It was a new unit set up to take on the growing number of robbery gangs. The General knew that his name was top of Ryan's list, so he decided to give his old enemy something to think about. One morning in 1976, Cahill's gang robbed the Werburg Street Labour Exchange of £100,000 – literally under the noses of the Flying Squad as the offices of the CDU overlooked the Exchange. Detectives drove past the front door every five minutes, going to and from Dublin Castle. It was considered to be the last place anyone would dare to rob. Cahill and his crew drove up to the front door and ran inside, armed with sawn-off shotguns and pistols. They knew exactly where to go as it was where most of them collected their dole every week. The gang were in and out in three minutes; they were speeding away as detectives raced down the stairs from their offices. Three years later they hit the Exchange again and got away with the more modest sum of £25,000.

By the mid-1970s, Cahill had turned Hollyfield into his own domain where he was the undisputed king of the castle. To illustrate his status, he erected a flag pole over his flat and hoisted a Tricolour, in an expression of solidarity with the nationalist minority in Northern Ireland. He also placed loud-speakers on the roof and played rebel songs at full blast, day and night. Whenever the cops came to make him turn the music off he went out and burgled some of the local big houses. With plenty of money coming in from the robberies, Cahill splashed out and bought himself a large Mercedes and a BMW. He also imported a custom-built 1100cc Harley Davidson motorbike for which he paid £4,000. He added other high-powered racing bikes to his collection. The flashy cars and bikes looked rather incongruous parked outside a rundown slum building, surrounded by ruptured sewers and piles of rubbish. His other indulgence was to buy a colour TV, which was considered a luxury item in Ireland in the mid-1970s. The TV aerial parked next to the flag pole and loud-speakers on the roof added to the surreal atmosphere in Cahill's squalid kingdom. One night, during a Garda raid, the colour TV landed in the courtyard below, smashed into several pieces. The cops had been attacked earlier when they'd driven into the complex and this was the return match. Cahill went out the following day and bought another TV. And when that suffered a similar fate he got another one. The General didn't believe in allowing his enemies get the better of him.

Money from the robberies was also used to open a pool hall in a disused warehouse at Raleigh Square in Crumlin. It became an ideal meeting place for the many gangsters living in the area. Sean Fitzgerald, John Traynor's best friend, was given the job of managing the place. The Fixer was a slippery con artist who nurtured an image as a respectable gent. He had the hall refurbished and bought 12 pool tables for cash. Inside the front door a porch was erected, so that when the police came in, the lack of natural light made it impossible for them to see the dodgy customers lurking in the shadows. Many years later when Fitzgerald was interviewed by this writer, he specifically mentioned the porch and explained why it was there. The duplicitous conman was very proud of his ingenuity. The pool hall became a magnet for Gardaí, who regularly sat outside watching who was coming and going. Members of the Flying Squad began to irritate their targets by going inside and playing pool for hours. The club was searched several times. Despite the unwanted attentions, legitimate business was soon booming.

The hall was also used for a most unusual money-laundering operation. A short time earlier, Cahill's gang had robbed a security van carrying the cash collected from Dublin Gas Company meters around the city. The General and his associates struggled away with £10,000 in silver 10p pieces – 100,000 coins – which they buried. They believed it would be easy to filter them through the successful pool hall. But when the gang dug up their hidden treasure the silver coins had turned black from the damp earth. The young hoods spent a whole night literally washing the coins in buckets. Then the coins were laid out on the pool tables, where they were polished up again with towels and blankets.

The criminal hotspot also became popular with young women who were groupies of the glamorous bad boys. Dozens of them had their first sexual experiences in a bed in a rear office at the pool hall. But one night things got out of control. Sean Fitzgerald described to this writer how Anthony Cahill took a young woman into the back room for sex. He became violent and sexually assaulted the woman with a pool cue. When the other gangsters heard the screams they ran in and found the girl hysterical and sobbing. Her clothes had been ripped and torn off her back. The General arrived later to calm her down but word about the incident leaked out, and after that people stopped going to the hall. Fitzgerald eventually shut it down.

One of the favourite targets of the armed gangs was factories, where cash payrolls were delivered on the same day each week. In the early hours of 12 May 1977, Cahill and five other gang members burst into the Ballyfermot home of Bernard and Elizabeth O'Neill and held the family at gunpoint. The General's target was the huge Semperit tyre factory, and its grounds bordered the O'Neills' back garden. Cahill had been planning the job for two months – monitoring the arrival of the security vans and scrutinizing how the money was handed over to the factory's security staff. A payroll delivery for the 1,000-strong workforce was due to arrive the following morning. During the night the gang cut a hole in the fence and then they settled in to wait.

The next morning, at 10.50 a.m., four gang members, including Cahill, struck with split-second timing, just as the cash was being transferred from the security van to the factory wages' office. The gang fired several shots in the air as staff tried to keep them out. They snatched the bags, containing over £50,000 in cash, and ran back to the fence, where high-powered motorbikes were parked for the getaway. As they ran away a security guard was shot and injured.

In the immediate aftermath of the Semperit job the Flying Squad stepped up their overt surveillance on Cahill. Det. Insp. Ryan had received information that the General was behind it. A month after the heist he was followed to Killiney Hill, in South County Dublin, by detectives who believed he was going to dig up the proceeds. As Cahill was coming down the hill, he met Ned Ryan and three of his men walking up to meet him. 'Now, Martin, you and I are going for a chat up that hill and when we come back down you'll have given back the Semperit money. It looks like this is the showdown,' Ryan later recalled in an interview for the book *The General*. Cahill turned and bolted back up the hill, with the cops running after him. At the top they tried to grab him. The paranoid General was terrified that he was going to be killed. He jumped off a steep cliff into the darkness below, after wriggling out of his anorak which was left in the hands of one of Ryan's men. The Flying Squad officers were sure Martin Cahill had been killed and began searching for his body.

The following day officers visited Cahill's wife Frances to see if she had heard from him and was he all right. They dropped in his jacket and the keys of his Mercedes which was still parked in Killiney. Incredibly, Cahill survived the fall and only suffered a fractured shoulder, with some cuts and bruises. He later claimed to his solicitor that the police had tried to kill him. There was no substance to his allegation.

Less than six months later, 28-year-old Cahill was given an enforced break from the attentions of the Flying Squad. On 24 November 1977, he was jailed for four years when a jury found him guilty of receiving a stolen car and two motorbikes which were intended for a robbery. Martin and Eddie Cahill had been arrested at the lock-up they were using to store the vehicles. He was joined in Mountjoy Prison by Eddie, who was also jailed for receiving stolen goods. A month afterwards, following two trials, Anthony Cahill was found not guilty of the Copeland murder. He had admitted burgling the dead man's apartment and was convicted of the lesser crime.

While inside, Martin Cahill was joined by Christy Dutton, a close friend since childhood who had taken part in a number of heists with Cahill and Henry Dunne. Dutton was a professional armed robber from Ballyfermot, with a reputation as a dangerous criminal. Cahill even named one of his sons after the mobster. He was also joined by another Ballyfermot hoodlum called Noel 'Noelie' Lynch, who was the same age as the other young criminals. Lynch was doing ten years for a pay-roll robbery at the Master Stevedores in Alexandra Basin in Dublin, during which shots were fired. At Lynch's trial in October 1972, the judge told him that it was 'one of the worst cases of armed robbery that has come before the courts in recent years'. Both Lynch and Dutton would later become integral members of the General's gang.

Another individual who would be important in Cahill's future plans also joined him in Mountjoy Prison. John Traynor was jailed in December 1977 for five years for possession of a firearm with intent to endanger life. The man, who would later be nicknamed 'the Coach' by journalist Veronica Guerin, had grown up in Charlemont Street, near Ranelagh in South Dublin, before his family moved to Crumlin. The two hoods had known each other from childhood and Traynor was a regular vis-itor to Hollyfield. When his family went to live in Kildare, he stayed in touch with his odd friend. It was Traynor who first helped Paddy Shanahan achieve his goal of becoming a gangster. Described as being 'extremely clever, manipulative and duplicitous', Traynor played games with everyone he ever did business with. Like Sean Fitzgerald, he worked hard to portray himself as a respectable criminal who was a cut above the rest of the underworld riff-raff. Ironically, he looked like a police-man and, being an inveterate opportunist, often posed as one, as did Sean Fitzgerald.

Traynor and Cahill formed a criminal partnership which was to last for almost twenty years. They had a strange relationship and were best summed up as gangland's odd couple. Traynor was everything that the General despised – a flash, hard-drinking chancer who only cared about saving his own skin. On the other hand, Traynor described Cahill as 'totally odd and very paranoid'. There was no written legal agreement between the unlikely partners. There was no need for one. Cahill knew that if there was a 'legal' problem he could sort it out in his own inimit-able fashion, and Traynor knew that Cahill was the one man in the world he could never rip off. It was a classic underworld version of a gentleman's agreement. Traynor became Cahill's adviser and organizer – in Mafia parlance, his *consigliere*.

In July 1978, Anthony and John Cahill robbed a £4,600 payroll at the Smurfit paper mill in Clonskeagh, South Dublin. Ironically Martin Cahill had worked in the mill for a short time after his release from Daingean – he never worked in gainful employment again. As the brothers drove off, they ran into two armed detectives who were escorting a security van. The cops and robbers exchanged gunfire and John Cahill was hit in the chest. The brothers managed to get away but were caught in Ballsbridge. The money and three firearms were recovered. In hospital 31-year-old John Cahill told detectives he had tried to pull the bullet out of his chest. Seven months later, in February 1979, the brothers were both jailed for ten years by the Special Criminal Court. When he was initially brought before the court, John Cahill objected to being there. He told the three judges in the non-jury court: 'I do not recognize the jurisdiction of this court. I am not political. I have no political association and have never had. It is wrong to bring me here. It is a bastardization of law to try me in this court.'

Four of the Cahill brothers were in prison by the late 1970s, but the General still believed he was king of the castle. A year earlier Dublin Corporation had finally taken action to relieve the squalid conditions in Hollyfield Buildings, which had become a health hazard. The 'Corpo' planned to demolish it and build again, but the General was not prepared to allow the destruction of his crumbling powerbase and he launched a legal bid from his prison cell to stop the demolition. A dozen families who refused to leave were served with eviction orders. After that the only flat left standing on the dilapidated site was Cahill's because he was still appealing the eviction in the courts. Eventually his wife Frances accepted a flat in Upper Kevin Street, in inner-city Dublin – across the road from the local Garda station. When he was released from prison in 1980, Cahill took on City Hall but he was forced to move into a caravan, after his flat was demolished one night. When the caravan mysteriously burned down, Cahill slept in a tent. Eventually the Lord Mayor of the time came to the site and pleaded with Cahill to allow the new building work to go ahead. After all, the new houses would be for Cahill's neighbours. The unemployed criminal backed down after he was promised a Corporation house in Rathmines.

Gangland was in the process of dramatic change when Cahill had walked out of Mountjoy Prison in 1980. Heroin had gripped the old neighbourhoods where he had grown up. His erstwhile friends, the Dunnes, had discovered a much more lucrative form of turning a dishonest pound. Cahill would later reveal why he refused to get involved: 'I was asked to go into drugs when I came out of prison but everyone was knackered. They would sit around all day talking about drugs and money, but they had no money. When I said "Yeah, let's do a robbery," they'd start talking about drug stores and I knew I was wasting me time.'

The General had other plans.

6. Turmoil

Des O'Malley had been a Fianna Fáil TD for less than two years when he was appointed Minister for Justice in May 1970. Within hours of sacking ministers Charles Haughey, Neil Blaney and Michael O'Morain over the 'Arms Crisis' (see Chapter 2), Taoiseach Jack Lynch gave O'Malley what would be one of the toughest jobs in Government from that point on. The 31-year-old Limerick man had a baptism of fire. He recently recalled: 'Being in Justice in the early '70s was like being in charge of the fire brigade, you were running around all the time trying to put out fires and you could do very little constructive work.'

The situation in the North rapidly deteriorated after the British Army shot 13 innocent civilians dead in Derry on 'Bloody Sunday', 30 January 1972. Before the year was out, almost 500 people had been killed in the violence that followed. After the announcement of a ceasefire by the Official IRA, the Provisionals became the main terrorist threat. The Provos were responsible for the bulk of the deaths and injuries, and they opened a new front south of the Border which threatened to destabilize Irish society. The serious security crisis inevitably distracted successive governments and forced them to take their eye off the looming menace of organized crime. In the shadow of the shadow of the gunmen, the gangsters were thriving.

The former Minister for Justice revealed in an interview for the RTÉ series *Bad Fellas*: 'All of these extreme acts of violence in the North and to a lesser extent down here, were all happening for the first time; people hadn't seen anything like that since the Civil War and not many people were still around who had seen the Civil War. It was a fairly frightening scenario and it meant that you had to concentrate all your efforts on that. I had hoped to engage in a lot of law reform which was tremendously necessary at that time but I never really got around to doing that at all.'

Brendan Halligan was a former Labour party Senator and TD during the 1973–77 Fine Gael/Labour coalition government. Halligan has no doubt about what the violence cost Irish society: 'The cost of the IRA and the security crisis they created is all the things that we did not do in health, in social welfare, in education, in housing, in infrastructure and simply building a better society. When they brought the bomb and the gun back into society things changed for ever. We would not have had the descent into organized crime to the extent that we have suffered from. It is inescapable that the direct causal link is the IRA and the introduction of the gun and the introduction of the bomb and the application of organization to criminal activity. The Gardaí didn't react rapidly enough to this new phenomenon of criminals organizing themselves. To our shame we have created a Mafia that is equal to any Mafia in Europe and have created an international crime problem of a high order.'

Former Justice Minister Paddy Cooney inherited the poisoned chalice from O'Malley in 1973. He found himself on the frontline in some of the worst days of the Troubles and recalled: 'Organized crime as we know it today had not emerged except in the ranks of the Provos. The cult of organised crime and the cult of the gun began in those times with the Provos and spilled over into gangland in cities like Limerick, Dublin and Cork. The appalling crime situation we have today can be linked quite clearly back to the Provos and their campaign of the '70s and '80s.'

Apart from armed robberies, the IRA also used the Republic as the logistical support base for their campaign in the North. The Provos set up training camps and smuggled munitions into Ireland which were stored in bunkers in the South and then moved to arms dumps in the North. In March 1973, the Government was given just cause to be concerned at the level of the threat posed by the terrorists. The Irish Navy intercepted a gun-running ship, the MV *Claudia*, off Helvick Harbour in Waterford. It contained a huge arsenal of weapons which had been sent to the IRA by the Libyan dictator Colonel Gaddafi. The haul included 1,000 rifles and anti-tank guns, 100 cases of landmines, 500 grenades and 5,000 pounds of explosives. The overall commander of the Provisional IRA, Joe Cahill, was caught with the weapons and was subsequently jailed for three years. It later emerged that a number of other large arms shipments had also been smuggled into the country during the 1970s.

The enormous financial cost of security during the Troubles put an

intolerable burden on an economy already on its knees. The 1970s in
Ireland were marked by industrial unrest and high unemployment,
amid a crippling recession caused by a worldwide oil shortage. In 1975,
Irish inflation was the highest in Europe when it reached 20 per cent and
once again emigration became the only option for tens of thousands of
Irish men and women. The only area that showed a growth in employment figures was the security forces. In a four-year period the strength
of the Gardaí and the Irish Army was increased by over 6,000 personnel –
2,000 Gardaí and 4,000 troops. A massive re-equipment programme was
launched to modernize the Irish Army and a number of new military
barracks were built. Dozens of dilapidated camps and barracks which
had not been used since the Second World War were also pressed into
service, to accommodate over 2,000 Irish troops who were permanently
garrisoned along the 280-mile Border. They provided armed support to
a force of over 1,000 Gardaí that was also on permanent border duty. In
addition, Gardaí and troops were providing an average of 5,000 escorts
every year, for the transport of cash, explosives and prisoners. The Army
also had guard posts on all of the country's electricity generating stations and other vital installations, to prevent bomb attacks by Loyalist
terror groups. In the early stages of the conflict, soldiers and armed
Gardaí were posted to protect the studios of the national broadcaster,
RTÉ, to prevent terrorists from trying to take them over. Extra armed
Gardaí were also required to protect members of the Government, who
were threatened with assassination by the IRA. At the height of the
Troubles the Irish Government was spending a much higher proportion
of GDP on security than the British.

The Troubles also placed tremendous pressure on the prison system
throughout the 1970s as hundreds of IRA and INLA members were
jailed for serious offences. Troops and Gardaí were deployed to guard
prisons, but there were still escapes. In one incident a hijacked helicopter was used to airlift top IRA figures from the exercise yard of
Mountjoy Prison. Attempts were also made to smash through the gates
of Portlaoise Prison, as the bulk of subversive criminals were held there.
The terrorists' activities provided a welcome relief for ordinary criminals, many of whom were freed on temporary release to make room for
the 'political' prisoners. Michael Noonan, who was Justice Minister in
the early 1980s, had no doubt of the overall effect this had on the growth

of organized crime: 'The IRA in particular put enormous pressure on the prison system and I believe that we released people who would later become key players in organized crime.'

On 12 March 1974, the Provos showed the depths of their murderous intent against the State when they gunned down Fine Gael Senator Billy Fox. The 35-year-old Monaghan Protestant had also served a term as a TD for the area. He was shot dead by a 13-member Provo gang at the home of his fiancée near Clones. It was the first murder of a serving member of the Oireachtas since the assassination of Kevin O'Higgins in 1927. Brendan Halligan recalled how the country teetered on the edge of anarchy after the killing: 'The IRA at that point did not recognize the legitimacy of the State, it referred to us all as quislings and traitors and at a point in this Government every member of the Cabinet was under threat of assassination which was not widely known for quite a while. That was the atmosphere in which you lived and the legitimacy of the State itself was being questioned. So there wasn't a day when you didn't expect the unexpected or something more dreadful or appalling than the day before.'

Paddy Cooney, who had been a friend of Senator Fox, still believes that the murder was a deliberate act of sectarian violence: 'It is inconceivable that the people who murdered him didn't know who he was. They [the gang] were neighbours; they were from the same locality. I am quite satisfied that they knew who he was and killed him notwithstanding his status as a member of the Nation's parliament.'

The Provo threat was a dominant factor throughout the 1970s. On 8 June 1972, 60-year-old Garda Inspector Samuel Donegan was blown up by an IRA booby-trap bomb on the Cavan–Fermanagh border. He was just two years from retirement. Garda Michael Clerkin was killed in another booby-trap explosion on 15 October 1976 near Portarlington, County Laois. The young officer was killed when he stepped on a flagstone, at the front door of a house. The booby trap was the work of the IRA and one of a number of breaches of their so-called code which forbade the murder of Gardaí or members of the Defence Forces. The police were lured into the trap by an anonymous tip-off. Three months before the Portarlington ambush, the IRA also assassinated the British Ambassador to Ireland, Christopher Ewart-Biggs. He was killed when his armour-plated car was blown up by a landmine, just 12 days after taking up his post. In 1979, Lord Louis Mountbatten and three other people, including two children, were killed when an IRA bomb exploded in his fishing boat at Mullaghmore, County Sligo.

At the height of the unrest, the Provos even got into the art business as part of their so-called war effort. On 26 April 1974, an IRA gang led by Rose Dugdale, the daughter of an English millionaire stockbroker, robbed 19 paintings. They were valued at £8 million and were stolen from the home of Sir Alfred Beit at Russborough House in County Wicklow. Shortly after the robbery the IRA demanded a ransom of £500,000 and the transfer from England to Northern Ireland of sisters Dolours and Marian Price, who were serving jail sentences for car bombings in London. Dugdale and her gang were to be the first victims of what became known in underworld circles as the curse of the Beit paintings – she was caught and the paintings were recovered. Dugdale was subsequently jailed for nine years by the Special Criminal Court after pleading 'proudly and incorruptibly guilty'.

In 1975, the Provos struck another blow to the floundering Irish economy when they kidnapped Dutch industrialist Dr Tiede Herrema in County Limerick. Herrema owned the huge Ferenka factory which employed 1,400 workers. The republican strategy succeeded in disrupting inward investment to Ireland for years to come, as foreign business executives began to fear for their safety. IRA members Eddie Gallagher and Marian Coyle held the industrialist for 36 days. They demanded the release of Gallagher's girlfriend, Rose Dugdale, and Coyle's IRA boyfriend, Kevin Mallon. Dr Herrema was eventually released following a 16-day siege in Monasterevin, County Kildare.

The Provos and the INLA also continued to rob financial institutions throughout the country. The terrorist gangs often took over entire towns and villages, using the same modus operandi as Saor Eire. But the republicans weren't the only source of the mayhem.

In the early 1970s the Loyalist terror groups launched bombing attacks on the Republic. Between 1972 and 1973, 12 people were killed and several more injured and maimed when Loyalist bombs exploded in Dublin, Dundalk and other border towns. On 17 May 1974, three, no-warning, car bombs ripped through central Dublin. They exploded at the height of the Friday evening rush hour, killing 26 people and injuring 300. A short time later, another car bomb exploded in the centre of

Monaghan Town. In all 33 people were killed that day – the highest number of casualties in a single day during the thirty years of the Troubles. No one was ever convicted for the atrocity and it took the Loyalist Volunteer Force (LVF) another twenty years to admit responsibility. The finger of suspicion, however, has always pointed to the involvement of British intelligence operatives in organizing the bombing campaign. The theory is that the offensive was timed to influence the Irish Government's plans for the introduction of tough, new anti-terrorism legislation. Strangely the atrocity was purposely played down by successive Irish governments. There seemed to be a fear that, if handled differently, the outrage would have played into the hands of the IRA and plunged the entire island into all-out civil war.

Amid so much turmoil and fear, the emerging criminal gangs managed to avoid the spotlight. Despite their own penchant for creating chaos, the activities of the Cahills, the Dunnes and their associates looked mild when compared to the Provos. As the 1970s came to an end, it was easy to see how tackling the organized crime gangs had slipped further and further down the list of pressing priorities – and Irish gangsters would not be the only ones to take advantage of an overburdened and distracted Irish State.

Oxford graduate Howard Marks was one of the first members of the international drug-trafficking community to realize Ireland's potential as a major European transit point. The Welshman was not a criminal in the traditional sense – he had no time for violence and most of those involved in his organization were toffs. Marks first got involved in the drug trade when he supplied hash and marijuana to fellow students while studying Philosophy at Balliol College in the 1960s. He went on to become one of the biggest cannabis suppliers in the world, smuggling individual shipments of up to 30 tons of hash and marijuana from Pakistan and Thailand into Europe, America and Canada. At one stage he was reputed to control 10 per cent of the world's hash trade. Once described in the English *Daily Mail* as the 'most sophisticated drugs baron of all time', Marks was said to have been involved with MI6, the Mafia, the CIA and the IRA.

The global dealer's association with the IRA and Ireland came in the person of James Joseph McCann, an incorrigible, publicity-hungry con artist from Belfast. McCann, who was in many ways not dissimilar in character to Christy 'Bronco' Dunne, projected the public image of a revolutionary folk hero. 'Just call me the Shamrock Pimpernel,' he once commented in a magazine interview. But unlike Christy Dunne, McCann had managed to hoodwink the media, governments, police, courts, customs and intelligence agencies around the world.

Jim McCann hit the headlines in 1971 when he was the first inmate to escape from the Crumlin Road Prison in Belfast. He'd been imprisoned because he was caught throwing petrol bombs at Queen's University for the benefit of the hippie magazine *Friends*. It was all part of a bizarre scam to con ex-Beatle John Lennon out of millions, by convincing him to support McCann's 'struggle' for Irish freedom.

One of Marks's associates, who worked at the magazine, reckoned McCann would be perfect for their plans to expand their hash business. Marks was introduced to McCann, who enthusiastically agreed to get involved. McCann helped Marks smuggle an estimated 15 tons of cannabis through Shannon Airport at various stages during the 1970s. The unpredictable 'IRA' man organized the collection of air freight carrying the hash, which he referred to as 'nordle', and Marks and his friends transported it back to England, hidden in cars and camper-vans.

No one suspected a thing until the early hours of the morning of 25 August 1979. Two uniformed Gardaí got a call about men acting suspiciously, at a lay-by near Kill, County Kildare. When the officers arrived to investigate, they found McCann and three others transferring boxes full of cans from a van into a container truck. During a scuffle McCann threatened the two cops at gunpoint. He was later arrested following a high-speed chase. At first the police assumed they had found a load of explosives and called in the bomb squad to carry out a controlled explosion on one of the cans. When it blew up, the air was filled with high quality, herbal cannabis. In all they found 890 lbs of Thai sticks. The Gardaí had just stumbled on to the biggest drug seizure in Irish history, and the arrest of the Shamrock Pimpernel made international headlines.

Drug Squad detectives recognized McCann from his many media interviews, although he wouldn't give them his name. 'My name is Mr Nobody, my address is the world, now fuck off,' he replied with typical bravado. McCann and the other three men were charged with possession of drugs with intent to supply. The 'Shamrock Pimpernel' was also charged with possession of a handgun. McCann's notorious reputation backfired on him when the court refused bail. Instead he was sent to Portlaoise Prison, as a high-risk remand prisoner. The 'IRA' man was naturally sent to the Provos wing of the prison, where he was at first warmly welcomed by his old comrades. But once the chancer had settled in, he was severely beaten by the Provos, using socks filled with billiard balls, for bringing the 'good' name of the organization into disrepute.

While awaiting his trial, McCann received a visit from one of his biggest fans, Christy Dunne. McCann was all Bronco wanted to be – a hell-raising international man of mystery. Bronco offered the Shamrock Pimpernel the services of his own international criminal organization, back in Dublin. But McCann, an accomplished con artist, spotted Dunne a mile off and politely turned down the offer. On the return journey to Dublin Dunne crashed his car and later contacted McCann, demanding that he pay for the damage. There was no further communication between the two villains.

In March 1980 McCann and two other defendants were acquitted, following legal argument about what constituted 'possession' of drugs under the existing legislation. McCann's counsel also argued that no evidence had been produced to prove he'd had the gun. He left the court a free man and promptly vanished.

The huge publicity surrounding the McCann bust indirectly led to the discovery of another major international drug enterprise based in sleepy Ireland. Residents in the village of Knocklong, County Tipperary were shocked at the news that Ireland had become a 'drug haven'. With so much talk about drugs, it was inevitable that people suddenly got suspicious about a number of Englishmen who'd moved into a rented farm house a year earlier. When they shared their suspicions with the local Gardaí, the Drug Squad in Dublin was called in to investigate. As a result they uncovered one of the biggest amphetamine manufacturing plants in Europe. They seized 160 kilos of the drug, known as 'speed', valued at £2.5 million. It was discovered that several consignments of the mind-altering drug had already been manufactured and smuggled back to London.

The operation was the brainchild of Londoner James Humphreys, who had once owned a sex empire in London's Soho. Dubbed 'the Emperor of Porn', he was at the centre of a massive anti-corruption purge at Scotland Yard's Flying Squad in 1977. Humphreys had agreed to testify against corrupt officers to whom he had been paying bribes, in return for his early release from prison, where he was serving seven years for GBH. As a result of his testimony, 48 senior policemen were jailed or forced to resign. When Humphreys finished cleaning up the 'Met' he decided to become a drug-trafficker. On 27 March 1977, just before his release from prison, the Thames Valley police Drug Squad had busted the most sophisticated drug manufacturing and distribution operation ever uncovered. In total 'Operation Julie' led to the seizure of 180 million 'dots' of LSD. The crime syndicate involved had been churning out an average of £20 million worth of 'acid' every year since 1970. As a direct result of Operation Julie there was a series of follow-up operations in several other countries and the worldwide supply of LSD was practically eliminated. Another synthetic substance, amphetamine, began to replace LSD on the streets and there was a huge, ready market for the stuff.

All Humphreys needed were a few good chemists, a laboratory and somewhere quiet to make the pills. He picked Knocklong because he reckoned no one would suss what he was up to, but then McCann and Marks indirectly scuppered his multi-million-pound plan. Three people were arrested and charged by the Drug Squad in 1979, including two English criminals who had been hired to make the drugs. The two Brits were tried and found not guilty by a jury. Local auctioneer Donie Ryan was the only person convicted in relation to the Tipperary operation. He got three years for aiding and abetting in the production and supply of a controlled substance. Humphries was never caught.

The McCann/Marks and Humphreys groups illustrated how easy it was to use Ireland as a major hub for international drug-trafficking and how, due to the ongoing turmoil, it was seen as a soft touch. The responsibility for the enforcement of the country's outdated drug laws initially fell within the remit of the Special Branch. Apart from terrorism and subversion, the Branch dealt with immigration and aliens – and because drugs were associated with foreigners they got the job. At this stage, the Garda Síochána as an organization did not consider drugs to be a matter for criminal investigation, and abuse was universally seen as a health problem.

In the late 1960s, however, one young Special Branch detective, the legendary Dennis 'Dinny' Mullins, took a particular interest in the new phenomenon of drug abuse. While the Justice Minister of the day was confidently declaring that there was *no* drugs problem in the country, Mullins knew better. The Limerick man possessed a deep social conscience and would rather bring a young addict to hospital for help than to a Garda station on a drug charge.

Mullins, a Detective Sergeant since 1965, lobbied his bosses in the Special Branch for a unit to exclusively focus on drugs. He was eventually given three detectives and the unit later became the Drug Squad, situated in Dublin Castle. The Squad was then transferred to the Central Detective Unit (CDU) in the mid-1970s. The fact that the highest operational officer in the Drug Squad held the rank of Detective Sergeant and, in later years, Detective Inspector, was an illustration of where it stood in the pecking order of An Garda Síochána. The Garda Band and the Press Office each had a Garda Superintendent at the helm. A Detective Superintendent was not appointed to the Squad until the late 1980s.

The fact that the main players in both the McCann/Marks and Humphreys cases had managed to get away was a bitter experience for the small Garda Drug Squad, and in particular for their leader. Mullins could see the slow, inexorable drift towards widespread drug abuse from the late 1960s onwards, and warned anyone who would listen of the looming social catastrophe. The response from his superiors was largely one of indifference and he was the butt of jokes among colleagues. When callers phoned CDU looking for him they were often told 'ould Dinny's out looking for a bucket of morphine'. Before the 1980s no one in the police wanted to know about drugs, and the Drug Squad didn't even have enough basic resources to operate properly.

When the Dunnes discovered heroin, everything changed; Mullins and his successor, John McGroarty, were given the job of putting them out of business. McGroarty replaced Dinny Mullins as the officer in charge of the Drug Squad in 1983. Former Chief Superintendent McGroarty retired from the Gardaí in 2000. He recently recalled how the drug problem took hold: 'The Drug Squad was set up in response to community concerns after the media highlighted how individuals, who came back from England with addiction problems, started breaking into pharmacies and chemist shops stealing drugs to supply their habits. When these people were arrested they were often found to be in the possession of other controlled substances as well, not necessarily substances supplied by chemists but other illegal substances such as heroin and cocaine. In the beginning the drugs problem was harmless enough in Ireland and was largely ignored. Special Branch got the job because drugs were deemed to be something foreign, nothing to do with Ireland or Irish society. For several years all investigations were carried out under the Dangerous Drugs Act of 1934, an ancient piece of legislation, which was very cumbersome and not suited for modern policing.'

Drafting new legislation to deal with the drug problem was also one of the casualties of the Government's preoccupation with subversion. A new Misuse of Drugs Act which was drafted in 1977 was not made law until 1979. By the time heroin hit the streets it was too late for the Irish authorities to do anything other than play catch up.

It was against this bleak backdrop of terrorism, social and economic problems and the authorities' indifference that the second decade of organized crime was about to dawn. According to a newspaper article at the time, crime was the boom industry of the 1970s. Gross turnover was up by 500 per cent; productivity in operational terms was up 300 per cent; operational failure rates had dropped from 70 per cent to 40 per cent. These statistics would have been welcomed with delight if Gangland Inc. had had the equivalent of a corporate board.

Official Garda figures had recorded upwards of 2,000 incidents involving the use of firearms during the decade and that did not include shooting incidents in Border areas. In a special news feature in the *Irish Times*, in December 1979, the paper's security correspondent and future editor, Conor Brady, asked a question that is still being asked in 2011 – why had it happened? He gave three reasons: the spill over of crime from the North, with crimes committed by republicans on the run in the South; a strong 'imitative trend' as local criminals adopted the methods of the 'people from the North'; and the 'substantial reduction of Garda strength and effort' in the South, as attentions were switched to the Border.

Conor Brady rather prophetically wrote: 'As we face into the 1980s one of the challenges facing the community is what it will do about crime and violence. The belief, widely held in some circles, that the problem will abate if and when the North settles down, is ill-founded. It is only partially a product of problems across the border and much more substantially one of our own making here in the South.'

PART TWO

The 1980s

7.   The Human Wasteland

James 'Jem' Dixon stared blankly out from two dark caverns in a withered, jaundiced face, etched with pain. A mutilated stump was all that remained of his right leg and the index finger of his left hand was missing. The decaying shell of a once tall, fit man sat slumped in an armchair, in a corner of his inner-city flat, waiting for death – and a release from his living hell. Dixon, like thousands of others, had fallen victim to the heroin plague unleashed by the Dunnes. The family's discovery of an easier, more profitable way of making dirty money had cost Jem his life. It was the summer of 1994 and the 41-year-old heroin addict and former pusher was dying from AIDS.

The story of Jem Dixon's life epitomizes the legacy of the underworld's move into hard drugs. He agreed to be interviewed for a newspaper feature which focused on the heroin scourge, 14 years after it had first taken hold. Jem was one of the last surviving members of a family wiped out by the 'smack' epidemic which struck Dublin like a tidal wave as the new decade dawned. The deadly drug first took a stranglehold on inner-city communities on the south-side of Dublin.

In the Liberties, South Dublin's oldest area, Eddie Naughton got involved in anti-drug campaigns when the heroin plague came to his door and claimed his daughter: 'When one of your children becomes a heroin addict the family just implodes, it isn't as if it's a sickness like cancer. People feeding a heroin habit get up in the morning and all they think about for the rest of the day is where are they going to get a fix. The world then just becomes a resource. The family is another resource for how they're going to get that fix. Nothing is safe in the house, pockets are picked, jewellery is stolen, and anything of value that can't be nailed down is taken and sold. We went through that hell with her for eight years but thank God our girl got through and turned her life around. But we were the fortunate ones; a lot of other families weren't so lucky.'

Just over a year later, in 1981, the drug-pushers hit the streets of the north side of the River Liffey, and heroin addiction took over with the same incredible speed. It feasted on the ingrained misery of high unemployment and a lack of opportunity, in a section of society that had been left to its own devices and conveniently forgotten by the Establishment. It was more than a coincidence that, fifty years earlier, ground zero for this new social calamity was also home to the worst tenement squalor in Europe.

In 1972, Father Paul Lavelle had been ordained as a priest and sent as a curate to Our Lady of Lourdes parish church in Sean McDermott Street. Fr Lavelle had no doubt why the inner-city was an ideal breeding ground for the plague: 'There was little opportunity for education and the standard of the local primary school, which was called the red brick slaughter house, was just awful, in spite of some wonderful teachers. So the children didn't get an opportunity to go further than primary school. Secondary school or university was just out of the question.'

The heroin epidemic brought devastation and despair on a scale never seen before in Ireland. It led to an unprecedented wave of crime, disease and death, creating a human wasteland, strewn with the debris of young, broken lives. Its tentacles then spread out to infect the poorly planned, working-class sprawls on the city's edge, places like the grim Ballymun tower blocks. And then the aftershock arrived – in the form of HIV/AIDS from the sharing of dirty, blood-filled needles. While there was a chance of surviving heroin addiction, AIDS was a death sentence.

Jem Dixon and his family were among the Dunnes' first clients. They were quickly addicted and, in order to feed their voracious habits, became notorious pushers. Jem and his brothers openly plied their trade on the streets of the north inner-city. In the early 1980s his brother Michael, nicknamed 'Snake', was exposed on the front page of a Sunday newspaper. He had been photographed selling heroin to two under-cover reporters. The deal was done in the middle of the day, outside the GPO in Dublin's O'Connell Street – the building synonymous with the fight for a free, better Ireland. The story caused a temporary public outcry, but the authorities continued to ignore the problem. By 1994, Jem Dixon's family had long since been surpassed by a new generation of drug-pushers trying to feed their habits.

Dixon's harrowing story reflected the life of thousands of other young addicts. Jem became involved in petty crime at a very young age and was punished with sentences in the industrial/reform schools. He was a 27-year-old thief when he first tried 'smack' in 1981.

'My brother Noel was injecting himself, along with a mate upstairs in a house in Matt Talbot Court and I said: "Give us a try at that to see what it does." I was hooked almost immediately and have been using ever since then. I felt like I hadn't a worry in the world when I took it. I was robbing at the time I took the heroin so I had plenty of money to buy stuff for a while. None of us knew fuck all about what smack could do to us and we shared needles with no worries about HIV,' he recalled, dragging on the butt of a rolled-up cigarette, held between skeletal fingers.

In 1985 he was diagnosed with HIV/AIDS – or 'the virus': 'Even then we didn't know much about what could happen to us when we got the virus. I knew of one bloke up in Mountjoy who got a syringe-full of blood from another bloke who had it. He injected it into himself so that he would be diagnosed [HIV positive] and then put in the segregation unit and probably get early release . . . the poor gobshite is now dying as well.'

To make matters worse Dixon used a dirty needle on the wrong blood vein and gangrene set in. Surgeons cut 20 inches off his right leg. Then he injected himself with a dirty needle in the hand and doctors had to amputate his left index finger. Every part of his arms, leg and groin were marked with black and blue sores where practically every vein had broken down from continuously injecting himself. When we met Jem he was taking the medically prescribed heroin substitute physeptone to feed his maniacal craving. But even then, despite all he had been through, he was still injecting the odd fix of heroin through a vein he'd managed to find in the stump of his leg. By then, heroin and AIDS had already wiped out the rest of his family.

In 1986, his brother Snake's wife died of an overdose, while she cradled her two-month-old baby in her arms. Five years later, Jem's brother-in-law, Thomas Curran, died from 'the virus'. The following year his sister Ellen, Curran's wife, and his brother Snake, both addicts in their early thirties, also succumbed to what the singer Prince referred to as 'the big disease with a little name'. A month later, another brother, Noel, followed them to the cemetery. He died when his head was smashed open with a hammer in a row over a heroin deal.

'Most of my family and friends are dead . . . I've been to about 30 funerals and I know that I'll be going to me own soon. If I see 45 then I'll be doing damn good; but I don't really care because since the day I was born life has been a pure disaster for me,' Jem reflected.

Dixon claimed that he had tried to educate other kids about the dangers of heroin. A picture of his shocking appearance, which accompanied the news feature, was enough to get the point across: 'I have fuck all sympathy for some of the youngsters who are on the gear today because they know what damage it can do and all about AIDS. But there is nothing for youngsters to do in these places except rob or steal. They get into serious drugs because they are constantly looking for a way out of the depression of the place. Things are going to get a lot worse in this town because there is little hope and no work for anyone . . . in a way I'm glad I don't have much longer left.'

In December 1995 Jem Dixon joined the rest of his family in the graveyard.

At the junction of Sean McDermott Street and Buckingham Street stands a sculpture of gilded bronze and limestone. It looks like a war memorial, but it is dedicated to the fallen from a different type of struggle. Simply called 'Home', it is a poignant reminder of the hundreds of young people from the local area, including the Dixons, who died as a result of the heroin plague.

The site of the memorial was a centre for drug-dealing in the early 1980s. Larry Dunne's lackeys used to drop off batches of heroin for the pushers to sell in the warren of surrounding streets. 'Home' stands as an eight-foot flame, housed in a limestone structure – a public acknowledgement of the grief still felt by the dead addicts' surviving loved ones. When the flame was smelted, relatives of the dead dropped cherished little mementoes into the molten metal – confirmation and communion medals and little toys from a distant childhood, a time of innocence before the heroin came. At its base are the simple words dedicating the memorial to 'Loved ones carried off by the plague'. The sculpture was unveiled in December 2000 by the President of Ireland,

Mary McAleese, at a deeply emotional ceremony, attended by hundreds of relatives. President McAleese told the gathering that the sculpture was a reminder of the 'tragic consequences, when a problem such as drugs is neglected'.

In Dublin's north inner-city, many of the older generation divide the history of the past fifty years into two distinct periods – life before the heroin came, and the nightmare that followed. Before the drug scourge life was already hard, with high rates of unemployment when the docks closed down. But the drug problem infected and corroded the fabric of the communities where it was sold. The plague had no regard for the traditional values that had held deprived communities together through the worst times of poverty and hardship – especially respect for their neighbours. Criminals had been accepted as part of the community as long as they didn't rob their own. But when heroin arrived communities were torn apart as young addicts stole anything of value they could find in the home to raise cash to buy drugs. They also targeted relations and neighbours. Violence was regularly used and sometimes people died. The plague spared no one. It caused bitter recriminations between families who had lived in harmony and stuck together during previous hard times.

As the plague spread door-to-door, soon practically everyone had a relative who was an addict. As younger kids grew up they too were sucked into this dark vortex of despair. And then the young addicts began having children. Hundreds of babies were on a loser from the moment of birth – inheriting HIV and a craving for heroin from their mothers. Once during the late 1980s, this writer interviewed a couple who were heroin addicts. I watched as they helped inject each other in the kitchen, while their three children, including a new-born baby, were left to their own devices in the sparsely furnished living-room. Pushers used their children to hide their drugs and even to deliver them for them. One notorious dealer, Tony Felloni, gave his son a fix to celebrate his fifteenth birthday.

Heroin created a health crisis across the city, as kids as young as 12 and 13 became enslaved to the elusive buzz. Apart from AIDS, addicts could contract diseases such as hepatitis and other infections, from using and sharing dirty needles. They died as a result of overdoses, contaminated 'gear' and suicide, when the sense of despair became too much.

Less than two years after heroin arrived in the streets of the north inner-city, the rate of drug abuse among teenagers and young adults was proportionately higher than in New York's notorious heroin wasteland, Harlem. The army of addicts resembled zombies. They were half-dead, mindless creatures with only one reason for living – getting 'fixed-up'. To feed their habit an addict needed the equivalent of an average industrial week's wages, each day. This meant a junkie had to steal and rob every day of the year, creating a predictable pattern of life. When a junkie wasn't stoned he was on the 'mooch'. Their time was divided between police stations and the courts and broken with spells in prison – where it was easy to get heroin.

Inevitably the growing number of addicts led to an unprecedented upsurge in street crime. Burglaries, muggings and 'jump-over' robberies in local shops and businesses became a part of everyday life. When AIDS arrived, the addicts found that they had a ready-made weapon which was as terrifying as a loaded gun – a syringe filled with their own blood. Young women and men also sold their bodies for sex on street corners. Drug addicts became the new underclass in Gangland's social structure. Junkies could be manipulated into doing the gangsters' dirty work in return for the price of a 'fix'. Heroin changed the underworld landscape for ever.

As a young community activist Mick Rafferty, who came from the same area as the Dixons, witnessed the tidal wave at first hand: 'The heroin problem just swept through the area like a prairie fire and we were all shocked. I think the reason it happened so quick was because the people knew and, in some sense, trusted the dealers. There was a culture of acceptance of criminality in the inner-city, and once the main criminals turned to drug-dealing there was a sense that this must be okay, if they say it's okay. These were very vulnerable kids who were effectively losing their childhood and they didn't know what they were taking. The values that we always pushed in our communities was respect, but that respect went out the window, because the heroin addicts would do anything for a fix. So a mother could come home in the evening and find her TV gone. An elderly woman could have her head smashed in for the few pounds in her purse. Then AIDS came and added to the misery.'

When AIDS arrived in the wake of the heroin epidemic, Father Paul

Lavelle officiated at the funerals of its victims: 'About 60 per cent [of drug addicts] became infected and I'd say most, if not all, of them have passed on because of AIDS. They were young, they were in their twenties; some were married. There's quite a lot of AIDS orphans around the place. For many of them getting HIV was just another part of the agenda of life; no school, no work, poor housing – into drugs, HIV, AIDS – pretty pathetic.'

Anti-drugs campaigner Eddie Naughton wrote a powerful novel, bluntly titled *Thank God Life Doesn't Go On Forever*, that was based on the realities of life in an inner-city community, besieged by drug-pushers. He recalled: 'I remember a local woman, whose three young children died from AIDS in their late teens, saying to my wife "thank God life doesn't go on forever, there has to be something better than this". She and her husband spent their middle years going between police stations, hospital wards, courts and counselling sessions until they were worn out. At the same time they buried their children one-by-one. This is what the drug culture and the drug-dealers have bequeathed, people in such despair that their only glimmer of hope is that the next life might be better.

'My most vivid recollection of the '80s and '90s living in this area is the funerals; attending funerals, seeing funerals, it was like there was a conveyor belt of coffins coming through the doors of our local church on Meath Street. You would see horse-drawn carriages, limousines and just ordinary funerals; poverty-stricken people who could barely afford it, burying their children. And behind the coffins you saw the procession of the friends of the dead, all of their faces with the same deathly pallor of the heroin addict, and wondered which one of them would be next. The kids who died were mostly between the ages of 15 and 25. If you lived to 25 you were doing well. At the time I don't think there was anyone in the Liberties area who didn't know somebody that was dying or [had] died of AIDS, or didn't know somebody who was heavily into drugs. It was the same in every working-class community across the city. When the criminals decided to get involved in drugs the first people they destroyed were their own.'

When heroin first struck the north inner-city, former Det. Supt Mick Finn had been attached to the local station at Store Street for almost twenty years. He had earned the respect of the local people and was known as a 'good copper', a relationship which was rare in the tougher neighbourhoods. Finn witnessed how the problem overwhelmed the police on his beat as hundreds of drug-pushers and addicts from all over the city began congregating around O'Connell Street and turned it into an open heroin market. He eventually took charge of one of the first permanent drug units outside the Drug Squad to tackle the heroin crime problem, and arrested Jem Dixon many times.

'The introduction of heroin brought devastation to the people who lived in the poorer areas. It became a great scourge in the north inner-city where I worked and it happened very quietly and very quickly,' Finn recalled. The prevailing policing philosophy was to treat crimes as individual one-off incidents. There was no room for long-term planning or strategy to prevent crime. The bulk of personnel and intelligence resources were still geared towards the Troubles.

'Many of the first people I saw using heroin had been incarcerated in institutions such as Daingean or Letterfrack or Upton and we didn't realize for a long number of years later what had happened to the children in those places. It had a major effect on how they led their lives after. Most of the addicts were unemployed and had been involved in petty crime. The area was socially deprived and perhaps for them the heroin was a form of escape. Over a period of time you could see the deterioration in the people using the heroin and their families, particularly their parents. And you see them every day hanging round waiting to buy or scrounge what they could off some other addict. There was a lot of fear both within families and on the streets, as people resorted to violence to rob money for drugs. It was a catastrophe.'

If heroin exposed the weaknesses within a dysfunctional society, then the reaction from the Government in the early 1980s highlighted an attitude of indifference. As long as the problem was contained within certain working-class areas and didn't seep into middle-class society, it was not considered a crisis. Drug addiction was still viewed as a personal choice and a medical issue. It would take years before any meaningful efforts were made to tackle its social roots.

The laws were also hopelessly out of date and the courts were being far too lenient with the big players. When the Dunnes were recruiting and enslaving the likes of the Dixons, John McGroarty was a senior detective in the small Drug Squad. He recalled: 'The politicians just didn't grasp what was happening: this was a fire that had just started downstairs and they're thinking that somebody will put it out and it will go away but that's not what happened. We suddenly had an epidemic of street crime as a result of the heroin epidemic. We had to put a lot of pressure on to get additional, more effective legislation and to increase the strength of the various drug units to take on the suppliers. But by then the drug problem was too well established to be eradicated.'

As the heroin plague seeped further into working-class areas across Dublin there was a commensurate improvement in the balance sheets of the Dunne family. Each batch of heroin they supplied created even more demand – and more profit. The family did not all become involved simultaneously, and neither did they operate together as a single organization. Serious cracks had already emerged in the ranks of the once-united clan and at the start of the decade they were going in their own directions. Shamie and Larry had separate international contacts and smuggling routes. They each had their own customers in the family and individually supplied Henry, Robert, Boyo, Charlie, Mickey, Collette and Gerard. These siblings in turn carved out their own drug patches, on both sides of the Liffey. Christy didn't get into the heroin trade and contented himself with importing hash.

The other family members supported one another by lending each other money and supplementing supplies after a Drug Squad bust. The Dunnes made full use of their fearful reputations for violence when it came to collecting money. If customers didn't pay up they were severely beaten and their lives were threatened. Larry and Shamie also sold heroin at wholesale prices to new dealers who began to emerge – criminals who were also looking for the easy money and wanted to set up their own operations. Drugs were sold openly in the flat complexes and in the streets. People of all ages, including 12-year-old kids and old-age pensioners, were being used to deliver the 'gear'. The infamous Jetfoil pub, owned by Martin Cahill and John Traynor, became a notorious hub for dealing. Very quickly an elaborate distribution network was established that stretched from Bray, County Wicklow up to Ballymun in North Dublin. This was the genesis of the criminal drug rackets in Ireland.

The people blamed the Dunnes and their army of dealers for the horror that completely demoralized a generation of people, but the family's legendary ability to rationalize their behaviour meant that they could easily detach themselves from the devastation they were causing. Anti-drugs campaigner Mick Rafferty recalls: 'I remember a meeting I was chairing in Rutland Street, and Larry Dunne stood beside me, to intimidate me, and he said "I've been accused of this, sure you all know me, I've only done good for the community".'

The Dunnes simply ignored the fact that they had introduced a new layer of misery into the lives of the already hard-pressed working classes. The family were allowed to blame society for not giving them a chance in life and turning them into criminals, but the same logic did not apply to their growing army of customers. As Mick Rafferty remembers it: 'They [The Dunnes] were a deprived family – we could argue about deprivation and criminality – and they got involved in crime, and crime can begin in working-class areas out of a sense of a need, but greed takes over, and the Dunnes introduced heroin into our communities . . .' The prodigious profits the Dunnes were suddenly making were all they cared about – and if the addicts could pay.

Within two years, the Dunnes were credited with controlling at least 50 per cent of the heroin trade in Dublin. Garda intelligence reports identified a total of 170 people involved in the entire Dunne network, 40 of whom were at the core of operations. As street crime spiralled, the Dunnes were also being paid for drugs with jewellery and other valuables stolen in thousands of burglaries. They were then fenced through separate networks in Ireland and the UK. Like armed robberies, the drug trade had created its own subsidiary industries.

The Drug Squad had an early break when they nabbed the main man, Larry Dunne. Larry was a fitness fanatic and was always immaculately groomed, wearing only Italian designer suits and shoes. His arrogance and a tendency to underestimate the police had brought about his downfall – he got sloppy. He had also developed a drug problem but didn't realize it himself – neither did his brothers, associates or the Gardaí. He picked up the habit by snorting tiny amounts of the drug to test the quality.

On 13 October 1980, Shamie Dunne took delivery of a consignment of heroin from their London-Irish partner in crime, Pat O'Sullivan.

The Drug Squad picked up the information on Shamie's phone and knew that he was arranging a meeting with Larry in the car park at the Burlington Hotel. At the last minute the venue was changed to Larry's house in Carrickmount Drive in Rathfarnham, South Dublin. John McGroarty got a search warrant and mobilized his team. At the same time Detective Garda Felix McKenna, who was attached to the Tallaght District Detective Unit (DDU), was investigating the armed robbery of £117,000 worth of jewellery from the home of Dominic Cafolla in Clonskeagh that September. The Dunnes and the Cahills were the prime suspects. Det. Gda McKenna had been a key member of Ned Ryan's Flying Squad in the CDU. Over the following 25 years McKenna would be a constant thorn in the side of organized crime gangs. The Tallaght cops got a warrant that evening and also headed to Carrickmount Drive.

Shamie and his sister Collette Dunne arrived at Larry's house around 7 p.m. Larry, his wife Lilly and a third man were waiting for them to arrive with the drugs. A short time later the Gardaí from Tallaght arrived to search the house. When Larry answered his door a member of McKenna's team presented him with a search warrant and told him they were looking for stolen jewellery. As Larry read the warrant, his hands started to tremble and his face went pale. When McKenna searched upstairs, he found 70 grams of uncut heroin hidden in a pillow in a child's bedroom. The detectives also found 30 grams of cocaine, a small amount of hashish and a set of laboratory scales. The haul, worth £60,000 (over €300,000 in today's values), was considered a major seizure. Larry, Shamie, Collette and Lilly Dunne were arrested and brought to Rathfarnham Garda Station for questioning.

The Drug Squad had arrived at the house during the raid, so when the suspects were released without charge on the Cafolla robbery, McGroarty re-arrested them for the drug seizure. The four Dunnes were then charged under the Misuse of Drugs Act and later released on bail. The charges against Shamie and Lilly, however, were dropped by the DPP and the Drug Squad was instructed to return £3,000 in cash they had seized from Shamie during the raid. Collette Dunne was convicted a year later for possession of drugs and weighing scales which were found in her car when it was searched at Carrickmount – she was jailed for two years.

Larry was in a state of shock after the bust. Thanks to his complacency, he was facing a serious charge of possession of drugs with intent
to supply – and the likelihood of a long stretch in prison. It also sent
shockwaves through the family network, who began to suspect there
was a spy in their midst. The home of a neighbour in Carrickmount
Drive, who was suspected of tipping off the police, was petrol-bombed.
But Larry quickly regained his composure and confidently predicted
that he was not going down and it didn't matter what he had to do to
achieve that.

In the meantime he made full use of the archaic justice system to
build a criminal empire. The courts were dreadfully slow in processing
trials and were lenient in granting bail. In the average two-year period
that it took cases to come to trial, the dealers and pushers were free to
ply their trade and build up a nest egg. That's exactly what Larry
planned to do. The bust had also taught him one essential lesson about
drug-trafficking – he had to insulate himself from his merchandise by
staying strictly hands-off. His catch phrase after the bust was 'Larry
doesn't carry'.

In May 1981, a Drugs Intelligence Investigation Unit (DIIU), con-
sisting of less than a dozen detectives, was set up at Garda HQ. The
purpose of the new unit was to carry out undercover work and gather
intelligence on the movement of drugs and the criminals involved. The
unit would also back up the Drug Squad, which still had just 20 personnel. Dinny Mullins and John McGroarty had repeatedly asked for a
major increase in Drug Squad numbers but had been turned down each
time. One member of Garda management once told McGroarty that if
they doubled the size of the squad, then they would double the number
of drug arrests. More arrests would signify a drug problem. The Gardaí
didn't need another problem.

The apparent lack of enthusiasm for a co-ordinated, focused approach
to narcotics-trafficking on the part of management continued throughout the early 1980s. But despite poor resources and little support, the
dedicated Drug Squad did try to take on the drug-dealers. In one initiative, a group of young officers based in city-centre stations set up an
undercover unit that became known as the 'Mockeys'. The modus operandi of the Dublin-born cops was to work undercover on the streets,
among the junkies and their dealers. The revolutionary approach, how-

ever, was viewed with suspicion and disapproval by the police hierarchy, who saw such methods as gimmicky and continued to largely ignore the growing epidemic.

By the beginning of 1982 there were an estimated 5,000 heroin addicts in the city, but this was a conservative figure because there were no adequate treatment centres available to record the true extent of the crisis. The Catholic Church had also become gravely concerned at the speed with which the heroin plague had taken hold. In April 1982, Fr Paul Lavelle invited Monsignor William O'Brien, who ran one of the world's biggest drug rehabilitation centres in New York, to visit Dublin. Monsignor O'Brien was stunned by what Fr Lavelle showed him. The pre-adolescent heroin problem was the worst he had seen and the strength of the heroin doses being sold was double the average on sale in most other countries.

The drug problem became so big that it could no longer be ignored by the Government. A young community activist and secondary-school teacher called Tony Gregory ensured that it was brought to their attention. Born in Ballybough, in the north inner-city, Gregory had been involved with Official Sinn Féin, and briefly the IRSP, before becoming an independent socialist politician. Mick Rafferty was a life-long ally and friend. Gregory was first elected as a TD for the area in February 1982 – a seat he held until his death in 2009. He fought his campaign on a promise to tackle the inner-city's chronic social issues, including poverty and drugs. In return for his support for Charles Haughey's minority Fianna Fáil Government, a £100 million package for the inner-city was agreed in the 'Gregory deal'.

In May 1982, the Taoiseach, Charles Haughey, and the Minister for Justice, Sean Doherty, called a meeting with Garda Commissioner Patrick McLaughlin and his deputy and assistant commissioners in Government Buildings. There were only two items on the agenda – drugs and the Dunnes. Haughey said he had never heard of the family and was unaware of the extent of the drug problem in the city until Tony Gregory told him. Of particular concern was Gregory's claim that the local people knew who was dealing and when drops were taking place. Gregory told Haughey the local police had little understanding of the problem and, when information was passed on, there were few arrests.

Haughey bluntly told the officers that he wanted the Dunnes put out of business and he would provide whatever resources were necessary. The Taoiseach said he wanted them all behind bars within 12 months.

The Gardaí had already dramatically increased their surveillance, both overt and covert, on the Dunnes and their associates. But their efforts gained momentum once the Taoiseach got involved. Shamie, who was normally cordial and friendly to the cops, went berserk and took a hatchet to detectives on one occasion when they were searching his house on Herberton Road in Rialto. He had been raided at least twenty times in less than two years and the pressure was getting to him. He was charged with assault and obstruction and picked up an 18-month suspended sentence. Shamie was a gregarious character and, like most of his other brothers, a ferocious womanizer. He'd left his English wife, Valerie, in 1978 and moved into a luxury apartment in Rathmines with Fiona O'Sullivan, a lover half his age. He could not read or write and was spectacularly vulgar. Shamie also had a fatal flaw for a gangster – he couldn't keep his mouth shut.

The Drug Squad placed taps on all the phones known to be used by the Dunnes. One former member of the squad still laughs today when he recalls Shamie's attempts to pass coded messages to associates on the phone: 'If he was giving someone another telephone number to ring, Shamie would call out individual numbers to the person at the other end. After each digit he would tell the other party on the line to add one or subtract one from it to get the real number – it didn't dawn on him that we could add and subtract as well.'

But by then the heroin trade had taken root and the Dunnes weren't the only suppliers. Many other dealers were getting involved and the situation had reached crisis point. People in the worst-affected areas decided it was time for them to take action.

Gregory's election initially gave the local people the confidence that they could do something about the misery, but little changed. The sense of shock and hopelessness in the communities hardest hit by heroin soon turned to rage. They were sick of the open dealing in their streets and the sight of addicts shooting up in the stairwells of the flats in front of their children. In the playgrounds and open areas, children were playing with syringes dumped by the junkies. As a consequence of the appalling crisis, and a total lack of effective State intervention, the residents of the worst-hit areas banded together in 1983 under the banner of the Concerned Parents Against Drugs (CPAD).

At first residents held meetings to discuss the problem; then they began to take action. Eddie Naughton became deeply involved in the CPAD in South Dublin. He recalls: 'There was widespread frustration right across the neighbourhoods and I think people just lost faith. I believe that the indifference of the police to the problem gave rise to the Concerned Parents. If the police had been on the ball there never would have been a need for the Concerned Parents.'

The CPAD took to the streets and marched, in large numbers, on the homes of known drug-dealers and evicted them. Drug addicts and pushers were summoned to mass meetings where they were confronted about their activities by the local community. Over time the tactic of marching on drug-dealers began to work, and they moved to other areas where the CPAD had not yet been mobilized. The protests rekindled community spirit and boosted people's morale. At night, men patrolled flat complexes and housing estates and set up road blocks, to prevent the addicts and dealers getting through. Several dealers and addicts were literally thrown out on the streets by the marchers. Faced with such people power, the pushers could no longer threaten or intimidate objectors with impunity.

Members of Sinn Féin and the IRA became involved and soon controlled the organization from behind the scenes. Many of their members came from the affected areas and genuinely wanted to do something about the appalling situation. The republican movement also saw the CPAD's war on drugs as an opportunity to build a political powerbase in Dublin's working-class areas, where traditionally they'd had no support. The presence of the terrorists in the shadows deterred the drug-dealers from taking action.

But the republicans encouraged the CPAD not to co-operate with the police, and deliberately worked to turn the communities against them. In Finglas in north-west Dublin, Brian Whelan was a dedicated community activist who wanted to do something about the spiralling drug crisis, but he was dismayed by this hidden agenda.

'The people who controlled the Concerned Parents [Sinn Féin/IRA] used it to push their agenda of further undermining the relationship between the people and the police. At every meeting their mantra was don't go to the Gardaí, the Gardaí are corrupt, the Gardaí are in league with the drug-pushers. It was reminding the children who were listening to this stuff at the meetings that the police were as bad as the drug-dealers. In reality the republicans were using the drug issue to control whole communities,' he recalled.

Some of the patriotic Provos saw another benefit of their involvement in the anti-drug movement – the chance to make money for 'the cause' and for themselves. Selected dealers were secretly given 'permission' to continue plying their trade in certain areas, in return for financial 'contributions'.

Eddie Naughton was a witness to this corruption: 'There were good people who joined the Concerned Parents but sinister elements, members of the republican movement, saw it as an opportunity to set up an alternative police force and controlled it for their own reasons. And people were going along with that but it was bound to fail. It soon became apparent that addicts were being beaten up for their money. After a while it was obvious that the organization was being drawn away from focusing on the people who were really doing the dealing, the major players in the area. It was a known fact around the area where I live that criminals of every hue were called in and they were told to pay a revolutionary tax to the Provos and those who didn't were shot. They weren't shot for dealing drugs. They were shot because they wouldn't pay up. And the Guards did nothing about it.'

Brian Whelan recalled: 'I was at the first meetings of the CPAD when it was set up in Hardwicke Street and I joined because a lot of good people were involved. At first there was tremendous work done on the ground and people started to reclaim their communities. But over time it became obvious that the people were being manipulated and exploited by well-known republicans and the only people being taken on were addicts or as they called them, "low-life junkies". I think the word scumbag was their favourite term of reference.

'But people began to notice that no major drug supplier was ever affected by the Concerned Parents, under the stewardship of the Provisional IRA. My suspicions were confirmed one night during a public meeting in a community centre in Finglas. I was in a toilet when a leading member of the IRA came in with a few local, petty criminals who were dabbling in the drug trade. He offered them a deal: stop joyriding in the area, stop breaking into houses and you can run the business of hash and Es. A weekly "tax" was to be paid over in return and as long as they stuck to the agreement no one would get hurt. That day those drug-pushers hit the big time because they had no worries about being marched on or targeted by the IRA. After that I left the organization with a sense of hopelessness. The ordinary people were being used and abused by everyone – the drug-dealers, the State, the Provos.'

The heroin plague had become a permanent feature of life thanks to the Dunnes and their army of dealers. But their days as the princes of the city's drug trade were numbered.

8. Going Down

Larry Dunne's wife, Lilly, had little empathy for the people impaling themselves on needles and shooting her husband's heroin into their veins. As far as she was concerned, her family weren't responsible. The junkies had no one to blame for their perilous predicament but themselves. They took drugs because they wanted to – no one forced them to do it. And Lilly had no difficulty sharing the family's viewpoint with anyone who had the bottle to ask.

When RTÉ reporter Brendan O'Brien door-stepped Lilly to get an interview, she dismissed his awkward questions: 'The drug-pushers don't go round beatin' people to buy it [heroin]; that's a choice of their own,' she said, in a tone that suggested this was so obvious that it didn't merit any further discussion. 'I wouldn't say Larry went about beatin' people to buy it.'

On 1 December 1983, O'Brien's uninvited intrusion into Lilly's detached world featured during a two-hour special investigation by the current affairs programme *Today Tonight*. The programme focused on the drugs trade and the growing culture of organized crime it had created. It also featured CPAD meetings and marches, including one that had been held outside Lilly's home a few weeks earlier. It was the first time that the drug crisis, and the involvement of the Dunnes, had been given such prominence by the national broadcaster.

By the time the programme was broadcast, the Dunne empire was in a steady decline and the underworld notoriety they'd once craved had turned them into the most hated criminals in history. Six months earlier Larry had done a runner from the Circuit Criminal Court, just before a jury returned to convict him on the Carrickmount Drive drug charges. His picture had been splashed across the front page of every newspaper, as the drug-dealer who'd brought the heroin plague to Ireland.

When he'd vanished in June 1983, Lilly had faced the press with the same characteristic Dunne bluster. 'Larry is well away by now. I hope he stays away. I have no idea where he is now. But wherever he is he should stay away – it's better than being locked up in jail,' she told an *Irish Press* journalist.

Lilly was equally unrepentant when the RTÉ men arrived at her door. When O'Brien asked her about her husband's reputation as the country's biggest heroin-trafficker, she side-stepped the issue: 'He has always been a kind gentleman and a loving father; he's never done us any harm,' she declared defensively.

'But the drug he was selling was doing people a lot of harm?' the journalist asked.

'Well, I'm only concerned about my family,' she replied.

Lilly was a disciple of the Dunne family doctrine, that they were blameless victims of an orchestrated conspiracy.

The Dunnes never saw themselves as bad guys – they were merely trying to get by in a cruel world where the game was always loaded against them. Larry and Shamie easily rationalized why they sold drugs: 'If I didn't do it someone else would; I don't force them to buy it,' Larry was once reported to have told an associate. In the early 1990s this writer caught up with Shamie, who was living in what he described as a self-imposed exile in London. The illiterate drug-dealer pointed out the health warning on the back of a pack of cigarettes he was smoking. 'Look at that,' he said, as he held the box upside down. 'They [the Government] say that these are bad for you but the people who sell them aren't criminals. More people die from lung cancer than drugs, so what's the difference? It's all right because respectable people are making money from it. It [heroin] is a commodity and if people want to take it that's their problem. There was heroin around before we became involved.'

In December 1983, however, the family was running out of road. The cops had declared war on them and were winning hands down. Henry, Mickey, their sister Collette and Shamie's wife, Valerie, were all behind bars, doing sentences for drugs, possession of firearms and receiving stolen goods. Shamie had been nabbed while cutting up £400,000 worth of heroin in his apartment and was awaiting trial. Others were also facing charges and eventually eight members of the family were in jail. Several of their main dealers and middle-ranking street pushers had also been rounded up and had either been convicted or were awaiting trial.

Christy Dunne hadn't been spared either. He and John Cunningham had been charged with three aggravated burglaries in which firearms were used in Meath and Dublin in November and December 1982. The crime spree was particularly nasty and terrifying for the victims. In the three incidents, Dunne and Cunningham had broken into people's homes and threatened them at gunpoint. In one of the cases a 71-year-old widow was grabbed around the neck and a gun was put to her head. Her 73-year-old sister was also held at gunpoint. In another incident a man lost the sight of one eye.

But that didn't deter flamboyant Bronco from mounting his own damage-limitation exercise a month after the *Today Tonight* programme, when he appeared on RTÉ radio and described himself as 'a good father – not a Godfather'. He took the opportunity to whine about how the authorities were making life difficult for his siblings and declared his loyalty to his fugitive brother, commenting: 'I'd die for Larry.' Bronco also managed to insult his brother Mickey 'Dazzler' Dunne, who had been jailed in October 1983 for seven years for dealing heroin. Mickey, he said, didn't have the IQ to be a criminal mastermind. There were few who disagreed with him.

A month later, on 4 January 1984, Christy's parents, Ellen and Bronco Senior, appeared on a Channel Four programme where they were interviewed about their family's involvement in the drugs crisis. Ellen cried when she talked about her boys. 'My sons were all gentlemen, beautiful men, beautiful manners, beautiful bodies. I never knew they were on drugs. I had to get work and I never had it easy with my husband either, son,' she said. 'I could never lay down and have my children in comfort. I lay down with black eyes. Now that's the truth, so don't talk to me about drugs, son.'

The most striking picture used to illustrate the newspaper coverage of Larry Dunne's flight from justice was a photo of his magnificent mansion in the Dublin Mountains. In August 1982, Larry had demonstrated his arrogance – and wealth – when he paid £100,000 (€350,000 today) up front for 'Gorse Rock' in Sandyford, County Dublin. It was there that the *Today Tonight* crew tried to interview Lilly. They used shots of the detached house as the backdrop to Lilly's comments about her husband, the loyal, family man. The image of the house was greeted with astonishment by a public trying desperately to make ends meet, at a time when the economy was on its knees and unemployment was spi-ralling. It confirmed how organized crime had taken root in Ireland.

Gorse Rock was one of the most ostentatious displays of ill-gotten gains by a Godfather in the history of the underworld. Dunne was tell-ing the world that crime certainly did pay. Pictures of the house were used over and over again by the media to illustrate what the narcotics trade was all about. In Larry's mind, however, it was a monument to his successful journey from the gutter. He'd come a long way since he first made newspaper headlines, with his brother Henry in 1960. Larry was like a prince, looking down from his lofty perch on his cash-producing kingdom below. The streets of the crime-ravaged estates were his domain and its army of addicts, pushers and dealers, his loyal subjects.

Larry's £100,000 cash purchase exposed the State's complete lack of power to go after the proceeds of crime. This would be a recurring theme in the story of organized crime until action was finally taken in 1996. Dunne didn't have to hide his drug money from anyone and lodged it in bank accounts held under his own name. But successive governments failed to come up with a solution. Around this time, Dunne was approached by a tax inspector one day, as he was going into court for a remand hearing relating to his outstanding drug charge. The taxman, who was accompanied by a Garda for his protection, asked Dunne how he could afford his mansion in the mountains, considering he was not in any kind of legitimate employment. 'Where do you fuck-ing think I got it?' Dunne snapped. 'I robbed it of course.'

Other members of the family had also been displaying their good fortune, but not on the same grand scale. Henry spared no expense when he completely renovated his home in Rutland Avenue, Crumlin. The house was extended while the front was given a mock-Tudor fin-ish, which looked incongruous in a terrace of Corporation houses. Inside it had a spiral staircase, bar and sauna. Henry even bought his wife, Mary, a race horse called 'Roebuck Lass'. Boyo also moved into a large house he acquired in nearby Weaver's Square, Crumlin and had it extensively refurbished. Some of the marble used was specially imported from Rome. He even gave it a grand-sounding name, 'Adam House'.

Gorse Rock had inspired Larry's siblings to dream about leaving the rat race to find peace in the mountains. In a cocaine-induced haze, the Dunne brothers would often take in the spectacular view and fantasize about building their own little community in the Dublin Mountains, on a site that Henry Dunne had purchased. They would invite close friends and associates to build alongside them. Eventually they would create their own little self-sufficient community, walled in and cut off from the hostile world. It would have its own shops and even a school – and a plentiful supply of drugs. They would install elaborate defence systems to keep their tormentors – the cops – on the other side. This new nirvana they would call 'Dunnesville'.

Apart from cornering the heroin business, the Dunnes were heavily involved in the importation of large quantities of hashish. They put together deals with other criminal gangs to invest in dope shipments.

Despite the shortcomings in the Gardaí's ability to adapt to the drugs' explosion, they were slowly starting to use a more modern approach against the Dunnes. The Drug Squad had managed to plant a number of paid informants within the organization. One of them was the Prince, who played on both sides of the fence – as long as the price was right. In 1982, the Gardaí paid him £25,000 for his invaluable assistance, but two years earlier he'd been involved in an operation that he didn't intend sharing with his Garda handlers.

A month after Larry's arrest in October 1980, Shamie had a set-back when a consignment of hashish worth £75,000 (over €380,000) was discovered in a lorry at Rosslare. Three associates were arrested and one of them was subsequently convicted for illegal importation. It was the second delivery of the drug from Patrick Quirke, an expat Irishman who was one of the biggest cannabis dealers in the world. Shamie had been introduced to Quirke as a member of the family who ran the Irish underworld. The following March, a truck containing one and a half tons of cannabis and £75,000 in cash was seized by police in Paris. It was the second load in a run from Holland into Ireland. When French police arrested the driver of the truck, they found a telephone number that linked the Dunnes to the Quirke syndicate in Amsterdam. At the same time Dutch police were looking for members of the group after an Amsterdam taxi driver was murdered when he stumbled upon members of the gang offloading almost two tons of cannabis.

The French and Dutch enquiries led back to Dublin. When the Drug Squad began to investigate they uncovered a huge international conspiracy, involving the Quirke organization and drug producers in Lebanon – and at the centre of it all were the Dunnes. They had hit the big time on the international drug-trafficking circuit. The man who helped broker the deal was the Prince. 'Operation Angel', the name given to what amounted to the biggest drug investigation in the history of the State, had a plot very similar to the one in the classic crime thriller *The French Connection*. A consignment of almost two tons of Lebanese hash – with a street value of just under £5 million – was to be shipped into Ireland by the Quirke organization in a deal with the Prince and the Dunnes. From there Larry was going to arrange its onward transportation to the UK. However, the plot thickened when the Prince brought two notorious members of the Mafia – one from Sicily and the other from the US – into the deal.

The plan was that the Dunnes and the Mafia would 'steal' the consignment from the Quirke group and ship it on to the UK. Unfortunately for them, the new Garda Drugs Intelligence Investigation Unit (DIIU) and the Drug Squad had rumbled that there was a conspiracy afoot. They began working with their colleagues in Europe to find out more. The Gardaí, however, had no knowledge of the involvement of the Mafia.

A large force of detectives was waiting on 9 September 1981, when the drugs arrived in Dublin. The huge shipment was in a container carrying 'household goods' on board a ship that originated in Lebanon. The Gardaí had put in place an elaborate operation, involving over forty detectives, and waited patiently for the mob to collect the load. But Dunne gang member Joe Roe was tipped off by a man working in the docks who spotted the police activity. After waiting two days the Prince, the Dunnes and the Mafia-men decided to try to snatch the dope from under the noses of the police, who were growing impatient. But before they could put the plan into operation the Gardaí had decided to move in and had seized the haul. Members of the Quirke group, who were staying in a house in South Dublin, were arrested, but they were released without charge because their detention was deemed unlawful. The Gardaí still made the most of a bad lot and proudly displayed the biggest drug seizure in the history of the State. The Mafia-men slipped out of the country when the heat died down and the Dunnes' flirtation with the Cosa Nostra was over.

In the meantime the family's drug operation continued to be a high priority for the Drug Squad, which began pulling it apart. In 1981, an ad hoc group of seven innovative, young, uniformed Gardaí, attached to Fitzgibbon and Store Street Stations, came up with a revolutionary new tactic to use against the Dunnes and their pushers. In their short time on the beat, the officers had realized how difficult it was to catch the dealers and pushers by conventional methods, so they volunteered to work undercover, posing as junkies. The team consisted of Mick O'Sullivan, Tony Lane, Aidan Reid, Oliver Claffey, Janet Russell, Jim McGowan and his fiancée, Noirin O'Sullivan. (In 2011 Noirin O'Sullivan became the first female Deputy Commissioner in the history of the Garda Síochána.) The fact that the officers were from Dublin was a major benefit and helped them to blend in. The vast majority of Gardaí at the time were from the country. Community activist Mick Rafferty explained the problems this caused. 'The basic problem was that the Guards from the country were suspicious of working-class communities; they almost saw everyone around them as a potential criminal and therefore they weren't willing to listen to us. They weren't used to an urban situation and the dynamics of a city.'

The team of undercover Dublin officers was given the cautious blessing of their immediate superior officers, who were desperate to drive a dent into the burgeoning trade by whatever means they could – just as long as it stood up to scrutiny in court. In just over a year the unit became the bane of the drug-dealing fraternity, who nicknamed them the Mockeys – or mock junkies.

Neither the Gardaí nor the underworld had seen anything like the Mockeys before. The Drug Squad soon realized their potential and began dipping into the huge amount of intelligence they were unearthing on the streets. In 1982, they arrested and charged 55 drug-pushers in the Store Street district alone. After a prolonged and patient surveillance operation, they busted several members of the Dunnes' drug-distribution network. Trusted lieutenants like Paul 'Gash' Ainscough, Thomas 'Bugsy' Kinsella and Paul Gallagher were all caught with large quantities of heroin, convicted and jailed. But their biggest prize was catching Mickey 'Dazzler' Dunne, who was openly dealing heroin from his flat in Fatima Mansions.

On the evening of 26 August 1982, Dazzler answered the door and barely looked at the dishevelled young guys standing outside. It had been a very busy day, with a constant stream of customers, and Mickey was running low on stock. 'Now lads I'm only doin' grams of heroin, I've no twenties,' said Mickey, before he noticed that the 'junkies' were holding up Garda ID cards. In seconds the entire Mockey squad burst in on top of him. As they searched the flat other pushers continued to call at the door looking for 'gear'. Each time they were invited in and promptly arrested. By the time the Mockeys ran out of handcuffs Mickey, his wife, Dolores, and nine customers were under arrest. Stolen jewellery and heroin had been seized. Dazzler had no choice but to concede defeat: 'Well lads, ye are the fucking best. Bugsy told me about ye but I didn't believe him. Ye caught me easy.' Mickey was charged with possession of drugs with intent to supply.

He joined his siblings, including brothers Larry and Shamie, and a string of their dealers who were already in the queue before the criminal courts. It wouldn't be long before Henry was also before the courts. The Dunnes were going down.

In January 1983, Christy's eldest daughter, Jacqueline, got married in Mount Argus church. The family's dear friend, Fr Michael Sweetman, officiated at the ceremony. It was a typically flamboyant affair, with the style and glamour of a high-society wedding. Over 400 guests were royally entertained in the Killiney Castle Hotel, in South County Dublin. It was the last time the entire Dunne family – three generations of them – were together in one place. A television camera crew and photographers turned up, to watch the jewel-laden, designer-clad underworld come out to play. The Gardaí also turned up with their long-lens cameras, to snap some of the most wanted gangsters in the country.

A month later, on 25 February, two of the wedding guests, Henry Dunne and Joe Roe, were both jailed in connection with an armed confrontation with members of the Garda Special Task Force (STF) on 26 May 1981. The STF was a specialist firearms unit which had been set up in 1979 to take on the growing threat from the IRA, INLA and 'crime-ordinary' robbery gangs. Armed with Uzi machine-guns and .38 Smith and Wesson revolvers, the unit was the first of its type in the Gardaí. At the time of the confrontation the two gangsters were planning to hold up a United Drug company van, carrying a £500,000 consignment of drugs. It was to be another Dunne family operation, involving a total of six robbers, including at least two other brothers. Around 2 p.m. that day Dunne met Roe at the North Strand and gave him an automatic pistol for the job. Dunne also carried a handgun under his coat. The four other gang members were in a car which was parked nearby. A shopkeeper who spotted the pair acting suspiciously called the Gardaí and the STF were sent to investigate.

Two STF patrols arrived in the area and checked out local premises. When the gang spotted them, the crew in the car pulled away quietly. The STF officers then spotted Dunne and Roe walking in the opposite direction, onto Charleville Avenue. The detectives recognized the two well-known villains and followed them. Roe and Dunne were getting into a car when the STF pulled into the road. Detective Garda Valentine Flynn got out and ordered the men to stop and put up their hands. Instead, Henry Dunne ran towards Flynn's partner, John Donohue, who was behind the wheel of the squad car. Dunne pulled his gun and ordered Donohue to drop his weapon. The pair began to struggle and Roe jumped into the squad car, beating Donohue over the back of the head with the butt of his gun. In the melee, Dunne fired a shot, hitting Donohue and severing an artery. He ran off and got away by vaulting a six-foot wall.

Roe also fled the scene, towards the North Strand, followed by two other STF officers. He turned and pointed his gun at Detective Garda Aidan Boyle, who fired a single shot over his head. Roe then tried to hijack a car but the detective caught up with him and ordered him to put the gun down. Instead the loyal Dunne henchman fired two shots at the cop. Detective Garda Boyle returned fire, hitting him in the side of the neck.

Roe was brought to hospital, where Detective Garda Donohue was already undergoing emergency surgery. He'd lost one-third of his blood and was lucky to be alive. Roe's injury was not serious and he was discharged the following day. Henry Dunne was found, within minutes of the incident, hiding under a bed in a house in Waterloo Avenue. Detectives fired a warning shot to show that they meant business. When Dunne looked up, he was greeted by a roomful of armed STF officers. When the detectives asked if the gun he was still holding was loaded, Dunne replied: 'I'll clear it for ye, lads, you can trust me.' As he was being taken into custody the armed robber said: 'Is he [the injured detective] badly hurt? I didn't mean to shoot him. He must have shot himself. It was an accident. It shouldn't have happened.' Forensic tests on the pistol later showed that it came from the batch stolen by Bronco Dunne from the Parker-Hale armoury in Birmingham in 1968.

The two gang members were charged with a number of offences, including possession of firearms with intent to murder, resisting arrest, causing grievous bodily harm and wounding. Despite the seriousness of the charges they were both released on bail, and weren't jailed until almost two years later in February 1983.

Two months after Henry's hearing, Larry Dunne's trial finally got underway, on 20 April 1983 – two and a half years after he was originally busted. He had hired the best defence counsel in the country and hoped they could get the case thrown out on a point of law. The drugs had actually been seized by Detective Garda Felix McKenna on foot of a warrant under the Larceny Act – not the Drugs Act.

On the first day of the trial Larry ensured the public gallery was filled with Dunne associates. They stared into the faces of every member of the jury in a bid to intimidate them, which is when Larry had a stroke of unexpected luck. One of his henchmen recognized one of the jurors. That night the juror was having a drink in his local when Dunne's lieutenant sat beside him. He got straight to the point. 'You will hold out, no matter what, for a not guilty verdict. You will say that Larry Dunne is innocent and you'll be paid for your services,' the henchman said, before getting up and leaving.

Each evening of the week-long trial the henchman met the juror. He reassured him that he could pull it off and convince the rest of the jury of Larry's innocence. When the jury retired to consider their verdict on 26 April, the same gang member ordered champagne for the planned party in the Legal Eagle pub, beside Dublin's Four Courts.

The juror did what he was asked. He held out against the other 11 members, who all agreed Dunne was guilty. But he could not convince them to return a not guilty verdict. When they didn't reach a unanimous verdict, the jury was discharged as the existing legislation only provided for unanimous jury decisions in criminal trials.

A new trial was set to take place on 21 June. For Larry it was a result of sorts and he had bought his freedom for a while at least. The juror was paid £5,000 for his trouble. But the prosecution counsel and the Gardaí smelt that something was amiss. Their suspicions were confirmed shortly after the collapse of the case when an angry juror approached the officer in overall charge of the investigation, Detective Inspector John McGroarty and told him what had happened in the jury room. It didn't take the Gardaí long to establish a link between the juror and one of Dunne's men. When detectives interviewed the man, he admitted that he had been put in fear of his life to bring back a not guilty verdict. The jury nobbling incident was brought to the attention of the Coalition Government. As a direct result provision was made in the new Criminal Justice Act in October 1983 to allow majority verdicts.

In the meantime Larry was back in business. A month before his first trial, Herbert da Silva, a Nigerian drug-trafficker, had arrived in Dublin to meet members of what he was convinced was the country's most formidable crime syndicate. Based in Paris, da Silva had been deported back to Nigeria from England when he was convicted on charges of drugs possession and conspiracy to rob. Da Silva was a drugs' wholesaler, buying directly from the heroin and cannabis producers in Lebanon, Pakistan and Afghanistan. He'd met the Dunnes through the Prince and their other continental contacts and accepted them for what they said they were – the Irish Mafia. He returned to Dublin again in May 1983, just weeks before Larry Dunne's second trial. Larry believed that he could beat the rap, although the rest of the clan told him he was going down.

Larry and Shamie met da Silva to discuss setting up a heroin route from Nigeria to Dublin. But the Nigerian had no idea how dangerous it was to be seen mixing with the Dunnes. He was put under surveillance by the Drug Squad and his hotel bedroom was bugged. He stayed in Dublin for a number of days and his every move was watched. At one stage he hired a prostitute and brought her back to his room in the Waldorf-Astoria Hotel on Eden Quay. Da Silva had three passions in life – sex, drugs and selling drugs in large quantities. One former member of the surveillance team later revealed how the Nigerian made a lot of noise while making love. As he was in the throes of passion, one mischievous officer held his walkie-talkie radio to the speaker receiving transmissions from the room. Every squad car in the city centre got a live feed from the action in da Silva's room that night.

On 18 May, Det. Insp. Dinny Mullins and his team raided the Nigerian's hotel room and found him with £45,000 worth of uncut heroin. In a notebook beside the bed the officers found telephone numbers for London, Italy, France, Greece, the US and Belgium. He also had Larry Dunne's number. When Mullins asked him why he had it the Nigerian replied: 'I do not want to talk about them. They are too big.'

Da Silva was charged and remanded in custody. Six months later, on 28 November 1983, he pleaded guilty to the drugs charges and received a 14-year jail sentence. However the court suspended the sentence on the condition that he took the next flight out of Dublin, which he gladly agreed to do. The sentence caused some controversy because two weeks earlier one of Shamie Dunne's couriers, Paul Preston, had been jailed for 14 years for possession of £18,000 worth of hash. The brothers' plans for a Nigerian supply route would never get off the ground.

On 21 June, Larry Dunne was back in the dock for his second trial at the Circuit Criminal Court. Christy and Shamie had advised him to take flight because he hadn't a chance, but Larry decided to bide his time. Before the trial, the prosecution requested Garda protection for the jury for the duration of the trial, so they wouldn't be got at.

Larry soon realized that his siblings were right. The court threw out a plethora of legal arguments and objections put forward by his defence team. He was going to be convicted. At lunchtime Dunne went to a local pub and ordered food. He went into the toilets and changed into new clothes which Christy had left for him. Larry slipped out a side door, into a waiting car and disappeared. He later dyed his hair and stayed in a safe house, before taking a ferry out of the country, armed with a large amount of cash and a few blank passports. The drug lord's disappearance dominated the national newspaper headlines and the Gardaí launched a massive search for him.

A month later another key player in the family's operation, Eddie Johnson, tried a similar stunt while awaiting sentence on drug charges in the Circuit Criminal Court. Johnson, from Fatima Mansions, had been one of the managers in the Dunnes' drug-distribution network in the south inner-city. An addict since 1972, Johnson ran a dry-cleaning business on Harold's Cross Road which had been financed by the Dunnes as a cover for the drug operation. The Dunnes' lieutenant managed to slip out of his handcuffs and bolted through the door. The prisoner he was handcuffed to, Jem Dixon's brother from Summerhill, also tried to escape but was caught before he got out of the courtroom. Johnson wasn't as well organized as his boss and was recaptured that night.

Johnson and his partner, William 'Blinkey' Doyle, used a lock-up garage on Meath Street as the gang's main storage depot. On 15 October 1982, Drug Squad boss Dinny Mullins and his officers raided the lock-up and caught Doyle and three other men in possession of £120,000 worth of heroin. One of the men arrested was INLA member Michael Weldon, who worked with Tommy Savage selling drugs and organizing bank robberies. It was an indication of the extent of the collaboration between the various criminal groups. The four men were charged but were subsequently acquitted, when the court found the Drug Squad had used a defective warrant. Less than a week after Doyle's arrest, the Gardaí raided the lock-up for a second time and caught Johnson with another large batch of heroin. The Dunnes' manager was charged, released on bail and went back to work. A month later the dreaded Drug Squad hit Johnson for a third time. This time he was busted with a large quantity of heroin and cocaine in his dry-cleaning premises in Harold's Cross. In total, he had been caught with over £400,000 worth of heroin (over €1.4 million in today's values) – the biggest seizure of the drug in Ireland at that time. In July 1983, Johnson pleaded guilty in the Circuit Criminal Court, where Judge Martin sentenced him to 12 years. Defence counsel pleaded for leniency on the grounds that he was a drug addict and was not the main player in the operation. The judge told Johnson: 'If the sentence appears to be merciless it is as near to merciless as possible. The drugs problem has reached such epidemic proportions that an entire generation of Irish youth is being destroyed.'

In October 1983, the Dunnes received another blow. Shamie's wife, Valerie, was jailed for three years for possession of stolen jewellery, which had been given to her husband as payment for drugs. Despite her husband's infidelities, Valerie still refused to co-operate with the Gardaí, who knew that he was responsible for it. Shamie decided to let his wife take the rap. A few days later Mickey Dunne was jailed for seven years after he pleaded guilty to possession of heroin with intent to supply. His mother Ellen sobbed when she heard the sentence being announced. 'It's all right, Ma,' Mickey said, 'I was expecting fourteen.'

The following February, Christy Dunne and John Cunningham stood trial on the aggravated robbery charges from two years earlier. During the trial there were allegations of intimidation of witnesses, and Judge Frank Martin complained of receiving threatening phone calls. As a result both the judge and the witnesses were given armed police protection. In the end Christy and Cunningham were acquitted.

Shortly after he was sent down, Mickey Dunne was in prophetic mood when he was interviewed by journalist Maggie O'Kane for the *Sunday Tribune*. Dazzler wanted the world to know that he became a dealer because there were no other opportunities for him in the employment market. 'I came back from England with ten years' experience in the brewing business and tried to get a job with Guinness but the manager was warned by the police that the wages would be robbed in a week because I was a Dunne,' Mickey moaned, in typical 'victim' mode. But then he made a chilling prediction. 'Things are going to blow up out there,' he warned. 'They're out there itching to step into the Dunnes' shoes – itching to get up the ladder. They're heavy and they're going to bring the gun back onto the streets.'

Fresh from his brush with the law, Christy Dunne went on holiday to Majorca with his partner Mary Noonan and friends in June 1984. On 20 June, he was arrested by Spanish police after detectives travelled from Dublin with information that Dunne had buried £130,000 worth of stolen travellers' cheques and false passports on waste ground near Illetas in Majorca. A young woman with a grievance against the philandering Bronco had travelled to Majorca with the detectives. She pointed out where the haul was buried and police dug it up. Dunne intended cashing the cheques on the island. They were part of a consignment of £500,000 worth of cheques, stolen from the American Express office in Grafton Street, Dublin, in March 1984. Five armed and masked men, one dressed as a Garda, had held the manager's family hostage overnight. The following morning he was taken to the office by the gang who tied up the staff as they arrived for work. Over the following months £150,000 worth of the cheques had been cashed in various European cities.

Dunne was remanded in custody while the investigation continued. He was later charged with altering his passport and his driving licence, and cashing some of the stolen cheques in Majorca. Bail was set at

£5,000 but Dunne didn't have the money to pay it. Back in Dublin, his family ignored his pleas for help. They were punishing their older brother for turning his back on them when they were in trouble.

In April 1985, Dunne had a short trial in a Palma court. He admitted altering his passport but denied he was a member of an international crime gang involved in large-scale robberies. The court convicted him of cashing the stolen cheques and he was jailed for two years and eight months. Gangland's first Godfather was 46 years old.

Christy could not handle being inside and started a desperate campaign to win his release. He sent a blizzard of letters to influential figures in Ireland, the Irish Consul and Amnesty International, protesting his innocence. Bronco also tried to use the media, employing his old reliable claim of being set up: 'I am a big fish according to the Irish police. They could never put me in this position but relied on innuendo and rumour as evidence against me.'

In another interview Dunne declared: 'I am going fucking mental in here.' He said he was now too old to 'do the time'. 'Jessie James and the other outlaws didn't keep going until they were fifty,' he said ruefully. On 29 October 1985, Christy Dunne was suddenly released unconditionally from prison. He was given no explanation for the surprise move. Ironically, on the day of his release another armed gang held up the same American Express office in Dublin. Bronco left Majorca on the first available flight.

Shamie Dunne had also been fortunate. The charge for possessing £400,000 worth of heroin was struck out on a technicality and he fled the country before the State had time to re-enter the case. He moved his operating base to London, where he remained in 'voluntary exile'. He claimed that if he returned home he would be 'harassed' by the police. Shamie chose not to attend the funeral of his father, Bronco Senior, who died in 1987 at the age of 72. Most of the Dunne siblings became drug addicts and some of them, including Anne and Gerard, died as a result. It also destroyed many of their children, including at least three, one of whom was Larry's daughter, who died from overdoses and AIDS-related conditions.

While Christy had been fighting an impossible battle to raise his bail money in Majorca, Larry was experiencing difficulties of his own. He was moving between Portugal and Spain to avoid being caught. But eventually the law caught up with him too when the picture in his pass-port aroused the interest of a Portuguese Immigration Officer. Larry was extradited back to Dublin where he was jailed for 14 years in April 1985. Hundreds of people from the communities worst hit by the her-oin plague turned up that day to see Larry Dunne get justice. The angry mob tried to block in the police van carrying him from court, in a bid to attack him.

On his way to join the rest of his brothers, Larry made a chilling prophecy, similar to the one Mickey had issued to the world in October 1983. Larry's words of wisdom would be used many times in following years to describe the changes that each new generation of villains brought to Gangland. 'If you think we were bad,' he said, 'just wait till you see what's coming next.' It was one of the few truthful statements Larry Dunne ever made.

On the ground, community activist Mick Rafferty could see the dir-ect link between what happened next and the situation we have today. He said: 'By the time Larry was arrested, he had built up a hierarchy of dealers, right down to the street, to user dealers. His prophecy about what was coming after him and his family was correct. Because what you got then were a new breed of dealers and a new breed of people in gangs that had absolutely no respect. Because whatever respect the Dunnes had for where they came from, the next breed of dealers had none, and they were ruthless, and that has led up the present . . . where life is cheap.'

9.   The Ultimate Price

Mickey Dunne didn't rely solely on his crystal ball when he arrived at his chilling prediction about the future of organized crime. The first few years of the 1980s had already witnessed some of the worst violence in the country's history, as terrorist and criminal gangs dragged Ireland to a state of near anarchy. By the time Dazzler was sent down in October 1983, gun law had been firmly established in Ireland and organized crime was moving to a new level of sophistication and brutality.

Since 1980, five Gardaí had been murdered by terrorist gangs during armed robberies. In less than two years after Dunne's incarceration, three more Gardaí and an Irish soldier were also murdered without mercy. Like Deirdre Fallon, their widows collected the posthumous Scott Medals for bravery. The police were paying a very high price in their battle with the underworld.

When Garda Dick Fallon was shot dead by Saor Eire in 1970, it had heralded the return of the gun to Irish streets and a rapid descent into violent crime over the following decade. The execution of three officers in 1980 heralded the bloody start of an even more violent era. The IRA, INLA and the 'ordinary' criminal gangs continued to rob financial institutions throughout the country with apparent impunity – and they were displaying a brutal determination to avoid arrest.

On the afternoon of 7 July 1980, a three-man INLA gang arrived in the small town of Ballaghaderreen, County Roscommon. They were there to rob the local Bank of Ireland branch. One gang member remained outside, covering the almost deserted main street while his two accomplices ran inside. The first raider fired a shot into the ceiling and ordered everyone to get down, while the other jumped across the counter. He handed the manager a bag and told him to fill it with cash from the safe. 'It's better to lose money than have someone killed,' he said, shoving a handgun in the banker's face. At the same time the man outside had intercepted two, unarmed Gardaí – Brendan Gilmore and Brendan

Walsh – as they arrived in a squad car to investigate. The officers were ordered at gunpoint to lie on the ground. Seconds later the other raiders ran to the getaway car and the gang drove off at speed, cheering loudly. It had taken them less than three minutes to rob £41,000.

Outside the town the gang changed cars. They sped off down a secondary road, in the direction of Frenchpark, but they met a patrol car at Shannon's Cross. It was coming from Castlerea in response to the robbery. Inside were three uniformed officers, Henry Byrne, Derek O'Kelly and Mick O'Malley and Detective Garda John Morley, who was armed with an Uzi submachine-gun. The getaway car smashed into the patrol car as the gang tried to get past. The INLA raiders jumped out and without warning opened fire on the police car. Garda Henry Byrne was shot in the head and died instantly as he tried to get out of the back seat. The 29-year-old was married, with two young sons, and his wife, Anne, was pregnant with their third child.

Detective John Morley returned fire with a burst from his machine-gun. The gunmen made a run for it on foot, followed by the 39-year-old former Mayo County footballer. Morley, who had been hit in the initial attack, fired another burst in the direction of one of the gang members who was hiding in a ditch. Further up the road, he levelled his machine-gun at the other two raiders, who were trying to hijack another car, and ordered them to stop. They opened fire, hitting the detective in the leg. He fell backwards, landing beside a ditch. Morley managed to fire a third burst at the terrorists as he fell. The two INLA men fired more shots as they tried to take the driver, who was fighting them off, hostage. A short distance later the terrorists crashed the car and took another vehicle.

Meanwhile one of the bullets fired by the gang had severed an artery in Detective John Morley's leg and he was bleeding to death. As he lay dying, Garda Derek O'Kelly urged him to hang on and tried to reassure him that help was on the way. 'Say goodbye to my wife and kids for me,' Morley whispered, as he lapsed into unconsciousness. The father of three died on his way to hospital.

The policemen's deaths were the first double murder of members of the Garda Síochána since the foundation of the State. It brought to six the number of police officers killed in the Republic in the 13 years since the gangs had first appeared on the streets.

The Roscommon murders were greeted with the same level of universal shock, revulsion and anger as that of Dick Fallon, ten years earlier. It also added to the growing sense of despair among the public because of the spiralling violence. There was a feeling that nothing could be done to stop the savagery. Thousands turned out to show their solidarity with the families and colleagues of the two men at their funerals in County Mayo. Morley and Byrne were buried side-by-side in a hillside cemetery overlooking Knock.

The investigation into the murders moved quickly, with hundreds of Gardaí and soldiers involved in the manhunt. They had already arrested the first member of the gang within an hour of the shootings. He was Colm O'Shea from Cork, a convicted armed robber with links to Saor Eire and the INLA. The 28-year-old had been shot in the chest by John Morley during the gun battle. The following day Patrick McCann, a 34-year-old from Dungarvan, County Waterford, was arrested near Frenchpark. Eight days later a third man, Peter Pringle, a 42-year-old former IRA man from Dublin, was arrested in Galway. The three men were charged with the capital murder of Garda Henry Byrne, possession of firearms and the bank robbery. A capital murder conviction carried the death penalty. Bizarrely, none of the suspects was charged with the murder of John Morley. The State's prosecution service felt that a conviction for the capital murder of Garda Byrne would be more likely because he was in uniform – so the killers would have been in no doubt that he was a Garda.

In November 1980, the INLA men were convicted of Garda Henry Byrne's murder, the armed robbery and possession of firearms. They were sentenced to death by hanging but this was later commuted to 40 years' imprisonment without remission. Peter Pringle, however, was granted a retrial 15 years later, when the Court of Criminal Appeal ruled that new evidence in the case cast doubt on his original conviction. The Special Criminal Court subsequently struck out all the charges against him and he was released. McCann and O'Shea were not deemed eligible for release as part of the Good Friday Agreement and spent over twenty years in prison.

Three months after the murder of the two Gardaí in Roscommon, on Monday 13 October, an IRA gang took over the village of Callan, County Kilkenny. During the audacious raid they held a number of soldiers and two Gardaí at gunpoint. The unarmed troops and police were in the process of delivering oil, during one of many nationwide strikes. The Provos first robbed the Bank of Ireland, then got into their getaway car, reversed 100 yards down the road and hit the Allied Irish Bank. When they were finished, the gang drove back down the street, picked up the gunman holding the Gardaí and soldiers, and sped out of town with £10,000 for 'the cause'.

Later that night, as part of the follow-up investigation, Detective Garda Seamus Quaid and his partner, Donal Lyttleton, were on the look-out for Belfast IRA man Peter Rogers. He ran a mobile greengrocery business from his home near Wexford Town. He was well known to the two local detectives who were tasked with monitoring the activities of terrorists in the area. Around 10.30 p.m. they spotted Rogers driving his van between Wexford Town and Duncannon. They pulled him over and asked him to open up the back of the van. Inside they discovered a small arsenal of explosives, electronic detonators, four guns, mercury switches and delay-action units for priming bombs. Rogers suddenly produced a gun and fired a shot over the heads of the detectives. He ordered them into a nearby quarry.

Seamus Quaid, who had been an All-Ireland Wexford hurler, produced his handgun. The detective pointed it at Rogers, ordering him to put his gun down. The Garda and the Provo then fired a number of shots at each other. At the same time Donal Lyttleton, who didn't have a firearm, was forced to dive for cover and went to get help. When the shooting was over, Seamus Quaid lay dying on the ground, while Rogers was injured in the leg. Despite his injuries the Provo made a run for it. The detective died 15 minutes later. He was 42 years old and the father of four children. Rogers later gave himself up and was charged with the murder of Seamus Quaid. In March 1981, the Special Criminal Court convicted the IRA man of the Garda's murder and sentenced him to death. Rogers was also convicted on the firearms and explosives charges. His death sentence was commuted to 40 years without the benefit of remission. The Provo was released 18 years later, under the terms of the Good Friday Agreement.

In response to the Garda murders, the Fianna Fáil Justice Minister, Gerry Collins, unveiled with much fanfare a £100 million security plan to tackle the increased threat of subversive and organized crime. The plan included provision for an increase in the overall strength of the force and an expansion of the Special Task Force (STF) – which was largely Dublin-based – to cover every Garda division in the country. The most exotic and expensive part of the plan was the provision of a dozen helicopters and light planes which would be used to back up Gardaí on the ground. (The Gardaí took delivery of the first police helicopter and surveillance plane in 1997.)

The murders of the three Gardaí had a major impact on the internal debate among detectives about carrying firearms. Apart from the Special Task Force and Special Detective Unit members, the rest of the plainclothes officers in the force were mostly unarmed and had expressed a wish to remain so. In a ballot held among detectives in Dublin in 1979 the vast majority had voted against being armed. In early 1981, however, there was a complete reversal of the earlier result, with 239 members voting in favour of carrying firearms, while 89 were against. Any remaining doubts there were about the need to be able to shoot back were erased in December 1980 when two more detectives were shot and critically injured, this time by a Dublin crime gang.

Frank Ward was one of the most dangerous armed robbers to operate in over four decades of organized crime. His reputation for violence was so great that even the other members of his gang were afraid of him. From the beginning of his criminal career Ward stood out for his obsession with planning and his sheer ruthlessness. One former associate recalled: 'Everyone went on jobs well tooled-up but Frank always brought a fucking arsenal with him – machine-guns, automatic pistols, rifles and grenades. Frank had no problem killing a Guard if one got in the way and he nearly always fired shots during a job. He was fucking mad.'

Born in Sligo, on 6 June 1953, Ward was a member of the travelling community. He had a dreadful childhood and spent a number of years in orphanages and the industrial schools. By the time he was a teenager, Ward was a reckless hood who was up for anything. He spent time living in Manchester and Belfast, before moving to live in Tallaght, West Dublin when he got married at 17.

An incident outside a Dublin nightclub in the late 1970s illustrated his volatility. Ward arrived at the club wearing an odd-looking cowboy hat and dark glasses. One of the bouncers laughed, saying: 'Jaysus, are you in disguise tonight, Frank Ward?' The armed robber didn't like the joke. He produced a handgun and shot the bouncer in the stomach. Although the Gardaí knew Ward did it, the bouncer wouldn't co-operate with the investigation. He was afraid that Ward would finish him off the next time. No one dared to jeer at his dress sense again.

Although Ward's first recorded conviction was not until 1978, when he got a suspended sentence for car theft, he was already a dedicated armed robber. He had originally been a member of the republican criminal mob, Saor Eire. Ward led a five-man gang which he organized like a terrorist cell. He picked the targets to be robbed and planned each job himself. The rest of the gang was not informed about the location of the job until the last minute. It ensured total secrecy about each heist and prevented tip-offs to the Gardaí. Ward's gang did scores of heists throughout the country, hitting factory payrolls, banks and post offices. According to Garda intelligence reports, Ward 'trained' criminals, teaching them how to rob. In one daring raid on 28 May 1979, his crew simultaneously robbed two banks in the village of Kilcock, County Kildare. During the heist, shots were fired from several firearms including a machine-gun, terrifying the hostages and forcing the police to back off. Ward told his victims that it was a job for Saor Eire.

The Ward gang included Johnny Doran from Ballyfermot, West Dublin. In Garda files Doran, who was a year older than Ward, was also described as a ruthless armed robber. He'd a long record for burglary before he moved on to more dangerous crime. Another member of the team was 32-year-old Anthony 'Tonto' O'Brien from the Oliver Bond House flats in Dublin's inner-city. O'Brien had a string of convictions, including one for manslaughter in 1969 for which he'd served four years in prison. Ward's second-in-command was 26-year-old James Daly from the north inner-city who Gardaí classified as 'very vicious'. Ward and his cohorts also took part in robberies with the Cahills and other emerging gangs. Doran was a close friend of George Mitchell and the Cunninghams.

In November 1980, Ward began plotting a robbery from the Bank of Ireland branch in Stillorgan Shopping Centre, South County Dublin. His plan was to hit the bank on 30 December, when it would be bulging with cash from the pre-Christmas spending spree.

Ward bought a green Volkswagen van from a used car lot owned by John Traynor. It could comfortably carry a group of armed men and the rear-mounted engine would provide protection if the gang came under fire. He equipped his crew with a total of eight firearms – a machine-gun, an automatic pistol, a revolver, two .22 rifles and three shotguns. Each weapon was loaded and had plenty of extra ammunition.

At 3.30 p.m. on 30 December 1980, the gang struck. Doran stayed with the van in the car park, while Ward and three others ran towards the bank. The sight of the armed and masked raiders, in combat-style clothing, caused panic among shoppers, who began running in all direc-tions to get away. The bank had just closed so the raiders ran up to the plate-glass window and used a sledgehammer to smash it in. Frank Ward and two others jumped through the broken window, while the fourth man covered the front. In less than three minutes the gang snatched over £102,000. The four reckless robbers then ran back through the car park and jumped into the waiting van.

Sean Keeley, an off-duty detective attached to the Special Detective Unit (SDU), heard the screams and went to investigate. He spotted the raiders running to the van. As they got inside the detective stepped into view and pulled out his .38 revolver. Ward and his men smashed the van's rear window and aimed their rifles at him. Keeley fired a shot and the gang responded with a volley of bullets, forcing the detective to duck down behind a parked car. The gang were still shooting as the van sped off, narrowly missing him.

Garda units across South Dublin had been alerted about the armed robbery. Detective Gardaí William Daly and Richard Curran were patrolling near Cabinteely Village when they heard the message. Daly, who was 43, had been in the force since 1959 and his 55-year-old partner had been in the job since 1947. William Daly drove their unmarked squad car, code-named Whiskey 8, through Foxrock Village in an attempt to cut the raiders off. They spotted the green Volkswagen and gave chase. The Garda car, which was more powerful than the van, began to close in. The gang fired a number of shots at the squad car, forcing it to drop back to a safer distance.

Ward was determined to shake off the police car permanently. When the van turned a corner Ward suddenly ordered Doran to stop. As the detectives drove up they saw the ambush – but were too late to do anything about it. Ward and his gangsters opened fire with a machine-gun, pistol and rifle, peppering the squad car and hitting the veteran detectives several times. Richard Curran was shot in the hand and fingers, while two more machine-gun rounds grazed the right side of his head. Another bullet ripped through William Daly's right forearm, causing extensive bone damage. Other rounds hit him in both legs. As the firing continued, Curran managed to open his passenger door and roll out onto the road, followed by Daly. The officers lay on the ground for cover and waited for the firing to stop. When the van sped off, Curran staggered to the side of the road and fell down. Daly, who was bleeding heavily, radioed in their position and the direction the van had taken.

Garda units converged on the area as Ward's gang headed into the Dublin Mountains. They abandoned the van on Glencullen Road and hijacked another car at gunpoint, but crashed it a few miles further up the road. They then hijacked a second car. Ward wanted to hold the driver as a hostage but there was no space for him in the car. At the same moment, Detective Garda Martin Doyle of the SDU arrived at the scene. He recognized James Daly who had taken off his balaclava. One of the gunmen aimed his rifle at the detective, as another armed raider walked towards him, brandishing a gun. The rifleman had to adjust the weapon so Doyle quickly reversed his car out of the line of fire. The gang members then crowded into the second car.

As the SDU officer reversed down the road, he met Detectives Martin Donnellan and Kieran Brennan, who'd arrived from Donnybrook Garda Station. Donnellan had survived an encounter with Ward's former Saor Eire comrades 12 years earlier, in Ballyfermot. The detectives blocked the narrow road with their two squad cars. Seconds later the gang drove round a corner at speed and ground to a halt, about 20 yards from the police. Doyle, the only one of the three detectives armed, took cover behind a tree and drew his automatic pistol. Donnellan and Brennan crouched behind their car and pretended that they were also armed. Brennan aimed his walkie-talkie, while Donnellan pointed his hands at the robbers to look like he was holding a weapon. There was panic in the getaway car and it reversed at speed back up the road, before sliding into a drain. The unarmed detectives then ran towards the five raiders as they clamoured to get out of the car.

The officers were still aiming their 'weapons' at the mob while

Detective Garda Doyle covered them. The gang thought they were out-gunned and made a run for it up the side of the mountain. As they did so, Doyle fired a warning shot over their heads while his colleagues continued their pursuit. He fired a second warning shot when one of the gang members turned and pointed a gun at him. The detective then fired another three rounds directly at the gangsters, hitting Tonto O'Brien twice in the knee. O'Brien and Doran dropped to the ground while Ward, Daly and the fifth robber continued running. A few yards further up Ward also stopped.

The three raiders were ordered to put their hands up as Donnellan and Brennan closed in, 'weapons' drawn. Doyle moved up to cover them as more units began to arrive. Brennan and Donnellan first arrested Doran and passed him back to another detective. They then arrested O'Brien, who was sitting with his hands in the air and screaming with pain. Donnellan then went for Ward, who was breathing heavily and in a distressed state. 'Shoot me now, I want you to shoot me now,' the robber, who was carrying a loaded pistol in his pocket, demanded. Donnellan grabbed him but Ward refused to walk and had to be dragged back down the mountain. All the way he kept repeating his request to be shot. An extensive search was mounted for the other two raiders but they managed to get away.

Doran later made a full statement to Donnellan admitting his part in the robbery. When the blagger was asked why the gang had done so much shooting, he admitted: 'We went mad shooting. We all lost our heads and started shooting. The gun I had blew up and I thought I was after shooting meself. I know I've been caught red handed.' Doran said he regretted that two officers had been shot. Detective Garda Curran left hospital two weeks later and recovered from his injuries. William Daly suffered serious damage to his arm and was hospitalized for almost a month. Technical examination of the squad car later confirmed that the two detectives had a miraculous escape from death.

On New Year's Eve Frank Ward and Johnny Doran were charged with the attempted murder of the two, injured detectives and the bank robbery. Tonto O'Brien was also charged with the same offences when he was released from hospital. In July 1981, Ward, Doran and O'Brien were jailed for 12 years each by the Special Criminal Court, after they were convicted of attempted murder and the robbery. James Daly fled

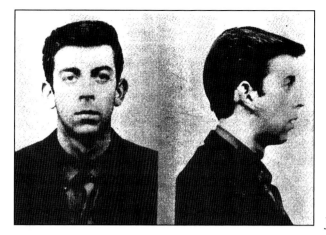

Joseph Dillon, Saor Eire.

Walsh, Liam. 50 Tyrone Road, Inchicore. Born Dublin 1933, 5' 8", Erect carriage, Dark hair, Grey eyes, Oval face, II stone in weught. Slight build.

Liam Walsh, Saor Eire member, blown up by his own bomb in 1970.

Casey, Martin. I9 Sandyhill Ave.,Ballymun. Born Dublin I94I. 5' 8½" in height, Erect carriage, Fair hair, Blue eyes, Oval pale face, II Stone weight, Strong build.

Martin Casey, who bought weapons from Christy 'Bronco' Dunne.

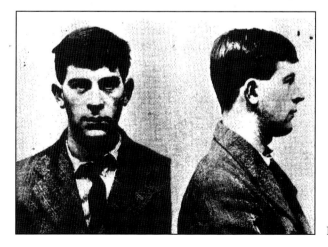

Patrick Dillon, Saor Eire.

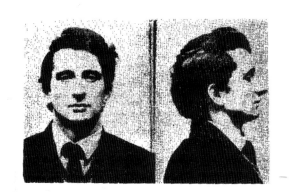

Dwyer, Patrick. I49 Harold's Cross Road, Dublin.
Born Kiltimagh, Co. Mayo in I939. 5' 8" in
height, Erect carriage, Dark Brown hair, Blue
eyes, Oval face, I2 stone, Medium build,
D.C.R. 862II.

Patrick Dwyer, Saor Eire.

64 Ard-Na-Greine, Clonmel. Born I944; Height 5'8" or 5'9"; Medium
build with slight shoulder stoop. Dark curley hair; sometimes wears
a beard; Blue eyes; Long thin face; II stone weight.
Semi-Professional ballad singer. Intelligent and well educated.

John (Sean) Morrissey,
Saor Eire.

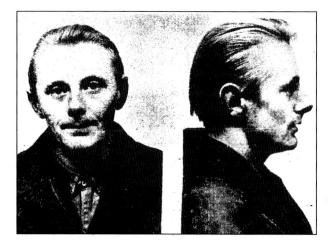

Simon O'Donnell, Saor Eire,
convicted of armed robbery
with INLA man Tommy
Savage.

(*Above left*) Christy 'Bronco' Dunne.

(*Above*) Christy 'Bronco' Dunne Sr and his wife Ellen, the parents of Ireland's first crime family.

(*Left*) Mickey Dunne (*left*) and Henry Dunne (*right*) with their mysterious business partner the Prince (*centre*).

(*Far left*) Larry Dunne, the man credited with bringing the first heroin shipments into Ireland, pictured in prison in 1992.

(*Left*) Henry Dunne at the funeral of Martin Cahill, 1994 (© Padraig O'Reilly).

(*Above*) Vianney 'Boyo' Dunne.

(*Right*) Robert Dunne (© Padraig O'Reilly).

(*Far right*) Charlie Dunne (© Padraig O'Reilly).

(*Above*) Joe Roe, Dunne family associate.

(*Right*) Christy Dunne Sr.

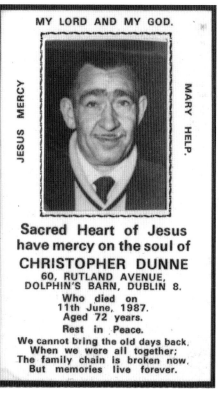

MY LORD AND MY GOD.

JESUS MERCY

MARY HELP.

Sacred Heart of Jesus have mercy on the soul of
CHRISTOPHER DUNNE
60, RUTLAND AVENUE,
DOLPHIN'S BARN, DUBLIN 8.
Who died on
11th June, 1987.
Aged 72 years.
Rest in Peace.
We cannot bring the old days back,
When we were all together;
The family chain is broken now,
But memories live forever.

(*Left*) Martin Cahill, the General.

(*Above*) Martin Cahill at home with his children in their rundown flat in Hollyfield.

(*Left*) Eddie Cahill, the General's brother (© Padraig O'Reilly).

(*Below*) Hughie Delaney, Martin Cahill's brother-in-law and member of the General's gang.

(*Below*) Family business: (*from left*) Eugene Scanlan, a member of the General's gang, and John Cahill, the General's elder brother.

(*Right*) Gang members in Portlaoise: John Foy (*back*) and Eamon Daly (*front left*) from the General's gang in Portlaoise prison in 1992 with Brendan 'Wetty' Walsh (*front right, dark shorts*) of the Athy Gang.

(*Above*) William Gardiner from the Athy Gang (*left*) and Albert Crowley from the General's gang (*right*) in prison.

(*Right*) Eamon Daly, member of the General's gang.

(*Far right*) Harry Melia, member of the General's gang.

Martin Foley ('the Viper'), member of the General's gang, who has survived one kidnap and four murder attempts.

Noel Lynch, convicted armed robber and member of the General's gang.

(*Above*) Martin Cahill murder scene, 1994.

(*Left*) Michael 'Jo Jo' Kavanagh, Cahill gang member (© Padraig O'Reilly).

(*Above*) Felix McKenna, retired head of the CAB who spent his career pursuing the crime bosses (© Padraig O'Reilly).

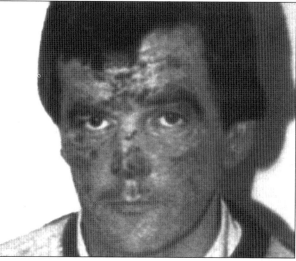

(*Right*) Seamus 'Shavo' Hogan, pictured with his own excrement smeared across his face while being questioned about the Paddy Shanahan murder in 1994.

(*Right*) Seanie 'Fixer' Fitzgerald, an associate of the General and John Traynor (© Padraig O'Reilly).

(*Left*) Tommy Savage, drug-trafficker, armed robber and former member of Saor Eire and the INLA.

(*Below*) Mickey Boyle: Garda mugshots from the early 1980s of the armed robber, kidnapper, extortionist and gangland hitman.

(*Bottom left*) Mickey Weldon.

(*Bottom right*) Paddy Shanahan.

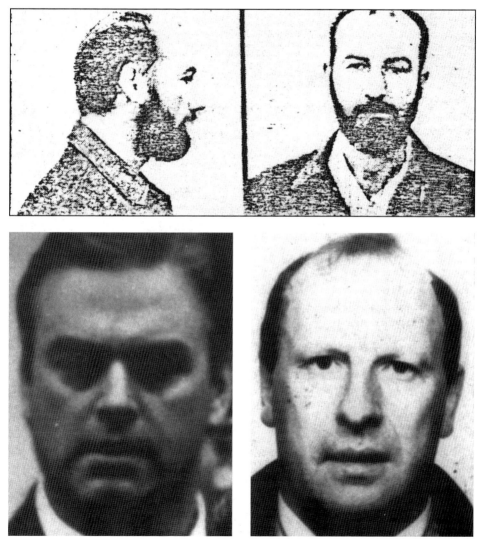

PJ 'the Psycho' Judge.

John 'the Coach' Traynor.

Pensioner and convicted drug-dealer Jimmy Edgeworth, who was involved in organized crime for over forty years (© Padraig O'Reilly).

(*Left*) Johnny Doran, associate of Frank Ward and George Mitchell ('the Penguin') (© Padraig O'Reilly).

(*Above*) Frank Ward, armed robber.

Retired Assistant Commissioner Tony Hickey, who spent forty years on the frontline against organized crime.

Retired Assistant Commissioner Martin Donnellan, who confronted Saor Eire and armed robber Frank Ward.

(*Above*) Eamon Kelly (© Padraig O'Reilly).

(*Right*) Gerry 'the Monk' Hutch.

John Gilligan in his Factory John years.

John Gilligan with Geraldine in the 1970s.

John Gilligan, Brian Meehan and Peter Mitchell with Frances Meehan (Brian's mother) at Sandals resort in St Lucia, 1996.

(*Above*) John Gilligan pumping iron.

(*Above right*) Peter Mitchell with his wife Sonya Walsh on the balcony of his luxury hideout in Spain (© Padraig O'Reilly).

(*Right*) Patrick Eugene 'Dutchie' Holland, armed robber and gangland assassin.

(*Right*) Brian 'the Tosser' Meehan, who was convicted of the murder of Veronica Guerin.

(*Far right*) Paul Ward, Gilligan gang member.

(*Right*) Veronica Guerin with husband Graham Turley and their son Cathal. Her bid to expose the truth about John Gilligan led to her murder.

(*Below*) The Veronica Guerin murder scene.

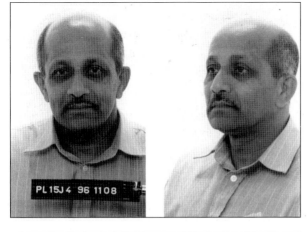

Simon Rahman, Gilligan's main supplier in Amsterdam.

(*Above left*) George 'the Penguin' Mitchell.

(*Above*) Paddy Mitchell, brother of George Mitchell.

(*Left*) John Noonan, Sinn Féin and IRA member who was a founder of the CPAD and later exposed for connections with drug-trafficker Martin 'Marlo' Hyland (© Padraig O'Reilly).

Austin Higgins, who was shot dead by Gardaí in Athy in 1990.

(*Above*) INLA terrorist Dessie O'Hare – 'the Border Fox'. Killer, armed robber and kidnapper.

(*Above right*) INLA member Fergal Toal, convicted of murder and kidnapping.

(*Right*) Danny Hamill, INLA.

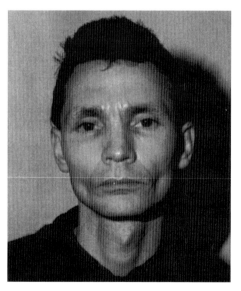

to the UK, where his luck eventually ran out. He was subsequently jailed for 16 years when British police caught him during a post office robbery. The fifth man was never located.

The Gardaí had been extremely lucky that day. In 1981 six detectives involved in the pursuit and arrest of Ward and his gang were awarded Scott Medals for valour in the course of their duties: Detectives Curran and Daly were awarded gold Scott Medals; Detectives Martin Donnellan and Kieran Brennan were decorated with silver medals; and Detectives Keeley and Doyle were presented with bronze medals.

The award ceremony in the Templemore Garda Training Centre that year was one of the most poignant in the history of the Garda Síochána. In all 14 officers were honoured at the medal ceremony, 3 of them posthumously. All the bravery medals awarded in 1981 resulted from confrontations between the Gardaí and armed robbers. The widows and children of the three murdered officers sat beside their dead husbands' colleagues. Martin Donnellan never forgot that day and recalled thirty years later: 'It was the most heart-breaking day in my career when I saw a little child of no more than four holding his murdered Daddy's medal. We were the lucky ones. It really drove home the fact that the subversives and criminals were trying to terrorize every citizen in the country.'

The murders of Gardaí in 1980 resulted in the issuing of .38 Smith and Wesson revolvers to most of the country's detectives. Together with the STF units, they began firing back and now posed a major threat to the armed robbers, whose chosen trade was becoming considerably more perilous. Henry Dunne and Joe Roe were among the first high-profile blaggers to have a run in with the STF when they were caught following a shoot-out in May 1981. It gave members of the Dunne family another excuse – they blamed the armed police for forcing them into the drug trade.

The Gardaí had already convinced another dangerous criminal to make the same career-altering decision. On 15 February 1980, Peter Joseph 'PJ' Judge from Finglas robbed Boland's Post Office in Ballyfermot, West Dublin with two other associates. During the robbery the 23-year-old up-and-coming drug baron demonstrated his violent disposition when he shot the post master, Michael Delaney, in the leg and chest. Delaney had tried to grab Judge's sawn-off shotgun as the robber jumped across the counter and grabbed £600. An hour later Judge and one of his accomplices, Willie O'Reilly, a violent criminal who had been reared in Artane Industrial School, were arrested by detectives. They were charged with attempted murder and armed robbery.

Judge, from Ballygall Crescent in Finglas, was already well known to the Gardaí. From an early age he displayed a tendency for extreme violence. His associates and the Gardaí described Judge as a natural-born killer. Many years later he would be known by his very apt nickname – 'the Psycho'. Judge had first demonstrated his capacity for violence in 1969 at the age of 14. He broke into a gunsmith's in Finglas, stole a shotgun and used it to shoot up the home of another teenager, who'd convinced Judge to dye his hair a day earlier. The Psycho got upset when other kids started laughing at him. Judge was later convicted for theft and possession of a firearm and rewarded with two years in a reformatory school. When he came out, he was even more dangerous and unpredictable.

The Psycho had no qualms about attacking the Gardaí if they got in the way. While on bail for the Ballyfermot robbery Judge held up a bank branch on Annesley Bridge in Glasnevin, North Dublin. During the heist Judge was confronted by an off-duty Garda. He aimed his gun at the policeman's head and squeezed the trigger. Luckily it jammed and the Psycho was arrested.

Judge and O'Reilly were jailed for ten years each for the Ballyfermot robbery. The Psycho later received another ten years for the Annesley Bridge hold-up. Like so many other ruthless villains before him, Judge swore that when he got out he would never again do serious time behind bars. The Psycho would leave his mark on the history of Gangland.

The increased number of armed Gardaí on the streets was beginning to make a difference – for a while at least – and there was a noticeable drop in the number of heists the following year. The number of serious criminals being brought before the courts also began to increase, as the Force adopted a more co-ordinated approach to tackling serious crime and learned some lessons from the mistakes of the past. There was now a realization that identification evidence and so-called 'verbals' – admissions made during interrogation – were not enough to sustain convictions in the courts. From the late 1970s, the Gardaí had also begun to rely more heavily on forensic science, as it often provided irrefutable proof against the gun gangs. The turn-around came in 1978, with the appointment of Dr James Donovan as Director of the Forensic Science Laboratory at Garda HQ, Phoenix Park. The deeply committed scientist spear-headed the advancement and modernization of forensic science in Ireland and used it as a vital weapon in the war against terrorists and criminals.

By the early 1980s, the State's Forensic Science Laboratory was a vital component of every major criminal investigation in the country. The scientist was the prosecution's key technical witness in several successful high-profile trials, including the IRA bombing of Lord Louis Mountbatten in 1979 and the murder of the three Gardaí in 1980. Dr Donovan was also a crucial witness in several trials involving the criminal gangs. What he found under the lens of his microscope was often more hazardous to a gangster or a terrorist than the business end of a cop's .38 revolver. The mobs had a new enemy and, inevitably, Dr Donovan began to draw unwanted attention.

10.   The Jewellery Job

On the morning of 6 January 1982, a powerful bomb suddenly exploded under a car driving onto the Naas dual carriageway at Newland's Cross, West Dublin. The force of the blast ripped the vehicle apart, lifting it off the road. The wreckage landed in a crumpled heap, several yards away. Shocked motorists ran to see if there were any survivors. Despite being critically injured, Dr James Donovan managed to stumble from the debris and collapsed at the side of the road. Somehow he'd survived the bomb that had clearly been meant to kill him. Before the dust from the explosion had settled the motive was clear – someone didn't want Dr Donovan to appear in the witness box.

The forensic scientist was rushed to hospital where surgeons worked for several hours to save his left leg and foot, part of which was blown off in the explosion. He underwent several other operations but never fully recovered from his appalling injuries. Almost thirty years later he is still forced to live on a daily cocktail of powerful painkillers. The courageous civil servant's legacy for excelling at his job was a lifetime of agony.

Dr Donovan still vividly recalls the incident. 'I was driving my car that morning when suddenly, as I looked through the windscreen, it disappeared into blackness. There was a cloud of dust with a tongue of red flame in the middle of it and after what seemed like a long time, I heard a loud noise. I put my hand down to my left side and felt a mixture of blood, gunge and broken bones. Since then the pain in my legs and hands and other places has gone on and on and on. The left foot gets infections and it just decides to bleed. It has to be dressed twice a day. I always thought I could put a square around it [the bomb] and forget but I cannot forget it . . . ever.'

The attempt to murder Dr James Donovan still stands out as one of the single worst acts of terrorism committed by organized crime gangs over the past four decades. The ferocity of the attack shocked a country that was growing accustomed to acts of extreme violence. Never before had an employee of the State, who was not involved in the security forces, been targeted in such a way; a government spokesman described the attack as a 'grave development and a serious departure from standard crimes'. It was a clear attempt to undermine the use of forensic science, at a time when it was becoming crucial to the investigation of serious crime. If scientists were too scared to do their jobs then the whole system could collapse.

Initially the finger of suspicion fell on the IRA and the INLA. Donovan's evidence had succeeded in securing the conviction of one of the Provo's top bomb-makers, Thomas McMahon, for the blast which killed Lord Mountbatten. His evidence had also been crucial in the Garda murder cases where members of both organizations had also been jailed for life. But, although they did not express any sympathy for what had happened, the two terror gangs issued curt statements of denial. The Provos declared: 'The IRA has more to lose by carrying out such an act because of the anti-republican hysteria it would arouse.' The INLA comment was even shorter: 'It serves no useful purpose.'

Garda ballistics experts and Dr Donovan's own staff later found evidence which seemed to corroborate the two denials. The device used was described in a Garda report as 'crude and unpredictable'. It was not as sophisticated as the timer and remote-controlled devices being used by both groups. The bomb, which was made of gelignite and petrol, had been attached to the exhaust pipe and was detonated after a build-up of heat from the engine, after it had been running for a while.

The Garda investigation soon found another suspect – Martin Cahill. Intelligence and underworld informants revealed that the sadistic gangster wanted Dr Donovan murdered. The scientist was all that stood between Cahill and a 12-year stretch behind bars for armed robbery. The underworld 'joker' who considered crime a 'game' had finally revealed his sinister side. The Donovan assassination attempt was the first clear evidence that ignoring the developing crime problem was creating a monster and that the ordinary villains were every bit as dangerous as the terrorists.

When Martin Cahill was released from prison on 11 January 1980, he wasted no time rebuilding his old network. He took full advantage of a demoralized police force, dealing with the murders of their colleagues and the subversive threat. The steady stream of criminal activity spilling south of the Border from Northern Ireland became a torrent in the 1980s as the Provos stepped up their efforts to fund the 'war'. As a consequence the General and his contemporaries thrived and prospered. On one job he joined forces with John Traynor, John Gilligan, George Mitchell and Paddy Shanahan for a warehouse burglary. Henry Dunne had introduced Shanahan to Cahill as a potential business partner. The crew robbed £100,000 worth of cigarettes from the ADC wholesalers in Johnstown, County Kildare. By the mid-1980s the hardcore of the General's gang included 30 of some of the most hardened and ruthless mobsters in gangland.

Cahill and his *consigliere* Traynor bought a number of properties to invest the General's money, including a dry-cleaner's on Dublin's Aungier Street. Traynor, who was the registered owner on the deeds, converted the upstairs section into a brothel. Unwitting customers were often secretly filmed enjoying themselves and blackmailed later. The voyeuristic General liked to shin up a drain pipe and watch the action inside.

In May 1981, Traynor and Cahill bought a grotty little bar at the North Wall near Dublin docks called the Jetfoil, which became a notorious haunt for drug-dealing. The money for the purchase came from one of Cahill's heists and Traynor fronted the bar. They bought it from another long-time villain, Niall Mulvihill, from the north inner-city. Mulvihill was a major player in organized crime and, like Traynor, was a facilitator for gangs. The bar's stock was either stolen by the General's men or bought at a competitive 'wholesale' price from John Gilligan or George Mitchell. Gilligan, in turn, had sourced the goods from one of the many warehouses he systematically plundered on a weekly basis, earning him the nickname 'Factory John'. Traynor used counterfeit or stolen bank drafts and false addresses to buy everything else. Gardaí from all over the city were regular visitors to the Jetfoil – and they weren't there for a quiet pint.

Cahill equipped his little army's arsenal with the unwitting assistance of the Gardaí. Over a period of several months, the gang repeatedly burgled the Garda Technical Bureau in St John's Road in Kilmainham where confiscated illegal firearms were stored. He took a large number of handguns, sawn-off shotguns, grenades and machine-guns. The paranoid General used the weapons for more than mere armed robberies. At one stage he conjured up a bizarre plot to embarrass the police by planting some of the stolen guns in the homes of journalists Vincent Browne and Colm Toibin. The two men had been involved in exposing allegations of State/Gardaí malpractice. Cahill plotted to tip off the cops about the guns. He hoped the Gardaí would search the journalists' houses, 'find' the guns, and then Cahill could reveal that the arms had been planted by the Gardaí in a bid to discredit the writers. It was one of many hare-brained plots concocted by Cahill and it came to nothing. In another stunt Cahill placed a sawn-off shotgun from the stolen arsenal in the boot of his car. He then 'found' it and contacted his solicitor, who in turn called the police. Cahill accused the Gardaí of trying to frame him and said they would probably find that the gun was from their arsenal. In his warped logic, Cahill believed that the discovery of the gun would discredit the cops in the event that he was caught with weapons in the future. He even ordered Martin Foley to phone the *Irish Press* at one stage and tip them off that he had proof that the Gardaí were trying to frame Martin Cahill. Later that night a reporter met a heavily disguised Foley in a pub car park in Tallaght. The General's henchman handed the reporter two guns – a sawn-off shotgun and a pistol – which he claimed two named detectives had given him to plant on Cahill. The burglary was not discovered until September 1983 when the Bureau was being moved to more secure offices in Garda HQ. Garda management didn't acknowledge reports that the guns had been stolen for several years.

In the meantime the Cahill gang were carrying out robberies and aggravated burglaries all over the country. On 29 January 1981, Cahill and Christy Dutton went out on a two-man job. Earlier that morning 45-year-old Dutton had been in the District Court, where he was remanded on continuing bail for a serious assault. Cahill picked him up on a motorbike and less than 20 minutes later they walked into the office of Quintin Flynn Ltd, in the Western Industrial Estate, Clondalkin. The company specialized in the sale and hire of computer games. They held up the company secretary at gunpoint and scooped a total of £5,724, including £1,000 in coins – Cahill didn't believe in leaving loose change behind. As they ran to their motorbike, the pair struggled to carry the heavy bag of coins between them.

A short time later they were spotted by a squad car in Rathmines but they gave it the slip. Forty-five minutes later detectives found the bike abandoned on a pathway along the Dodder River, behind Bushy Park in Terenure. As officers began a search of the area, Cahill and Dutton walked around the corner, carrying two helmets, and were promptly arrested. While in custody, officers from the Technical Bureau took possession of the men's helmets, gloves and jackets, for forensic examination. They also took Dutton's shoes which had melted onto the motorbike's exhaust pipe. Throughout the 48 hours he was being held, Cahill continuously repeated his mantra: 'I don't want to talk to youse men . . . leave me alone.'

At the same time Detective Garda Felix McKenna, one of Cahill's old adversaries, located the money from the robbery in a ditch along the Dodder River. The Gardaí didn't find the guns as they'd been retrieved earlier from another hiding place in the park.

Cahill and Dutton were charged with armed robbery and possession of firearms on 31 January. Detectives ensured that Cahill wouldn't be able to accuse the cops of a frame-up this time. They were going to use their new weapon to put Cahill away – forensic evidence.

Dr James Donovan examined 58 pieces of evidence upon which the State's case would be largely based. He established scientific evidence, linking the criminals to the spot where the Quintin Flynn money was recovered and to the stolen motorbike. The forensic analysis could also make a link between the men's clothes and helmets and the actual crime scene. As far as Detective Inspector Ned Ryan was concerned, Martin Cahill was going down. The General, however, didn't agree.

On 11 October 1981, Cahill and Dutton were returned for trial from the District Court to the Circuit Criminal Court. Later that night Cahill broke into the office of the clerk of the District Court on Chancery Street. He dug out his own file and three others, placed them in the middle of the floor and set them alight. The office was completely destroyed in the blaze. A new file had to be constructed by the Gardaí and the DPP and lodged in the more secure Four Courts. Cahill expressed his dissatisfaction by dispatching two of his men to set fire to that building. The blaze cost the equivalent of at least €1 million in today's values and forced the closure of some of the highest courts in the land for over a month. The last time the building had suffered such an attack was during the Civil War. The Four Courts was again at the centre of a violent conflict – Martin Cahill's war against the State.

The General realized that the arson attacks were not going to prevent his trial from going ahead and he was running out of options. When he consulted his legal advisers and studied the Book of Evidence, it was obvious that the State's case was based mainly on compelling forensic evidence. Dr James Donovan was the witness who could put him away, so Cahill decided that the scientist would have to die.

Dr Donovan was already well known to members of the Cahill gang. He'd testified at Anthony Cahill's trial for the murder of John Copeland, where fibres from the dead man's flat were found on Cahill's clothing. It was this evidence that resulted in Anthony's conviction for burglary. The forensic expert was also due to testify in an aggravated burglary case involving Eddie Cahill and gang member Harry Melia. In 1978 the two violent criminals had attempted to rob Ambrose Sheridan, manager of The Belgard Inn in Tallaght. Sheridan and his wife were badly beaten with iron bars and kidnapped from their home. A jacket Eddie had left behind provided the forensic key which clinched the State's case against him.

Martin Cahill first considered abducting and killing the scientist or assassinating him in the street but decided there was too great a risk of being caught. He then looked to the example of the IRA. They had been using car bombs as an effective murder weapon in the North and Britain. A booby-trap device would get rid of Cahill's enemy and he reasoned that the Provos would be blamed because they also had a motive.

Cahill and his henchmen began to watch Dr Donovan's movements and soon worked out his routine. The scientist was provided with an armed Garda driver only when he was testifying in court – the rest of the time he had no protection. Every morning he left his home shortly after 8 a.m. and travelled the same route to the Phoenix Park.

According to a report on the investigation, which emerged for the first time while researching this book, a total of seven individuals were later identified as being involved in the bomb plot. A number of named informants, including one of the men involved, revealed that Cahill had approached INLA members Thomas Healy and Thomas McCarton and offered them £5,000 to make the bomb. Healy, who was described as a van driver from Clondalkin in south-west Dublin, was well known as an armed robber who worked with criminal gangs in the city. In 1977, he was convicted in the Special Criminal Court on charges of possessing firearms with intent to endanger life. McCarton, an ex-Provo from Belfast, had been jailed in the late 1970s. He was part of a team sent to murder the founder of the IRSP, Seamus Costello, in the first of many internecine INLA feuds. Following his release, McCarton moved to live in Crumlin, beside his friend Martin Foley, and took part in heists with the Cahill gang. According to the documents, both men agreed to help Cahill as long as he gave an undertaking that blame for the 'operation' would not be passed onto the INLA. At one meeting a well-placed informant quoted Cahill as saying the scientist 'will have to be done and we [Cahill's gang] will see that he is put away'.

Henry, Christy and Larry Dunne were also involved in the plot. According to the confidential information, the Dunnes were asked to obtain explosives for the bomb in November 1981. Christy Dunne bought a small consignment of explosive from an underworld arms-dealer who was based in the north inner-city. The dealer had been a member of Saor Eire.

A device was constructed which Cahill and another associate then attached to Dr Donovan's car outside his home on the night of 24 November. The following morning Dr Donovan was driving to work when he heard what he later described as a slow, rolling explosion. In his rear-view mirror, he also saw a flash on the driver's side of the car. Donovan pulled in and examined underneath the car but could see no damage. The explosive substance had been faulty. The scientist had no idea that he had been the victim of a bomb attempt and passed it off as a mechanical fault.

Martin Cahill, his associate Noel Lynch, Healy and two of the Dunne brothers then recruited INLA member Gerry Roche, who was a bomb-making specialist. From Dun Laoghaire, Roche was described in Special Branch reports as an 'extremely dangerous terrorist' who was one of the founder members of the INLA. Acknowledged for his unique 'leadership and organisational abilities', Roche was the INLA's Chief of Staff, for two terms in the 1970s and 1980s. Three years earlier he was suspected of plotting to murder the British Ambassador, when he placed a radio-controlled bomb under the Ambassador's church seat. Luckily it failed to explode. In 1981 Roche had served a short sentence for taking part in riots outside the British Embassy in Dublin, in support of IRA hunger-strikers in the Maze H Blocks. He gave Cahill a quantity of gel-ignite and the components which McCarton used to make a second bomb. This time there would be no mistakes.

In the early hours of 6 January 1982, Cahill and his associates fixed the bomb under Dr Donovan's car. At 8.30 a.m. it exploded with devastating consequences and sparked a new crisis for the Government. Over sixty detectives were assigned to the investigation. It involved one of the biggest trawls of the criminal and terrorist community yet seen. Within weeks Gardaí had a full picture of how the crime was organized and who had been involved. Martin Cahill, Noel Lynch, Thomas Healy, Gerry Roche and Henry and Christy Dunne were among ten suspects arrested for questioning about the outrage under the Offences Against the State Act.

Detectives were forced to drag Cahill kicking and screaming from his flat in Kevin Street. At Ballyfermot Station it took ten Gardaí to pin him down to get his finger-prints. When they tried to take his mugshot he rubbed the finger-print ink all over his face. They never got the picture. From then on Cahill began disguising his face from public view, covering it with his hand or wearing balaclavas. Whenever the police raided his home over the next 12 years they were met by a grinning Al Jolson look-alike. The police had very few decent pictures of the General, which meant that most of them didn't know what he looked like. Throughout the rest of his detention, Cahill sat in a corner with his hands over his face repeating the mantra: 'I don't want to talk to any of these men'.

No one was ever charged with the bombing because, ironically, there was no forensic evidence to link any of the suspects with the crime. The assassination attempt should have been a wake-up call but there were no new measures for a more targeted approach to tackling the growing menace of organized crime.

The need for serious action was reinforced two days after the bombing when an elderly security manager, Gerard Crowley, was shot dead when he tackled robbers stealing the payroll delivery at Clerys' Department Store in O'Connell Street. A month later the INLA gunned down another unarmed policeman. Garda Patrick Reynolds, who was attached to Dr Donovan's local station in Tallaght, died on 20 February after he was shot in the back by the gang. Reynolds and four colleagues had been sent to investigate suspicious activity at a flat in Avonbeg Gardens. Two days earlier the gang, led by notorious INLA member Sean 'Bap' Hughes from Belfast, had carried out an armed robbery in Askeaton, County Limerick. The brutal murder of another Garda, so soon after the bomb attack and the killing of the security manager, put a huge strain on already over-stretched resources – which more than suited Martin Cahill and his mob.

For the gang it was business as usual. A few days after his release from custody in February 1982, Cahill took part in a robbery from the Allied Irish Bank in Drumcondra, during which a security guard was shot and injured. Three months later, a teenager called Gerard Morgan was shot dead in Crumlin after one of the men involved in the robbery accused Morgan's brother of 'stealing' his share of the loot, which had been hidden in a local garden. On 12 February, Thomas Healy and another man, Sean McKeon, were arrested and charged with armed robbery in Clane, County Kildare. The INLA man was jailed for 12 years for robbery and possessing a .38 revolver. In April, the General's gang held the family of an amusement arcade manager hostage in Clonmel, County Tipperary, and robbed £4,500. Some hours later Cahill and his associates dumped the body of their pal Tony Doran on a road in Clondalkin. On the way back to Dublin, he'd drunk a bottle of brandy and choked on his own vomit.

On 16 July, the gang struck again when four armed and masked men held up the staff in the post office sorting office in Mallow, County Cork. The blaggers – including Martin and Eddie Cahill and Michael and John Cunningham – got away with over £116,000 in cash (over €400,000 today). On 3 August, they raided the home of another arcade manager in Ardmore, County Waterford, during which the victims were assaulted and tied up. The gang stole jewellery, cash and a firearm. A month later they scored another spectacular jackpot when they got away with £133,000 in cash. This time a member of the gang simply walked into the Central Sorting Office at Sheriff Street in Dublin, dressed as a postman. The cheeky crook had no need for a gun. He told the duty clerk that he was there to collect the money for post offices in Tallaght, Clondalkin and Lucan. The only use his trigger finger got that day was signing the dispatch sheet, as he was handed three cash bags.

The bomb attack on Dr Donovan earned Cahill a reputation among the Gardaí and the underworld as one of the country's most formidable and dangerous criminals – but he was about to commit his most audacious robbery yet.

The Thomas O'Connor and Sons jewellery factory in Harold's Cross in Dublin, which supplied jewellers' shops throughout the country, was an Aladdin's cave for an ambitious robber. In January 1983, John Traynor brought Cahill information which set in train one of the most spectacular robberies in Irish criminal history. For months the Coach had been nurturing a relationship with an inside man who worked for O'Connor's. The corrupt employee was selling Traynor small quantities of uncut jewels and gold dust he'd pilfered from the factory. Traynor showed Cahill a matchbox full of gold dust which the employee had given him, worth £1,000. 'I told him that if this was what you could pick up off the floor in a tiny box then imagine what you would get if you robbed the place,' Traynor later recalled. The employee had agreed to provide photographs and detailed plans of the security system and lay-out of O'Connor's, in return for a share of the loot.

O'Connor's had been a source of intense interest to Cahill and other criminal groups for some time. The IRA had cased the factory, but abandoned their plans because the high-tech security systems made it practically impregnable. In 1982 Henry Dunne had also considered hitting the place. To get around the security, his team had planned to dress as Gardaí and simply walk in and rob it. Henry also discussed the job with Cahill and they made a half-hearted attempt to tunnel underneath the factory but only succeeded in alerting the Gardaí. Detectives from the Serious Crime Squad had staked out the premises, on and off for a number of months, but gave up when no one showed.

Studying the data supplied by the informer, Cahill began working on a plan to hit the factory. Over the next six months, he planned every aspect of the O'Connor's heist, including organizing a fleet of stolen cars and a van. Traynor and Cahill also did the surveillance, sitting in a park across the road. Cahill assembled a group of 12 criminal associates to take part in the job. He could no longer look to his immediate family to make up the bulk of the team. His brothers Eddie and John were both in prison, and his brother-in-law, Hughie Delaney, had been jailed in January, as had Harry Melia. Henry Dunne had also been jailed in February. A month later, 31-year-old Anthony Cahill died from a drug overdose in prison. Martin dedicated the O'Connor's heist to his memory.

Cahill drummed every last detail of the job into the gang members, making them repeat over and over again what each individual had to do. It was during this job that the hoods nicknamed him 'the General' because of his military approach. Cahill's second-in-command was John Cunningham, and they dubbed him 'the Colonel'. The other members of the O'Connor's team included Cahill's brother Michael, brother-in-law John Foy, Noel Lynch, Christy Dutton, Thomas McCarton, Martin Foley, Seamus 'Shavo' Hogan and Jimmy Edgeworth. In 2010, at the age of 73, Edgeworth would become the oldest person ever convicted of heroin-trafficking in Ireland.

Armed with the inside information, the General decided to do the robbery on Tuesday, 26 July 1983 because most of the staff would be on holidays. Cahill even planned an alibi for the raid because he knew he would be one of the Gardaí's prime suspects. For two days beforehand he made himself as conspicuous as possible. He staged a one-man picket outside the Department of Justice and the Dáil, protesting about forensic evidence connected to the Clondalkin robbery, which he claimed had been planted on him.

On the Sunday before the robbery, Traynor called to see Michael Egan, an aluminium window-fitter from County Offaly, who lived on Sundrive Road in Crumlin. Egan was a 'Walter Mitty' character who was drawn to the company of flash criminals like Traynor and the fraudster was happy to exploit him. Egan was told that Cahill needed to hide a van in the workshop at the rear of the house which was accessed by an alleyway. There was 'a small stroke going down' and members of the gang would be hiding there the night before. The following morning, at exactly 9 a.m., Egan was to open the workshop doors.

On the evening of the robbery the gang gathered in the Dropping Well pub in Milltown in Dublin. On Cahill's orders, they turned up dressed like a football team and he handed each one a sports bag. Inside each bag were a handgun, balaclava and gloves. The sports bags also carried an assortment of hand-grenades, smoke bombs, walkie-talkie radios and coal sacks for the loot. Nothing was overlooked.

The members of the 'soccer' team broke into the O'Connor's complex from the rear and hid in a boiler house that was not alarmed. The following morning Cahill and the rest of the gang watched as the manager arrived to open up. When he turned off the security system and opened the gates for the staff, the gang made their move. Once inside, they rounded up the employees as they arrived and locked them in a room. A car and a van were driven into the complex with other gang members on board. Cahill remained outside on his motorbike controlling the operation on a walkie-talkie. Other hoods sat in two cars on nearby roads, watching for Garda patrols. The O'Connor's job was a flawless operation. Within 35 minutes, they removed the contents of the strong room, including gold bars, gems, diamonds and thousands of gold rings. The haul weighed over half a ton and was valued between £1.5 million and £2 million (€4.5 million and €6 million in today's values). After the robbery, O'Connor's was forced to close down, with the loss of over a hundred jobs.

As the gang jumped into their vehicles Cahill set off a smoke-grenade to warn staff not to call the police. Then he led his convoy out into the morning rush-hour traffic. At the same time a car was set on fire two miles away in Walkinstown. Cahill believed the decoy would send the Gardaí in the wrong direction. The loot was driven to the workshop and Egan closed the doors behind the gang.

Cahill, Cunningham, Traynor and Lynch spent the following day and night sorting through the mesmerizing array of gold and jewels. At one stage they were almost caught when two detectives, who were hunting for the robbery gang, were heard searching the alleyway behind the workshop. If they'd decided to search the building there would have been a shoot-out – Cahill and his men were all armed and ready to open fire.

While the loot was being sorted, Traynor took a break and went for a coffee in nearby Crumlin Shopping Centre. As he walked in, a detective he knew strode towards him with a broad smile. Traynor reckoned his number was up. But instead of clasping handcuffs on the fraudster, the cop was anxious to share the good news – Shamie Dunne had been caught red-handed by the Drug Squad earlier that morning. They'd burst into his luxury apartment in Milltown and found him cutting up 32 ounces of high-quality heroin.

Despite his difficulties with the law, Dunne still helped out his old friend by putting him in touch with London fence Les Beavis. The Dunnes had done plenty of business with Beavis, who bought jewels that had been stolen in various robberies or handed over as payment for drugs from them. He was one of Scotland Yard's 'most wanted' criminals. On the black market the O'Connor's haul was worth only a fraction of its legitimate value. Eventually Cahill and Traynor agreed to sell the sapphires, rubies, emeralds and diamonds to Beavis for £100,000. The money was divided equally among the gang members, who also had a bag of gold each which the fence agreed to buy for £40,000 a go. Some gang members opted to swap their gold for heroin and cannabis, through contacts in Manchester's Quality Street Gang. The Dunnes had also introduced Cahill to the English mob.

Over the next six weeks the gold and jewels were smuggled to London on the Cork to Swansea ferry, concealed in the panels of a car. The operation was a complete success. Some time later Cahill sold Beavis another bag of gold from the robbery haul. This time a mechanic from South Dublin, who was on the periphery of the gang, agreed to do the run. The gold was hidden in the car and taken on the same route to London. However, when the door panels were opened it was discovered that the loot had been 'stolen' from the robbers. What happened next became part of gangland folklore and added to the General's reputation as a sadistic thug.

The mechanic made the fatal mistake of not contacting his boss to offer an explanation. Instead he stayed in London for two weeks. His reluctance to face the music convinced the General that the mechanic was guilty. When he eventually surfaced, Cahill had him abducted and taken to a derelict house in Rathmines, where he interrogated the suspect for several hours.

'Tell me what you done with the stuff and who ya gave it to,' the General demanded, over and over, as the mechanic was slapped around by two of his henchmen. The terrified driver protested his innocence, as he was knocked to the ground. Cahill produced a staple gun as he stood over the suspected thief, who was pinned down by the henchmen. He stapled each of the mechanic's fingers to the wooden floor. Before he stapled a finger, the General asked the same question and each time the terrified suspect screamed that he didn't do it.

Cahill then produced a claw-hammer and two, six-inch nails. He placed the point of the nail in the palm of the man's stapled hand and held the hammer in the air. He repeated his question. When he got the same answer, Cahill hammered the nail down, as the suspect let out a blood-curdling cry. The General struck again, punching the nail into the floor. Then he moved to the other side of his victim. As he asked the question again, Cahill ignored the agonized pleas for mercy. He drove the second nail through the other hand and completed the crucifixion.

When the harrowing ordeal was over Cahill and his henchmen were satisfied the mechanic was innocent. No one could endure such torture for a mere £40,000. The General's court of rough justice had found the man not guilty. But he had to endure even more excruciating pain as Cahill used a pinch-bar to pull the nails out of his hands. The General gave his victim some rags to soak up the blood and brought him to the casualty unit of Meath Hospital. The mechanic never made an official complaint to the Gardaí. One crucifixion had been enough. As Cahill later commented, 'People remember pain. A bullet through the head is too easy. You think of the pain before you do wrong again.' It sent a clear message to other gangsters that the General would tolerate nothing less than total loyalty.

It hadn't taken long for word to filter through the underworld network about who was responsible for the O'Connor's job. From his many underworld informants, Detective Inspector Ned 'the Buffalo' Ryan, the man in charge of the Garda investigation, soon pieced together the whole plot. His men had even succeeded in recovering some of the stolen loot when they dug up a grave in Mount Jerome cemetery, across the road from the factory. A special squad was formed to target the gang and all the suspects, with the exception of Cahill, were arrested and questioned. Much to Ryan's intense annoyance, his superiors would not give him permission to arrest the gang leader. The Buffalo always maintained that the top brass held the bizarre belief that by arresting Cahill they would in some way be giving him public recognition for a job well done. But the police were not the only ones interested in Cahill's landmark stroke.

A week after the heist, two senior IRA figures in Dublin arranged a meeting with the General and Traynor in a coffee shop in Crumlin Shopping Centre. When the niceties were out of the way the Provos

got down to business. They demanded half of the O'Connor's haul.
The IRA badly needed funds to fuel their killing machine and, as a
result, were also planning a number of high-profile kidnappings (see
Chapter 12). Cahill was having none of it and smiled across the table at
them: 'If you want gold then go out and rob yer own gold like we did.'
The Provos were agitated by Cahill's complete lack of fear and respect.
They reminded him that there would be very serious repercussions if he
failed to comply with their demand. The General stood up and moved
his face closer to the IRA men: 'You do your strokes and we'll do ours.
Ye'r not gettin' a fuckin' penny.' Then he stormed out of the coffee
shop with Traynor in tow.

The General and his army were on a collision course with their terrorist counterparts and the Provos had no intention of letting Cahill off
the hook. Nor could they allow his temerity and lack of respect go
without sanction. They bided their time and began building up intelligence on the General's large criminal network. They met with the
INLA and other criminals to share information on Cahill's gang and to
ascertain what they had done with the O'Connor's money. One of their
sources was the General's bomb-maker, Thomas McCarton. He was
supposed to take part in the robbery but had failed to turn up. When
McCarton demanded a share of the loot anyway, Cahill refused. The
Provos soon had an excuse to make their move.

The Concerned Parents Against Drugs (CPAD)'s tactic of patrolling
the streets of the inner-city communities and marching on the homes
of known pushers and addicts had resulted in the latter's exodus to the
relative peace of the working-class suburbs. The area worst hit by the
migrating junkies was Crumlin, where the heroin plague quickly spread.
In February 1984, the CPAD was organized in Crumlin and immediately found itself on a collision course with the large local criminal
population. The principal organizers of the group were IRA/Sinn Féin
member John Noonan from Tallaght and John 'Whacker' Humphrey, a
convicted armed robber with close ties to the republican movement.

Rumours soon began to circulate that Cahill's gang had invested the
O'Connor's loot in drugs. The gossip was corroborated by the fact that
some of them were closely associated with families suspected of heroin-
dealing, and Jimmy Edgeworth, Martin Foley and others were involved
in the drug trade themselves. It was also widely known that the Dunnes

and the Cahills had been partners-in-crime. Curiously, Christy Dunne agreed to assist the Provos in their investigation of the heroin trade. He nominated several drug-dealers but failed to mention anyone from his own family circle, even though Larry and Shamie were facing drug charges. Instead loyal Bronco named Cahill and members of his mob.

On the night of 19 February, the CPAD marched on the homes of suspected drug-dealers in Crumlin. The protesters also stopped outside the homes of several criminals suspected of involvement in the trade. One of those visited was Shavo Hogan's in Rutland Grove. The robber had a blazing row with Humphrey and other protesters on his doorstep. The marchers then made their way to the home of Thomas Gaffney, whose family was heavily involved in heroin-pushing in the area. Gaff-ney, a drug-abuser with a reputation for violence, was a close friend of both Cahill and Foley. Gaffney and his brothers sold heroin for Ma Baker, a notorious drug-dealer from Crumlin, whose family were long-time friends of Martin Cahill. The granny had no scruples and paid children to sell her 'gear'. She reputedly even sold it to her own kids. Gaffney confronted the CPAD marchers and exchanged threats with Whacker Humphrey. Later that night, Foley and Hogan ran into a CPAD picket in Rutland Grove and ended up in a fist-fight.

As tensions rose, Cahill and his gangsters met the following morning and decided to take retaliatory action. The General decided to organize a counter-protest and hurriedly formed the preposterously named Concerned Criminal Action Committee (CCAC). The 60-strong criminal group then marched on the homes of several CPAD members to intimidate them. The following night the homes of a number of CPAD members, including Humphrey's, were smashed up. Armed and masked men then ambushed two other activists in St Theresa's Gardens, shooting one of them in the legs. The General had declared war.

The CCAC gave press interviews as the area became a tinderbox. Foley and Hogan, who acted as spokesmen, complained that the CPAD pickets and marches were affecting the activities of 'ordinary decent criminals'. Cahill gave an interview to *Irish Times* journalist Padraig Yeates, on the understanding that he would not be identified, commenting: 'I hate drugs; they have ruined members of my family.'

After a number of other confrontations, meetings were held between the CPAD, represented by the Provo John Noonan, and the CCAC spokesmen Foley, Hogan and Gaffney. At the peace talks it was agreed that any further incidents would be sorted out, with each side carrying out its own investigation into the source of the problem to prevent an escalation. The gangsters left, happy that they had secured a truce. But the terrorists had other ideas.

On 11 March, Tommy Gaffney was abducted by a four-man IRA gang, outside the Park Inn pub in Harold's Cross. The General's friend was taken out of Dublin and brought to a safe house, where he remained handcuffed to a chair for 12 days. He was repeatedly questioned about the drug trade by the cash-hungry Provos. But they were more interested in Martin Cahill and the O'Connor's loot.

The Gaffney kidnapping seriously escalated an already tense situation. Extra Gardaí and Special Task Force units were drafted into South Dublin to avert an outbreak of all-out warfare between the two sides. Hogan and Foley were taken in for questioning about the shooting of two CPAD members. The CCAC also marched on the homes of anti-drug protesters. Threats were made and shots were fired at the homes of republicans suspected of involvement in the abduction. As the days went by, with no word about Gaffney, Cahill believed that the IRA had murdered him. The General took the precaution of moving between safe houses, to avoid an assassination attempt. Then the Provos launched another strike in the simmering war.

On the morning of 22 March 1984, Martin Foley was in bed at home in Cashel Avenue, Crumlin, when four IRA men burst into his home. The super-fit gangster put up a ferocious fight with his attackers. After a violent struggle, the IRA men managed to put handcuffs on Foley and drag him to a waiting van. The Provo kidnap gang included university graduate and self-employed butcher Sean Hick from upmarket Glenageary Avenue, Dun Laoghaire. Twenty-two-year-old Liam O'Dwyer, from Castleknock, was also university-educated and from a family, later described by his defence counsel, 'of impeccable respectability'. In contrast, the youngest member of the snatch squad was Derek Dempsey, a petty criminal from Raheen Drive in Ballyfermot who was a recent recruit to the IRA. The leader of the team was 33-year-old bar manager James Dunne, from Finglas, north-west Dublin, a long-standing IRA member.

As the kidnappers drove onto the Crumlin Road, they were spotted by a Garda patrol car that had been alerted to the disturbance in the area. The cops followed the van as it drove at the speed limit in the direction of Sundrive Road. Other Garda cars joined the slow-moving convoy. When a squad car moved to stop the van on the South Circular Road the IRA gang tore off, sparking a dramatic high-speed chase. By then, all nearby police units had been alerted about the Foley abduction. They joined in the pursuit as the van drove towards the Phoenix Park. As it sped through the main entrance from Conyngham Road, Dempsey and O'Dwyer fired shots at the pursuing patrol cars. Two unarmed officers had a narrow escape when a bullet bounced off the windscreen wiper in front of them. The van was eventually hemmed in on Wellington Road by all the squad cars that had descended on the area. The gang got out and tried to drag Foley with them but abandoned the idea. They fired shots at the police as they made a run for it, down steps leading onto Conyngham Road. But they were out-gunned and out-numbered, as over a hundred Gardaí arrived on the scene. The gang surrendered when members of the STF returned fire on them with Uzi machine-guns. Twenty-five minutes after it had begun, the kidnap drama was over.

Foley, who was still in his underpants, was battered and bloodied, but safe. He was brought to hospital and treated for a fractured jaw and several cuts and bruises. For the first time in his criminal career he was glad to see the police. It had been a fruitful day's work for the Gardaí – an entire IRA Active Service Unit had been caught red-handed. But it was a devastating blow for the Provos, who had already lost five members in another shoot-out with the STF seven months earlier (see Chapter 12).

Later that night, the Provos released Tommy Gaffney. Before they set their hostage free they told him they were releasing him on the condition that he told the Gardaí he had been abducted by a group 'concerned about the chronic drug problem in Dublin'. Shortly after midnight on the morning of 23 March he was left near Abbeyfeale, County Limerick.

Gaffney's release, Foley's rescue and the capture of an IRA cell brought one of gangland's most dangerous episodes to an uneasy end. An all-out bloodbath had been avoided, but the Provos also told Gaffney to deliver a final message to the General: 'Tell Cahill that we will never kidnap him – we'll stiff him on the street.'

Shortly after the incident, Cahill gave an interview to the *Irish Times* in which he claimed that the crisis had been caused because the Provos wanted a share of the O'Connor's loot and that it had nothing to do with drugs: 'They can't go out and rob for themselves any longer. They have to rob ordinary criminals who have done the work and taken the chances. There's nothing lower than someone who robs a robber.' Cahill confirmed that he had been prepared to go to war with the Provos in Dublin. He was telling the underworld that he was afraid of no one. The General's exploits gave him an air of invincibility. His reputation was reaching legendary status in the underworld. His attack on Dr James Donovan, his war with the police, facing down the Provos, the crucifixion and the O'Connor's heist had all made him seem untouchable.

As tensions eased Cahill got back to life as normal. He used some of his ill-gotten gains to buy a four-bedroom detached house at Cowper Downs, an upmarket corner of Rathmines. It was the last place anyone expected the General to live, but it was close to his beloved Hollyfield. Although officially on the dole, he paid £80,000 in cash – approximately ten years' dole money and almost €250,000 in today's values – for his new home. And there was nothing anyone could do about it. He registered the house in Noel Lynch's name. Cahill was also a keen pigeon fancier and he paid tens of thousands of pounds for racing birds and, much to the chagrin of his neighbours, built a large loft in the back garden. The General's pets were an unwelcome sight in the quiet, middle-class neighbourhood but no one was in a position to complain. Life was good for the General, but he still faced the prospect of a lengthy prison sentence.

Martin Cahill and Christy Dutton stood trial for the Clondalkin armed robbery before Judge Frank Martin in May 1984. The General was still determined not to go down without a fight. For the first two days of the four-day hearing, gang members crowded into the courtroom to try to intimidate the jury. At one stage two of Cahill's men suddenly began shouting abuse. 'Martin Cahill, ye'r only a dirt bird drug-dealer who killed my sister,' one of them roared. 'Ye'r a murderin' bastard,' shouted the second heckler, as they were both herded out of the court by Gardaí. It was a blatant stunt to have the trial aborted, on the grounds that the comments would prejudice the jury. Cahill had pulled a similar stunt during the 1970s. On that occasion a man stood up in the public gallery and confessed to the judge and jury that he had committed the burglary and not Cahill. It worked and Cahill eventually won an acquittal. But this time, Judge Martin saw through the blatant stunt and allowed the trial to continue. Next Cahill sacked his defence team and tried to conduct the case himself, cross-examining Garda witnesses in the box. After a half-day on his feet, however, he realized that he was no 'Rumpole of the Bailey' and re-appointed his legal representatives.

The most dramatic moment in the trial came when Dr James Donovan was called to give the evidence which had almost cost him his life. Ironically this was to be his first appearance in court since the bomb attack and the significance was lost on no one, especially Cahill. James Donovan had courageously returned to work several months earlier. The tough Cork man was determined to show the gangsters that they had not won. In October 1982, evidence from his laboratory had helped to convict Eddie Cahill and Harry Melia, when they were tried in the refurbished Central Criminal Court. They'd each received seven years.

There was total silence when the heroic public servant entered the courtroom. He was flanked by his armed Garda bodyguards, who were now with him round-the-clock. Despite being in agony from his injuries, Dr Donovan was determined to deliver his forensic evidence in this particular case. As he hobbled on his crutches to the witness box, he passed Cahill sitting in the dock with Dutton. The General was studiously avoiding making eye contact with his victim. Judge Frank Martin broke the silence and conveyed to the scientist the court's sympathies for his injuries and congratulated him on his courage in returning to work.

In the end neither a bomb nor intimidation helped Cahill to win his freedom. When the case for the State closed on 1 June, defence counsel for the two gangsters argued the technical legal point that the State had failed to prove a vital ingredient in the charge of armed robbery – in her evidence to the court, the victim of the robbery had not been asked if she had been put in fear of her life during the heist. In the circumstances Judge Martin was left with no option but to acquit the two men. Cahill couldn't believe his luck. The law had worked in his favour.

Afterwards Cahill celebrated with his henchmen in the Tilted Wig pub, across the road from the Four Courts. He sat grinning at the downcast members of the Garda investigation team who had come so close to ending Cahill's criminal career. As he got up to leave, Cahill spotted his adversary, Detective Inspector Dick Murphy, who was in charge of the case. Murphy had been the first, and only, cop who ever got Cahill to admit to a crime. With a beaming smile Cahill shouted across the bar: 'Hey, Murphy! Get up ya. See ya again.' Then he gave the detectives the two fingers and walked out. Martin Cahill's reputation had grown to almost mythic proportions in gangland.

Two months later, on 3 July 1984, the four IRA members went on trial in the Special Criminal Court for kidnapping Martin Foley. They were also charged with shooting at Garda Tony Tighe, possessing firearms with intent to endanger life and using them to resist arrest. In the three months since his abduction, Foley had been placed in the rather awkward position of receiving 24-hour armed police protection. It was a situation that both sides could have done without. Foley had declared his determination to testify against the men who he believed had intended murdering him. When his INLA friends suggested he might develop amnesia about the incident, he'd stubbornly refused. In the hours after the abduction he formally identified the four Provos on an identity parade. Gardaí had to pull him back when he'd spat at the terrorists and tried to punch one of them. He'd also made three detailed statements. In the meantime, however, the Provos had sent him a message. If Foley didn't keep his mouth shut he would receive another visit, but this time he wouldn't be going for a drive.

By the time Foley was called as the principal prosecution witness, he had suffered a complete change of attitude. When prosecuting counsel asked the Viper to recall the events at his home on the morning of the incident he replied: 'I was half asleep and I can't remember what I did. I don't know if I was standing up or still in bed. I remember some noises in the bedroom. What I remember after that was sitting in a patrol car in dense fog with, I think, a lot of police around me. I was on a tarmac road in dense fog and there were fields and trees and a lot of uniformed Gardaí around.' When asked if he recalled making a statement to the Gardaí he replied: 'I don't remember. I remember one of the Gardaí telling me that I had been kidnapped or something.'

The court agreed to an application from the prosecution to have Foley declared a hostile witness so that they could then cross-examine him. In criminal trials counsel cannot cross-examine their own witnesses, unless they have been deemed to be hostile. When pressed again about his signed statements, Foley claimed: 'I was in court when it was read out and it is completely untrue.'

In Foley's original statement, he had been very clear about what had happened during the incident. 'The van stopped and one of them dragged me on to the roadway and he wanted to bring me with him, but my legs were taped and I fell on the ground. He [one of the Provos] ran away from me, the tape was down from my eyes and I could see everything. I was in the Phoenix Park. I could see the four men running to the left of the van, going down a hill, towards the wall of the Park. They were firing shots. I could see uniformed guards running after them. There were detectives there with guns in their hands. It was foggy but I could see everything that was happening.'

In any event the prosecution had overwhelming evidence with which to prove their case against the Provos. On 26 July, they were found guilty of kidnapping the cowardly gangster. Derek Dempsey received a nine-year sentence; Sean Hick and James Dunne got seven years each and Liam O'Dwyer got five.

With the case out of the way, an uneasy peace returned to Gangland and it was business as usual for the mobsters. A week after the trial Martin Foley married his girlfriend, Pauline Quinn. Both the Provos and criminals stood back from the brink and got on with their separate wars. But the Provos would not forget the former burglar from the rundown tenement who had humiliated them. For his part the General was on top of the world, and could barely keep the sneering smile off his face.

11. Murder in Gangland

The drug trade transformed Gangland and, in the process, undermined the old ethics of so-called 'ordinary decent criminals'. As former professional armed robber and drug-dealer Dave 'Myler' Brogan once lamented: 'When drugs came everything changed. There was no loyalty and people who had once been friends started turning guns on each other because one thought the other had ripped him off. Fuck it, it just wasn't worth the hassle any more.'

The smashing of the Dunne criminal organization was a victory of sorts. But while they'd been taken off the stage, the demand for heroin had been consolidated and so had the supply network they'd created. Putting the family out of business had created a new problem – and pushed Gangland to a different level. The Drug Squad's John McGroarty, the man who played a major role in the Dunnes' downfall, explained: 'Putting away the Dunnes led to a fragmentation of the drug trade and led to a multiplicity of gangs, who saw this as an opportunity to get into the big time. It ushered in a new phase in the story of organized crime in this country.'

As a steady stream of mobsters decommissioned their balaclavas and getaway cars for the much more lucrative narcotics trade, a new gangland phenomenon was created – the contract killing. The prodigious profits from the trade made people greedy and they began using violence and murder to protect their interests. The gun became the corporate tool of choice for the ambitious gangland businessman.

By comparison the armed robbery gangs which had previously dominated the crime scene had little to fight about, as long as the proceeds of a job were divided up equally. Any rows were generally sorted out with a 'straightener' and the number of criminals being murdered by their counterparts was very low. Their preferred victims were the Gardaí, security guards and innocent bystanders.

In the early years of the drug trade, the small number of gangs involved observed the equivalent of gentlemen's agreements when it came to business and territory. The Dunnes rarely used guns to sort out issues over drug patches – as there was plenty to go around for everyone. Former *Irish Times* journalist Padraig Yeates was one of the first reporters to cover the emerging gangland in the early 1980s, at a time when the media, like the Government, was preoccupied with the Troubles. Yeates commented on the arrival of the contract killer: 'Dublin was still quite a small place and everyone knew everyone else. If there was a row over turf the criminals knew each other and could meet to sort it out. But as the years progressed there was a proliferation of gangs and the scene became much more fragmented and violent.'

By the time Larry and Mickey Dunne made their dire predictions about the underworld's violent future, the first gangland executions had already taken place.

In 1983, a hash-dealer called Gerard Hourigan officially became the first victim of a professional gangland hit man. A small-time crook from Ballymun, Hourigan was typical of hundreds of other young men who would perish in gangland in the years of bloodshed that followed. He was brash, ambitious and didn't mind whose toes he stood on, as he made his way to the big time. The 25-year-old from Balcurris Road was in charge of distributing hashish and heroin in the grim flats complex for Myler Brogan. Ballymun, once seen as a revolutionary new approach to public housing in the 1960s, had become a haven for junkies and their suppliers. The estimated 1,000 heroin addicts living in the concrete wasteland added to the grinding misery of its inhabitants. But for Hourigan's boss this was a hugely lucrative patch and one that Brogan would not give up without a fight. Myler, who was in his thirties, was a former member of Saor Eire and a key member of a large drug-smuggling network that controlled the narcotics trade in North Dublin.

Brogan's partners were Tommy Savage and Michael Weldon, hardened criminals and terrorists from Swords. Savage, nicknamed 'the Zombie' because of his unpredictably dangerous personality, was also a former member of Saor Eire who had later joined the INLA. Weldon joined the terrorist group in the late 1970s, while serving as an infantryman in the Irish Army. Described as a 'top-class' soldier, Weldon had been promoted to the rank of corporal. He was suspected of stealing a number of weapons from his battalion, including a rifle and machinegun, which he threw over the barrack wall for 'the cause'. Another

member of the drug gang was INLA man Danny McOwen, from the
north inner-city, who cut his teeth with Savage in Saor Eire.

Brogan, Savage and Weldon, all of whom were associates of the
Dunnes, established major international supply routes for cannabis into
Ireland. Some years later Brogan described to this writer how he established the gang's contacts with hashish producers in Lebanon's Bekaa
Valley and international dealers in Holland: 'I knew people who knew
people and I was introduced to the producers in Lebanon when I travelled there. Savage would never have gotten into the business as much as
he did if it hadn't been for me.'

In Ballymun, Hourigan used local youths to distribute Brogan's
drugs from a club in the basement of the Joseph Plunkett Tower. The
ambitious lieutenant seized an opportunity to branch out on his own,
however, when Myler was arrested in France in January 1983, as part of
a drug investigation. It created a shortage of cannabis in Ballymun and
Hourigan had to source the product elsewhere. He decided to set up his
own operation and began eating into Brogan's patch. He also approached
the Dunnes with a view to doing business and told them of his plans to
oust Brogan. When one of the Dunnes' men warned Hourigan that he
had dangerous ambitions, the young hood arrogantly laughed if off.

Brogan was held for three months but released without charge in
early April. When he returned to resume his role, his old friends in the
Dunne family tipped him off about his former lieutenant's plans for the
future. Myler sent word to Hourigan that he was sacked and that people
were talking about shooting him. In retaliation, Hourigan and his associates raided the home of Brogan's parents in the north inner-city,
looking for the proceeds of drug deals. On 7 April, he robbed Myler's
prized silver BMW from outside the Penthouse pub in Ballymun and
rammed it into a wall. Hourigan returned the crumpled car to its park-
ing spot and visited one of Brogan's henchmen, to let him know what
he had just done.

In September 1992 this writer interviewed Brogan, who had moved
to live in London and had cut his ties with his former partners-in-crime.
Myler revealed how he and two other well-known criminals dealt with
the errant underling: 'We went to see him and gave him a hiding because
he was trying to muscle in on our patch. He was getting too big for his
boots and he had to have manners put on him. I warned him that he was

messing with the wrong people especially Tommy Savage.' Myler then went to his partners in the gang and told them of Hourigan's impertinence. They laughed off the mouthy hood, describing him as a 'souped-up granny-basher' and told Myler to deal with it himself. But then Brogan claimed the situation changed: 'Savage and the lads heard that Hourigan was going around laughing at them.' The young drug-dealer sealed his fate with another act of foolhardy bravado. He went looking for members of the gang in Swords, where most of them lived, armed with a handgun and a sawn-off shotgun. Hourigan had taken a step too far.

Shortly after midnight on 10 April, Hourigan and four of his friends returned to Ballymun, after spending the day drinking in the city centre. Earlier he had bragged to his mates about the death threats from his old associates. The young crook joked he'd get a haircut and wear his best suit, so he looked well when he got shot. But the hit man, on the back of a waiting motorbike, wasn't going to give Hourigan the chance to dress up for his execution. The killer got off his bike and fired a shot at the drug-dealer. Hourigan ran for it and tried to hide in the basement club. The hit man followed him inside. He fired two shots at close range into Hourigan's chest, killing him instantly. Then he calmly walked out and jumped on the back of the waiting bike.

When we met in London, Brogan was adamant that he had not been responsible for Ireland's first gangland murder. 'I was one of the prime suspects and I was lifted for it but I had absolutely nothing to do with it. I heard about it a few days later,' he claimed. 'After that I got out of the hash business and went back to robbing.' Savage and Weldon, however, continued in the drug trade and were among the most successful traffickers in the country. By the late 1980s they controlled a large portion of the drugs market in Dublin and Cork.

No one was ever charged with Hourigan's murder, although the Gardaí and the underworld knew who had been involved. During our meetings Brogan named the two hit men, both associates of his, who carried out the murder. Police sources in Dublin later confirmed that the two men were the prime suspects. Gangland murders would remain the toughest crimes to solve. Professional hit men have a tendency to disappear behind the biggest wall this side of the Wall of China – the wall of silence.

The public didn't realize the significance of the Hourigan murder and it didn't receive much media attention. Less than 24 hours earlier, Sergeant Patrick McLaughlin was shot and fatally injured by two men who called to his home in Dunboyne, County Meath. This time there was no hit man or terrorist gang involved. Two local men, Joseph Green and Thomas McCool, both drunk and with minor grievances against the Sergeant, were responsible for the shooting. They were both subsequently convicted for the murder.

Two months later the gangland hit man struck again. Danny McOwen had fallen out with Savage and Weldon and had set up his own armed robbery gang – the Gang of Six. In 1980, McOwen had refused to take the rap when he and Savage were caught in a stolen car together. McOwen was driving the car at the time and broke with the villains' code that the driver put his hands up for the crime. McOwen also began moving in on their drug-dealing territory. Like Hourigan, McOwen made no secret of his ambition to build a criminal empire. In the process he was making a lot of enemies. He'd also involved himself in a row between associates of a gang led by a young criminal called Gerry Hutch from Buckingham Street, in the north inner-city. One of McOwen's friends had an affair with the girlfriend of a member of the Hutch gang. The criminal concerned was the prime suspect in a number of gangland hits over the following years.

On 7 June, 29-year-old McOwen discovered he was being actively targeted for assassination and went into hiding. But despite his precautions the would-be crime boss was a creature of habit. On the morning of 14 June 1983, he turned up to collect his dole in the Cumberland Street Labour Exchange, in the inner-city. He made the same trip to the city centre every week from the comfortable detached home he'd bought in 1982 at Cloghertown, Clonalvey, County Meath. Although officially unemployed, he paid £25,000 in cash for the house. That morning McOwen collected more than he'd bargained for. As he left the Exchange, a lone gunman suddenly appeared and shot him four times in the head and chest. McOwen died in the street. No one was ever charged with the hit although Gardaí had a number of strong suspects.

On St Stephen's Day 1983, heroin-dealer Eddie Hayden, a former international amateur boxer, also became a gangland murder statistic.

A lone gunman emerged from the shadows as Hayden left a girlfriend's flat in Ballybough, in the north inner-city. The killer, armed with a sawn-off shotgun, blew half Hayden's head away, when he fired at point-blank range. Hayden had been arrested in relation to the McOwen murder six months earlier but it was never established if the two killings were connected. The era of the hit man had arrived.

Hayden was one of 17 people who had been questioned about the McOwen murder. Included among them were McOwen's armed-robber friend George Royle, veteran gangster Eamon Kelly and his protégé, 20-year-old Gerry Hutch. Despite his young age, Hutch was considered to be a serious criminal. The unholy villain would later become known as 'the Monk'. A year earlier Kelly and Hutch had also been arrested in Crumlin, after they were accused of threatening a 17-year-old called Alan Morgan. The teenager had been threatened over money that had been 'stolen' from their associate, after he'd taken part in a hold-up at the Allied Irish Bank in Drumcondra with Martin Cahill in February 1982. The teenager's younger brother, Gerard Morgan, was shot dead on 26 May as he was about to answer the door at the family home in Lismore Road in Crumlin. Investigating Gardaí believed that the murdered youth was mistaken for his older brother. Cahill's associate was later charged with the murder but the case was dropped by the DPP because a witness had refused to testify.

In a Garda file on that case, Eamon Kelly was described as having involvement in 'major criminal activity' and being 'a constant associate of hardened criminals'. 'He [Kelly] has Godfather status among city criminals and through fear and intimidation maintains this status,' it read. The same document contained the following observations on the Monk. 'Although of tender years, Gerard Hutch is much respected and feared by the criminal element on account of his previous exploits and violent disposition. He is full-time involved in the organisation of major crime.' Gardaí had spotted Hutch's 'talent' early on.

Gerard Hutch was born into poverty in Dublin's north inner-city in April 1963. His family lived in a flat in Corporation Buildings, a run-down tenement where a communal toilet served the whole block. In 1971, they moved to a pokey Corporation flat at Liberty House on Railway Street. Like most of his peers, the future criminal mastermind first ran into trouble with the law for petty theft at a very young age. He received his first conviction in the Children's Court when he was eight years old.

Hutch hung out in a gang of tough teenagers who terrorized the city centre in the late 1970s. They were nicknamed 'the Bugsy Malones' after the famous children's spoof gangster movie of the same name, in which the bad guys were armed with machine-guns that fired cream cakes. The Bugsys, however, preferred bullets. As a result of their exploits they attracted considerable media attention. On one occasion Hutch was interviewed for RTÉ radio: 'I can't give up robbin'. If I see money in a car I'm takin' it. I just can't leave it there. If I see a handbag on a seat I'll smash the window and be away before anyone knows what's goin' on. I don't go near people walking along the street . . . they don't have any money on them. They're not worth robbin'.' And when he was asked what he wanted to be when he grew up he giggled: 'I'd like to be serving behind the bank . . . just fill up the bags and jump over the counter.'

Gerry Hutch notched up over thirty convictions for burglary, assault, larceny, car theft, joyriding and malicious damage over the 12 years following his court debut. He was jailed 11 times and served his sentences in the notorious St Lawrence's Industrial School in Finglas, St Patrick's Institution for young offenders and, later, Mountjoy Prison. The institutions were the equivalent of his primary, secondary and third-level education. While inside he taught himself to read and write. From his late teens, Hutch stood out from the rest of his peers as different and much cleverer. He was sensible with the money he stole. When he became a dad for the first time at the age of 18, he paid £10,000 for a house for his new family on Buckingham Street, in the heart of his old neighbourhood. The quiet, intense young man didn't drink and assiduously avoided the heroin scourge that devastated his neighbourhood in the early 1980s. Jem Dixon and his siblings were his first cousins. Several of Hutch's friends became addicts and at least four of them died as a result.

Eamon Kelly and his brother Matt, who were from the north inner-city, first noticed that Hutch was wiser than a lot of the other young thugs in the neighbourhood and decided to take him under their wing. The young Monk ran 'errands' and worked in the Kellys' large carpet business on the North Circular Road. Eamon Kelly was a former member of the Official IRA and an armed robber with a fearsome reputation for violence. Garda intelligence at the time believed that the business was being used as a front for criminal activity.

In 1981, the carpet company was wound up by the High Court and a liquidator was appointed on behalf of the Revenue Commissioners over unpaid taxes. In a controversial, landmark case the liquidator issued proceedings against the brothers, to have them held personally responsible for huge debts. A year later the premises mysteriously burned down.

In November 1982, Hutch's friend Eamon Byrne, a fellow member of the Bugsy Malones, died when he was accidentally shot in the back of the neck by Gardaí during a botched robbery in Dublin docks. Around the same time a criminal mob calling itself the Prisoners' Revenge Group (PRG), of which Martin Cahill, George Mitchell and John Gilligan were leading members, carried out several attacks on prison officers and their homes.

The long-running Kellys case hit the headlines again in 1983 after several people involved were threatened and intimidated by the brothers and their associates. On the first morning of the hearing the home of the leading counsel for the liquidator was targeted in an arson attack. The State's legal team, revenue officials, witnesses and Mr Justice Declan Costello were all given armed police protection for the duration of the hearing.

The Kellys' former accountant, Brendan McGoldrick, who agreed to testify, told the court that he had been threatened with murder if he opened his mouth. He said Matt Kelly and an associate, Mickey Deighan, had made the threats. As a result the two hoods were jailed for contempt of court. The accountant then admitted falsifying company documentation on behalf of the brothers. Gerry Hutch's mentors had such a reputation for violence that McGoldrick was forced to live under armed police protection for several years, as there were fears that a contract had been put out on him.

The court later held that the business of the company was carried on with 'intent to defraud creditors' and for 'other fraudulent purposes'. It ruled that both brothers were 'knowingly parties' to the carrying on of the business in that manner. Both men were held liable for all debts, including a £1.8 million tax bill, and Matt Kelly was made a bankrupt. In 1984 Eamon Kelly, who lived with his family in Clontarf, was charged with stabbing a 21-year-old man in the chest outside the old Workers' Party Club on Dublin's Gardiner Street. He was subsequently convicted of wounding and jailed for ten years. However, the case was appealed and, after a retrial, he was convicted of assault and his original sentence was reduced to three years.

Gerry Hutch was jailed for the last time six months after the McOwen murder, in December 1983, when he got two years for malicious damage. When he was released in May 1985, like all the other gangsters, Hutch promised himself that he would never do time again. But unlike so many of his contemporaries the Monk achieved his ambition. Very soon he had earned a reputation as a clever blagger who carefully planned robberies down to the last detail. But he was also regarded as a potentially dangerous enemy.

Myler Brogan spent much of his criminal career working with Hutch and his brother Eddie. 'We were all good mates for a long time. Gerard was a very cold fish and very calculating. He didn't go looking for trouble and minded his own business but if you fucked with him you were walking on thin ice,' he revealed. 'Whenever they [the Hutches] needed a gun man on a job that they could rely on they came to me. During the '70s and '80s I went on several jobs with Gerard Hutch, Thomas O'Driscoll and others. I was always the first one in the door of the bank or wherever it was we were robbing. In December 1985, we went to rob a security van which was delivering wages at the Initial Laundry in Rathfarnham. It was supposed to be carrying £1 million in cash. There were three of us waiting for it and I ran over and fired a shot into the van to scare the crew and they threw the bags out to us. When we looked inside there was a £1 million all right but it was in cheques and there was just £25,000 in cash.'

The relationship went sour, however, when Brogan failed to come up with the cash he'd agreed to pay for a shop the Hutches were selling in Killarney Street: 'I was supposed to make the money from a couple of strokes but I didn't get it. When I said I wanted out I was told that I would have to answer to Gerard if I didn't pay up. That was when I decided to leave Dublin. I was sick of it.'

Gerry Hutch meanwhile gathered a tightly knit team of other hard-nosed young criminals around him. They were about to make the big time. On the evening of 26 January 1987, the crew of a Securicor van made their last pick-up from the Bank of Ireland at Marino Mart, Fairview in North Dublin. As the front seat observer was getting back into the van, a red BMW pulled up and three armed and masked men jumped out. One of the raiders, armed with a handgun, pointed it in the security guard's face, shouting: 'Get out or I'll blow your fucking head off.' A second raider, armed with a rifle, joined the first. They pulled the security officer from the van and threw him onto the ground. He was kicked and warned to stay down or he'd have his head 'blown off'. At the same time a third raider appeared at the opposite door and pointed a gun at the head of the driver. He was ordered to hand over the keys and get out.

The Monk and one of his accomplices jumped in behind the wheel of the van and they drove off. The other two robbers got into the BMW and followed. They stopped briefly and pushed out a third security officer whom they'd discovered in the vault in the back of the van. The gang drove the van a short distance into school grounds off Griffith Avenue, and unloaded the bags of cash into a waiting car. They vanished as Gardaí were being alerted to the robbery.

Hutch and his crew later met in a safe house to count the cash. They'd expected to get between £25,000 and £100,000. But it took them the whole night to count the money. When they finished the large stack of money came to £1,357,106 (over €3.1 million today). The young villains couldn't believe it – they had just pulled off the largest cash robbery in the history of the State. The Monk and his mates had elevated themselves to the top tier of organized crime. It would be remembered as the Marino Mart job.

Garda intelligence nominated a number of possible suspects for the audacious crime. Martin Cahill, as a matter of course, was high on the list, but even the General was curious to know who had done it. As a consummate professional he could appreciate a skilled job. With Matt Kelly's guidance the Monk took charge of disposing of the money. The plan was to simply lodge it in a number of financial institutions across the Border in Newry, County Down. Hutch used two men to move the cash – Francis Joseph Sheridan and Lonan Patrick Hickey. They were perfect for the job as they weren't known to the police and had no criminal records.

Four days after the robbery, Hutch gave Sheridan £320,000 in cash and told him to hide it in his home. Over the next two weeks, Sheridan received instructions from Hutch, directing him to deliver quantities of the cash to Hickey. In turn Hickey brought the money to Newry, where it was lodged in building society accounts opened by Hickey and Hutch. But the Serious Crime Squad had picked up information about the cash movements and began watching the bagmen.

On the fifth trip to Newry the Garda team investigating the robbery moved in on Hickey. He had £80,000 on him which was to be lodged in the bank accounts. Sheridan was also arrested and he showed detectives the rest of the loot, £129,361, which was hidden in his attic. During questioning Sheridan admitted that the cash was from the Marino Mart job. Detectives also found two building society books, one in Hickey's name, and the other in Hutch's. The two men later admitted to Gardaí that they had been working for Gerry Hutch. They subsequently pleaded guilty and were each sentenced to 21 months in prison. They were the only people ever charged in connection with the heist. In the Circuit Criminal Court defence counsel for the pair claimed 'dangerous and ruthless men' had used Sheridan and Hickey. Hutch was referred to as 'Mr X', and described as being particularly dangerous.

At the same time the Gardaí contacted Securicor, who obtained an order in the Belfast High Court freezing the accounts. A Sterling bank draft Hutch had withdrawn was also cancelled. In total the authorities located £320,000. The remaining £1 million was never recovered. A file was forwarded to the Director of Public Prosecutions recommending that Hutch be charged with handling the proceeds from the heist, but it was decided not to proceed with the case because the bagmen were too scared to give evidence against him.

In September 1987, the Monk suffered another setback when two of his partners on the Marino Mart job, Thomas O'Driscoll and Geoffrey Ennis, took part in a hold-up at the Cumberland Street Labour Exchange where Danny McOwen had been murdered. The heist went terribly wrong when the raiders were confronted by a detective who was on duty inside the building. O'Driscoll and a third raider opened fire on the Garda, hitting him in the face and body. The injured detective fired all six rounds in his revolver, hitting O'Driscoll five times. The third raider dragged the injured gangster to the waiting getaway car, which was being driven by Ennis. A short distance away they left O'Driscoll on the side of the road, in the hope that he would get medical attention. He died minutes later.

Meanwhile Hutch was putting up an extraordinary legal fight in the Belfast High Court for the return of his 'hard-earned' cash. It was one of the many blatant examples of how criminals were prepared to exploit the law. In the days before the establishment of the Criminal Assets Bureau (CAB) and adequate anti-money-laundering legislation, the Monk was quite literally untouchable. In evidence, he claimed that Lonan Hickey had been acting as his agent when he lodged the money in the Anglia Building Society. Hutch insisted that the money was his but couldn't offer a credible explanation about where'd he got it.

On 30 July 1992, the Right Honourable Lord Justice Murray ruled that the money was the proceeds of the Marino Mart heist and ordered the return of the cash to Securicor. Hutch then appealed the case to the Appeal Court of Northern Ireland, which upheld the earlier decision. The relentless Monk then appealed the case again, this time to the House of Lords in London. On 23 February 1994, the Lords' Appeal Committee unanimously refused the Monk leave to appeal the case and ordered that the criminal mastermind pay all costs in the various actions. After that Hutch threatened to bring the case to the European Court, but he later dropped it.

By then Hutch had laundered his share of the Marino Mart robbery and several other heists he'd masterminded. In 1987, he and Matt Kelly went into business with the armed robber Paddy Shanahan, who'd moved into the construction industry. The former member of the Dunne 'Academy' was considered a good businessman and through his construction firm, Manito Enterprises, he began laundering money for a host of major gangland players. In October of the same year Shanahan started refurbishing Buckingham Buildings, a tenement complex in the heart of the north inner-city, to turn it into modern apartments.

It was to prove to be a profitable relationship – until another hit man upset the partnership.

12.   The Kidnap Gangs

Throughout the 1980s terrorist and criminal gangs used a terrifying new method of raising cash – kidnapping for ransom. Scores of abductions were carried out, mainly in Dublin and the Border region, which were never reported to the police. In 1985 alone, Gardaí revealed that there were 37 unreported kidnapping cases in the Republic. And the trendsetters for this terrifying crime were the Provisional IRA.

In the early 1980s, the IRA's terror campaign was conservatively estimated to be costing them at least £1 million a year, mostly funded by criminal rackets. The money was used to pay members of Active Service Units (ASUs), buy weapons and organize bombing missions in Northern Ireland, Britain and Europe. Money from the annual 'budget' was also spent on the dependants of prisoners, full-time Sinn Féin staff and the IRA propaganda machine. The costs kept mounting, but increased security measures at financial institutions and more armed Garda and Army escorts for cash-in-transit vans throughout the country dramatically reduced the Provos income from armed robberies. By the time the ASU was captured abducting Martin Foley, the IRA was already well practised at using the sinister tactic of kidnapping to raise funds.

In the first three years of the 1980s the Provos were responsible for a string of abductions which netted the organization ransoms worth over £3 million. In the process they murdered two members of the Irish security forces, stole the world's greatest racehorse, and left Ireland's international reputation as a place to do business in tatters.

At first the terrorists used kidnapping as a weapon to highlight the conditions that their so-called Prisoners of War were enduring in English jails. In December 1973, the IRA abducted Thomas Niedermayer, the Managing Director of the Grundig plant in Dunmurry, West Belfast, which employed 1,000 people. The 45-year-old was also the honorary West German Consul in Northern Ireland. He was taken from his home at gunpoint and there was no further trace of him. In 1980 his remains were accidentally uncovered during excavation work on a building site, less than a mile from his house. His captors later claimed Niedermayer died from a heart attack. The IRA had planned to barter the industrialist in return for the release of the Price sisters. They were among ten terrorists convicted for a car-bombing campaign in London in early 1973, and were on hunger strike, demanding to be sent back to serve their time in Northern Ireland. (Rose Dugdale also stole the Beit paintings in a bid to have the women repatriated, see Chapter 6.) One of Niedermayer's kidnappers was subsequently convicted for the abduction.

In June 1974, Lord and Lady Donoughmore were kidnapped from their home, Knocklofty House, near Clonmel, County Tipperary. They were held for four days before being released unharmed. The couple later revealed that their captors told them they weren't interested in money but wanted the repatriation of the Price sisters, who were only alive because they were being force-fed. Over a year later the Provos struck again when they kidnapped Dutch industrialist Dr Tiede Herrema, the CEO of the Ferenka plant in Limerick. The IRA now demanded the release of three of their members, Rose Dugdale, Kevin Mallon and James Hyland, from prisons in the South.

The terrifying tactic was dropped by the IRA Army Council after that because it was seen as ineffective and counterproductive. There was a change of heart, however, as it became more difficult to make 'expropriations' and there was an increasing demand for cash, as they tried to expand their war. The Provos resorted to kidnapping again and were responsible for a number of abductions where they held bank managers' families hostage, while forcing the bankers to withdraw cash from the premises. These were among the first so-called 'Tiger kidnappings' in the country. The most dramatic of these took place in January 1980. The family of a Dublin bank manager was held while a ransom of £30,000 was handed over. A year later the teenage daughter of the manager of the Bank of Ireland in Dundalk and her friend were kidnapped at gunpoint and a £50,000 ransom was demanded. The girls were released the following morning in Crossmaglen in South Armagh, however, after the British Army intercepted a car carrying the ransom. In February 1980, a wealthy Belfast coin-dealer was murdered, nine hours after he'd been abducted and a ransom of Stg£1 million was demanded for his safe return. On the morning of 16 October 1981, the terrorists struck again. Ben Dunne Junior, who ran the family's successful Dunnes

Stores chain, was kidnapped on the northern side of the Border, on the main Dublin to Belfast road. Dunne was grabbed at gunpoint when he stopped to give assistance at a faked accident. The IRA demanded a £500,000 ransom, which his distraught family immediately tried to raise. Gardaí learned that they had arranged the withdrawal of £300,000 from a bank that afternoon. They intercepted a car being driven by a company employee the following day, on the way to South Armagh with the cash. The Government was determined that no ransom should be paid, fearing that it would only encourage further high-profile abductions which would have catastrophic consequences for the already troubled economy. The Dunne family made a number of further attempts to pay the ransom but each time were prevented from doing so by the authorities. Ben Dunne was released unharmed six days later, amid Garda suspicions that £500,000 had somehow been handed over to the Provos.

Then in February 1983 the republicans sunk to new depths when a Dublin-based IRA gang kidnapped the £10 million racehorse Shergar from Ballymoney Stud, County Kildare. It was another attempt by the Provos to destabilize the economy with an attack on the country's horse-breeding industry. The terrorists demanded a £2 million ransom for the safe return of the world-famous horse, which was owned by a syndicate that included the Aga Khan.

According to former IRA commander Sean O'Callaghan, who was also a Garda Special Branch agent, Shergar injured himself within hours of the abduction. Another credible Provo source later claimed the prized animal was gunned down in an isolated shed by a gutless patriot using a machine-gun. Shergar was then cut up with a chain-saw and buried, either in County Leitrim or in the Arigna Mountains in County Roscommon. To avoid international outrage the IRA and the INLA regularly denied committing atrocities during the Troubles – the murder of Shergar was one of them. The organization never publicly accepted responsibility for the crime and Shergar's remains have not been found.

After the Shergar fiasco, the eight-man IRA gang involved in his kidnapping were ordered to target Canadian millionaire Galen Weston. He was the joint owner of Associated British Foods (ABF), the parent company of the Quinnsworth and Penneys chains. Weston was to be kidnapped for a ransom of £5 million. The organization planned to use the money to purchase more sophisticated weapons, including surface-to-air missiles and other armaments. However, the gang had been under intense surveillance since the Shergar abduction and Garda Special Branch were aware that they were plotting something big. The Gardaí were also tipped-off by a number of high-level informants in the Provos, including Sean O'Callaghan and a prominent member of Sinn Féin who has never been publicly exposed as a spy. The plan was to take Weston at his home on the morning of Sunday, 7 August 1983.

Around 4 a.m. that morning, the IRA unit cut the phone wires to the Westons' mansion near Roundwood, County Wicklow. Shortly before 8 a.m. the Provos, armed with automatic pistols, machine-guns and Armalite rifles, made their move, but 13 members of the Special Task Force, carrying pistols and Uzi machine-guns, were waiting for them in the house. Galen Weston and his family had been warned of the attack and had secretly flown to England for the weekend. As the Provos were walking into the trap, the millionaire was preparing to play polo with the Prince of Wales. When five members of the gang appeared, the waiting detectives ordered them to put down their weapons. Two of the Provos opened fire on the Gardaí, who began shooting back. The three other Provos also began firing down at the house from higher ground. An intense gun battle ensued during which the STF officers fired a total of 185 rounds in less than five minutes. When it was over, four of the would-be kidnappers lay wounded. Five members of the gang were arrested while the remaining three escaped. Three of the men detained at the scene were from Belfast: John Hunter, Gerald Fitzgerald and John Stewart. Fitzgerald was the IRA's intelligence officer. The two others were Nicky Kehoe from Cabra in Dublin and Peter Lynch from Derry. Kehoe, the only one of the five who was uninjured, had a previous conviction for possession of explosives in 1974. Lynch also had previous for firearms' offences and possession of explosives.

The operation was another disaster for the Provos and a huge victory for the Gardaí, who had shown that they were now more than a match for the terrorists. On 4 November 1983, the Special Criminal Court convicted the Provos for a series of charges, including possession of firearms with intent to endanger life. They were jailed for terms ranging between ten and fourteen years. As the five terrorists were being led down from the dock they gave clenched fist salutes and shouted 'Up the Provos'.

Gerry Adams, who was the Sinn Féin vice-president at the time, acknowledged the salute from the public gallery.

The IRA had suffered a humiliating defeat but it didn't deter them.
Less than three weeks later, on 24 November, the Provos launched a
second attack on the Weston business empire. Forty-nine-year-old Englishman Don Tidey, CEO of the Quinnsworth chain, was taken at
gunpoint as he left his home in Rathfarnham to bring his daughter to
school. His kidnappers, three of whom had shot their way out of the
Maze Prison in Belfast two months earlier, had set up a fake Garda
checkpoint as Tidey approached. He was bundled into a car and driven
off at speed, while a ransom demand for £5 million was delivered to the
headquarters of ABF in London.

The search for Don Tidey was one of the biggest ever mounted in the
history of the State. It involved over 4,000 Gardaí and troops. To add to
the pressure on the security forces, an intensive nationwide search was
also being conducted to locate a dangerous terrorist, the notorious
leader of the INLA, Dominic 'Mad Dog' McGlinchey, who had been
on the run since December 1982.

McGlinchey was one of the most psychotic killers to emerge during
the Troubles and by his own admission, had been responsible for at least
30 murders and 200 bombings. He'd skipped bail while awaiting the
judgment of the Supreme Court when he challenged his extradition to
Northern Ireland on murder charges. A close friend of Martin 'the
Viper' Foley and Thomas McCarton, Mad Dog also lived in Crumlin
and organized several armed robberies with local criminals. Foley and
his wife looked after McGlinchey's children when he went into hiding.
While on the run Mad Dog was involved in the abduction of relatives
of INLA member Harry Kirkpatrick. In the first of the infamous
'supergrass' trials that took place in the 1980s, Kirkpatrick had turned
State witness against his former comrades. McGlinchey was still in hiding when the Tidey manhunt almost cost him his freedom.

On 2 December, two uniformed Gardaí who were searching for
Tidey stumbled across the INLA mass-murderer when they inadvert-
ently visited the safe house he was using in Carrigtwohill, County
Cork. The policemen were held at gunpoint, stripped of their uniforms
and left bound and gagged, before Mad Dog made his escape. Five days
later, he did the same thing to two other unarmed officers when they

tried to arrest him in Wexford. By the time McGlinchey was finally cornered, following a shoot-out in County Clare in March 1984 during which a Garda was shot and injured, he had left a trail of chaos around the country, including armed robberies and other shooting incidents.

In the meantime Garda intelligence confirmed, through their informants on the IRA Army Council, that the supermarket executive was being held near Ballinamore, County Leitrim. On 13 December, hundreds of extra police and troops were drafted into the area. They began focusing the search operation on woodland in isolated countryside, some miles from the northern end of the town. Ten search teams, made up of armed and uniformed Gardaí backed up by troops, were deployed to comb the area. Garda recruits from Templemore were also drafted in to boost up the numbers. It was to prove a disastrous decision.

On the afternoon of the third day, one of the search teams stumbled on to the hide where Don Tidey was being held. Recruit Garda Gary Sheehan was the first to spot an IRA man. As he turned to tell Private Patrick Kelly, the soldier covering him, the IRA men opened fire, unleashing mayhem. The rookie Garda and the experienced soldier were gunned down as a hail of bullets zipped through the woods. Gary Sheehan was 26; 36-year-old Patrick Kelly was the father of four children, the youngest born 11 weeks earlier. Sheehan was the tenth member of the Gardaí to be murdered since 1970. Private Kelly was the first soldier to be killed by the terrorists since the start of the Troubles.

In the confusion that followed the initial gun battle the gang, who were also dressed in combat clothing, took a number of Gardaí and soldiers as hostages. The terrorists forced their captives to run in front of them, as the Provos fired at the other search teams in the area. The gang hijacked a car and got away. At the same time the supermarket executive, who was dressed in the same garb as his kidnappers, managed to escape. Tidey was lucky that a Special Branch detective recognized him or he might have been shot in the pandemonium. He had been held captive for 23 days.

The Tidey kidnap drama was a disaster for the security forces and resulted in bitter recriminations between the Army and the Gardaí. It led to a complete overhaul of operational procedures between the two organizations. Some time later it was also discovered that Associated British Foods had secretly agreed to pay the IRA over Stg£2 million to ensure that none of its executives, including Tidey, were kidnapped again. The money was paid into a Swiss bank account controlled by the IRA and it was then transferred to a bank in Navan, County Meath. When Garda Special Branch and MI5 traced the money, the Government rushed legislation through the Oireachtas to freeze the funds. In February 1985, the State seized £1.7 million of the money.

No one was ever convicted of the double murders in Ballinamore or the kidnapping of Don Tidey. It was the last high-profile kidnapping carried out by the Provos although they continued to be heavily involved in protection and extortion rackets. But they had given other criminals the template for an alternative method of raising easy money.

Mickey Boyle from Bray, County Wicklow, was a one-man serious crime wave. Over four decades he did it all – progressing from burglary and armed robbery to extortion, kidnapping and gangland murders. But, like Paddy Shanahan or Dutchie Holland, Boyle did not fit into the stereotypical profile of a career gangster. Born in November 1946, he came from a respectable family background. The second eldest of six children, Boyle's father was a sergeant in the Irish Army and his mother was a legal secretary. He grew up in Scott Park, a modest terrace of ten houses in the seaside town. In his early years Boyle was described as a quiet, intelligent young man who played hurling and football for his county. He was a hard-working, trouble-free student who could have achieved considerable success. When he left school, however, Mickey Boyle quickly showed where his real talent lay.

He immersed himself in crime and by the age of 22 his CV included dozens of convictions for larceny, burglary and car theft. Boyle was a complete maverick who mostly operated alone and earned a reputation as a dangerous, unpredictable villain. In 1969, he received his first four-year jail term for armed robbery when he held up an elderly widow at gunpoint in her own home. While inside Boyle married his girlfriend, Breda Moran, from Dundrum, and the couple would have two children together.

In prison Boyle's reputation as a young desperado impressed the older lags. He befriended Saor Eire members, including Simon O'Donnell and Joe Dillon, and learned a lot from his new admirers. But Boyle didn't like prison and hatched an elaborate escape plan. He inveigled his way into the Central Mental Hospital in Dundrum when he convinced doctors that he was unstable – something that former associates and Gardaí would agree on. He absconded but was recaptured and returned to Mountjoy.

After his release in 1972, Boyle briefly joined the British Army but deserted. When he returned to his wife and family in Bray he went on a crime spree, committing burglaries, armed robberies and shootings. His reputation as a head-case grew and he was eventually charged with robbing two banks in Enniskerry and Rathdrum. Boyle had no intention of making things easy for the Gardaí. When he was arrested he told them: 'I think the best chance I have is to keep my mouth shut. I have nothing to gain by helping and nothing to lose by not helping.'

In April 1975, he stood trial in the Central Criminal Court, Dublin. On the second day Boyle, who was heavily guarded because of his earlier escape, asked to be escorted to the toilets. The officers dutifully stood outside a lavatory cubicle while he relieved himself – and retrieved a pistol which had been hidden in the cistern. Boyle flushed the toilet and walked out, holding the gun. He ordered the wardens to lie on the ground, slipped out a door to a waiting car and vanished. He was recaptured two months later at a race meeting and jailed for a total of ten years.

When he was released in 1982, Boyle decided to apply his criminal mind to taking advantage of an opportunity his native county offered in abundance – North Wicklow is a kidnapper's dream. Some of the country's wealthiest businesspeople live there, in magnificent mansions, nestled into the breathtaking landscape. Mickey Boyle spent his childhood trekking through the hills and mountains and knew every back road in the region. Within weeks he was back in business.

In March, Boyle and his accomplice, Eugene Prunty, a 32-year-old unemployed fitter from Old Court in Bray, forced their way into the home of Belgian-born publisher Albert Folens and his wife, Juliette, near Enniskerry in the foothills of the Wicklow Mountains. After the Second World War, Folens was jailed for ten years for collaborating with the Gestapo against his own people. He escaped and made his way to Ireland where he made a fortune as a publisher of educational books. Boyle took Juliette Folens from the house and told her husband that she would be held in the woods until £25,000 (around €90,000 today) was handed over. If Folens called the cops, his wife would be shot. The publisher was instructed to collect the cash from his bank in Tallaght and deliver it to a pre-arranged location. Boyle reckoned that £25,000 would not arouse suspicions at the bank. After the money was paid Folens was told where his wife was being held – she'd been locked up in their garage.

In April 1983, the daughter of businessman Peter Simms was abducted at their home in Shankill in South County Dublin, and a ransom of £10,000 was paid over. Garda intelligence reports from the time suggested that there had been four other similar abductions in the same area but the victims had not contacted the police. Boyle was soon nominated as the most likely suspect – after the IRA – and was taken in for questioning. He told the police nothing and was released without charge when two people provided him with alibis, one of whom was a well-known Provo.

After his release Boyle began looking for a new target and quickly found one. William Somerville was a wealthy solicitor with a successful law practice in Enniskerry. He lived with his family at Dargle Hill, a large house on a 50-acre farm less than a mile from the picturesque village. In July, Boyle put them under surveillance, logging all their movements. A few weeks later, at 10 p.m. on 9 August, William Somerville and his wife, Manon, went for a short drive, leaving their 14-year-old son, James, feeding his dogs in the backyard. As the Somervilles' car pulled out of the driveway, Boyle appeared from the undergrowth, wearing a combat jacket, a stocking over his head and carrying a sawn-off shotgun. He ordered the startled teenager back inside.

When the Somervilles returned an hour later they found Boyle holding a gun to their son's head. The kidnapper told the terrified couple that he was taking the kid hostage and demanded a ransom of £50,000 for his safe return. James's father pleaded with the kidnapper to take him instead and Boyle agreed. He ordered Somerville to drive his car to a lane near Stillorgan, in South County Dublin. A plastic bag was placed over his head and he was bundled into the back seat of another car. Boyle and Prunty drove to a forest near Kilpeddar, County Wicklow, where they tied the solicitor to a tree. They taped his knees, ankles and hands together and gagged him before leaving. At 2.15 a.m. Mrs Somerville called the Gardaí and arranged to meet them away from her home, in case the kidnappers were watching from the hills.

Detective units across South County Dublin and North Wicklow were alerted. Later that morning Boyle phoned the Somerville home. He told Mrs Somerville her husband was in good health and, if she did as instructed, he would remain so. The ransom was to be in £10 and £5 notes and placed in two sacks. A location for the drop-off would be given later. By then the Gardaí had a tap on the phone and detectives instantly recognized Boyle's voice. Surveillance teams were ordered to locate the violent criminal and keep him under observation until the solicitor was rescued.

At noon, when Boyle called again, Mrs Somerville wanted assurances that her husband was safe. She told Boyle that her husband's business partner was arranging the collection of the ransom from the Northern Bank on College Green and it would not be ready until 4 p.m. Ten minutes before the phone call, a team of surveillance officers had spotted Mickey Boyle with Prunty, walking along the Main Street in Bray. The officers had watched the two hoods making the call to Mrs Somerville. The pair were tailed to Wicklow Town, where they stopped for lunch. Later they drove back to Bray, where Prunty called into the local Garda station – the headquarters of the kidnap investigation – to present his driving licence and insurance documents. Sometime earlier he had been stopped at a routine Garda traffic checkpoint and told to present his documents under the Road Traffic Act.

When the kidnappers had gone, their victim's business partner was brought into the Garda station, through a side door. The ransom money was then initialled, photographed, and the serial numbers were noted. The evidence against Boyle continued to mount, as the surveillance units watched him make another phone call to the Somerville home from a phone box on Putland Road in Bray. He again reminded Mrs Somerville of the consequences for her husband if she didn't follow his instructions. Forty minutes later Boyle made a fourth call and spoke to Mrs Somerville's brother, Norman Brittain. He informed the kidnapper that the money was ready and asked about the drop-off. The gangster said he would call back at 5 p.m. with the location.

Shortly after 5 p.m. Eugene Prunty phoned and instructed Brittain to leave the cash in a burned-out car on Sandpit Lane, near Enniskerry. Boyle watched from a hide in the bushes as Mrs Somerville and her brother dropped off the money. When he saw that the coast was clear the kidnapper snatched the bags. At the same time, a team of heavily armed police was ordered to move in on the kidnapper – but they'd surrounded the wrong area. By the time they discovered their mistake Boyle was well away. There was considerable embarrassment among the Garda top brass that Boyle had managed to escape with the ransom money. A major search operation was ordered across Dublin and Wicklow to find him.

A short time later, one of the surveillance teams spotted Prunty in Bray and he was promptly arrested. At 12.10 a.m. that night Boyle phoned the Somerville home and told them where William could be found – he had been tied to the tree for almost 24 hours. On the same day, without Boyle's knowledge, Prunty was charged with demanding money with menaces from Norman Brittain.

On the morning of 12 August, the Serious Crime Squad located Boyle's safe house in Harold's Cross, South Dublin, and raided it. As they burst through the front door, the kidnapper jumped out the back. He was chased and managed to escape, after scaling several walls. Four days later the cops finally caught up with him when he was arrested in Mulligan's Pub on Poolbeg Street, Dublin, wearing a wig and glasses. When he was taken to Bray Station for questioning, Boyle at first refused to say anything during the 48-hour detention period. However, the officer in charge of the investigation, Detective Inspector Mick Canavan, convinced him that he had nothing to lose by giving up the ransom money. Boyle eventually brought Gardaí to the spot where it was hidden. He was charged with the false imprisonment of William Somerville and demanding money with menaces. Incredibly, despite strong Garda objections, the kidnapper was released on £10,000 bail.

On 21 October, he was due to appear in the local District Court for a further remand. But Boyle had a prior engagement of a less legal nature to take care of first. At 7 a.m. that morning, 46-year-old businessman Robert Manina and his wife, Alma, woke up in their home on Somerby Road in Greystones to find a masked man standing at the bottom of their bed, pointing a gun at them. A second man stood at the bedroom door, cradling a rifle in his arms. Boyle ordered the couple to turn on to their faces and demanded to know if they had a safe – there wasn't one in the house. The gunmen rummaged through the house to see for themselves. After about ten minutes the couple were ordered to dress, told to 'keep your fucking mouths shut', and herded downstairs. One of the raiders grabbed Robert Manina by the back of the neck and began choking him. When he let go, Alma Manina was ordered to put on a coat and flat shoes and to wear a scarf over her face. Before leaving, Boyle warned Alma's husband not to phone the police and told him that if he wanted to see his wife alive again he would have to a pay a £60,000 ransom. The kidnappers brought their terrified victim to a disused shed near Enniskerry and locked her inside. Meanwhile, a distraught Robert Manina called a friend and asked for help in raising the ransom money. The friend decided to raise the alarm. The police knew straightaway who they were looking for.

Less than three hours later, detectives from the Special Task Force got a call to go to Stylebawn near Enniskerry. A local man had reported spotting two men acting suspiciously. Four officers, with their weapons drawn, approached an area around a farmhouse called 'Cataldus'. Behind the house, they saw Mickey Boyle standing beside the door of the concrete shed where he had imprisoned his latest hostage. Detective Garda Michael Merrigan shouted: 'Drop the gun Michael.' Boyle crouched down and darted across a garden, diving for cover between a wall and another shed. He lifted a gun to aim at the pursuing cops who fired two warning shots in the air. Boyle bolted across a road and fired a number of shots as he struggled to shake off the cop who was on his tail. He ran through thick, thorny bushes, but as he reached the roadway Detective Sergeant Basil Walsh jumped on him.

At the same time his colleagues found Alma Manina in the shed – she was shaken but uninjured. Had things gone according to plan, Boyle could still have made it to Bray Court for his remand hearing. As he was being placed in a squad car, he pleaded with the detectives: 'Shoot me, shoot me, I will get life for this anyway. I may as well be in now, there is nothing else left for me now, come on, come on do me a favour, shoot me now.'

Back in Bray Station he told Detective Inspector Canavan: 'It's all over as far as I am concerned, I don't wish to talk about this thing any more; what is the point. I have let down everybody that meant something to me.' Boyle buried his head in his hands and refused to speak any more.

The Gardaí ensured Boyle still made it to the District Court on time.

He was charged with four charges: of false imprisonment, demanding money with menaces, possession of a firearm with intent to endanger life and using a firearm to resist his arrest. Spotting that the game was up he did not seek bail. In July 1984, Boyle pleaded guilty to a total of six charges relating to the two kidnapping incidents. While awaiting trial he suffered from depression and tried to kill himself. The judge described his crimes as 'detestable, appalling and horrid' and sentenced him to 12 years. Boyle's partner in the Somerville kidnap, Eugene Prunty, was also convicted and sentenced to ten years in prison. Mickey Boyle spent the rest of the 1980s behind bars.

But Boyle's incarceration and the obvious risks inherent in kidnapping people for ransom didn't deter other gangsters, who thought they could do better.

John and Michael Cunningham were no different to other criminals – they dreamed of pulling off one big job which would set them up in the good life, permanently. Living the great 'underworld dream', the brothers, like the Dunnes, enjoyed wining and dining in the best restaurants, bars and clubs. They drove big cars and regularly brought their families on lavish holidays in places like Barbados, Florida and Spain. But the high life was a big drain on cash and took a lot of armed robberies – and risk – to sustain.

The O'Connor's heist was the last major job John 'the Colonel' Cunningham took part in with the General. He didn't agree with Cahill's modus operandi, which invariably involved large teams and meant that the share of the loot was much less than it could be with a smaller group. Instead, the brothers teamed up with another armed robber from Tallaght, Tony Kelly. Thirty-two-year-old Kelly, who was originally from Dublin, had spent most of his life in Leeds in the north of England. He had a string of convictions for larceny, forgery and burglary and had served seven years behind bars. Like the Cunninghams, Kelly had expensive tastes and was known for his flashy *Miami Vice* suits and relaxing sojourns in the Bahamas.

In the early 1980s, the three partners began doing armed robberies in Leeds, where Kelly had extensive underworld contacts. Back in Dublin the extra armed cops on the streets were making life hazardous for the ambitious blagger. The gang adopted a business-like approach to their

work and regularly commuted between Dublin and England to do robberies in Yorkshire – taking a flight from Dublin in the morning, doing
a job and then catching a return flight home the same day. Business was
good. Police estimated that the 'Irish crew' had robbed in the region of
Stg£1 million from banks and security vans during a three-year period,
up to 1984. They became so successful that a special police squad was set
up to target them. In October 1984, however, the lucrative day-trips
came to an end when the three hoods were named as the chief suspects
for the murder of Police Sergeant John Speed, shot dead during a chase
after a robbery in Leeds. After that the hoods decided to do their robbing at home.

Early in 1986, the West Yorkshire police, who had been building a
case against the gang, decided they had enough evidence to charge the
three hoodlums with Sergeant Speed's murder. While awaiting extradition warrants, they requested assistance from the Gardaí in arresting the
Cunninghams and Kelly. The three robbers were tipped off that they
were about to be pulled in and the Colonel decided that they needed to
pull one big job as soon as possible. This time the money would be used
to skip the country with their families. Their new home would need to
have plenty of sun – and no extradition agreements with the UK or
Ireland. The Colonel had read the newspaper reports about how the
IRA had been secretly paid up to £3 million from the Dunne and Tidey
abductions alone. He knew that the only realistic chance of a massive
payday was to kidnap a member of a family worth millions. He was also
aware of the large number of kidnappings that had never been reported.
The confident crook reckoned he could do a better job than the Provos
or Mickey Boyle.

The gangsters began leafing through magazines and newspapers, to
pick a target. Among the short list of possible hostages was Susan
O'Reilly the first wife of Independent Newspapers' Dr Tony O'Reilly.
Norma Smurfit, the ex-wife of business tycoon Michael, and Guinness
heiress Miranda Guinness were also considered. Eventually they chose
Jennifer Guinness, the wife of John Guinness, Chairman of the Guin-
ness Mahon Bank. The couple lived in a mansion, Censure House, at
Baily near Howth, North County Dublin. They were well known in
the sailing world and participated in the Round Ireland yacht race.
Cunningham had read a magazine feature about them and decided that

they would have little difficulty raising a large ransom. However, he had picked the wrong Guinness family – the banker was not a member of the fabulously wealthy brewing clan.

In early March 1986, the three robbers began watching Censure House to monitor the family's routine. They rented a number of safe houses, including a flat above a shop in Arbour Hill in Dublin and a fisherman's cottage near Drumconrath, County Meath. Tony Kelly hired a hatchback car, in his own name, to transport their victim. The Colonel decided that they would kidnap either Jennifer Guinness or one of her two daughters and demand a £2 million bounty for her safe return. He was confident that if they convinced the Guinness family that they were the IRA, they would be too scared to call in the police. Cunningham obtained a hand-grenade, a replica Uzi and three handguns for the job. He also made up two devices to look like bombs, complete with 'remote-controls'. The Colonel believed that a bomb would scare people out of their wits and focus their minds on paying the ransom.

On the afternoon of 8 April 1986, the three hoods barged into the Guinness family home and held 48-year-old Jennifer Guinness at gunpoint, along with her daughter Gillian, their housekeeper, Patricia Coogan, and her 15-year-old daughter. The four women were herded into a TV room, while the gang waited for John Guinness to come home. An unfortunate book-dealer, Simon Nelson, was also held when he called to the house.

The kidnappers deliberately gave their hostages the impression that they were from the IRA by referring to the 'organization' and their 'fund-raising mission'. If everyone behaved then no one would be shot. Jennifer Guinness told the 'terrorists' that they had picked the wrong family. The gang said they were 'following orders' and addressed each other with military titles. Cunningham was the Colonel and his brother Michael was the Sergeant. While they waited, the gang took Jennifer's jewellery, which was valued at £50,000.

When John Guinness returned home later that evening the Cunninghams pounced on him. They told him they wanted a £2 million ransom and brought him into the kitchen. They produced two bags containing the fake bombs. John Guinness tried to grab the Uzi which had been left on a table by the Colonel. Cunningham punched Guinness to the ground and pistol-whipped him. He cocked the weapon and fired a shot past the banker's head. Cunningham then told him that the 'bombs' would be strapped to his wife and daughter and could be detonated from a half mile away. The banker, who was bleeding heavily from injuries to his eye and nose, was asked how long it would take to raise the money. He replied about a week. Cunningham told him he would phone him using the code word 'Jackal'.

The gang opted to only take Jennifer with them after she convinced them that one hostage would be easier to control than two. The woman's extraordinary strength and courage throughout her abduction would astonish even her abductors. When the kidnappers had left, Gillian managed to free herself and the other hostages and the Gardaí were called. Scores of detectives were mobilized, along with the Serious Crime Squad and the Special Task Force. A pre-arranged plan called the 'National Cordon', which had been devised after previous kidnappings, was put into operation, with checkpoints throughout the country.

The police had three objectives: the safe return of the hostage, the capture of the gang and the prevention of a ransom payment. The INLA and IRA were quickly ruled out as suspects when informants in both organizations were quizzed. The other obvious suspect was Martin Cahill, who had the capacity, personnel and resources for such a crime. Detective Inspector Gerry McCarrick of the Serious Crime Squad, however, quickly nominated the Cunninghams. He had picked up intelligence that the brothers and Kelly were planning something big in June, possibly a kidnapping. His surveillance team had also spotted John Cunningham meeting with a guns-for-hire dealer whom they had been monitoring. McCarrick took on the task of trying to track the brothers down.

Over the following seven days Jennifer Guinness was moved between three different locations while efforts were made by her family to raise the ransom, which, after negotiations, had been reduced to just £300,000.

On the evening of 15 April, McCarrick's surveillance team discovered that the Cunninghams were holding the hostage in a house on Waterloo Road, South Dublin and the Gardaí decided to surround it. As squad cars containing armed police raced there, John Cunningham got a call at the house warning him that they were on the way. Minutes later members of the STF were knocking at the front door. When the kidnappers tried to get out through the back they were met with more detectives and there was a brief exchange of gunfire. Kelly was arrested and the brothers retreated inside. They dragged Jennifer to an upstairs bedroom and threatened: 'We will blow her fucking head off if you don't get out of the house.'

A ten-hour stand-off followed, during which John Cunningham threatened to blow himself up with a hand-grenade. As police negotiators tried to convince them to surrender, the brothers discussed killing themselves. The Colonel's wife, Mary, was due to give birth to his first child and in a telephone call she urged him to think of his unborn baby. The kidnappers finally agreed to give themselves up, unloaded their weapons and put them on the floor. They shook hands with Mrs Guinness and gave her back her jewellery. As they walked out of the house to the waiting police Michael opened the door and smiled to Jennifer Guinness saying, 'Ladies first.' It was 6.24 a.m. on 16 April and the kidnap drama had ended, along with the Cunningham brothers' aspirations to the big time.

As he was being brought away by police, detectives asked the Colonel if he really believed he could pull off the crime. 'We wouldn't have done it if we didn't think that we were going to get the money. Two million was only a starting figure . . . it was going to be the big one but it all went wrong,' he replied ruefully. Instead of the large ransom, John Cunningham received a hefty 17-year sentence. His brother and Tony Kelly were each jailed for 14 years.

Jennifer Guinness's courage made her a national heroine and her resilience was universally admired. Within two weeks of her ordeal she and her husband took part in the Round Ireland yacht race. Tragically John Guinness was killed two years later while mountain climbing. For many years she devoted her energies to helping the victims of crime.

The capture of the Cunningham gang and the long jail terms they received did not act as a disincentive to other criminal gangs. Instead, they just chose to target less high-profile victims, for more realistic ransoms. In the six months before the Cunninghams' court appearance in June 1986, there had already been 14 unreported abductions. Then, in 1987, the country was struck by another extraordinary kidnap drama. This time the mastermind was a sadistic, mass-murderer called Dessie O'Hare, aka 'the Border Fox'.

Even by INLA standards, O'Hare, from County Armagh, was one of the worst killers to emerge from its stable of psychopaths. Born in 1958, he joined the IRA at 16 and quickly proved himself a ruthless killer. In 1979 he joined the INLA and that same year was sentenced to nine years for possession of a firearm by the Special Criminal Court. When he was released in October 1986, O'Hare told Gardaí that he had become a pacifist after studying the works of Martin Luther King, Mahatma Gandhi and Owen Sheehy-Skeffington. But his pacifism didn't last long.

Based on first impressions, baby-faced O'Hare came across as an inoffensive, gentle soul who would be more at home running a crèche than a blood-thirsty terrorist gang. But in reality he made his comrade Dominic McGlinchey look almost normal.

On New Year's Eve 1986 he attacked a Protestant neighbour in Ballymacauley, County Armagh. He was a member of the Ulster Defence Regiment (UDR), a controversial, part-time military unit which backed up the security forces. O'Hare wounded the soldier before turning the gun on his victim's 72-year-old mother, whom he shot and killed.

The murderer also immersed himself in a ferocious blood feud between two INLA factions. Martin Cahill's bomb-maker, Thomas McCarton, was the first to be killed and in early 1987, 13 terrorists were gunned down by former comrades. The Border Fox claimed responsibility for four of the murders. In one incident he shocked even his psychotic comrades when he abducted INLA member Tony McCloskey in Monaghan. O'Hare used bolt-cutters to cut off McCloskey's ear and some of his fingers. Then he and a female companion took turns pumping bullets into McCloskey's mutilated body. He later told a newspaper that he was happy to give McCloskey a hard death. O'Hare was also a suspect for the murder of McGlinchey's wife, Mary. In January 1987, two men shot her nine times – including seven in the face and head – in front of her two young sons.

O'Hare's gang robbed a string of banks in towns along the south of the Border, during which unarmed Gardaí were fired on. He even robbed weapons from a Provo arms dump in South Armagh and attempted to murder Official Unionist MP Jim Nicholson. The Provos were concerned that the Border Fox's unpredictable behaviour was jeopardizing their own operations in the area. They told the INLA that if they did not do something about O'Hare then the Provos would do it for them. On 11 September 1987, O'Hare was expelled from the organization and immediately set up his own mob, which he called the Irish Revolutionary Brigade. But he needed cash to run his killing machine and decided that kidnapping was the best way to get it.

His gang consisted of fellow ex-INLA men Fergal Toal from Armagh and Eddie Hogan from Cork, both violent, reckless thugs. Jimmy McDaid was a Dublin INLA man who'd first suggested a kidnapping campaign. Another member of the team was Tony McNeill, a young militant republican from Belfast. McNeill in turn recruited the help of a 45-year-old barber called Gerry Wright from Parkgate Street in Dublin. Wright agreed to help organize safe houses in the city. O'Hare eventually chose his target – Dr Austin Darragh.

The doctor was the wealthy owner of a medical research company in Dublin and O'Hare planned to snatch him in October 1987. But in the weeks before the abduction, O'Hare was showing the signs of a man going completely out of control. He even executed Jimmy McDaid. The INLA man signed his death warrant when he refused to take part in the kidnap, which rendered him a traitor in O'Hare's eyes.

The erratic terrorist's plan was in disarray from the start. When the gang stormed into Dr Darragh's mansion in Cabinteely, South Dublin, on the night of 13 October, he had not lived there for four years. Instead it was the home of his daughter Marise and her husband, dentist Dr John O'Grady.

Unperturbed by his error, the Border Fox decided to kidnap John O'Grady instead and demanded a £1.5 million ransom. It was the beginning of an intensive six-week manhunt during which O'Hare managed to stay one step ahead of the security forces. At one stage he chopped off the dentist's two little fingers and left them in an envelope behind a statue in Carlow Cathedral, to show the family how serious he was.

The kidnap crisis ended on 5 November, when detectives arrived at a house in Cabra, West Dublin on a routine enquiry. Toal, Hogan and McNeill were there with O'Grady when the Gardaí knocked on the door. In the confusion that followed Eddie Hogan shot Detective Garda Martin O'Connor in the stomach, seriously injuring him. The three kidnappers escaped but were later captured and John O'Grady was rescued.

Detective Garda O'Connor later underwent six major operations to save his life. John O'Grady also spent two weeks in hospital after his dreadful ordeal. O'Hare, who'd been away from the house arranging the collection of the ransom money, was arrested three weeks later, on 27 November. He drove into an ambush set up by Irish Army snipers in County Kilkenny. The Border Fox was critically injured when he was hit several times with high-velocity bullets. His companion, Martin Bryan, was shot dead. O'Hare's survival was nothing short of miraculous.

On 13 April 1988, Dessie O'Hare and his gang were convicted of the O'Grady kidnapping in the Special Criminal Court in Dublin. He was jailed for a total of 40 years for the false imprisonment and the malicious wounding of O'Grady. Eddie Hogan also received a total of 40 years for false imprisonment and the attempted murder of Detective Garda O'Connor. Fergal Toal was given 20 years for the kidnapping charge and a 15-year concurrent sentence for possession of a firearm with intent to endanger life. Toal had already received a life sentence in March for the murder of a man in Dundalk. Tony McNeill was given 15 years for kidnapping and possession of a firearm. Gerry Wright got seven years. Handing down the sentences, Mr Justice Liam Hamilton described the crime as 'one of the most serious cases to come before the courts of this State'.

O'Hare then made a ten-minute statement: 'The time has come for republican freedom-fighters to turn their guns on members of the Irish Establishment, particularly the judiciary, members of the prison service, the Navy, the Army and the Gardaí for carrying out their dirty work which will determine their fate in years to come. It is morally wrong for republicans to eschew retribution against figures in the South. It will always be justifiable and morally right for Irishmen and women to slay those who collaborate with British rule.'

The dangerous psychopath was eventually released from prison in 2006, when he joined forces with one of the country's largest criminal gangs.

13. Crime Incorporated

On 9 April 1985, a secret dossier on the activities of Martin Cahill and his gang was forwarded from the Serious Crime Squad (SCS) in Harcourt Square to Garda HQ. It was the culmination of a year-long, undercover investigation which had commenced shortly after the General and the Provos went to the brink of war over the O'Connor's heist. It was the first time that such a methodical, comprehensive investigation of the gangster's operation had been undertaken. It detailed the General's crimes, his associates and how powerful he had become. It even focused on the money trail – something unheard of at the time.

The report made for disturbing reading, so much so that the detective who wrote it was hauled up before the top brass and accused of 'empire building'. It was then buried by a management ideologically opposed to more imaginative methods of tackling the growing threat of organized crime. Twenty-five years later it was resurrected during research for this book.

For the 12 months running up to April 1985, the Squad collated every surveillance report, enquiry, sighting and piece of confidential information received about the gang, in the dossier. The investigation revealed that the General's mob was carrying out at least two armed robberies or aggravated burglaries every week. The report described an extremely well-organized crime syndicate. It listed the names of over thirty members of the Cahill organization who were active at that time but did not include his brothers John and Eddie, and other members of the gang who were serving prison sentences. The list was a 'who's who' of organized crime's future Mr Bigs.

The report stated: 'Cahill has gathered a substantial core of trusted and hardened criminals, from all areas of the city, around him. Cahill instils a deep-rooted fear in all the people who associate with him. This, coupled with the blood relationships of a lot of its members, and his ability as an organiser, seem to ensure loyalty to him. All the members of his gang are ruthless thugs who, when confronted in particular circumstances would not hesitate to maim or murder civilians or members of the force. Their crimes are planned meticulously and carefully. High-powered motor-bikes and/or cars are used. Radio-receivers tuned to Garda frequencies are used and monitored. Disguises and protective clothing are worn (such as) bullet-proof vests. An array of firearms is always carried. The targets of these crimes are well surveyed beforehand. Safe houses and flats are used as pick-up and drop-off points. They use gullible or blackmailed couriers to their own ends. This, taken with other reliable information received, accounts for a considerable portion of serious crime over the last decade.'

The report also exposed a secret that Martin Cahill managed to take to the grave with him – he was a drug-trafficker, involved specifically in the supply of hash. The Squad discovered that one of Cahill's closest associates, Noel Lynch, was regularly dispatched with large bank drafts to Manchester, where members of the Quality Street Gang organized shipments. The hash was then smuggled into the country by couriers. Cahill sold the drugs to loyal members of his gang but never came into contact with the actual shipments. Martin Foley and armed robber Thomas Tynan were identified as being among the gang's dealers. It was noted that they regularly called to Cahill with large amounts of cash.

The investigation team also focused on the General's business and property interests. They verified his investment in the Jetfoil pub and a number of shops, which were in the names of associates and family members. The investigation discovered that he'd opened a petrol station in Ranelagh with Noel Lynch, through which stolen fuel was sold. The gangsters even set up an oil company in Kildare and used an alcoholic technician to take the dye out of cheaper agricultural 'red' diesel which was then sold as more expensive 'white' diesel. When things went wrong the man was shot and injured.

The dossier also made it clear that the Gardaí had no powers to uplift sensitive financial information from the banks, which had simply refused to co-operate with the discreet enquiry. A criminal's bank accounts could not be frozen or seized but the State did have some powers to go after dirty money. In the 1983 Financial Act, Ireland became one of the only countries in the common law system with powers to tax the pro-ceeds of crime. There was no record of this power ever having been used, however, until the establishment of the Criminal Assets Bureau 13 years later. In the 1980s the Government was reluctant to use the legislation because making criminal activity taxable could be seen as legitimizing it.

The Squad also ran into difficulties when dealing with other agencies of the State. The report revealed: 'Requests to both the Revenue Commissioners and Dublin Corporation to investigate Cahill's gross abuses of the system have proved unfruitful. This is in no doubt through fears of reprisal and/or intimidation of the various departmental staffs involved. This, coupled with the widespread notoriety of the Cahill gang, seems to have closed down this avenue of investigation.' Martin Cahill would soon justify those fears.

The ten-member detective squad involved in compiling the dossier offered strategic recommendations on how Cahill could be put out of business. In the report's conclusions they made a number of practical recommendations. These included additional personnel, a secure radio channel, more surveillance vehicles, and a co-ordinated investigative strategy going forward.

The Squad's immediate superior, Detective Inspector Gerry McCarrick, gave his full backing to the report and its recommendations. Garda management classed McCarrick as a loose cannon and a maverick because he challenged the archaic views in the force. In reality he was a hugely talented thief-taker and a man before his time.

Throughout the 1980s it was Garda policy to refuse to acknowledge the term 'organized crime'. Garda management tended to adopt the ostrich approach to the unfolding crisis on the streets – they stuck their heads in the sand hoping it would all go away. The prevailing ethos was indirectly helping the gangs to prosper and thrive. Around the same time there was an infamous internal report, colloquially known as the 'Three Wise Men report', which directed a move away from specialist squads. The theory was that every man and woman in the force should be able to fulfil any policing role that the job required. The first casualty had been the disbandment of the 'Mockey' squad. Despite the impressive number of drug-dealers it caught, the ad hoc undercover unit was derided as gimmicky. The Drug Squad was also still being starved of personnel. The deployment of resources was a critical issue at a time when the Troubles were still draining available manpower. During the Cahill enquiry the members of the team had been redeployed to investigate the murder of their colleague Detective Garda Frank Hand, who was shot dead by an IRA gang on 10 August 1984. The 26-year-old officer had just returned to duty after his honeymoon when he was gunned down while providing an armed escort for a cash-in-transit van at Drumree Post Office in County Meath. A year later an INLA gang shot dead Sergeant Patrick Morrissey following a bank raid in County Louth. He was the twelfth member of the force to be murdered since 1970.

Despite the stultifying atmosphere and poor resources, the SCS still enjoyed a number of notable successes against Cahill's mob. They located a flat in Dartry and a yard in Templeogue which were being used as logistical bases for the gang's operation. The detectives discovered stolen motorbikes, false number plates, scanners, balaclavas, postmen's uniforms, a bullet-proof vest and tools used for fixing weapons. They also seized a number of weapons from the gang's awesome arsenal. Members of the Squad also arrested Cahill's brother-in-law, Eugene Scanlan, and Harry Melia in October 1984, following a shoot-out near Rathfarnham Shopping Centre. Both men, who were on their way to rob a security van, were on temporary release from prison to make room for IRA prisoners.

The detectives compiling the dossier also discovered that Eamon Daly and Cahill had been using a man to store firearms, motorbikes and stolen money for them, as well as moving weapons before and after robberies. The man, who was gay, was being blackmailed by Cahill and his mob over his sexuality, which was illegal in Ireland until 1993. Although the blackmail victim gave detectives detailed statements, he was too terrified to testify against the gangsters in court. The investigation also led to the discovery of a former Saor Eire member who ran an extensive 'guns-for-hire' racket from his business premises in the inner-city and the Squad gleaned valuable intelligence when he was put under surveillance.

Garda management would not be able to ignore the General and his mob for much longer.

On 21 May 1986, Cahill strolled into Russborough House near Blessington, County Wicklow and stole 11 of the most valuable paintings in the world. In the process he became an international gangland celebrity with the second-biggest art heist in history. Vermeer's 'Lady Writing a

Letter' was among the Dutch Old Masters stolen. It was conservatively valued at £20 million and the only Vermeer in private hands in the world, aside from one owned by Queen Elizabeth. The collection belonged to Sir Alfred Beit, a former British MP, whose family made their fortune mining diamonds in South Africa. He'd brought the priceless art collection with him when he moved to the Palladian-style mansion near the Blessington lakes in 1952.

Ironically Cahill had again proved himself to be a more accomplished thief than the Provos. In April 1974 a gang led by Rose Dugdale also took the paintings, after holding Sir Alfred and Lady Beit at gunpoint. But in less than two weeks Dugdale was in custody and the paintings were recovered. It was one of the reasons why Cahill was attracted to the Beit heist when Paddy Shanahan approached him with a plan.

The armed robber from Kildare still had a keen interest in art and antiquities, even though they had cost him dearly. In 1980 he'd been arrested with two accomplices in England after the robbery of antiques from the Staffordshire home of collector Sam Firman. Shanahan received a six-year sentence and returned to Ireland after his release in 1984. After his return he burgled a number of stately homes around the country and off-loaded the stolen art and antiquities through his contacts in London. They tapped into the huge black market for stolen heirlooms across Europe. Shanahan had first discussed the prospect of robbing Russborough with his English contacts after Sir Alfred featured in a TV documentary about his priceless treasures. Shanahan and his partners were more interested in the furniture, clocks and Ming porcelain than the paintings, which were so well known they'd be impossible to sell. Shanahan asked Cahill to do the actual robbery while he would then sell the valuables through his contacts.

But the General had other plans. He confidently predicted that the paintings would fetch millions on the black market or in a ransom demand. Over a two-month period, Cahill and John Traynor made several visits to Russborough House, which was open to the public. He planned the art robbery down to the last detail. When Shanahan went to England to get an underworld alarm expert, Cahill did the job behind his back.

The Beit art robbery was a precision job and immortalized Cahill's reputation as a craftsman thief. Up to 12 gang members were involved, including Martin Foley, Christy Dutton, Noel Lynch, George Mitchell, Shavo Hogan, Eamon Daly and Rossi Walsh, a violent armed robber from Pearse Street Flats in the south inner-city. Cahill got around the alarm system by carefully removing a pane of glass in a window. He then deliberately stepped in front of an infrared sensor and, in the next few seconds, disabled the sensors in the section of the house he wanted to rob. The glass was replaced and the gang retreated into the trees to wait for the police to arrive. After inspecting the house with the caretaker, the police decided that everything seemed to be in order and left. Cahill and his gang then simply walked back in and took what they wanted. After the robbery the paintings were stashed in two stolen jeeps which were driven in the dark through fields, guided by plastic bags the gang had placed on sticks at regular intervals along the way. The paintings were then taken to a bunker which Cahill had built in the Dublin Mountains before the job.

Cahill was stopped by uniformed Gardaí in Terenure on his way home, just over an hour later. The General never missed an opportunity to give himself an alibi. When the officers tried to search him Cahill began peeling off his clothes and shouting at the top of his voice, 'I'm being harassed by the police . . . I don't want to talk to youse . . .' Then for good measure he went to his local Garda station in Rathmines and alleged that the officers had assaulted him at the checkpoint. He reckoned that the incident would be helpful, in the unlikely event that he was charged with the robbery. The fact that he was in Terenure so quickly afterwards would surely put a doubt in the minds of a jury. Gardaí knew, however, that whenever Cahill made an uninvited visit to his local station it meant he was up to something – and the alarm was raised to expect another serious crime.

Weeks before the heist, Noel Lynch had registered a bogus security company with the Companies Office. The plan was for the company to approach the Beit Foundation and offer to help 'find' the paintings, for a suitable reward. The security firm even had its own card with the letters, 'RIP' emblazoned in gold on a black background. Apart from the 'recovery' of stolen goods, the company specialized in the movement of 'large amounts of cash' and 'debt-collecting'. But the Beit Foundation refused to have anything to do with Lynch and informed the police. The Gardaí were now in no doubt about who they were dealing with and

Cahill was not unhappy about that. At the time the Beit Foundation was in the process of donating the collection to the State. Robbing the paintings was another two fingers to the Establishment, especially the police. It was also a blow against the wealthy, whom Cahill regarded as the real criminals.

The Beit art robbery was to be the beginning of a fascinating and complex story of international intrigue, involving police forces and criminal organizations in several countries. In the many efforts to off-load the priceless collection, the General had to play his game of wits with the FBI, Scotland Yard and several other police agencies who participated in various Garda stings to recover the art. On more than one occasion the General's sixth sense forced him to pull out of deals at the last minute. In his paranoia he also believed that the South African Secret Service, BOSS, had put a contract on his head because of the Beit family's connections in that country. Several villains were involved in efforts to sell off the haul, including Drogheda-based fence Tommy Coyle, who had contacts all over the globe. Coyle dealt with paramilitaries and criminals on both sides of the Border – and the sectarian divide. He was also an informant who worked with MI5 and Garda Special Branch. One of the great gangland mysteries is how he was never shot before he died from cancer in 2000.

The Beit paintings were blamed for putting a jinx on Cahill and any criminals who came into contact with them. Shavo Hogan would later recall of the robbery: 'It was a really simple robbery. Robbing the paintings was the easy bit. Everybody thought they were going to be millionaires. But after that night everything went downhill. There was a curse on those paintings.'

One of the first gang members to suffer from the curse was John Traynor. In August 1986, Gerry McCarrick's men in the Serious Crime Squad raided a shop which was owned by a relative of Traynor, off Dublin's George's Street. But instead of finding Dutch Old Masters the cops recovered £33,000 worth of stolen cigarettes. They were part of a haul stolen earlier by 'Factory' John Gilligan and his gang. Traynor was arrested and accepted responsibility for the cigarettes. He was charged with receiving stolen goods and released on bail. He was also facing charges for receiving over £15,000 worth of video game-machines which Gilligan had also purloined.

To add to the pressure, one of his stolen cheque scams came back to haunt him at the same time, when the Fraud Squad traced revenue cheques that had been lodged by one of his runners. Twenty-five-year-old car salesman Brian Healy from Tallaght was arrested after cashing four of the forged cheques for nearly £5,000 between July and August 1986. Healy told detectives that he got them from Traynor. The runner was convicted and given nine months in prison while the Fraud Squad caught up with their old adversary.

Traynor then ran into more trouble than he could handle. In January 1987, Eileen Egan, the wife of Michael Egan whose workshop was used after the O'Connor's robbery, decided to spill the beans about his involvement. When Egan was arrested he told the police that he had only been paid £5,000 from the robbery. 'I have ended up with no financial gain of any kind from this incident. All I have had from this is trouble and threats,' he said.

When Cahill heard that Egan had been duped out of his share of the loot he was furious with his erstwhile partner. Cahill also suspected that Traynor had ripped him off in a property deal. The Jetfoil pub had become the biggest drug-dealing centre in the north city and there was constant hassle from the police, so Cahill and Traynor burned it down in May 1984. They'd estimated they could claim £50,000 for the 'malicious' damage to the property from Dublin Corporation. The premises were also the subject of an impending compulsory purchase order by the Dublin Port and Docks Board. In his paranoia Cahill believed that Traynor had secretly sold the place to them behind his back and had pocketed his share.

One night in March 1987 the General went looking for his partner, in the company of John Foy and Martin Foley. Cahill was armed with a gun and he intended punishing his *consigliere*. But the conman had fled town and gone to England, just in the nick of time.

In England, Traynor teamed up with an old fraudster friend, James 'Danger' Beirne, from Elphin. Traynor and Danger Beirne began operating with a number of other English and Irish fraudsters, dealing mostly in stolen and counterfeit bank drafts and cheques. A central figure in the fraud syndicate was John Francis Conlon from Westport, County Mayo. Conlon, who was born in 1940, emigrated to the USA in 1959. He'd become the quintessential international man of mystery who dabbled in the high-stakes world of spying and gun-running. He had documented links with several 'spook' agencies, including the Israeli secret service Mossad, the CIA and MI5. The arms-dealer also had contacts in the American Drug Enforcement Agency (DEA) and the major Colombian drug cartels. Conlon did international arms deals in the Middle East and Eastern Bloc countries. The former East German secret police, the Stasi, held an extensive file on the Mayo man which detailed deals he'd negotiated, including the supply of weapons to Iraq during the Iran–Iraq War and also to the Afghan rebels. Conlon bought his own private Learjet for his jaunts across the world. At one time, he dealt with a notorious Syrian arms-dealer, Monzer al-Kassar, but the Syrian placed a contract on Conlon's head after the Mayo man tipped off Mossad that al-Kassar was planning to murder two of its agents in Amsterdam. The following year Conlon, who was an old acquaintance of Danger Beirne, obviously decided to take a break and indulge in some old-fashioned criminal activity with his countrymen.

In 1990, the three cronies came into possession of a batch of stolen treasury bonds, registered with the Bank of England. They planned to obtain millions of pounds by placing the bonds with a bank as collateral for a mortgage on a huge international 'development'. In London, a crooked official who worked for a Swiss bank had been offered a cut if he helped them out. Conlon, who had a base in Miami, Florida, produced plans for a huge holiday complex on a Caribbean island which required a Stg£100 million mortgage. As collateral, the stolen bearer bonds, which had had their numbers altered, were produced and a deal was agreed.

The fraudsters managed to draw down an initial payment of around Stg£200,000, which was collected by a runner from the Swiss bank's headquarters in Geneva. But in the meantime the City of London Police and the Serious Fraud Office had been tipped off and an investigation begun. Traynor and company made another application to draw down Stg£1 million of mortgage funds from the Geneva bank in July 1990 and Traynor dispatched his courier to collect the new funds for the 'Caribbean project'. When the courier went to the bank in Switzerland, he was told that there would be a slight delay with the paperwork and he was asked to wait. The courier rang Traynor, who was sitting on a park bench near Bayswater Road in London. As they were talking,

Swiss police arrested the courier for fraud. At that same moment the City of London police swooped on Traynor. He was charged with handling stolen bearer bonds and remanded in custody to Wormwood Scrubs. On 18 October 1991, Cahill's *consigliere* was sentenced to seven years for his part in the international operation. He was shattered when he was sent down and blamed Conlon for setting him up.

Five months after Traynor's sudden departure, Cahill dealt his most humiliating blow yet to the police. On the night of 29 August 1987, his crew broke into the offices of the Director of Public Prosecutions on St Stephen's Green in Dublin. Cahill had already visited the offices on a number of previous occasions. He knew how to get around the security system and where to find what he was looking for. In the ultimate act of provocation he stole the files and Books of Evidence pertaining to some of the State's most sensitive criminal cases.

Among the files he was most anxious to get his hands on was the one on the O'Connor's case against Michael Egan and the file dealing with the death of his brother Paddy, who'd been stabbed in Ballyfermot in December 1986. Paddy Cahill had become partially crippled after falling off a motorbike during a getaway. Despite being on crutches, he was still a notorious burglar and drug-abuser who terrorized the people in his neighbourhood. A month before the visit to the DPP's offices, Paddy Cahill's killer had been acquitted by a jury after he told the court he was acting in self-defence. Within hours of the result the family had packed their belongings and left for England. That night their house burned down. The General believed that the acquittal was the product of a conspiracy between the police and the DPP. He imagined they were getting at him – so he decided to get back at them.

Cahill also stole important files on major armed robberies, assault and drug cases. Included in the haul of 145 files were documents relating to a number of Garda corruption cases and the controversial death two years earlier of wealthy Midlands priest, Fr Niall Molloy.

Like so many other strokes by Martin Cahill, the infamous 'files' became the stuff of gangland legend. Cahill ensured that word filtered back to the DPP and the Gardaí that he was responsible for stealing them. He wanted the Establishment to know he had a bargaining chip. The files were to become a valuable currency in the underworld, with criminals offering them in return for charges being dropped or reduced. The thefts were extremely embarrassing. But the police reckoned they already had a surprise in store for their nemesis.

Since the Beit robbery several traps had been laid for Cahill, but he hadn't fallen for them. But then the elusive gangster began to nibble on some new bait. In Holland, a Dutch fraudster called Kees van Scoaik, who had problems with the local police, offered to help snare Martin Cahill in return for the charges against him being dropped. Before running into trouble with the Dutch police the conman had met with Rossi Walsh to discuss a possible deal to sell the paintings. As proof that he had access to the collection Walsh had given the fraudster one of the paintings. When the Dutch police contacted Garda HQ it was agreed to set up a sting operation. The anti-terrorist Special Detective Unit (SDU) was put in charge of the Irish end of the operation. Through an intermediary, van Scoaik agreed to pay £1 million for four of the paintings. After a number of false starts the Dutchman finally got to meet Cahill with Lynch, Daly and Hogan, in the Four Roads pub in Crumlin on 26 September 1987. It was agreed that the gang would show the paintings to van Scoaik's French 'art expert' the following day. The 'art expert' was an undercover agent with Interpol. He was to be picked up by the gang from the Burlington Hotel that afternoon. The police were getting tantalizingly close to catching Cahill – and possibly retrieving the DPP files.

The following day Shavo Hogan picked up the undercover cop and drove him to Killakee Woods in the Dublin Mountains. Cahill and Eamon Daly were there to meet him with the paintings. At the same time a British surveillance aircraft flew high over head. It was supposed to pick up the signal to move when the art expert flashed a special torch he was ostensibly using to inspect the paintings. A large force of armed members of the SDU was standing by, at Bridget Burke's pub in Firhouse, waiting for their cue from the surveillance plane. The main players of the biggest crime gang in the country were within minutes of being nabbed with some of the most valuable paintings in the world.

But it all went horribly wrong. The police's radio network broke down, causing utter confusion. As that was happening Cahill's survival instincts kicked in and he became suspicious of the 'art dealer'. The undercover cop was pushed into Shavo Hogan's car and driven back to the city. Cahill and Daly meanwhile put the paintings into a car and headed back towards Tallaght. On their way, they drove past the assembled army of confused detectives who were still trying to work out what was going on. When he later discovered how close he had come to being caught Cahill could not believe his luck. And instead of keeping his head down he couldn't help taunting the Gardaí about their botched efforts to catch him.

For the second time in a month the Gardaí had suffered a humiliating defeat at the hands of their hated enemy. Both Interpol and the Dutch police expressed their anger at the way the operation had been mishandled. They accused the Gardaí of putting the life of the undercover agent in danger. There were also bitter internal recriminations. Incredibly, the Serious Crime Squad had been kept out of the loop and didn't know that the operation was even going on. Detective Chief Superintendent John Murphy who was in overall command of the Central Detective Unit (CDU), which included the SCS, was furious at the deliberate snub. The investigation to recover the paintings was the responsibility of his officers, who knew Cahill and his gang much better than the anti-terrorist SDU or Garda HQ. It also later transpired that the officer in charge of 'M' District, where the rendezvous took place, Superintendent Bill McMunn, had not been informed about the operation either. If he had known, McMunn could have informed the SDU that he had recently called in experts who had identified radio black-spots in the area around Killakee Woods.

Cahill was getting cocky to the point of recklessness and had pushed the patience of his enemies to breaking point. He was making such a nuisance of himself that he could no longer be ignored by the people who'd buried the SCS's report two years earlier. Now everyone in the Gardaí – including the intransigent management – realized that the General had to be taken on.

Garda Commissioner Eamon Doherty, who was appointed in November 1987, had wasted no time in getting to grips with the gangland problem. He asked for a detailed intelligence report, listing all known criminals involved in organized crime in the city. In 1987 alone there had been almost 600 armed robberies in the country, 500 of which had happened in Dublin. Only 100 had been solved. Armed crime could no longer be overlooked because it wasn't going away. A large dossier was compiled and this time it was not going to be buried. There were, the report concluded, three major gangs operating from bases in Dublin and carrying out robberies throughout the country. Gerry Hutch's mob, who had started the year with the biggest cash heist in the history of the State, was one of them. The other was John Gilligan's Factory Gang. But top of the list was the General's gang.

After the Killakee fiasco, the CDU's Chief Superintendent Murphy sent one of his officers to meet Martin Cahill. The gangster was bluntly told that he had a few days in which to return both the paintings and the DPP's files. There was something about the cop's demeanour that rattled Cahill. The gangster's instinct told him there was trouble ahead and he cautioned his troops to be extra vigilant. But before the Gardaí could get stuck into the 'ordinary criminals', they first had their hands full with the nationwide search for Dessie O'Hare and John O'Grady, which kept them busy for weeks. In the meantime a new terrorist-related crisis had hit the country. On 1 November 1987, the French Navy intercepted the gun-running ship the *Eksund*. It was carrying a cargo of over 100 tons of weapons and ordnance, destined for the IRA, from Colonel Gaddafi in Libya. There was panic in the Government when it was discovered that two, similar-sized shipments had already been successfully smuggled into the country over the previous two years, under the noses of several international security agencies. The Government called a national security emergency and the biggest search operation in the history of the State was launched. 'Operation Mallard' involved over 8,000 police and soldiers who searched 50,000 properties across the country, looking for underground weapons bunkers. In the midst of the distractions the General's gang continued their operations.

On 31 November, the postmistress at Kilnamanagh Post Office in Tallaght was taken hostage by armed and masked men in her home in Inchicore, West Dublin. The following morning, she and another hostage, who had a 'bomb' attached to his chest, were ordered to go to the post office and withdraw £30,000. It was a carbon copy of a similar robbery two years earlier, at Killinarden in Tallaght, which was also the work of the Cahill gang.

For Ned Ryan, the Kilnamanagh robbery was the last straw. He had been promoted to the rank of Detective Superintendent for the Southern Division, which included Tallaght. Ryan was an old adversary of the General's and, years earlier, had tried to warn his superiors that Martin Cahill would be a major problem. Members of the gang now considered themselves so untouchable that they even visited one of Ryan's detectives at his home and threatened to kill him.

The Serious Crime Squad team who'd been involved in the 1985 report on the mobster were also vindicated by the sheer volume of Cahill's audacious and brutal crimes. Cahill was also drawing the attentions of the media on himself. The first major exposé about gangland's elusive General appeared on the front page of the *Sunday World* in October 1987. Cahill was now becoming an embarrassment to the political establishment. The time for action had finally arrived.

On the morning of 2 December 1987, Commissioner Doherty held a conference in his office with the chief superintendents in charge of the Dublin Metropolitan Area's five Garda divisions and Detective Chief Superintendent John Murphy of CDU. Doherty sat back in his chair and asked the question that was about to change the General's life: 'What are we going to do about this man Cahill?' Murphy replied that if he was given the resources and the time he could smash the General's gang within six months. It was decided that it would get whatever resources were needed.

The next issue was how they would go after Public Enemy Number One. It was eventually decided to use overt, close-up surveillance which was designed to harass and antagonize the targets as much as possible. In the military it is referred to as reconnaissance by fire. Each division in the Dublin Metropolitan Area was to produce 15 candidates for the new Squad which was to be attached to the Serious Crime Squad in CDU. It was called the Special Surveillance Unit (SSU).

Those selected were young cops, many of whom had only been in the Gardaí a short time. They were to augment the more experienced detectives in the Serious Crime Squad. The SSU was divided into four teams. Each team was headed by an experienced detective sergeant from CDU – DS Felix McKenna, DS Noel Keane, DS Martin Callinan and DS Denis Donegan. The four sergeants were well acquainted with the Cahill gang. Callinan, who was appointed Commissioner in 2010, had been one of the officers who compiled the poorly received intelligence dossier on Cahill two and a half years earlier.

There were to be seven main targets in the initial operation, Martin Cahill and six others – Daly, Foley, Foy, Hogan, Lynch and Dutton. The number of targets would vary as the operation progressed and surveillance would be extended to other criminals as they came into the picture. The plan was to place up to six Gardaí in three squad cars, covering each target. Each target was to be given a codename. Cahill was 'T One' or 'Tango One'. The SSU were to make life as unbearable as possible for the gangsters.

Over the last weeks of 1987, the SSU officers underwent firearms training and were fully briefed on every piece of intelligence that existed on the Cahill gang. The SSU was poised and ready for action. The famous 'Tango Squad' had been born.

On 1 January 1988, the seven 'chosen' gangsters woke up to a major New Year's Day surprise. When they looked out their bedroom windows the Squad was there waiting for them. When the hoods stood at their doors and stared at the fresh-faced cops, they were greeted with grins and little waves. Wherever the mobsters went, the T Squad went with them, stopping and searching them several times on a typical journey.

The mobsters were well used to police surveillance but had never seen anything like this before. Shavo Hogan would later recall: 'The first week it started we thought this is great craic. But it became a nightmare: beeping horns and shining torches into the house at night. It really fucked up everything. You could not go out for a drink without a cop sitting beside you.' Tango One was the only member of the gang to take up the challenge to play mind games. He once joked: 'I'm thinking of getting involved in the security business. No one is going to rob me with all these armed police around.'

Over the following six months Dublin witnessed an extraordinary game of cat and mouse, played out on the streets between the Tango Squad and the gangsters. The Cahill mob resorted to trying intimidation and threats against their tormentors. As the intense war of wits escalated, hundreds of car tyres were slashed by Cahill's people in middle-class neighbourhoods of South Dublin. Then the cars belonging to the criminals were also smashed-up and their tyres were slashed. Tough, young thugs who were part of the new generation of serious criminals were employed to ram squad cars off the road. One of them was a particularly violent 22-year-old hood from Crumlin called Brian Meehan. He had already cut his teeth as a member of the General's organization and taken part in a string of armed heists. Meehan, who later earned the nickname 'the Tosser', had tried to shoot an unarmed officer during a robbery five months earlier with his mentor, Michael 'Jo Jo' Kavanagh. When the T Squad appeared he was facing a charge for an armed robbery in December 1987 from a bank on Grafton Street.

Soon the targets turned nasty and the SSU members were given details about their families and warned that they would be 'got at'. While he was being followed by the Squad, Cahill would drive through estates where members lived and flash his hazard lights outside their homes. Members of the unit began wearing balaclavas to hide their identities from the criminals. In one incident Martin Foley smashed a detective's jaw and left him unconscious, after he'd crashed into a squad car. As a result Foley was arrested and charged with serious assault. In another act of retaliation, Cahill dug up the greens at the Garda golf club in Stackstown, County Dublin. In a sinister twist, he also ordered a murder contract on Det. Supt Ned Ryan, whom he blamed for all the hassle. A hit team was brought in from Manchester and the veteran detective was placed under armed protection.

But the campaign of harassment by the police soon succeeded in making the hoodlums careless and, one by one, they were caught for armed robberies and firearms offences. Foy and Hogan were the first to be arrested after they opened fire on unarmed officers when they were intercepted on the way to a hold-up in Walkinstown. Daly was caught following an armed stand-off with the Tango Squad during a heist three weeks later. Over the following months a string of other associates were also rounded up. Harry Melia and Eddie Cahill were caught red-handed when the Drug Squad discovered them sorting through a £50,000 consignment of heroin in Cahill's home. The General's brother-in-law, Eugene Scanlan, and Harry Melia, both of whom were on bail, were caught that year by Detective Inspector Tony Hickey's Serious Crime Squad team. They had just collected guns which had been stolen during a raid organized by the General.

Cahill's brother John, who had been released from prison in 1986, had set up his own armed robbery gang. It included Albert Crowley and

Noel Gaynor, who were part of the General's core gang. Gaynor was married to the Cahills' sister and the Crowleys were also related through marriage. Lone raider Dutchie Holland, who was also released from prison in 1986, joined the gang, as did two notorious IRA members, PJ Loughran and William Gardiner. Martin Cahill had presented his sibling with a 'coming out' present of six handguns, a Thompson and an Uzi machine-gun, to help get him started again. The new gang became very active, and inevitably attracted the attentions of the Tango Squad.

John Cahill, Crowley and Gaynor were arrested following a £107,000 robbery from a security van in September 1988. The gang struck with military precision, as the van delivered cash to an employment exchange on the Navan Road on the city's north-side. One Garda was held at gunpoint and shots were fired at another. Three of the gangsters were found hiding in a shed at a house in Ballyfermot after a high-speed chase across the city; the other three managed to escape the net. Cahill, Gaynor and Crowley received prison sentences ranging from seven to twelve years. The man who owned the house where they were found was also jailed for seven years. The Serious Crime Squad caught up with Holland a year later. He was arrested with three other men while in the process of delivering explosives which he intended selling to the IRA. Dutchie and his pals were each jailed for ten years, but the sentences were later reduced to seven.

Despite all the police attentions, Martin Cahill was still involved in organizing robberies and 'tie-ups'. In the winter of 1988, he organized a number of tie-up robberies from the homes of wealthy business figures, stealing jewellery and paintings. Undeterred by his experiences so far in the art world, he also robbed the £500,000 Murnaghan art collection, which belonged to the family of the deceased Supreme Court judge James Murnaghan. The Tango Squad recovered the stolen art and one of Cahill's associates, Wally McGregor, was charged and subsequently jailed. At the same time a number of the Beit paintings were also recovered in London and his salesman, John Naughton, was convicted of possessing the stolen art.

Another unwelcome consequence of the Tango Squad investigation was that the main targets suddenly found themselves in the full glare of the media spotlight. Brendan O'Brien, who had exposed the Dunnes and the drugs crisis some years earlier, highlighted the Cahill gang in a riveting hour-long *Today Tonight* show special. It was watched by over a million viewers and made the General a household name overnight. O'Brien and his crew encountered the General when he turned up at Werburgh Street Labour Exchange to collect his weekly dole money. Despite his wealth Cahill always collected his £90 each week – it was something that he never missed. He was determined to collect every penny he was entitled to from the State.

The reporter stopped Cahill outside the Exchange, which the General had robbed several times, while members of the Tango Squad stood nearby. Cahill decided to bluff it out and gave an impromptu interview. When asked was he the General or did he know who the General was, Cahill glibly replied: 'I don't know, some army officer maybe? Sure the way the country is goin' these days you wouldn't know what way to think.' On the subject of the Beit paintings, Cahill claimed that Noel Lynch had appointed him a private detective to recover the art collection. 'I am on standby with Martin Foley and Eamon Daly for a job to get them [the paintings] back,' said Cahill.

Cahill even became the subject of debate in the Dáil. The mob's social welfare payments became the topic of most concern, at a time of high unemployment and recession. It was also a source of embarrassment that the most successful criminal in the country was, effectively, on the State's payroll. The Minister for Social Welfare announced that there was to be a full investigation. This decision would have dramatic consequences.

The Tango Squad ultimately succeeded in breaking up the General's once powerful criminal network and within two years at least a dozen of his closest lieutenants were serving long sentences for armed crimes in Portlaoise maximum-security prison. Other gang members like Lynch, Dutton and Shanahan, fed up with Cahill's antics and his games with the police, decided to go their separate ways. But the operation failed to put their primary target out of business. In the summer of 1988 he served a few months' imprisonment on Spike Island in Cork for refusing to enter a bond to keep the peace after threatening his neighbours in front of the T Squad. Cahill later claimed that he had enjoyed the break on what he described as his 'treasure island'. When he got out he continued to organize robberies, but not on the same scale.

The police operation had also instilled mistrust and suspicion among the members of the mob. Shavo Hogan was accused of giving the police information which led to John Foy being arrested for a second time. Foy was on bail when he was caught collecting guns for another robbery. One day Hogan was attacked in the prison exercise yard by Harry Melia and other former friends. They used a homemade knife to slice off the top of one of his ears. It was the gangland symbol of the rat. Martin Foley went on the run to avoid his trial for assaulting the Tango Squad member. He was extradited from England and given a two-year sentence in 1990. In an interview for London-based GQ magazine in 1991, Cahill claimed that Foley was a police informant and had tried to set him up during the Tango Squad operation. In one of his bizarre conspiracy theories, Cahill even claimed that Foley's 'assault' on the detective had been a 'set-up'. During that interview he referred to Foley by the nickname 'the Viper'. It would be the General's legacy to his former friend.

Other members of gangland's brat pack had also ended up in prison by the end of the 1980s. George 'the Penguin' Mitchell and Gerard Hopkins went on trial for armed aggravated burglary and false imprisonment, when they robbed a truckload of cattle drench worth over £100,000. The two friends, who were working with John Gilligan, held the truck driver at gunpoint. Then they locked him in a refrigerated container where he almost froze to death. Despite serious attempts to intimidate jurors and witnesses, Mitchell and Hopkins were each jailed for five years. The Penguin's brother Paddy had even organized the theft of files from a court clerk – but it turned out they were for a different case.

The Tango Squad had also concentrated their efforts on John Gilligan, who had been systematically robbing warehouses and factories throughout the country for years. Any commodity which could be sold, from washing-powder to colour TVs, Factory John robbed it. He later bragged of that time: 'It was great fun and I got a buzz out of it. Sometimes we got stuff and other times nothing. We were chased by the cops now and again and we had plenty of near misses. There were a lot of times when we were in and out of a place and no one knew a thing for ages afterwards. The strokes were a win-win situation for everyone. The victims, the owners of the truck or the factory got the insurance money . . . and me and the lads got a few bob. It was the perfect crime and doing no harm to anyone.'

By the time the Garda operation started against Cahill, Gilligan was already facing a number of charges for burglary. These included one for the theft of £80,000 worth of chocolate from a warehouse in Tallaght in 1987. While on bail in January 1988, Gilligan and two associates were arrested with goods stolen from a hardware store in Enniscorthy, County Wexford. This time he was arrested by Detective Sergeant Felix McKenna and his T Squad officers. McKenna had had a personal interest in Gilligan since his time stationed in Tallaght. The dangerous Godfather had plagued the hundreds of warehouses and factories covered by the Garda 'M' District. He treated the area like his kingdom and if anyone else decided to rob there, then they had to deal with him.

The diminutive gangster used every tactic, both legal and otherwise, to thwart criminal prosecutions against him. He threatened to murder anyone who crossed him or might consider testifying against him in court. On a number of occasions, cases were dropped after Gilligan visited vital witnesses and bluntly told them he would kill them. One terrified witness told Gardaí the thug had placed a shotgun in his mouth and threatened to blow his head off on the morning of the trial. On another occasion Gilligan blamed one of his gang members, David Weafer, for informing and doing a deal with the police after they were caught with a load of stolen Nilfisk vacuum cleaners. During that 'job' Gilligan and his crew burst into the Nilfisk warehouse in Tallaght and held up the staff at gunpoint, while they loaded a stolen 40-foot container with hundreds of the machines. Cops caught Gilligan and Weafer in another warehouse unloading the vacuum cleaners. Twenty-two-year-old Weafer, from Finglas, aroused the mobster's suspicions when he subsequently pleaded guilty to a charge of receiving the machines and got a relatively light two-year sentence. An angry Gilligan organized for some of his associates in prison to slash Weafer's face with a knife in the showers.

Gilligan made no secret of the fact that he was involved in threatening people. He reckoned that the more people who knew he was dangerous, the easier it would be to convince them to stay at home. Factory John would mock the police whenever he successfully thwarted a trial or investigation. And he had no difficulty threatening anyone in authority who stepped on his toes either.

In May 1988 Gilligan was jailed for 18 months for the chocolate robbery. At his hearing in the Circuit Criminal Court in Dublin, Detective Inspector John McLoughlin described the General's associate as 'one of Ireland's biggest criminals in organized crime'.

Factory John was released in July 1989 but a few months later he was due to go on trial for the Nilfisk robbery. He had used the law to delay the case going ahead for over three years. Inevitably intimidation and threats had been issued against witnesses. Staff at the Nilfisk HQ in Dublin had received anonymous calls, warning them that the place would be burned down if employees gave evidence at the trial. The matter was reported to the police and Gilligan's bail was revoked. The trial lasted for two weeks, during which the bully boy openly tried to intimidate jurors by staring menacingly at them. In the end Gilligan didn't need to scare anyone – he got off on a legal technicality.

Factory John grew even more arrogant about his chances of beating the Enniscorthy robbery rap. He'd already 'got at' the State's main witness, the owner of a yard where he stored the loot. But DS Felix McKenna had other ideas. In the run up to the trial, McKenna furnished an extensive report on John Gilligan's history for the Director of Public Prosecutions. In it, he itemized the number of times Factory John had used intimidation to get off various charges and when he was suspected of threatening jurors. McKenna also outlined Gilligan's associations with other major criminal groups and republican terrorists. He urged the DPP to have the thief returned for trial to the non-jury Special Criminal Court, like the members of Cahill's gang.

At a pre-trial hearing for Gilligan and his co-accused, James 'Fast-40' Kelly, Robbie O'Connell and Christy Delaney, their lawyers argued that there was insufficient evidence with which to try any of them. The judge disagreed and promptly returned Gilligan's three associates for trial in the Circuit Criminal Court. When it came to Gilligan there was a surprise in store. The DPP had sent him forward for trial in the Special Criminal Court. Gilligan went white with rage.

On 7 November 1990, after a day-long trial, Gilligan was convicted of receiving stolen goods and jailed for four years. Factory John could not believe what he was hearing. In passing sentence the presiding judge remarked: 'He has been involved in serious crime for many years and it appears that he has never had lawful employment.' Gilligan was sent to join the rest of his pals in Portlaoise Prison.

In the meantime Martin Cahill showed the world that the Garda crackdown on his operation had not reduced his propensity for sickening violence against anyone who crossed him. In January 1989, as a result of the Dáil-driven Department of Social Welfare investigation into his affairs, he received a letter informing him that his unemployment benefit was to be discontinued. Cahill had already received a visit from a tax inspector, whom he'd invited to meet with at Cowper Downs. The General soon stopped talking about 'taxable earnings' and began discussing the problem with crime and anti-social behaviour. Pointing out the window, he'd said to the nervous official: 'Now, d'ya see what I mean? Just look out that window and look what those bloody vandals have done now.' Outside the tax inspector's car had been set on fire. The General had made his point and he'd received no demand for unpaid taxes.

The letter informing him that his dole had been cut was signed by a Higher Executive Officer called Brian Purcell. Cahill appealed the decision and came face to face with the dedicated public servant at the hearing. Purcell outlined the reasons why the payments had been stopped, namely that Cahill's means showed that he did not qualify for social welfare benefits. On 9 May, the social welfare inspector appeared on behalf of his department at another appeal hearing, this time for Cahill's sister-in-law and lover, Tina Lawless, whose social welfare payments had also been cut as a result of the Cahill investigation. The General decided that he was going to have revenge.

Shortly after midnight on 29 May 1989, Brian Purcell was watching TV and reading the Sunday newspapers at his home in North County Dublin. His pregnant wife and two children were asleep upstairs when the front door bell rang. Purcell opened the door and one of Cahill's henchmen shoved a gun in his face, pushing the civil servant back into the house. His wife was awoken and brought downstairs, where she was tied up and gagged. The four-man snatch team spent an hour in the house, searching for documentation relating to Cahill's case. They then tied-up, gagged and blindfolded Brian Purcell and took him away in his car. They drove to Ailesbury Gardens in Sandymount, where he was left lying near railway lines. After a while the kidnappers frog-marched him a further 20 yards and put him sitting against a wall, with his legs out in front of him.

The General emerged from the shadows with a .38 revolver in his hand. This was how Cahill dealt with his problems. He didn't like confrontations or 'straighteners'. His preferred modus operandi was to turn up in the depths of the night when his victim had no way of protecting himself or retaliating. Cahill shot the terrified civil servant once in each leg and then ran off with his men. Miraculously neither bullet hit an artery or bone.

Brian Purcell managed to work the pillowcases off his head and called for help. He was rushed to hospital where he underwent operations on his legs and recovered from his appalling ordeal. It was a horrifying crime but it succeeded in achieving what Cahill wanted – to send shock-waves through the entire Irish public service. Even when the civil servant was recovering from his injuries, he received an anonymous get well card which read: 'The General prognosis is good.' Armed Garda protection was placed on all Department of Social Welfare officials dealing with the Cahill case. Brian Purcell made a full recovery from his injuries and courageously returned to work. In 2011 he was appointed Secretary General of the Department of Justice.

For the second time in seven years, the General had sent a chilling message to the Irish State on behalf of Crime Incorporated. In the final years of the 1980s Cahill had shown, yet again, that organized crime was getting out of control, and that he'd lived up to the predictions in the Serious Crime Squad's 1985 dossier.

The General's actions would encourage and embolden his former partners and the new generation of hardened, young criminals who would live up to Larry Dunne's infamous prophecy. In the 1990s Gangland would be transformed, as the drug trade became a multi-million-Euro business. Organized crime was about to get a lot more sophisticated and violent.

PART THREE

The 1990s

14. End of an Era

'I'm packin' in this fuckin' game. If I get away I'll never rob a fuckin' bank again.'

Martin Cahill made this solemn promise to himself as he desperately tried to outrun the Garda who was closing in fast behind him. At the age of 40, Gangland's notorious General had just realized that he was too old for pulling heists. The years spent gorging himself on cakes and fizzy drinks had taken their toll on his ability to literally stay out of the hands of the law. Cahill was unfit, overweight and suffering from diabetes. As he gasped for breath, the most wanted criminal in history, who had escaped so many times in the past, was only a few steps away from capture. If the Garda caught him, Public Enemy Number One could be sure that the State would help him keep his promise – for a possible 15 years. The General called to his pals running ahead: 'Lads, come back, come back.' Then he turned around and shot the unarmed officer twice, at point-blank range.

It was Monday, 8 January 1990, and Cahill had fired the first angry shots in what would go down in gangland history as the 'Year of the Gun'. The first year of the 1990s was one of violence and bloodshed, marked by a number of dramatic shoot-outs between the police and the armed robbers. This time, however, the Gardaí were the victors, as they took on the gun gangs with a determination not seen before. They measured their victories by the bodies of dead and wounded blaggers who had decided to shoot it out, rather than put their hands up. In 1980, three Gardaí were gunned down when they faced the gangs. But the tables were turned in the first six months of 1990. Three armed robbers were shot dead, several more were injured and a number of major gangs ended up behind bars. The turnaround forced the Godfathers to consider less hazardous and more profitable means of turning a dishonest buck. Over the following years, as the drug trade expanded, most robbers changed job descriptions.

As a detective inspector in charge of the Serious Crime Squad (SCS) in 1990, Tony Hickey was in the thick of the action. He witnessed how the year of the gun brought significant change to Gangland. 'We had plenty of evidence at the time that criminals exclusively involved in armed robberies looked around and said this is a dangerous business,' he recalls. 'The Gardaí had shown the criminal fraternity that they had the ability to take them on and quite a lot of them decided that there was an easier way to make money with less risk, and that was drug-trafficking.'

The armed Gardaí would also have a major effect on Tango One. At 7.35 a.m. on the morning of Cahill's life-changing decision, porter Willie Blake arrived to open the Allied Irish Bank in Ranelagh, Dublin. He turned off the alarm system, opened the shutters and went out to open the gates to the staff car park at the back of the building. As he did so, Blake was grabbed by Eddie Cahill and Eugene Scanlan, both of whom were armed and masked. They pushed him back inside and demanded to know who had the keys of the safe. Martin Cahill joined his crew about ten minutes later and took over the interrogation. He held a grenade up to the terrified porter's face and told Blake he would be blown up if there was 'any messin'. Over the next 50 minutes the porter admitted staff, as Cahill stood behind Blake holding a noose around his neck and a gun in his back. The staff members were ordered to lie on the ground while they waited for a manager to arrive with the keys to the night safe. Outside the bank, a fourth member of the gang suddenly banged on a rear window, to relay some kind of signal. The General obviously wasn't aware the window was connected to a silent panic alarm. The Gardaí were immediately called from a central monitoring station. Within minutes Martin Cahill could hear the sirens.

When he looked out he spotted the first squad car, containing uniformed officers John Moore and William Joynt, as it pulled up outside. The three men in the bank dropped everything, including a bag of guns, and ran out through the back door onto Ranelagh Avenue. When they spotted Garda John Moore at the front door, they ran in the opposite direction towards Ranelagh Park. Moore ran after the raiders, who headed for the Chelmsford Avenue exit. The General started to lag behind and couldn't keep up. Moore closed in on him with the intention of rugby-tackling him to the ground. Cahill later recounted what happened to his old pal John Traynor, and said it was in those seconds that he decided that it was a younger villain's job.

Cahill shot Garda Moore in the right arm and then continued running. With the adrenalin rush, the brave young officer didn't realize that he had been hit and kept chasing the potential killer. At the same time, Eddie Cahill, who was much fitter than his older brother, had doubled back behind John Moore. Eddie shot the Garda again, this time grazing his right leg. Martin Cahill also fired another shot at Moore. He later told Traynor how close he'd come to killing the unarmed cop when he'd aimed a fourth shot at Moore's chest but the gun's trigger broke off. Ironically the old gun was part of the consignment of weapons he'd stolen from the Garda depot, less than a decade earlier.

Garda Moore kept up his pursuit until he collapsed on the pavement at the park gates of Chelmsford Avenue. The young officer was rushed to hospital, where doctors took a bullet from his arm and treated him for a flesh wound to his leg. He was lucky to be alive. In the ensuing confusion the gang escaped. The General was last seen running through the grounds of the Royal Hospital in Donnybrook. He was puffing and panting and holding his stomach. But he managed to get away.

The investigation into the botched robbery soon uncovered the General's involvement. At the time his gang had been seriously depleted thanks to the efforts of the Tango Squad and the SCS. But he still had a number of associates at liberty as a consequence of the bail laws – both Scanlan and Eddie Cahill were both awaiting trials for serious offences, including armed robbery, possession of firearms and drugs. Just over a month later they were arrested in connection with the Ranelagh incident. Martin Cahill wasn't lifted because, in the absence of forensic evidence or a positive identification, senior officers believed there was no point. No one was charged with the incident. Cahill had a lucky escape, but the same could not be said for some of his associates.

Thomas Tynan, Austin Higgins, Brendan Walsh, PJ Loughran and William Gardiner were a potent, deadly mixture of criminals and republican paramilitaries – forever remembered in gangland folklore as the Athy Gang. They formed the nucleus of an overall team of ten criminals whose members came from both sides of Dublin. During 1989 there were a total of 49 armed robberies from banks in Ireland. The Athy Gang accounted for 32 of these, taking over £300,000 in the process. By September they had already carried out 20 robberies. Over the next four months they carried out another 12. Even by the General's standards, the gang had become one of the most prolific teams of blaggers ever seen.

PJ Loughran and William Gardiner, both IRA members, were the leaders of the motley collection of mavericks. Loughran, who was 29 and originally from Dungannon, County Tyrone, was one of the many republicans on the run in the South. He'd moved to live in Coolock, North Dublin, to hide from the authorities in Northern Ireland where he was wanted for terrorist offences. Gardiner, who was from Cabra and aged 37, had also been an active member of the organization. They were both experienced armed robbers and had worked with John Cahill and his crew for nearly two years. That partnership had ended when Gardiner, Loughran and Dutchie Holland escaped after the security van job went wrong in September 1988 and John Cahill, Albert Crowley and Noel Gaynor were arrested.

After that the Provos teamed up with other members of the same criminal pool, including Brendan 'Wetty' Walsh and Thomas Tynan, both members of the General's gang. Walsh was 34 and from the Charlemont Gardens Flats in the south inner-city; Tynan was 29 and from South Circular Road. Walsh was a brutal hoodlum with a long criminal record for armed robbery, violence and false imprisonment. Tynan was a heroin-user with form for violence, theft, burglary and drugs. Despite his habit, Tynan was trusted because he kept his mouth shut and he was an adroit robber. The fifth member of the soon to be infamous mob was 26-year-old Austin Higgins from Donaghmede. He came from a respectable middle-class family but had decided, like Mickey Boyle, that he wanted to be a criminal.

The five robbers made up what Garda intelligence would later identify as the 'A' team in the 'firm'. Five other hoods made up the 'B' team. Gardiner and Loughran used their IRA training to organize the gang like an Active Service Unit. Secrecy and meticulous planning were the hallmarks of their modus operandi. They began targeting banks, mostly branches of the Bank of Ireland, within a 120-mile radius south of Dublin. The chances of running into armed Gardaí in country towns were substantially less than in the capital, and the cops weren't geared up for the same level of rapid response as their city colleagues.

There was also the added incentive of getting more cash. By 1990 there were two types of robberies taking place: those carried out by well-organized, professional gangs and strokes by strung-out addicts, desperately looking for money to buy heroin. The majority of robberies were being carried out by junkies, armed with a syringe, knife or gun, who might do two or three 'jump-overs' in a typical day. The Athy Gang knew that, as a result of all the hold-ups in Dublin banks, limited amounts of money were now being kept behind the counters – and Garda response times had dramatically improved.

Gardiner and Loughran had plans for up to four robberies in different counties at any one time. Detailed reconnaissance was carried out on each target and they made sure they knew every back road in the area. The IRA men treated the rest of the gang on a need-to-know basis and, to prevent careless leaks, only informed them of the location on the morning of a heist. The gang had a pool of five or more stolen high-powered cars, fuelled up and stashed in hotels and apartment blocks around the south-side of Dublin. The gangsters had a large arsenal of powerful firearms and used scanning equipment to listen in on the Gardaí. Wigs and false beards were used as disguises. The weaponry and the cash from each robbery were hidden by Loughran and Gardiner in pre-planned hides, in a number of forests along the getaway routes.

Loughran was normally the 'wheels man' on each job while the other four sprinted into the bank, ordering staff and customers to lie face-down. They threatened to shoot anyone who moved. Each raider would carry a hold-all bag, strapped across his body. Three of them would vault the security screens and empty the tills while the fourth covered the terrified occupants. The gang were in and out of a bank in between two and four minutes. One or more of the other high-powered, stolen cars would be parked within a ten-mile radius of the job. The team would split up and make their way back to Dublin along separate routes; sometimes they even took the train.

The gang's modus operandi became their calling card and it soon became obvious to the Gardaí that the same gang was responsible for most of the bank jobs taking place. In September 1989, the Central Detective Unit (CDU) launched 'Operation Gemini', tasked with spearheading the investigation to catch the gang. The CDU had already enjoyed considerable success apprehending a string of major criminal players and the man in overall command of Operation Gemini was Detective Chief Superintendent John Murphy. He appointed his deputy,

Detective Superintendent Noel Conroy, to lead the operation. The officer in charge of the investigation on the ground was Tony Hickey. Gemini was launched on 4 September at a special conference of detectives held in the CDU's offices in Harcourt Square, Dublin. A few hours before the conference started, the gang hit another bank in Edenderry, County Offaly. It reinforced the urgent need for the investigation.

Four days later the gang struck again, this time at the Bank of Ireland at Emily Square, Athy. In less than four minutes they got away with £47,000 – it was their largest score yet. Three days after that, the bearded robbers vaulted the counter of the Bank of Ireland in Coolock – Loughran's local branch. This time they got just £3,000. On 14 September, the gang hit the Bank of Ireland branch in Dunmanway, County Cork and a week later the Bank of Ireland branch in Gorey, County Wexford. During one month their haul from five robberies was almost £100,000.

The initial breakthrough in the case came from an informant. He tipped off the Squad that Thomas Tynan and another robber from Dolphin House Flats were involved in the robbery spree, which was the talk of gangland. Another source revealed that Brendan 'Wetty' Walsh was involved with Tynan. The Operation Gemini team mobilized the Squad's surveillance unit to monitor the three suspects, in a bid to identify the rest of the gang, but it was difficult because the gang members employed counter-surveillance techniques. Eventually, however, the discreet watch paid off.

Tony Hickey recalled the challenge his unit faced: 'When Operation Gemini was set up in September 1989 the Loughran/Gardiner gang were our top priority. In the beginning we didn't have very much intelligence to go on but after a period of time we identified the gang members and mounted a surveillance operation. Loughran had been a hardened terrorist and so was Gardiner. They used the expertise they gained in the IRA. They were very conscious of surveillance and good at counter-surveillance. When they left Dublin, they invariably travelled over the Dublin Mountains and always used back roads. During the robberies they used gratuitous violence on bank staff and fired shots. We also had high-grade intelligence specifically stating that they intended using lethal force if they were confronted by Gardaí either going to or coming from a robbery. If we were to put them out of action we knew we had to catch them carrying weapons. It was a very difficult operation from the start and there were plenty of wild goose chases during the five months we were after them. But they had to be lucky all the time and we only had to be lucky once.'

Covert surveillance was going to prove extremely difficult, especially in the case of trained professionals like Gardiner and Loughran. The Squad would have to be innovative if they were going to catch the mob.

In the meantime the Athy Gang continued their robberies, unaware the Serious Crime Squad was on to them. In the first two weeks of October they carried out another four heists from banks in counties Kilkenny and Tipperary. It was after the last one in Roscrea that their luck began to run out. Austin Higgins and another gang member were arrested when they were stopped in County Offaly on their way back to Dublin. Two detectives from Operation Gemini were sent to interview the pair in Portlaoise Garda station. During his interrogation Higgins began to talk and admitted his part in the robbery. There was a single piece of forensic evidence that directly linked him with the robbery – a boot-print on the bank counter he had vaulted in Roscrea. The other robber was released because of a lack of evidence and Higgins was charged with the robbery the next day. He had never faced a serious charge and the prospect of a long stretch behind bars before. After his release on bail he agreed to turn informant.

In the initial stages Higgins gave the Operation Gemini team an invaluable insight into the operation of the gang. But he couldn't give them what they needed most – specific information on a target – because he never knew until the morning of the job. Three days after Higgins's arrest, Loughran, Gardiner, Walsh and Tynan robbed the AIB in Rane-lagh, Dublin to get his bail money. They got just £4,622. Two weeks later, on 3 November, the gang hit the Bank of Ireland in Bray, taking £11,693. Following the 'job' the Gemini team raided the homes of all the gang members, including Higgins, but found nothing to connect them with the heists.

After assessing what they knew of the gang's behavioural patterns, the officers in charge of Operation Gemini realized that they would need serious armed help if they confronted the robbers. They requested the assistance of a newly formed specialist Garda unit called the Emergency Response Unit (ERU). It had been quietly established a year earlier and was intended to eventually replace the Special Task Force. In

1990 most members of the force were unaware of its existence. Its incep-
tion followed a recommendation in an internal review that the force
needed a more specialized squad to deal with sieges, hijackings and
heavily armed gangs. Membership of the unit was, and still is, a closely
guarded secret. Members were handpicked, after undertaking a rigor-
ous selection course, and were intensively trained in tactics and firearms.
The ERU was based on similar police SWAT-style teams in America,
Germany and Britain and members had additional training with the
Irish Army's Special Forces unit, the Army Ranger Wing (ARW). The
ERU's 32 members were equipped with the Smith and Wesson Model
59 semi-automatic pistol, Uzi submachine-gun, Heckler and Koch
assault rifle and the Winchester pump-action shotgun. A major shock
was in store for the criminal underworld.

The ERU and the Operation Gemini team drew up an elaborate plan
to intercept the gang. A list was drawn up of 165 potential targets within
the gang's operational radius. It detailed banks in ten counties and each
bank branch/town was given a specific code name. All the gang members and cars being used also had codes, to prevent the robbers
identifying themselves when they tuned into police frequencies. Loughran was VIP 1, Tynan was VIP 2, and so on. The plan also identified
every road leading from the towns listed. It was an awesome task and
there were several false starts.

On 14 November, the investigation team learned that the gang
planned to rob the bank at Mountrath, County Laois the following day.
A major operation was put in place around the town as SCS and ERU
officers waited for the raiders to turn up. The surveillance team confirmed that the gang had left Dublin in a stolen red car around dawn,
but they couldn't follow them without being spotted. The Laois tip-off
came to nothing as, that afternoon, the 'A' team hit the Bank of Ireland
in Tullow, County Carlow, 35 miles away. The extraordinary game of
cat and mouse continued.

Meanwhile the investigation team had located four of the gang's getaway cars. They planted a number of eavesdropping devices in one of
them, as it was used to carry out surveillance on targeted banks. A homing device, which could be monitored by air, was also placed on one of
the vehicles. The Air Corps made a Cessna spotter-plane available for
the job. It was one of the first occasions that the Gardaí had used such

sophisticated electronic equipment in their fight against organized crime. But unfortunately they didn't have enough equipment to bug all the cars. The operation then ran into trouble with Garda management. The SCS, the CDU surveillance team and the ERU were gobbling up considerable resources in their efforts to catch the blaggers. The top brass was still averse to long-term operations and wanted to see results. As Christmas approached there was mounting pressure to call it off. Chief Superintendent Murphy pleaded for more time.

Operation Gemini was given a reprieve when, that December, the gang pulled another two heists in Enniscorthy, County Wexford and Thurles, County Tipperary. The investigation and ERU teams watched an area of the Killakee Woods in the Dublin Mountains and waited for the gang to return with the money and weapons, but they never showed. The detectives later learned that Loughran was using another hide, in a wooded area near the village of Windgap, County Kilkenny.

Loughran and Gardiner continued to identify new targets during the Christmas holidays. Loughran called the gang together for another job on 28 December and Higgins dutifully relayed the information to his Garda handlers. He didn't have a specific location for the raid so squads of officers were dispatched to cover banks in counties Wicklow, Wexford, Waterford and Kilkenny. The homing device was no help because the military plane was unable to operate in the poor winter conditions. The ERU watched the two wooded areas in Dublin and Kilkenny – and waited. Loughran decided to abort the robbery, however, when the gang failed to rendezvous at a pre-arranged time in Kilkenny. Higgins later revealed that Loughran would have been prepared to carry out the raid, even though there were Gardaí near the bank, if the rest of the team had turned up on time. The gangsters took a break for the New Year and the waiting game dragged on into a fifth month.

The breakthrough finally came on 4 January 1990. The gang were planning to hit the Bank of Ireland in Athy for a second time. This time the intelligence was rock solid – the information came from a tape-recording of a conversation which took place on the reconnaissance run to Athy. The investigation team sat back and listened as Gardiner and Loughran unconsciously shared the whole plan with them. If the local Gardaí appeared the ex-Provos had a brutal contingency plan ready for them: 'We'll blow the fuckers away; take them out; shoot them.'

The robbery was set for the following morning. The Operation Gemini and ERU teams took their positions around Emily Square – but the gang aborted the raid at the last minute. There was a second false alarm on 8 January, the same day that Martin Cahill almost got caught.

Four days later the gang finally walked into the trap in Athy. Eleven members of the ERU were deployed in the local fire station and a nearby yard at Leinster Street, while 15 members of the Serious Crime Squad were positioned in an outer cordon. The local uniformed and detective units were also alerted and on standby around the town. A detective sat in a car facing the bank, ready to raise the alarm when the gang arrived. At 12.20 p.m. he gave the signal as the raiders drove into Emily Square in a stolen BMW and parked outside the bank. 'The eagle has landed, the eagle has landed,' he calmly reported. Loughran stayed behind the wheel, while Gardiner, Higgins, Walsh and Tynan walked quickly towards the front door. They wore long coats, false beards and wigs. As they got to the door, they took out their guns. They pushed the porter, Noel Reddy, back inside and ordered staff and customers, including young children, to get down. Three gangsters vaulted the counter and emptied the tills, just like they had done four months earlier.

As soon as the signal was given all hell broke lose. Detective Sergeant Nacie Rice and his team of five ERU men sped from the yard. They raced down Leinster Street into Emily Square in two cars, blocking the BMW from the rear. Simultaneously the second ERU team, under Detective Sergeant Michael Shanahan, sped from the fire station and cut the raiders' car off at the front. Loughran frantically tried to shunt his way out from between the ERU cars, by driving backwards and forwards. The screams of the car engine and the squeal of tyres added to the confusion.

The armed detectives fired a total of 20 shots at the wheels of the getaway car to immobilize it. When Loughran was ordered to put his hands up and get out, he lifted a pistol and pointed it at the driver of the squad car in front. Two officers opened fire on him at the same time, hitting him in the neck and head. The leader of the Athy Gang, who'd vowed to fight his way out, slumped sideways in his seat seriously injured.

Inside the bank the gang heard the gunfire and began to panic. Brendan Walsh looked out and shouted to the others: 'We're set up, we're set up; the cops are everywhere.' Higgins cried: 'It's over, it's over, we're fucked . . . I don't want to die anyway. They're shooting on the street, I don't want to die.' Walsh shouted at Higgins: 'It's not over, get a hostage . . . get a fucking hostage.' Higgins turned and grabbed bank official John Condron, holding his neck in an armlock. William Gardiner grabbed a customer and Walsh pulled the porter off the ground. Tynan lurked among the terrified hostages.

The group shuffled to the front door. Higgins was very agitated and shouted at the police: 'Get back or we'll shoot.' The ERU officers told them to put down their weapons. But in the confusion of the initial confrontation with Loughran the keys had been left in one of the squad cars and the engine was still running. The rear door of the car nearest the bank was open and the gang began to inch towards it. The cops continued shouting at the gunmen to give themselves up. Then Higgins moved his gun to the back of John Condron's head and screamed: 'I'll blow his fucking head off if you don't move back.' As the robber moved his finger to the trigger, Detective Sergeant Rice took aim and fired a single shot, hitting Higgins on the right side of his forehead. Other detectives fired at the wheels of the abandoned police car to immobilize it. At the same moment Tynan was shot four times when he turned and aimed his gun at the officers.

The shooting was over in seconds. Tynan, Higgins and their hostage John Condron were lying seriously injured on the pavement. Three of the detectives involved in the operation were also hurt. Two of them suffered minor grazes and the third had a shotgun wound to the left leg. A pedestrian who was standing on the street 300 feet away suffered a graze when he was hit by a ricochet.

Walsh and Gardiner retreated back into the bank with their hostages. The two hoods were in a panic and sweating so much that their disguises fell off.

Gemini's Tony Hickey took command of the situation and phoned the bank from the hotel next door. During an hour-long stand-off, he calmly negotiated with Brendan Walsh and assured him that no one would be harmed if they surrendered. Walsh said that he wanted a priest and an ambulance. Hickey first convinced the robber to agree to hold fire while the injured men lying on the pavement were moved for urgent medical attention. The gangsters also allowed eight of the hostages to leave. Hickey contacted the local priest, Father Patrick Mangan, who volunteered to go into the bank and bring Walsh and Gardiner out with him. Before they gave themselves up, Gardiner laughed as he dumped his weapon and fixed his hair. Walsh handed a bullet to the prettiest lady in the bank as a souvenir. Then they walked out on either side of the priest and were promptly arrested.

Austin Higgins never regained consciousness and died some hours later in hospital. Hostage John Condron, who was hit by one of the rounds from the Garda guns, never fully recovered from his injuries and was left partially disabled. Loughran was also left disabled from his injuries and as a result never stood trial. Emergency surgery saved Thomas Tynan's life and he later recovered. Tynan, Walsh and Gardiner were subsequently sentenced to 12 years each.

The infamous Athy incident caused some controversy when it was discovered that the ERU had done all the shooting and the gang hadn't fired a single shot. The gangsters' weapons were, however, found cocked, loaded and ready for use. But the controversy faded within days as the public showed overwhelming support for the police action. There was little sympathy for gangsters who wanted to fight back.

The dramatic debut of the ERU made them a household name overnight and they were commended for their courage and professionalism. The bank staff, customers and even the family of the injured bank official, paid tribute to the Gardaí who took on the Athy Gang. An internal inquiry later found that the Winchester pump-action shotgun, responsible for most of the collateral injuries, was not suitable for confrontations in built-up areas. A new system of communication was also introduced for such situations and ERU training methods were modified. As news of the Athy gunfight spread, the three-letter abbreviation burned itself into the minds of the criminal gangs. For the first time the cops had shown the gun gangs that they were more than a match for them. Armed robbery was becoming an extremely dangerous business.

On May Day 1990 a seven-member IRA gang from Dublin raided the AIB in Enniscorthy, County Wexford. Armed with two sawn-off shotguns, three handguns and two replica weapons, the gang got into the bank by climbing through an upstairs window after scaling scaffolding. They tied up bank staff on the first floor and then forced staff and customers downstairs to lie on the ground. But the inexperienced Provo thieves spent too long in the bank. A member of the staff, who was on the phone when they burst in, managed to raise the alarm.

At the local Garda station Superintendent Michael Murphy issued a machine-gun and three revolvers to four uniformed officers: Thomas Millar, Thomas Dunphy, Michael McGinley and John Barron. The armed officers arrived at the bank as the raiders were getting into a get-away van. As they tried to drive off, the IRA unit fired three shots at the Gardaí. The four cops returned fire, hitting the driver, Kenneth Bolger, in the head. The raiders threw out their weapons and promptly surren-dered. Bolger, who was from Sandymount, Dublin, underwent a number of operations and survived his injuries. Dominick Adams, Brian Kenna, Pamela Kane, Anthony Beggs and Patrick Lavin were each jailed for ten years after they took the unusual step of pleading not guilty but admit-ted through their counsel that they had taken part in the heist. The seventh member of the crew, Gerard Kearns from Tallaght, received a 12-year sentence. When Bolger recovered from his injuries he was jailed for eight years. It was another stunning victory for the police.

Just over two months after the rookie IRA unit pulled their ill-fated robbery, two more hardened and reckless gangsters decided to take on the law. Their names were Thomas Wilson and William 'Blinkey' Doyle.

During Christmas week 1989, while the Athy Gang were planning more armed robberies, Thomas Wilson was enjoying his first taste of freedom in 12 years. Originally from Ballyclare, County Antrim, the 38-year-old had been involved in petty crime from the age of 14. After joining the IRA, he spent most of his adult life behind bars. In July 1972, a month before his twenty-first birthday, Wilson was convicted of two cases of armed robbery and jailed for three years. Shortly after his release, he was caught again and charged with attempted armed robbery in Belfast. For that he got a ten-year stretch in October 1975. In prison, Wilson went on hunger strike and later escaped from hospital. He was recaptured in 1977, after doing another heist in Belfast. In 1978 he was sentenced to 18 years for that robbery, to run consecutively with his earlier sentence. The school drop-out decided to knuckle down in prison and do something constructive. He received a degree in math-ematics and was considered a model prisoner. He left the North shortly after his release and moved to live in Dublin. But instead of using his maths degree, Wilson went back to doing what he knew best – robbing banks.

He joined the gang led by former INLA men Tommy Savage and Michael Weldon. The terrorist partners-in-crime had moved on to the Irish Peoples Liberation Organization (IPLO), which was a breakaway group that emerged from the ashes of the INLA feud in the late 1980s. And, like the INLA, it attracted only the dregs of republicanism. In addition to their 'political' struggle, Savage and Weldon were also operating a thriving drug business and organizing armed robberies to raise money for further shipments of cannabis and heroin. They ran a tightly knit, well-organized group and worked closely with a number of other criminal mobs, particularly the one led by Gerry Hutch and Eamon Kelly.

The Savage/Weldon gang included two other former INLA members from Northern Ireland. Thirty-one-year-old Danny Hamill from Portadown – nicknamed 'the Rabbit' because of his prominent front teeth – was as violent and unpredictable as his Dublin comrades. In 1981 he appeared before the Special Criminal Court on kidnapping, explosives and firearms charges. On another occasion he was jailed for five years for robbing a jewellery store. He was classified by Garda Special Branch as 'a dangerous armed criminal'. Patrick Pearse McDonald, a professional barber from Newry, was also enjoying his freedom. He'd been released from Portlaoise Prison in August 1989 after serving a sentence for kidnapping and firearms offences. According to his associates, he was the IPLO's second-in-command in the South. McDonald was as colourful as he was brutal, and was an incorrigible womanizer. Soon after his release he set up a hairdressing salon in Marino, on Dublin's north-side and earned the nickname 'Teasy Weasy', after a famous London coiffeur to the stars.

The gang operated in groups of between two and four members, concentrating on banks on the northern fringe of Dublin. Like most robbery teams, they were creatures of habit. They preferred stealing getaway cars from car parks at train stations. On 5 March 1990, Wilson and Hamill were arrested when they were caught stealing a BMW from Bray Railway Station, County Wicklow. During a violent confrontation, the two terrorists assaulted and seriously injured an unarmed officer with a concrete block. Wilson and the Rabbit were charged and remanded in custody.

While on remand on B-Wing in Mountjoy Prison, Thomas Wilson met William 'Blinkey' Doyle, a former graduate of the Dunne 'Academy', who'd been caught with over £200,000 worth of heroin in 1983, along with Mickey Weldon. When the Drug Squad warrant was found to be defective and the charges were dropped, Doyle had continued his involvement in the drug trade and armed robberies.

On 1 February 1990, Doyle was arrested and charged in connection with an armed hold-up at a bank in Celbridge, County Kildare. While being questioned, he admitted taking part in five other heists across West Dublin in January. But members of the gang suspected that he had been sharing a lot more information with the police and accused him of being a tout. Their suspicions had been aroused the previous October, when Doyle had been charged with a similar job in Newbridge and detectives had recovered the money and guns. Another notorious armed thug from the north inner-city, Larry Cummins Senior, was also charged with the Newbridge job. While awaiting bail, Doyle was attacked by Cummins's associates and his face was slashed with razors. Blinkey had received over a hundred stitches.

Doyle was released on bail on 20 June and immediately joined up with Wilson and his associates. During the next 16 days the gang robbed 5 banks in Meath and Kildare. At 10.15 a.m. on 26 June, Doyle and Wilson hit the Bank of Ireland in Leixlip, County Kildare. They considered it such an easy target that they returned again on 6 July. The raiders, who were carrying three firearms – two pistols and a shotgun – parked their getaway car outside the front door and ran inside, leaving the engine running. The same car had been used by a four-man gang two days earlier, in a robbery in Dunshaughlin. In the bank they ordered staff and customers to lie down and one raider vaulted the counter. They left a few minutes later with just over £3,000 in cash. Outside they jumped into the getaway car and sped back towards Dublin. By then the Gardaí had been alerted and specialist squads from the ERU and STF were heading for the area.

The robbers were spotted by an ERU officer as they drove near the Hole in the Wall pub, beside the Phoenix Park. One of the most reckless car chases ever seen in Dublin began when the Garda tried to stop Doyle and Wilson. Over the next 15 minutes the two desperados reached speeds of up to 100 miles per hour, as they tried to shake off the squad cars closing in on them. Wilson, who was the passenger, fired several shots through the side window, as the police tried to hem the car in. Bullets bounced off the pursuing cars as the chase continued along Ratoath Road and then onto Griffith Avenue. When the robbers drove onto the dual carriageway in Finglas, there were up to ten police cars on their tail. A squad car driving ahead of the getaway car tried to prevent them from overtaking. Doyle attempted to ram it out of the way. When he couldn't get past, he swung over to the other side of the carriageway and sped off towards Glasnevin against the oncoming traffic, forcing drivers to swerve out of the way. Wilson fired more shots at the squad cars which were keeping abreast of them on the correct side of the carriageway.

The high-speed convoy caused havoc in the morning traffic, as it continued through Botanic Avenue and onto Richmond Road. Pedestrians and motorists were stunned by the real-life 'cops and robbers' drama as Wilson hung out of his window, firing more shots in the direction of the convoy of blue lights and wailing sirens. The robbers then sped into Fairview Avenue, which is at the centre of a warren of narrow side streets. The getaway car collided with a parked car and spun around, facing back at the convoy of squad cars which had stopped behind it.

Doyle drove back in the direction of the police and mounted the pavement to get past the first car, while Thomas Wilson fired more shots. One of the detectives fired back. The car careered another 50 feet down the street before ramming into the side of another squad car, trapping the four unarmed officers inside. One of the raiders could be seen lifting a weapon to open fire on the cops. Two members of the ERU, one of whom was armed with an Uzi submachine-gun, fired a burst into the getaway car. Doyle was hit by five bullets while Wilson died from a gunshot wound to the head.

It had been another fatal day for criminals who thought they could still fight the law and win. What became known as the Fairview shootout had provided more food for thought for the community of blaggers. The deaths of the two men in July 1990 marked the first year of the third decade of organized crime. It would ultimately be remembered as the end of an era for armed robbers.

15.   An Evil Empire is Born

Portlaoise Prison has been Gangland's premier educational academy for over twenty years. The heavily fortified prison complex, on the edge of the Midland town, is the underworld's Alma Mater; and its alumni include some of the best-known gangsters in Ireland and Europe. In the early 1990s the future direction of organized crime was mapped out behind the grim, stone walls which are patrolled by heavily armed soldiers. The E1 wing was where contacts were made, plans laid and gangs formed. The gangland equivalent of a university atmosphere prevailed as criminal concepts were debated, new trends explored and experiences shared. The most popular subject on the curriculum was learning from the mistakes that had won the 'students' their State-sponsored 'scholarships' in the first place – and how to avoid them in the future. Another area of debate was how dangerous the business of armed robbery had become since the bloody shoot-outs in Dublin, Athy and Enniscorthy. Ireland's maximum-security prison is where the story of modern Gangland begins.

Up to the late 1980s, Portlaoise was almost exclusively used to house members of the IRA and the INLA. In the annual prison report of 1988 the average daily population in the prison was 196, 40 of whom were so-called 'non-subversive' prisoners. They were mostly petty criminals and drug addicts from Dublin, who received 50 per cent remission in their sentences in return for working as glorified servants for the terrorists, who refused to do domestic chores. In November 1973 the decision had been taken to send all republican prisoners to Portlaoise, following the escape by helicopter of three senior Provos from Mountjoy. Terrorists were also moved from other detention facilities because the authorities deemed Portlaoise, which was built in 1830, to be the most secure institution in the country.

But the Provos soon proved them wrong. In August 1974, 19 IRA prisoners escaped when they overpowered prison warders and used explosives to blast open a gate. Soldiers who were guarding the perimeter of the prison fired warning shots to prevent the rest of the inmates from also making a run for it. The 19 Provos got to the main Dublin Road, where cars were waiting to whisk them away. While most of the escapees were recaptured, the incident was hugely embarrassing for the Government, which was desperately grappling to contain the terrorist threat to the State.

Gardaí had also discovered an underground tunnel, dug from outside, a month earlier. On 17 March 1975, 18 Provo inmates attempted another mass breakout, during which they used more explosive charges to blast their way through a locked steel door and a gate into the recreation yard. At the same time, IRA members positioned outside the complex opened fire on the troops standing guard on the prison rooftops. A truck that had been specially modified to act as a battering ram smashed through a closed gate. It drove in the direction of the prison wall, where the inmates were waiting on the other side. The plan was to ram a hole in the wall but the improvised 'tank' ground to a halt when the wheels became entangled in a wire fence. Its crew was arrested. In the meantime soldiers fired several warning shots and forced the prisoners to retreat back into the building. One IRA member, Thomas Smyth from Dublin, was killed when he was injured by the ricochet of an army bullet.

As a result Portlaoise was transformed into a maximum-security prison and is still one of the most impregnable in Europe. The ratio of prison officers to prisoners was the highest in the country and they were backed up by a large number of Gardaí. An air exclusion-zone was ordered around the complex and a detachment of 120 troops, armed with rifles and anti-aircraft machine-guns, patrolled the perimeter walls and rooftops and others manned watchtowers. The complex bristled with CCTV cameras and sensors, both above and below ground; and lines of tank-traps stood guard around the prison's entire boundary. There were no further escapes.

From 1988 onwards, it was decided that hardened criminals who were convicted by the Special Criminal Court would also be sent to Portlaoise. It was deemed the most suitable facility to accommodate the increasing number of dangerous villains being jailed as a result of the Tango Squad and other offensives against organized crime gangs. The new category of high-risk, violent prisoners was a reflection of the changes that had taken place in Gangland. On the E1 wing they were segregated from their republican neighbours, who didn't see themselves as gangsters. In less than two years, the wing became home to a fearsome collection of Ireland's most dangerous drug-dealers, robbers and killers.

The long-stay residents on E1 included most of the General's gang – his brothers, John and Eddie Cahill, and trusted lieutenants Eugene Scanlan, Albert Crowley, Noel Gaynor, John Foy, Eamon Daly and Harry Melia. Seamus 'Shavo' Hogan was moved from E1 to the prison's segregation unit in October 1990, after the gang accused him of being an informant and tried to slice off the tops of his ears. Also in residence were the three surviving members of the Athy Gang, and 'Factory' John Gilligan, Dutchie Holland, Larry Dunne, Brian Meehan and his close pal Paul Ward. Another resident shifted to E1 was John Cullen, a notoriously brutal Dublin pimp, who was serving life for the triple murders of prostitute Dolores Lynch, her mother and her aunt in 1983. Cullen burned the women to death as they slept in their home. Dessie O'Hare and Fergal Toal were also moved to E1 after being ejected from the INLA's wing.

In January 1992, they were joined by Christy 'Bronco' Dunne, who arrived with a hefty 11-year sentence. At the age of 53, the Godfather who had ushered in a new era of crime in Ireland had finally been forced into retirement by his hated enemies, the police. Dunne's last crime was a typically nasty and cowardly one. It completely debunked Bronco's claims that he was an ordinary, decent criminal. He had been convicted of holding Finglas postmaster Rocco Cafolla and his family hostage, before forcing Rocco to take £80,000 from his post office and hand it over to the gang. During the terrifying ordeal in December 1988, the family was held at gunpoint overnight and the following morning a 'bomb' was strapped to Cafolla's back when he was sent to collect the cash. Bronco had organized the crime to look like a paramilitary operation and he recorded instructions which Rocco Cafolla had to follow. Afterwards he gave his three accomplices £24,000 to divide between them and kept the rest for himself. From his point of view the 'job' had been a complete success. But the irony was that heroin, which Bronco had avoided, would play a major role in his downfall.

A clear sign of the suave Godfather's decline was that he'd been forced to recruit two of his teenage nephews for the job and they were both junkies. Isaac Turner and Ryan Dunne looked up to their Uncle Bronco, who filled their heads with nonsense about forming the new generation of the powerful Dunne 'family'. Turner was the 18-year-old son of Christy's sister Anne. His brother, Abraham, a convicted killer and drug-dealer, and his mother were also heroin addicts. Seventeen-year-old Ryan Dunne was the son of Bronco's brother Robert, who was serving a sentence for armed robbery. Ryan and his father were also junkies. The third recruit, 27-year-old Raymond Roberts from Dolphin House Flats, was also a drug-abuser.

After almost three weeks of investigation the Gardaí had drawn a blank on identifying the suspects. But the Serious Crime Squad got a lucky break when Detective Garda Tom Barbour pulled in Isaac Turner, who was wanted for another offence. When he searched Bronco's nephew, the cop found a wad of £1 notes in an envelope and a building-society book showing that Isaac had lodged £4,000 a few days after the Cafolla kidnapping. When the notes were checked, it was established that they came from a consignment of cash that had been delivered to the post office just before the robbery. When he was questioned about the money Turner cracked and spilled the beans.

Turner and Roberts subsequently pleaded guilty while Ryan Dunne fled to England, and Turner agreed to testify at his uncle's trial. It was the final shame for a family who had once lived by a code of *omertà* – and it was Bronco's ultimate nightmare. At Isaac Turner's court hearing, the judge noted that his evidence might make 'a major professional criminal amenable to justice for this heinous crime'. Turner was given a four-year sentence and segregated in prison for his own protection.

Christy Dunne used every legal mechanism at his disposal to prevent the trial going ahead. Typically, he even tried to mount another media campaign, claiming, yet again, that he had been stitched up. He also tried to intimidate his nephew to prevent him taking the witness stand. But that also failed. When Bronco finally stood trial, Turner testified against him.

During the two-week trial in the Circuit Criminal Court, Bronco put on one of his finest performances for the jury. But in the end they didn't believe him and he was sent down for the longest sentence he'd received in his thirty-year career as a professional criminal. He was devastated. During a subsequent court appearance, the one-time gangland hard-man whined to a judge about his predicament: 'If I don't get just-ice in this case I'll be leaving Portlaoise Prison in a coffin.'

Dunne continued to plead his innocence twenty years later, despite the overwhelming evidence against him. In his mind he was the victim of a nefarious plot by the police. On E1 in 1992, however, no one was interested in listening to Bronco's tale of woe. As far as the younger hoods were concerned, he was a burned-out, over-rated has-been. The most infamous of all the Portlaoise alumni, John Gilligan, was already planning a very different type of evil empire to the one the Dunnes had once aspired to. Factory John dismissed Bronco and his family as 'mup-pets' – and instead focused on implementing his future plans.

A prison sentence is a sanction where a malfeasant loses his liberty for a set period of time. It is also intended to convince the gangster to change his ways and reform. But rarely has any career criminal exited a prison's gates as a law-abiding citizen. In fact, an analysis of the records of any committed gangland player shows that his crimes tend to be better organized after a spell behind bars. Gangs formed on the prison landings and exercise yards are more ruthless and loyal than most. Retired Chief Superintendent John McGroarty witnessed the development of the mobs during his forty-year career. 'Gangs normally come from blood relationships, from localised areas in the neighbourhood and particu-larly prison,' said McGroarty. 'You invariably find that they've served time in prison together and that is where strong bonds of friendship are forged. The criminals assure each other that when they get out they'll have a bigger and better plan. A gangster will have some information or an idea which he will develop and bring other individuals into the mix. Between them they will hatch a wonderful plan to do highly profitable crime and next time they won't get caught. That's what so many of them like to think. And that is how the John Gilligan gang got started, on E1 in Portlaoise.'

While the likes of Eddie Cahill, Larry Dunne and John Cullen took art classes, and others learned how to play guitars or to read and write, Gilligan was busy networking, making contacts and winning the respect of his fellow inmates. Factory John already enjoyed a formidable repu-tation. One former inmate recalled: 'For a small fellow Gilligan had a tougher reputation than some of the biggest fellahs on E1. He was known for having mad bottle and he was a violent bastard who wasn't afraid to do anyone who fucked around with him. It was like he always wanted to make up for the fact that he was so small. Gilligan was a big mouth and was always demanding to be the centre of attention but he was still well-liked. He was always slagging the other lads and having the craic and trying to help out. But he was making connections; nurturing fellahs who could help him on the outside. Gilligan was a great grafter.'

A video of a soccer match that took place in Portlaoise Prison on 23 May 1992 is a remarkable piece of gangland memorabilia. It provides a rare insight into how Gilligan ingratiated himself with the rest of the prison population. The match was between the criminals on E1 and a team from the IRA. Gilligan lavishes praise on his team of violent hoods: Brian Meehan, Paul Ward, Harry Melia, Eugene Scanlan, Martin Farrell, Fergal Toal and Warren Dumbrell. Harry Melia is 'man of the match' as he scores most of the goals. The criminals eventually win by an impressive 16 goals to 5.

Gilligan prompts the cameraman to film the Provos and walks over to commiserate with them. Dessie O'Hare, who had missed the match, then appears in the yard and Gilligan shouts: 'It's himself, the Border Fox, would you come over here, Dessie, and say a few words to us or I'll blow the whistle on ya!' It is obvious that Gilligan is working hard to be everyone's favourite lag. Four years later, the same tape provided the Gardaí with important corroboration of the close relationship between Gilligan and his co-conspirators in the murder of journalist Veronica Guerin.

On E1 wing, Gilligan developed a close relationship with Brian Meehan and Paul Ward. He'd known Meehan for a number of years and treated him like a son. He admired the young criminal's 'bottle'. Meehan and Ward had a lot of potential and Gilligan would make them wealthy beyond their wildest dreams. In return the two hoods were staunchly loyal lieutenants and became the backbone of his criminal organization. They epitomized the new breed of ruthless young criminals Larry Dunne had prophesized would take over when his career as a Godfather came to an end. Ironically Larry was rubbing shoulders with his successors as he served his 14-year sentence on E1.

Gangland's new brat pack grew up in a world where organized crime was already well established and they had plenty of role models to choose from. Meehan in particular had a natural talent for serious crime. Born in Crumlin in April 1964, Meehan was a joyrider from his early teens, robbing high-performance cars and having dangerous high-speed chases with the police. He was known as 'Meenor' to his friends but was later dubbed 'the Tosser'. He became very proficient at ramming squad cars and showed no fear. Older criminals who heard of his prowess as a 'wheels man' soon took notice of the reckless youngster. A member of the General's gang, Michael 'Jo Jo' Kavanagh, took Meehan under his wing, using him to rob getaway cars for heists. Then he began using him as a driver. By his twenty-first birthday, Meehan was an accomplished armed robber.

The young thug had a fascination for guns – and had no compunction about using them. In February 1987, Meehan tried to shoot an unarmed Garda. He held a gun to the head of the officer who was trying to arrest him after a robbery, but the weapon misfired. As Meehan ran away, he pointed the weapon at another officer but it misfired again. The third time it worked and he fired a warning shot in the air. A month later Meehan and Kavanagh were part of a four-man gang, who held up a wages' delivery at the Ringsend Bus Depot, East Dublin. As the gang was escaping, the raiders were confronted by an armed detective who was protecting the premises. He fired several shots at the gang, who had pointed their weapons at him. Two members of the gang were later arrested and charged. Kavanagh had been wounded by the detective and Meehan brought him to a corrupt vet in County Wexford, who gave him medical treatment.

By the late 1980s, the young thug was attracting the attentions of the Serious Crime Squad. He was regularly spotted by Gardaí in the company of Gilligan, Kavanagh and Martin Cahill. It was obvious to them that he was being groomed for greater things. On one occasion Meehan was stopped at a Garda checkpoint in Clontarf, driving a high-powered, stolen jeep. He was with PJ Loughran, the head of the Athy Gang, on their way to take part in a robbery. When Meehan was asked for his name, he pulled a pistol and pointed it at the cop. He told the guard to 'fuck off' before driving away at speed. On 21 December 1987, Meehan, Kavanagh, Paddy Shanahan and Canadian-national Norman McCaud pulled a daring daylight robbery from the Allied Irish Bank on Grafton Street, Dublin. McCaud was a Mafia hit man who was on the run from

Canadian police who wanted him for murder. He and Shanahan provided back-up, as Meehan and Kavanagh posed as window-cleaners.
They gained access to the bank using a ladder and crossing a number of
roofs. When they were over the cash-counting room, they broke
through a skylight and lowered themselves down using ropes. They
held staff at gunpoint and took £55,000 before climbing back up the
ropes again and escaping.

But Meehan had become a major target of Detective Inspector Tony
Hickey's Serious Crime Squad. A week later he was arrested for the robbery and was subsequently charged. In a bid to save his neck, Meenor
offered his services as an informant. He told detectives where they could
find a number of weapons he'd hidden, including the one he threatened
the cop with in Clontarf. He was released on bail.

Brian Meehan continued to take part in robberies with members of
the Cahill and Gilligan gangs. He was arrested for questioning following the robbery of £1 million worth of pharmaceuticals from the
Dublin Drug Company. There was insufficient evidence with which to
charge him but he agreed to continue working as a tout. As part of the
arrangement, Meehan was placed back in custody while awaiting his
trial for the Grafton Street bank job. A few days later he simply walked
out of prison, by arrangement with his Garda handler, and went into
hiding. But he was soon 'recaptured' when the detectives realized he
was playing for time.

Meehan's trial for the AIB robbery was aborted a number of months
later, when two female jurors told the police they'd been followed home
from the court and intimidated. Gardaí identified associates of Cahill
and Kavanagh as the culprits, but the jurors were too scared to give evidence in court against them.

A second trial was set for April 1989. Meehan pleaded guilty and was
jailed for six years and sent to Mountjoy. He was one of the ring-leaders
of a full-scale riot in the prison in the summer of 1990. Millions of
pounds worth of damage was caused when the gangsters staged a roof-
top protest. The riot won Meehan his 'promotion' to gangland's Alma
Mater and he was moved to Portlaoise's E1 wing.

Paul Ward's involvement in the Mountjoy riot also earned him a
place in Portlaoise with the big players. Ward was the same age as Meehan and came from Windmill Park in Crumlin. The two young thugs

had been pals since they were kids, and Ward was going out with Meehan's sister, Vanessa. Ward had graduated from car thief to armed robber alongside Meehan, and in November 1989 he'd been sentenced to four years for a hold-up in Crumlin. Known as 'Hippo', Ward had a reputation for violence and had a heroin habit.

In the early 1990s, Gilligan would sit in his cell with Meehan and Ward, discussing the future. Everyone on E1 had found out the hard way that the cops were getting much better at catching the robbers. The Athy Gang had shared their experiences of what it was like to get up close and personal with the new ERU. But they had been luckier than Doyle and Wilson in the Fairview shoot-out. The gangsters had also heard that a new squad, called the Cobra Unit, had been set up in Dublin to specifically target armed robberies. Teams of heavily armed officers, wearing bullet-proof vests and driving high-performance cars now cruised every division in the city. Their rapid response times shocked the serious blaggers and forced them to look around for an alternative source of income. The former warehouse robber realized that in such circumstances moving into drugs was a no-brainer.

Meehan told Gilligan about how his best friend, Peter Mitchell, was running a very lucrative business selling hashish and a new drug called ecstasy, which had arrived with Dublin's rave scene. He also dealt in cocaine, which was becoming increasingly popular with Ireland's growing number of recreational drug-users. Known as 'Fat Head' or 'Fatso', with a reputation as a loud-mouthed thug, Mitchell was from Summerhill in the north inner-city. He was five years younger than Meehan. Physically big, with a violent reputation to match, Mitchell had befriended Meehan while they were both in Mountjoy. Fatso also took part in the infamous riot but wasn't sent to Portlaoise because he'd been due for release. When Mitchell got out he began dabbling in the drug trade, but steered away from heroin because it was considered too troublesome. Junkies were difficult to deal with and the trade was loathed in the working-class communities. Mitchell controlled an area that stretched from his own neighbourhood in the north inner-city out as far as the working-class suburb of Coolock. During visits to Meehan in Portlaoise, he would brag about the huge money he was making. One good deal could yield more hard cash than a whole fleet of Factory John's stolen trucks. And there was a lot less risk and aggravation.

The decision of Gilligan and his protégés to become drug-dealers would have a profound effect on the future of organized crime. Taking Mitchell's advice, the new gang opted to get heavily involved in cannabis and to explore the ecstasy and cocaine markets. They'd also learned from Larry Dunne's fatal mistake. Gilligan vowed that he would never come into contact with his own supply.

From when he joined the force in the 1970s, Assistant Commissioner John O'Mahoney spent most of his career in the Serious Crime Squad and witnessed first-hand the evolution of organized crime. O'Mahoney was a member of the CDU team who first targeted the Cahill gang in 1984. He was also a team leader in the Tango Squad and recalls: 'When John Gilligan came out of prison he identified a niche in the market and decided that cannabis resin was to be his business. He decided that for a number of reasons: one was that he felt that by operating in the area of cannabis that he would not be as big a target for law enforcement as if he was dealing in heroin. He also saw that there were more people in this country using cannabis and the people who were using it had more money to spend. This was also the beginning of the Celtic Tiger era.'

John Gilligan already had ambitious plans for the future before he was jailed in November 1990. His wife, Geraldine, was the driving force behind her husband. She acted as his secretary and adviser in his criminal activities and was later described in court as her husband's partner-in-crime. In September 1987, he paid £7,000 in cash for a derelict farmhouse called 'Jessbrook', on five acres of land at Mucklon near Enfield, County Kildare. The Gilligans immediately began reconstructing the house and building stables, as Geraldine's dream was to turn it into a world-class equestrian centre. When he was in the company of his law-abiding acquaintances, Gilligan preferred to describe himself as a horse-breeder rather than an armed robber.

Geraldine's plans for Jessbrook put huge pressure on her husband. Factory John switched his attentions to hardware outlets and warehouses to rob the materials he needed for the reconstruction work. His efforts were interrupted in May 1988, at the height of the Tango Squad's operations, when he was jailed for 18 months, and again when he was convicted and jailed for four years in November 1990 for the Enniscorthy robbery.

With Gilligan in prison, Geraldine had to take over some of his operations. In late 1989, Detective Superintendent Noel Conroy and Detective Inspector Tony Hickey had learned of Gilligan's involvement in a proposed deal to sell the Beit paintings. Drogheda fence Tommy Coyle had been finding it very difficult to set up a deal with a buyer who was not an undercover cop. Then he discovered that the Loyalist terror group the Ulster Volunteer Force (UVF) was interested in buying the paintings to raise cash to buy arms and explosives from a South African gun-runner. The UVF and the other Loyalist terror groups, the Ulster Defence Association (UDA) and the Ulster Resistance, had pooled their resources to boost their arsenals, after revelations that the Provos had received tons of weaponry from Libya. Coyle had arranged a number of meetings between Martin Cahill and a representative of the UVF. The General, who was desperate for cash, thought the Loyalists' blood money was as good as the Provos', and had appointed Gilligan to act as a go-between in the complex negotiations. Cahill also agreed to hand over the least valuable painting in the collection, 'The Letter Writer' by Gabriel Metsu, so the Loyalist middlemen could show it to a prospective buyer, as proof that they had the collection.

When Gilligan was jailed, Geraldine took his place in the discussions with the UVF and Conroy and Hickey began watching her. In January 1990, a surveillance team watched as a representative of the Portadown terrorists visited Geraldine at the family home in Corduff Estate in Blanchardstown. The UVF man actually asked one of the undercover men for directions to Gilligan's house. The police secretly monitored a number of other meetings between Geraldine and two Loyalists, which took place in pubs on the outskirts of Dublin. She would then visit her husband in Portlaoise and report on progress.

A month later, however, the jinx of the Beit paintings struck again when the conspiracy with the UVF went disastrously wrong for Martin Cahill. Two of the Loyalists travelled to Istanbul to do a deal with a Turkish businessman. He claimed he represented a sheikh who was interested in buying the collection. On 24 February 1990, the terrorists gave 'The Letter Writer' to the businessman to prove their bona fides. But before they could be lured further into the trap the UVF men were tipped-off and advised to get out of Turkey. As they headed to the airport they were arrested by the 'businessman' and his associates, who were all undercover policemen. It was later suspected that the operation had been compromised by British intelligence.

The seizure of the stolen Beit painting, and the connection with the most notorious sectarian terror group in Northern Ireland, made big news back in Ireland. It was the last type of publicity that the General wanted and it gave his old enemies in the Provos a new reason to watch him.

After the fiasco, there was no further contact between the Gilligans and the UVF. In Portlaoise John Gilligan continued his Machiavellian manoeuvring and spent his time plotting his next move. When John Traynor returned to Dublin in 1992 and visited Portlaoise, Gilligan shared his future plans with him. The Coach had already come to the same conclusion about the drug trade and he was delighted to get on board. Traynor was back in business again, after sorting out some problems of his own.

Traynor had hated every day he'd spent in custody in England since his incarceration in July 1990. He soon started working on a cunning plan to get himself out as quickly as possible. The conniving fraudster was a model prisoner and soon got moved from Wandsworth Prison to a more relaxed regime in Highpoint Prison in Suffolk. He then started working on becoming eligible for temporary release so that he could go home and see his family. But before he could make his move Traynor had a few things to deal with first – especially his relationship with Martin Cahill.

In 1992, the compulsory sale of the Jetfoil pub to the Port and Docks Board was finalized for £180,000, half of which Traynor organized to be paid to the General. Cahill forgave his old pal and sent word to England that the Coach would not find himself nailed to anything when he came home. Cahill also organized money for Traynor's wife and children, who were finding it difficult to make ends meet.

Once Traynor had that difficulty out of the way, he still had to sort out the problem of the outstanding charges against him for receiving stolen cigarettes. He couldn't face the prospect of another stretch in prison. Traynor contacted a detective attached to the Central Detective Unit who, by coincidence, had moved into the same cul-de-sac where Traynor's wife and kids lived in Rathfarnham, Dublin. The officer had befriended Traynor's family and helped the kids to collect vouchers for cheap flights, so they could visit their father in prison. Traynor greatly appreciated the kindness and invited the officer to visit him to discuss where he stood on the outstanding criminal charge. When the detective reported back to his superiors, the Coach's invitation was seen as a welcome and unexpected development. The outstanding charge was based on a weak case and it was likely that the fraudster would walk. But they weren't prepared to share that information with him. The charge could be used as leverage to get Cahill's *consigliere* working for them.

When the detective and a senior officer visited the Coach in the UK, over a two-day period, Traynor suggested that he was prepared to do a deal of some kind if the charges were dropped against him. He was bluntly told that the State wanted the return of the DPP's files which Cahill had taken in 1987. In particular, they wanted the file relating to the suspicious death of Father Niall Molloy in 1985. The battered body of the Roscommon priest was found in the bedroom of wealthy landowners and horse-breeders Richard and Therese Flynn, in County Offaly. Fr Molloy, who was a close friend of the Flynns, had been involved in a number of horse and land deals with Therese. The killing of the priest had all the ingredients of a steamy scandal – money, power, religion, sex and secrecy. Richard Flynn was subsequently charged with manslaughter but was unexpectedly acquitted in 1986. The court ruled that the priest could have died from a heart attack and not his head injuries. At the time there were widespread allegations of a cover-up. The file in the General's possession contained notes and statements that certain people in power did not want in the public domain. The authorities wanted the file back at all costs.

Traynor was informed that his outstanding warrants would be 'looked at' if the file was returned, but no other assurances were given. The Coach replied that Cahill had absolute control over the files and all he could do was talk to the man whenever he got home. When the cops left, the slippery conman was satisfied that he was ready to go home. He consulted a lawyer, who assured Traynor that he could not be extradited back to the UK on the charge he had been convicted of because the law didn't cover it. By November 1992, the fraudster had convinced the prison authorities that he had gone straight and could be trusted with a week's temporary home leave. Traynor jumped on a flight back to Dublin – and didn't return to the UK for another 18 years.

Traynor had also received some comforting news two months earlier, when his former business partner, John Francis Conlon, was arrested in Dublin. Mayo-man Conlon and veteran villain Eamon Kelly, Gerry Hutch's mentor, were arrested after they'd collected £500,000 worth of high-quality cocaine from a courier who had arrived in Ireland on a flight from Miami. Conlon had sourced the drug through his Colombian connections. It was the biggest seizure of cocaine yet recorded in Ireland. In the early 1990s, the Colombians had begun targeting the European market as a new outlet for cocaine. It was partly as a result of a huge crackdown on the South American cartels by the US Government, in its much hyped 'war on drugs'. Kelly and a group of North Dublin criminals had decided to invest in the new cocaine trade. The deal for the kilo of the drug, which was 85 per cent pure, had been done through Traynor's two old associates, Conlon and James 'Danger' Beirne. Unfortunately for Kelly and company, someone tipped off the Gardaí.

A large surveillance team from the CDU and the Drug Squad were watching on 3 September 1992, when Conlon arrived in Dublin on a flight from London. As he walked into the arrivals hall he made eye contact with Eamon Kelly, who was waiting for him. Neither man spoke; they walked out separately to the car park and got into Kelly's van. They were kept under observation as they drove around the city. The investigation teams, who were under the command of Detective Inspector Martin Callinan (the current Garda Commissioner), watched as Conlon withdrew £2,000 from a bank and then drove to Jury's Hotel. A short time earlier, a Cuban woman called Elizabeth Yamanoha had checked into the hotel. She had been recruited as a courier by Conlon in Miami. The portly 40-year-old had smuggled the kilo of cocaine in the folds of her body fat. She handed the drugs to Conlon, who gave her the £2,000 and went back to Kelly. Callinan gave the order for his officers to move in and arrest the drug-dealers as they crossed the River Liffey at the East Link Toll Bridge. Now Kelly, as well as Traynor, was accusing Conlon of setting him up. During his trial in 1993, the violent, ex-Official IRA member also implicated Danger Beirne in the drug plot, when he revealed that the Roscommon rogue had asked him to collect Conlon at Dublin Airport. Kelly was eventually jailed for 13 years for the cocaine rap.

Conlon, who had left the jurisdiction while out on bail, was re-arrested in England in December 1994 and extradited to Dublin the following May. At the time Conlon's arrest created a considerable stir in intelligence circles. He later told journalist Sean Boyne of the *Sunday World* that MI5 were in contact with the Garda top brass to 'discuss' the case. Conlon claimed MI5 had promised him that he would not serve time in an Irish jail because of his value to them as a spy. In 1998, he pleaded guilty to the cocaine charge. The court was told that he had accidentally contracted Hepatitis C while in custody and was also suffering from a bad heart. Conlon was given a ten-year sentence on the charges, with the last five years suspended because of his age, health and 'peripheral role' in the crime. He was spirited away from the court following the hearing and quickly vanished. Members of a number of intelligence agencies had been in court to listen to the proceedings.

James Beirne had not been so lucky. A year earlier he was jailed for 17 years for his role in a conspiracy to smuggle a multi-million-pound consignment of cocaine into Britain.

When John Traynor returned home in November 1992, the General welcomed him with open arms. Gangland had changed completely since Traynor had fled to England in 1987. The hardcore of the General's gang were behind bars and Cahill had had to organize a new gang around him. Always anxious to portray himself in a good light, Traynor later claimed to this writer that Cahill confessed to him that 'everyone let me down except the fraud man I didn't trust'. The General regaled his *consigliere* with stories of the dramas that had befallen the gang in the intervening period. When he reckoned the time was right, Traynor broached the tricky subject of his proposed deal with the police. The manipulative fraudster was astonished when Cahill, who harboured a pathological hatred of the State, actually agreed to co-operate and return the contentious file. Despite his unpredictable nature, the General was a pragmatist and he knew he needed Traynor on his side.

A few weeks after his return, the Coach called the young detective who had helped his family at his office in Harcourt Square, Dublin. It was late in the evening when the phone rang. Traynor had a brief message. 'I think that we can do that bit of business tonight. Meet me outside the Garda Club.'

Ten minutes later the detective found Traynor sitting in a car outside the Garda Social Club on Harrington Street, around the corner from Harcourt Square. He instructed the detective to walk to Stammer Street. There was no one in sight when the detective walked into the dimly lit side street. He felt for his revolver as a shadowy figure suddenly emerged from a bush about 300 feet down the road. It was Martin Cahill. He walked over to the cop and handed a plastic bag to him. There was a strong, damp smell coming from the bulky file inside. It had obviously been buried somewhere for a long time. Cahill was brief and to the point. He didn't waste time on small talk with the enemy. 'I'm doin' this for John. I appreciate what you did for his family. This is where you and me start and finish.' The General turned and disappeared into the night. It was the one and only occasion when Martin Cahill had given the police anything other than grief. The State kept its side of the bargain and the charges against Traynor were subsequently dropped.

The Coach was finally free to make a new start in life. And like Gilligan, he had no intention of doing time ever again. Instead, to raise some cash, he immersed himself in the ongoing efforts to sell the Beit paintings. Traynor made a tentative approach to the CDU officers with an offer to sell the masterpieces back to the police. The opening demand was for £1.6 million. He gave an officer a photograph of one of the paintings, by Rubens, called 'Portrait of a Man'. The negotiations, which involved the National Gallery and the Beit Foundation, fell through after six months.

At the same time Cahill had concluded a deal with a Belgian criminal syndicate, brokered by veteran villain Niall Mulvihill. He'd been a business associate ever since he sold the Jetfoil pub to Cahill and Traynor in the late 1970s. Mulvihill, like Traynor, had always been heavily involved in the background of various criminal rackets, including organizing logistics and money-laundering services for different mobs. Mulvihill, who was a Fianna Fáil activist and known as 'the Silver Fox', was not a violent criminal, but his list of associates included all the major players, as well as members of the INLA and IRA.

A month before Traynor's return to Ireland, Mulvihill paid Cahill £500,000 as a down-payment for a £1 million deal for eight of the paintings. The handover took place in Rathfarnham and the priceless art was later smuggled out of the country by trucker and Gilligan gang operator Liam Judge, from Allenwood, County Kildare. Mulvihill and a Belgian underworld art dealer intended selling the paintings to a German national for £1.5 million. But the deal fell through when Mulvihill's Belgian partner became suspicious that the German was an undercover cop.

As part of the same deal, Cahill loaned Mulvihill £100,000 to buy 125 kilos of cannabis in Spain, which was to be driven to Ireland via London. Cahill never got back the money he loaned, or the profit he was promised, from the hash deal. Even though the Silver Fox claimed that he had been stung by some of his associates, the General and other underworld sources believed that Mulvihill had ripped him off.

Cahill demanded the return of the eight paintings from Mulvihill, who agreed on the condition that the General return the rest of the down-payment. In the end a compromise was reached: four of the paintings were returned to Cahill and Mulvihill hung on to the other four.

Over the following months, the Beit jinx struck again when three of the paintings were recovered in London: two were found when a burglar stole them from an apartment and then tried to sell them; the third, the Gainsborough masterpiece 'Madame Bacelli', turned up in a left-luggage office at Euston Station.

Mulvihill later claimed that he and Cahill patched up their differences and a new deal was negotiated to sell the remainder of the paintings and a number of works by Picasso to two criminals from Belgium and England. Payment was by means of £1.5 million worth of high-quality heroin, which was to be shipped into the UK by a Turkish gang. Mulvihill assured the General and Traynor that they would finally get their slice of the profits. On 1 September, Mulvihill and two Irishmen arrived at Deurne Airport outside Antwerp for the handover. As they passed the paintings to the criminals, they were arrested by Belgian police who had been waiting for them. The two criminals turned out to be cops – one from Belgium and the other Scotland Yard. Mulvihill was held in custody for three months but was released when the charges were dropped on a legal technicality.

Just over a week later, on 9 September 1993, John Gilligan was granted temporary release from prison. He'd served the remainder of his sentence in Cork after he'd assaulted a chief officer in Portlaoise in November 1992. The short-tempered thug said he 'lost the rag' when he had to wait for some paperwork. Gilligan was convicted of the assault and given an additional six months. The conditions of his temporary release were that he signed on each week at Portlaoise Prison, until his full release on 7 November. Three days after Gilligan got his freedom, Brian Meehan was also granted temporary release. His full release date was set for April 1994. Paul Ward had finished his sentence six months earlier.

As John Gilligan walked through the prison gates for the last time, he made a promise to himself that would have major repercussions for Irish society. He swore that he would never again serve another jail sentence. Gilligan was determined to become the most powerful figure in Gang-land.

16.   A New Order

In the 1990s organized crime moved into a new, more dangerous phase, as narcotics became the stock in trade for the vast majority of gangsters. Despite the economic difficulties in the early part of the decade, there was a steady increase in demand for all types of drugs among Ireland's large population of young people under the age of 30. In time it would become a billion-Euro industry and pose a major threat in the dramatic escalation of violence, as rivals were prepared to kill over turf.

A sinister trend emerged as drug-suppliers in Holland and Spain began throwing automatic pistols and machine-guns in with shipments for their Irish customers. It was akin to a 'sales incentive scheme' for drug-traffickers – get a free shooter with every ten kilos purchased. The first proof of this came in 1990, when a large consignment of hashish was washed up in two barrels on a Dublin shoreline. The haul had been dropped from a larger ship off the coast but the gang missed the rendez-vous. There were six 9mm automatic pistols and ammunition hidden inside the barrels.

The evolution of the Gilligan gang typified the changing face of organized crime in Ireland. Gilligan and Traynor wasted no time organizing their exciting new business venture together in the autumn of 1993. The Coach did his own research into the trade by drinking and socializing with the new breed of drug-dealers. The clever crook studied the dynamics of the business and the methods used to launder the profits. With this in mind he opened a second-hand car dealership near the site of the old Hollyfield Buildings, and began importing Japanese cars which were very popular at the time. Like Gilligan, Traynor was reluctant to dabble in heroin – not as a result of any deep-rooted revulsion at the devastation it caused on the streets, but because heroin-dealers were classed as the scum of the earth and attracted too much media attention. Traynor simply didn't need the aggravation. Dealers down the heroin distribution chain also tended to be addicts themselves and prone to 'ratting' to the police. The Coach preferred to be the one talking to the cops. Through his one-to-one relationship with his Garda handlers, Traynor could gauge what they knew.

Little John and Big John were the perfect partnership and they were totally dependent on one another. They had been close friends since they'd worked on the B and I ferry together. Gilligan, Traynor and a small group of crooked employees had controlled a major fraud racket that eventually ran the company aground. Traynor even bluffed his way into a senior position in the Seamen's Union, which effectively controlled B and I. At one stage, the Government commissioned a secret survey among passengers on a typical sailing. While the manifest recorded 220 passengers, an actual head count found that there were more than 700 people on board.

In the new business Traynor needed a partner with clout in the underworld whom he could trust. The Coach was then happy to stay out of the limelight and live the high life on the proceeds. He once described Gilligan in an interview with this writer in 1995: 'He is the best grafter I have ever met. In criminal terms he is a great businessman. He can turn money into more money, no problem and is prepared to be hands on if necessary. But he is very dangerous if you fuck with him.'

In return, Gilligan needed Traynor's planning to get his new empire off the ground. Always the cunning chancer, the Coach had worked out the gang's strategy. He advised Gilligan that they should vary the size of the drug shipments. Each large consignment should be followed by a smaller one in case the route was compromised and the drugs seized. It would also give them the breathing space to collect their money. Traynor suggested operating a cash base, or what is known in bookie circles as a 'tank'. The gang would start with an initial cash injection as the 'tank'. After each shipment the money would be collected and the original investment money would be returned to the 'tank' to pay for the next one. As business prospered, the 'tank' increased to cushion the financial loss if a shipment was seized.

But getting started in the narcotics trade is an expensive business and Gilligan and Traynor needed the start-up capital for their venture. They turned to the General for help.

Two months before Gilligan's release in September 1993, Traynor and Martin Cahill had started planning one of their most ambitious strokes yet. Through an inside source, Traynor had compiled information on the main cash-holding centre of the National Irish Bank (NIB), in Dublin. At certain times of the week there could be as much as £10 million in cash in the vaults. The difficulty was how to get their hands on it. A traditional armed hold-up would be pointless because of the location and the level of security. To get away with it, they'd need to be able to enter the building unchallenged and ensure that the police weren't called.

Traynor and Cahill came up with a plan to abduct a senior NIB executive and make him collect the cash. After preliminary surveillance the General selected the bank's CEO, Jim Lacey. They plotted to hold the banker and his family hostage overnight. Lacey's wife and four children would then be taken to a hiding place with Lacey left under no doubt that the lives of his family were in his hands. Meanwhile a member of the gang, posing as another kidnap victim, would convince the banker that his family had also been abducted. Lacey would have to ensure the cash was handed over, to secure the safe return of both families.

Brian Meehan was already recruited for the job, along with Jo Jo Kavanagh, who would pose as the victim. Kavanagh, the last remaining member of Cahill's original gang still free, was facing a serious criminal charge in the courts and had fallen out of favour with many of his former associates. The widower felt he had nothing to lose.

On 5 September 1993, three armed and masked men burst into the Crumlin home of Kavanagh's mother-in-law, Esther Bolger, with whom two of his five children were living. His wife, Marian, and her brother Derek had both been killed in November 1988 when Kavanagh drove a van they had been passengers in into a parked truck while drunk. In the house one of the masked men put a gun to the grandmother's head when she confronted them. He warned her: 'This is serious. Open your mouth and you're dead. I mean what I say. Don't make a sound.' But by then Mrs Bolger had recognized two of the gunmen – Martin Cahill and her hated son-in-law. She identified them and pointed a gold sovereign she was wearing around her neck at Cahill, saying: 'You know who gave this to my dead daughter, Cahill? It was your wife, Frances.' Cahill ignored her and produced a Polaroid camera. He took pictures of Kavanagh's two scared children to be used by Kavanagh to convince Jim Lacey that his children were also being held hostage. Then, on 15 October, Kavanagh was 'abducted' by his associates.

Meanwhile Cahill and his gang had been watching the movements of Jim Lacey and his family. Two other executives at the bank had also been monitored in case the choice of hostage changed. Cahill even tested the security system at the Laceys' home in upmarket Blackrock, when he purposely activated the alarm to test police response times.

Traynor had organized most of the logistical support for the operation, but the born coward preferred to stay a safe distance from the action. Just to cover all eventualities the duplicitous rogue even tipped-off the detective he was dealing with in the Serious Crime Squad that there was 'a big stroke' being planned involving a bank. Traynor knew that the police did not have the resources to mount a major surveillance on such vague information. He made it clear that he'd only heard a 'whisper' and was simply doing his duty as an informant. If he was involved then why would he tip-off a cop that something big was going down? On the day of the crime he made sure he was at a safe, highly visible distance and was seen walking through O'Connell Street with John Gilligan and visiting a bookie's shop.

On the night of 1 November 1993, Cahill and six members of his gang went about their brutal work. The gang was lying in wait for Jim Lacey and his wife, Joan, when they returned to their home at 1.25 a.m. on the morning of 2 November, after attending a bank function. The hoods rushed the couple as they walked through their front door and there was a violent struggle as the Laceys fought back. Jim Lacey was struck across the head with a pistol which left a large gash in his forehead. The family's babysitter was ordered to lie on the ground at gunpoint and the Lacey children were awakened and ordered out of their beds by the men in masks. Brian Meehan was one of the most aggressive members of the kidnap gang. He delighted in causing terror. The Tosser cocked a gun over the heads of the Lacey children for added emphasis, as Cahill warned Jim Lacey he would never see his family again if he did not follow instructions.

The level of organization that went into the crime would later help identify Cahill as the prime suspect. Each gang member was dressed in a two-piece overall, balaclava, knitted gloves and white runner boots – all of which were to be disposed of after the job. They also each had a number, between one and seven, sewn onto their overalls and they addressed each other by number only. Around 6 a.m. Joan Lacey, her children and their babysitter were hooded and taken away in a van driven by Brian Meehan. He brought them to a disused stable at Black-horse Avenue, North Dublin. Around the same time, Kavanagh was dumped on the floor beside Jim Lacey. To keep up the 'hostage' pretence, the gangster was tied up and had a hood over his head. Cahill gave Lacey strict instructions. He was to go to the NIB cash-holding centre with the other hostage and organize for a van that would be provided to be driven inside, where it was to be filled with cash.

'I don't want any bollix about time locks. We know all about this place and the amount of cash there, which is millions. I don't want any small stuff. We want fifties and twenties. You're to make sure the place is totally emptied – the big room, the secret room, all the rooms, right? Because if it's not we'll kill your children. We've already shot your son in the hand just so that you know this is serious,' the General blustered. They had faked a shot to convince Lacey they were serious. When the gang left, Kavanagh told the bank executive that he'd been detained 'for at least two weeks'. He showed Lacey the fake pictures that Cahill had taken of his kids two months earlier. Kavanagh kept saying, almost in desperation, 'They have my kids.' Lacey showed Kavanagh pictures of his own children and the criminal began playing on the banker's fears.

Later that morning Kavanagh drove with Jim Lacey to pick up a van that had been left for them at Merrion Road Church. Cahill had even strengthened the suspension system in the van to ensure it could carry the huge amount of cash.

When Lacey and his fellow 'hostage' got to the NIB, the executive told his senior manager of the unfolding drama and the instructions he had been given to ensure the safe return of his family. Despite being terribly shaken by his ordeal, Jim Lacey outwitted the General's other 'victim'. The banker told his staff to take £250,000 or so in the vaults and put it in bags. Kavanagh was handed three large bags, stuffed with cash and told that was everything from the vaults. In reality there was £7 million in the NIB vaults that morning. The 'victim' grew impatient and angry and kept repeating that there was supposed to be millions there. He warned Jim Lacey that his family would be killed if the gang's orders were not followed. But to maintain his story Kavanagh couldn't push the issue and he left with the money.

Later that afternoon one of the gunmen holding the Lacey family in

Blackhorse Avenue told them that everything had gone to plan and they had got 'more money than you could dream about'. The gang left and a few hours later the hostages managed to break free.

It had been a bad day for Cahill and his mob. They got away with just £233,000 – a fraction of what they had been after. Cahill and Traynor were furious the next day when the newspapers reported that the gang had missed the £7 million. They had been outfoxed by their courageous hostage.

Over the following two months the gang members, including Cahill, Meehan and Traynor, were identified, arrested and questioned about the kidnapping, but with no success. Cahill had even left a box of chocolates with the Laceys' babysitter to give the Gardaí a clue that it was his 'job'. The same officers who had dealt with Meehan during his earlier stint as an informant interviewed him but this time he wasn't opening his mouth. Meehan was confident that they had nothing on him and the gang members were released without charge. But there was strong circumstantial evidence against Jo Jo Kavanagh and he was charged with the crime. The case eventually came to trial in the Special Criminal Court in October 1997 and he was jailed for 12 years.

The Lacey kidnapping was to be Martin Cahill's last major crime. After the kidnapping, Cahill agreed to loan Traynor and Gilligan just over £100,000, for which he was promised a return of at least half a million. They used the cash to buy their first drug shipment.

Towards the end of November, Gilligan flew to Amsterdam with his childhood friend from Ballyfermot, trucker Denis 'Dinny' Meredith, who had been a member of the Factory Gang for years. He had impressive criminal connections and had used his contacts to smuggle cigarettes, booze and small amounts of drugs into Ireland from Europe. His contacts then put the gang in touch with one of the biggest international drug-traffickers operating in Holland at the time – Simon Ata Hussain Khan Rahman.

Born in Surinam in 1942, Rahman was a major league criminal who made gangsters like Gilligan, Traynor and Cahill look like schoolboys. He had criminal connections throughout Europe, the old Soviet Bloc countries, the Middle East and North Africa. His criminal empire, based in The Hague, dealt in narcotics, fraud and firearms. His front was that of a legitimate millionaire businessman who specialized in the import and export of goods, from foodstuffs to furniture. Rahman nurtured a veneer of respectability and was Chairman of a Muslim cultural association called Jamaat Al Imaan. In 1994 the Dutch authorities estimated that the practising Muslim was worth between £20 and £50 million. Rahman had well-established supply routes and smuggled cannabis into Holland from Nigeria and Morocco, disguised as cargos of foodstuffs and furniture. He supplied gangs in England, France, Belgium, Germany and the Eastern Bloc countries.

One of Rahman's closest associates was Johnny Wildhagen, a Dutch national from The Hague. The 40-year-old was a violent cocaine addict who worked as Rahman's enforcer and manager. Wildhagen organized shipments of drugs and guns for export, using invoices from bogus companies. Rahman also appointed one of his associates, Martin Baltus, as the Gilligan gang's liaison man. Rahman was not impressed by Gilligan and referred to him disparagingly as a loud-mouth and 'De Klein' ('the little one'). He didn't trust Factory John or his gang members, like Meehan, Ward and Mitchell, whom he dismissively described as 'the others'.

At their first meeting, Rahman informed Gilligan that each deal would have to be paid for up front, in cash. The price of the first shipments of hash was in the region of £1,300 per kilo, but it would be cheaper depending on the quantities being ordered. Rahman also explained that, as trust and goodwill developed, the payment for shipments could be broken into three parts: a portion would be paid in advance, upon delivery and shortly after the drugs were sold.

Gilligan and Meredith returned to Dublin the following day. The negotiations and talks continued. A week later, on 29 November, Traynor and Gilligan travelled to Amsterdam where Traynor, who controlled Cahill's £100,000, finalized the first deal for 170 kilos. Rahman and Wildhagen were impressed by Traynor, describing him as 'Big John, the real boss of Gilligan'. Traynor, it is understood, convinced Rahman that if he reduced the price of the initial shipment from £1,300 to around £1,000 per kilo, as a sort of introductory offer, it would mean more cash for the businessman in the long run. The gang invested every penny they could steal, borrow or con into the first deal. It would be the start of a very lucrative relationship.

On 5 December the first consignment of drugs arrived in Dublin

Port, on a transport truck organized by Dinny Meredith. The 150 kilos of hash were packed into six boxes, specially sealed, labelled as leather jackets and addressed to an engineering works in Chapelizod, West Dublin. The truck delivered the boxes to the transport company's main warehouse. The following morning the boxes were picked up by a courier and sent to Chapelizod. Gilligan and Traynor had the truck followed to ensure that it was not under surveillance. When it stopped at traffic lights, Brian Meehan knocked on the window and told the driver he had been sent to collect the boxes for the engineering works. He signed for them using the fictitious name 'Frank O'Brady'. The deal went off without a hitch.

On 12 December the second part of the deal, 20 kilos, arrived on a transport truck from the same haulage company. This time it was packed in one box, labelled 'compressor parts'. The Gilligan gang were in business.

In the early days of the operation, Gilligan and Traynor distributed the hash through Peter Mitchell, Brian Meehan and Paul Ward. They in turn had set up a network of dealers who bought the drugs from them. Over the following months the operation expanded rapidly, with dealers throughout Ireland buying from them. Peter Mitchell recruited Charlie Bowden, a flash, arrogant character with a natural talent for organization, who had no previous involvement in crime. Bowden was a hard man with military training who'd left the army with an 'unsatisfactory' discharge. He eventually became the gang's manager.

When one of the earlier shipments was intercepted by Customs at Dublin Port in February 1994, Gilligan and Traynor decided to switch smuggling routes. Dinny Meredith introduced them to 38-year-old John Dunne. He was operations manager with the Sea Bridge shipping company, at Little Island in Cork. Dunne, who was originally from Finglas in Dublin, asked no questions when Gilligan and Traynor offered him £1,000 to handle each shipment. Like Bowden, Dunne also became a vital cog in a well-organized machine.

Before each drug shipment, various members of the gang would travel to Amsterdam where they exchanged large quantities of Irish and UK currency for Dutch guilders at Bureaux de Change in the city. The cash was then handed to either Rahman or Baltus. The Dutch mob packed the drugs in crates, labelled 'machine parts', and shipped them to

Cork. John Dunne would then arrange to have them delivered to the car park at the Ambassador Hotel on the outskirts of Dublin, where Bowden would be waiting. The crates were taken to Greenmount Industrial Estate in Harold's Cross, where Bowden checked the load and divided it into individual orders. The gang then delivered the drugs to its customers in a van bought specially for the job – it was dubbed the 'dope mobile'.

Gilligan's operation became one of the most secure and lucrative illegal drug-smuggling operations in gangland history. In 1996 the newly formed Criminal Assets Bureau (CAB) and the Gardaí investigating the Veronica Guerin murder painstakingly compiled a detailed document on the gang's activities. It was uplifted from flights taken by various gang members to Holland, the amounts of money they each exchanged and the weight of the shipments arriving in Cork. They conservatively estimated that between April 1994 and October 1996 over 21,000 kilos of hashish arrived through Cork, in 96 individual shipments, none of which was detected. Large quantities of automatic pistols and machine-guns were also sent.

The figures involved were staggering. In two years Gilligan's mob had exchanged £11.5 million alone at Bureaux de Change in Amsterdam and had paid Simon Rahman over £25 million. With an average price of £2,000 per kilo, Gilligan had made a personal profit of £16.8 million, with Traynor's take also running into millions. The five core members of the mob – Meehan, Ward, Ward's brother Shay, Mitchell and Bowden – made an estimated £8.5 million between them. But these figures did not include a number of other large consignments of cocaine, ecstasy and cannabis which had been smuggled through other routes. It was the first time that anyone in Ireland discovered the real value of organized crime. It completely dwarfed the profits being made in the early 1980s by the likes of Larry Dunne.

When Charlie Bowden subsequently turned State's evidence against his fellow gangsters, he admitted in the Special Criminal Court that he had made between £150,000 and £200,000 in just over a year. He explained what he did with it: 'I spent a lot of money on cocaine. I bought designer clothes and went on foreign holidays. I would go out. I would live well. I would buy stuff for the kids.' He also revealed how handling the bundles of drug cash became a problem for the gang: 'This was a constant refrain throughout the whole time when we were earn-ing this type of money, where to put it. I used to stuff it in a laundry basket. When it got full I got another one. We spoke about offshore accounts and how we would go about doing it. We were thinking about getting the money into bank accounts in the Isle of Man.'

Gilligan decided to launder some of his loot by gambling in Dublin betting shops. Sometimes he'd bet on all the horses running in a race, at up to £10,000 a time. Some of the larger bookmakers conducted dis-creet enquiries but could not detect any pattern suggesting a scam. One major bookmakers' chain eventually limited the amount of money he could wager at any one time. Between 1994 and June 1996 Gilligan wagered a total of £5,480,849, which included the betting taxes. His return was £4,860,714, after a loss of £620,135. Laundering his cash this way cost him 13.5 per cent. On the surface he appeared to have been unlucky. But when it was measured against the lowest standard rate of taxation, Gilligan's laundering operation was providing superb value for money.

Detective Chief Superintendent Tony Quilter, the head of the Garda National Drug Unit (GNDU), which had taken over from the old Drug Squad in 1994, described the operation. 'The Gilligan gang brought drug-trafficking to another level in this country. They brought a highly organized, businesslike structure to their empire. They dealt directly with associates on the Continent. They bought in bulk and they had a sophisticated and logistical distribution network.'

Traynor and Gilligan also established a partnership with the INLA, who were heavily involved in organized crime rackets, including drugs. Gilligan had developed a close relationship with Fergal Toal while he was networking in Portlaoise Prison. In fact the friendship was so strong that at one stage other inmates began to joke – behind their backs – that they were lovers. At the same time the Coach acted as a liaison between the Gilligan gang and INLA boss Michael Kenny and his sidekick Declan 'Wacker' Duffy. Kenny would meet Traynor and Gilligan on an almost daily basis. The gang supplied drugs and guns to the INLA, who effectively became Gilligan's private army. At the same time the hypo-critical thugs were in touch with the media to claim that they were involved in 'anti-drug' activities in South Dublin.

The Coach reckoned that he was closer to the terror group than his partner. He once told his Garda handler that if it came to a row between himself and Gilligan then the INLA would back him. The terrorists would prove to be very helpful to the crime syndicate, especially when it came to one of their creditors – the General.

Martin Cahill had noticed how well his associates were doing in the drug trade. He began putting pressure on Traynor for a return on his investment, demanding over £500,000, which he reckoned was a fair return.

Traynor called to see Cahill every day and put him off. He assured him that, despite the gangland rumour machine, the gang was not yet in profit. But Gilligan had decided that they were not going to pay Cahill his money. Traynor disagreed and wanted to pay him something. After all, Cahill might be a major mobster in decline but he was still a potentially dangerous man. Chronic diabetes, for which he had refused treatment, had made him even more irrational and unpredictable. Since the Lacey kidnapping he had confined his criminal activities to arson attacks and tyre-slashing sprees around South Dublin. The focus of his anger was the construction of three houses at the back of one of his homes at Swan Grove. In his volatile state of mind, the General suspected that the houses would be used by the Gardaí to keep him under surveillance. As Cahill's demands for his money became more threatening, Traynor and Gilligan knew that the only way to sort him out was with a bullet in the head – but they had to bide their time.

Their lucky break came on Saturday, 21 May 1991. A three-member hit team from the Ulster Volunteer Force attacked a Sinn Féin fundraiser in the Widow Scallans pub on Dublin's Pearse Street. The function, in aid of the 'Prisoners of War Department', was targeted by the Belfast gang after they read about it in the Sinn Féin/IRA propaganda sheet, *An Phoblacht*. The UVF had dramatically escalated sectarian violence in the North and had been planning a bomb attack in Dublin. At 10.50 p.m. two members of the hit team arrived at the door leading to the upstairs function room, which was packed with over 300 people. One of the terrorists carried a handgun, the other a bag containing an 18lb bomb. Thirty-five-year-old IRA man Martin Doherty from Ballymun tried to stop the two men getting in. In the scuffle that followed, Doherty was shot five times in the chest and died instantly. A second man, Paddy Burke, was injured when he was shot through a locked door leading to the function room. When they couldn't get through the door the UVF men abandoned the bomb and made their escape. Their getaway car was later found burned out off the North Strand. Miraculously the bomb failed to explode. If it had, the blast would have been powerful enough to kill everyone inside and demolish the building.

The following day the UVF issued a statement to the BBC in Belfast claiming responsibility for the attack. In it they said they had struck at the 'heart of the republican movement in its own backyard'. In the wake of the Widow Scallans incident there was intense speculation that a criminal gang from Dublin had assisted the hit team. The Provos soon pointed the finger of suspicion at their old adversary Martin Cahill. After the ill-fated attempt to sell the Beit paintings, the General had form with the Loyalist terrorists. At the time the bomb attempt was blamed on the Billy Wright UVF group in Portadown, whose members had been involved in the Beit deal.

However, neither Cahill nor any other Dublin criminals were involved in the attack. During research for this book it was revealed that both the RUC and the Gardaí established that a UVF group from Belfast was actually responsible. They considered the operation a success, even though the bomb had failed to explode. The fact that they'd murdered an IRA member was a bonus. The killers were, however, upset that the Billy Wright group was blamed, and made efforts to make it known that they had carried out the 'brave' act of war. The Belfast UVF gang was heavily involved in organized crime, including extortion, hijacking and drugs.

One of the claims made in the wake of the attack was that Cahill's gang had supplied cars to the UVF. This is also untrue. The car used in the attack was a Northern-registered gold Triumph Acclaim. It had been purchased the day before the attack, from a car-dealer in Lurgan. In the hours preceding the incident, a number of Gardaí had spotted the UVF car, as it appeared to be driving around lost. Also of significance was the presence of a Northern-registered red Ford Fiesta. It was spotted near the Widow Scallans pub an hour before the attack. It was later discovered that the leader of the gang drove a similar car, and he had driven to Dublin to pick up the hit team.

The explosives used in the attack had been stolen from a quarry in the North of England and smuggled to the UVF through contacts in Scotland. But the most interesting information to emerge in connection with the Widow Scallans attack related to the 9mm automatic pistol used to murder Martin Doherty. Ballistics and forensic checks revealed that, over the previous six years, it had been used in three other murders, two attempted murders and one punishment shooting in Belfast. The UVF didn't believe in disposing of their scarce firearms. In April 1995 six members of the gang, all of them from Belfast, were arrested for questioning by the RUC. There was insufficient evidence to charge any of them.

Hard evidence was the last thing that Gilligan, Traynor or the Provos needed. In the weeks that followed the Widow Scallans attack, the Provos launched an in-depth 'investigation' to find out who had helped their enemies. Criminals and drug-dealers were 'invited' to be interviewed by the IRA. In later years it would emerge that the terrorists were merely using the conspiracy as an excuse to muscle in on the various drug rackets and to extract 'donations' from organized crime gangs. The patriots were preparing for peace and wanted to feather their own nests. At the time their propagandists claimed that they were doing what the cops couldn't – clearing up the crime scene. The fact that organized crime continued to thrive over the following years proved that they were lying.

Gilligan and Traynor were two people the Provos didn't have to approach for information. The drug-dealers knew that the General had made many enemies in the underworld and were happy to volunteer their belief that Cahill had been involved. Factory John and the Coach had begun plotting the murder of their former pal but if the Provos – or the INLA – did it for them, then so much the better.

Cahill's troubles with the INLA began in 1992, when one of his most trusted lieutenants was charged with raping and buggering his own 14-year-old daughter. Despite Cahill's revulsion at his henchman's crime, he was determined that the matter would not be dealt with in the courts. In the General's warped logic the terrified teenager had committed a greater crime by 'ratting' to the police. Shortly after the father was charged, Cahill offered the child £20,000 and a new home – if she withdrew the statement she'd made to the police. He assured her that her father would be punished and would never go near her again. When she refused, Cahill turned up the heat.

One of Cahill's former associates, John Bolger from Crumlin, who was close to the victim's family, stepped in to protect her from the General. The 31-year-old father-of-three was a hard-drinking gambler and petty thief who lived in the shadow of bigger gangsters. But he was well connected. He and his wife, Jean, were good friends of John and Geraldine Gilligan. Bolger also regularly took part in various scams and robberies with the INLA and provided safe houses for their members. He socialized with Michael Kenny's thugs and loved the respect and clout it gave him.

In the spring of 1993, Martin Cahill and the rape victim's father had approached Bolger to discuss the problem. Bolger had taken part in numerous strokes with the two men in the past. Cahill offered Bolger £10,000 in cash, as an incentive to convince the girl to drop the case. But Bolger told Cahill and the rapist to fuck off and walked away. The General had another face-to-face meeting with Bolger, who hadn't changed his mind. In the weeks that followed Bolger, his family and the victim were subjected to a campaign of intimidation by Cahill's men. Slogans were daubed on the walls outside Bolger's home and detectives placed protection on the house. In the end Michael Kenny and his INLA henchmen visited Cahill at his home in Cowper Downs, in Rathmines. They warned him that there would be 'major problems' if he didn't stop the intimidation. Surprisingly it worked and Cahill ceased his efforts to stop the rape investigation.

Traynor had managed to stay out of the row but continued to carry stories from one side to the other. Gilligan sided with Bolger but hadn't shared this information with Cahill. Gilligan and Traynor were also involved in a lucrative fraud with Bolger and the INLA. Shortly after Gilligan's release from prison, he and Traynor had come into possession of a large number of stolen bank drafts. The INLA, through Bolger, had organized a system of laundering the valuable pieces of paper throughout the country. It proved to be a lucrative scam and everyone was earning from it.

Bolger and his INLA pals had another scam on the side as well. Bolger had come into possession of a key to open post boxes. The gang would simply open the boxes and steal envelopes containing cheques and bank drafts. Everyone was a winner but it all went tragically wrong for Bolger on the night of 21 July 1994. He was shot dead, following a drunken row with other INLA members over money which had gone missing. INLA boss Michael Kenny was also hit when Belfast INLA thug Ricky Tobin opened fire on their car with a semi-automatic rifle. Tobin later told detectives: 'It was him or me – I had to do it.' He later retracted the comment and said: 'All I'm saying now is that I was there and I had a gun.' Tobin was subsequently charged with Bolger's murder but skipped bail and moved to England. His companion during the attack, Bobby Tohill, presented himself to Declan 'Wacker' Duffy for his punishment – being shot in both ankles. Tobin was eventually jailed for five years in the Special Criminal Court after he pleaded guilty to the lesser charge of possessing a firearm for an unlawful purpose on the night of John Bolger's murder.

That same month, the INLA found itself involved in fresh conflict with the General. In July 1994 one of Cahill's relatives was evicted from a Dublin Corporation flat, off Charlemont Street in the south inner-city, where she had been squatting for over a year. The flat had been allocated to INLA killer Joe Magee, who intended moving in. Martin Cahill had other ideas. After issuing threats to Magee, the mob boss burned the flat to ensure no one could live in it. For the INLA it was the final straw – Kenny and his troops decided that it was time Cahill met his maker.

At the same time the General ratcheted up the pressure on his former friends. He demanded his share of the drug money. Traynor later claimed to this writer that Cahill was becoming increasingly prone to unreasonable temper-tantrums. The General's relationship with Gilligan was becoming particularly fraught. Cahill had several meetings with Little John and Big John, and confided to one of his associates that he had thrown Gilligan out of his house.

In the middle of August 1994 a Garda surveillance team watched as Gilligan visited Cahill at the home of his sister-in-law and lover, Tina Lawless, in Rathmines. On both occasions Gilligan went to great lengths to avoid being spotted, arriving on foot after walking through side streets to avoid detection. Gilligan and Traynor were determined not to pay the General, and the greedy pair didn't mind if it took murder to hang on to their cash. It would be a recurring theme in the story of modern Gangland.

At 3.10 p.m. on the afternoon of 18 August 1994, Cahill emerged from the home of Tina Lawless, where he spent most nights, and looked around to see if the Gardaí were watching him. Earlier a motorbike courier had parked at the end of Swan Grove and pretended to examine a street map. Cahill would probably have reckoned the biker was yet another young cop, hoping to nab the big-time Godfather – like so many other cops over the previous twenty years. The General climbed into his black car and drove onto Oxford Road. Seconds earlier the 'courier' had driven by the Stop sign to alert his accomplice that their target was on his way. The killer had been standing there for most of the afternoon, dressed in a fluorescent jacket with a clipboard in his hand, supposedly conducting a traffic survey.

As the crime boss slowed down at the junction, the hit man dropped the clipboard. He stepped over to the driver's door with a .357 Magnum revolver in his hand. Before Cahill could do anything the window exploded into a thousand tiny shards, as the first shot was fired. The bullet ripped through his shoulder and head, forcing him to one side. As the car chugged slowly across Charleston Road, Ranelagh, the hit man walked alongside and fired another three shots into his victim. When the car collided with railings under a large chestnut tree, his executioner leaned inside and pumped another round into the gang boss, to make sure Cahill had finally met his maker.

The gunman appeared to be in no hurry to get away. He walked to the waiting motorbike and climbed on the back. The hit team sped off as residents out enjoying the sunshine began dialling the emergency services. Like their victim, the killers successfully covered their tracks and disappeared behind gangland's wall of silence. In a strange way Cahill would probably have appreciated their professionalism – it would not have been a fitting end if he'd been whacked by mere amateurs.

When Gardaí arrived at the scene of the most significant murder yet in gangland history, they took blankets from an ambulance and covered the body of their former adversary. It was the ultimate irony that in death the Gardaí were the ones preventing the press photographers from getting a final picture, when, for the past twenty years, the police had been trying to unmask the bogeyman of organized crime. Now that the game was over they allowed him to die as he had lived – a faceless man.

Before the body had even grown cold, the INLA and the IRA rushed like vultures to claim the kill. Ninety minutes after the shooting the INLA contacted a Dublin radio newsroom and claimed responsibility. But then, at 7.28 p.m. the same station was contacted by the IRA, using a recognized code word, 'Eksund'. The Provos claimed responsibility and then took the extraordinary step of attacking the INLA's claim, describing it as mischievous and false. The same organization which had so often denied some of their worst murders, helpfully described the weapon used to shoot Cahill, to expunge any doubt about their involvement. Seventeen minutes later the INLA spokesman phoned the newsroom again, and this time denied that the organization had been involved at all. At 8.27 p.m. the *Irish Times* received two typed statements, purporting to be from the IRA, which again claimed responsibility for the high-profile hit. The next day the Provos contacted the same radio newsroom and this time gave details of how the murder had been carried out. Even in death, Martin Cahill had succeeded in causing confusion and farce. He would have found it all very amusing.

In the next edition of *An Phoblacht* the terrorists issued another statement, in which they gave the reason for their patriotic act: 'It was Cahill's involvement with, and assistance to, pro-British death squads which forced us to act. Cahill's gang was involved closely with the Portadown UVF gang which, apart from countless sectarian murders in the 26-Counties, was responsible for the gun and bomb attack on the Widow Scallans pub. The IRA reserves the right to execute those who finance or otherwise assist Loyalist killer gangs.' Then the statement issued the underworld with a not-so-subtle warning. 'We have compiled a detailed file on the involvement of other Dublin criminals with Loyalist death squads. We call on those people to desist immediately from such activity and to come forward to us within fourteen days to clear their names.'

The murder of Martin Cahill sent shock waves through his beloved gangland. Some criminals went into hiding, fearing that they would be next in line for a Provo bullet. The IRA was clearly setting itself up for the future and remains heavily involved in organized crime rackets today. Calm returned a few weeks later, when the Provos announced the first ceasefire in the Peace Process.

Few close observers, including seasoned detectives and veteran criminals, believe that the IRA actually killed Martin Cahill. The smart money is that the INLA did it with the involvement of the Gilligan gang. Gilligan successfully ended the reign of the one criminal who posed a threat to him. Now nothing could stand in the way of his ascent to the top of the gangland pile. The new Godfather of organized crime had allowed the publicity-hungry Provos to claim the kill – as a kind of goodwill gesture. Two years later, the diminutive thug remarked mysteriously to a journalist: 'I know who murdered the General and it wasn't the IRA.' In 1997 a woman who'd witnessed the murder of Martin Cahill came forward to the police when she saw a picture of Brian Meehan in a newspaper. It was the first time his picture had appeared in public. The woman was absolutely certain that Meehan was the man she'd seen near Oxford Road, just before the hit.

In the wake of the Cahill murder, Paddy Shanahan, the General's one-time partner-in-crime, appeared to be extremely stressed. In recent years, underworld sources have claimed that Shanahan was involved in business dealings with Gilligan. It's been alleged that at one stage Gilligan suspected that Shanahan was secretly a police informant, and tested him by revealing the whereabouts of a hash shipment. According to the sources, the 'drugs' were actually sods of turf which had been packed to look like hash. When the haul was found by the Gardaí, Gilligan was convinced of the builder's guilt.

At the time, Shanahan was still working closely with Gerry 'the Monk' Hutch and his mentor Matt Kelly. The Buckingham Buildings project had been a great success and the crooks invested in another venture with the 'legitimate' builder. In 1993, Shanahan commenced the construction of a shop and apartment complex called Drury Hall in Dublin's Stephen Street. When the CAB was established three years later they identified Hutch and Kelly as being among the project's secret underworld backers. They traced two Sterling bank drafts, worth £130,000, which had been withdrawn from a Belfast bank account held in the name of Hutch's wife, Patricia Fowler. The drafts were then lodged into the accounts of a company owned by Shanahan.

On Friday, 14 October 1994, Shanahan worked late on the building-site. Shortly after 7 p.m. he arrived with a friend at his gym in Crumlin. As he walked to the front door, a lone gunman emerged from the shadows and shot the former gangster once in the face, at point-blank range. Shanahan fell to the ground, seriously injured. The hit man casually walked out the pedestrian exit and disappeared. Two days later, the Dunne family's one-time student, who had graduated to become a major-league gangster, died from his injuries.

Shanahan's death brought to 11 the number of gangland murders which had taken place in Ireland since 1990. Five of the murders took place in 1994, making it the most violent year yet recorded. The bloodshed had started in February with the murder of former INLA boss Dominic 'Mad Dog' McGlinchey in Drogheda, County Louth. The mass-killer was gunned down after he made a phone call to Gilligan's associate, Martin 'the Viper' Foley, from a public coin box. As Mad Dog was about to make a second call, two armed and masked men jumped from a car and began pumping rounds into their target. McGlinchey was shot at least 11 times. In a brutal twist of fate his son, Dominic Junior, witnessed his father's death. Seven years earlier he had also witnessed his mother being shot dead by her former INLA comrades.

The previous year, 1993, there had been three gangland murders in Dublin. Two of them were directly linked to the burgeoning drug trade. Michael Godfrey had been executed by PJ Judge (see Chapter 21), and heroin-dealer Fran Rodgers was gunned down in front of his young daughter, as he was lighting a Halloween bonfire in the Coombe, Dublin. The third fatality was Sean Clarke, who had been suspected of molesting children. The modus operandi of the murders of Clarke and Rodgers had striking similarities. In both cases the killer was armed with a shotgun and first disabled his victim by shooting him in the legs, before finishing him off with a blast in the head. Detectives believed that the same assassin did both hits. The gun would remain the corporate tool of choice in gangland's new world order.

The detectives investigating the murder of Paddy Shanahan sent a file to the DPP recommending murder charges against one of the criminal associates for whom he had been laundering cash. The man was never charged. During the police enquiries, Dutchie Holland emerged as the suspected hit man and was arrested for questioning. He was released without charge. Dutchie had been freed from Portlaoise Prison a month earlier and was living in the Crumlin home of Seamus 'Shavo' Hogan at the time. Shavo was also arrested in the swoops that followed the Shanahan hit. Unlike Martin Cahill, who used black polish to hide his face, Hogan smeared his with faeces. When the hoods were finished with the police they both got involved in the drug trade. Dutchie became an important member of Gilligan's gang.

Over the following years the murder rate steadily rose, as the drug trade flourished. With Martin Cahill out of the picture and the INLA and the Provos in his pocket, John Gilligan emerged as the strong man of the Dublin underworld. Gangland had a new master.

17.   The Munster Mafia

The fake tax disc in the windscreen of the BMW aroused the suspicions of Customs officers monitoring the cars arriving in Rosslare on 5 March 1990, off the ferry from Cherbourg. The eagle-eyed officers ordered the female driver to pull the car to the side. They summoned Jake, the sniffer dog, to conduct a spot check for drugs. Mary Vesey had no reason to be concerned and believed it was just routine. But then she realized she had driven into a nightmare as the dog started to bark and enthusiastically wag his tail, indicating he had made a hit. The civil servant was frozen with shock, as the Customs team uncovered a secret compartment, containing a stash of 76 kilos of cannabis. The 44-year-old would never forget her weekend in Paris with former priest John McCarthy.

Mary Vesey was immediately arrested by Gardaí and charged with importing the drugs which had a street value of £700,000 (€1.5 million today). It was a major seizure. She protested her innocence and profound shock when she was brought before Wicklow District Court to be formally charged. 'I was used as a tool to bring drugs into the country,' Mary Vesey told the judge. She said she had driven the car back to Ireland to oblige a 'friend' after they'd spent the weekend together at a rugby international. Vesey had arranged to meet the man in the Talbot Hotel in Wexford but he never turned up. 'Now I know why,' she remarked ruefully. Vesey had been duped by the enigmatic, international drug-trafficker dubbed 'Father Hash'.

As far as Vesey was concerned, 50-year-old McCarthy was a well-educated, charming gentleman. But the truth was a lot more sinister than that. The ex-priest was a key figure in a Cork-based international crime syndicate that had a major influence on developments in the drug trade in Ireland. They became known as the Munster Mafia. Like most of his associates, McCarthy had successfully operated under the radar until his car was stopped in Rosslare.

Father Hash was probably best described as the Irish underworld's equivalent to Oxford graduate Howard Marks. Neither man could claim that they were driven into crime through social deprivation or lack of opportunities in life. John McCarthy was born in 1940 and grew up on the Western Road in Cork, where his family were wealthy farmers. After school he studied for the priesthood and was ordained in Rome. He was fluent in French, German and Italian and held a Doctorate in theology. He ministered in Rome and Paris for a number of years before returning to Cork, where he was appointed Curate to the villages of Ballinspittle and Ballinadee. He also worked as a teacher and was Chaplain to the local convent school in Bandon.

McCarthy became the subject of scandal for the first time when he fell in love with a local woman and left the priesthood in 1981. His former parishioners remember him as the 'priest who ran off with the woman'. A few years later the couple had a daughter, married and settled in Waterfall, outside Cork City. Father Hash earned a living as a cattle-dealer but then he decided to cater for the needs of another flock – dope-smokers.

McCarthy became a partner in one of Ireland's first well-organized drug-smuggling syndicates. It had extensive international contacts and was operating long before John Gilligan switched from stealing hardware to selling hash. In the early 1980s, the Munster Mafia identified the craggy coastline of the south-west as an ideal route for smuggling multi-million-pound drug shipments for European markets. One of his business partners was fellow Cork man Paddy McSweeney, who was probably the most successful drug-trafficker in the history of organized crime in Ireland.

Successive Garda intelligence reports identified Patrick Anthony McSweeney as a major player in the global drug trade. An extremely clever and sophisticated operator, McSweeney painstakingly avoided any public connection with organized crime – and his only criminal convictions were for road traffic offences. Born in 1949, he shunned the company of anyone who risked drawing him into the spotlight. The secret of his success was that he trusted no one, never opened his mouth and, unlike the Dunnes and the General, didn't attract attention. He observed a strict rule of maintaining a safe distance from his product and customers. To the outside world he was a wealthy businessman, who frequently travelled throughout Europe, Asia and South America.

Gardaí claim that McSweeney imported some of the first shipments of heroin into Ireland in the late 1970s, and by the end of the 1980s he had become one of the biggest Irish operators. Although he was well known to the police and was the subject of many undercover investigations, he always escaped the net. It wasn't until the Criminal Assets Bureau (CAB) investigated McSweeney's vast wealth that he finally lost his cherished anonymity – they hit him with a tax bill for almost €2 million.

Another central figure in the Munster Mafia was Alan Buckley, a well-spoken antiques dealer based in Kinsale. Buckley, who was ten years younger than McSweeney, had been equally successful at maintaining a low profile and also hid behind the image of a respectable businessman. Buckley held shares in a number of front companies owned by McSweeney. Like his partner, he had featured in several major drug investigations through the years but avoided getting caught. Intelligence analysis of his role in the operation determined that he was the organizer and logistics manager. But he too was eventually forced out into the open when the CAB came calling – and served him with a tax demand for over €350,000.

By his own admission he became a full member of the Munster Mafia in the late 1980s. In an interview with this writer in 2002, Buckley admitted: 'For eight years I was involved in that [the drug trade]. It was pure greed mixed with the excitement.' He claimed that he was out of the drug business, which he would only refer to as 'that': 'It is six years since I had any involvement in any of that [drug crime]. I don't want to go into specifics about what I did and I do not have a problem with anyone from my past. I have no need or desire to go near that life again.'

One of the better-known members of the group was Cork crime figure Thomas Francis O'Callaghan, who was the front man in McSweeney's secret empire. Tommy O'Callaghan had progressed from robber to drug-dealer after a string of convictions for theft and burglary, both at home and in the UK. Originally from the Churchfield area of Cork's north-side he was first incarcerated in 1969, at the age of 15. Like many of his underworld counterparts, he was sentenced to two years in Daingean Reformatory School.

O'Callaghan was a shrewd crook who played his cards close to his chest and also studiously avoided attention. His criminal gang controlled a huge slice of the drug market in Munster and by the 1990s was classified as one of the country's top ten operations. Despite being unemployed all his life, O'Callaghan enjoyed a lavish lifestyle and bought a luxury home in upmarket Buxton Hill in the city in 1987, where he lived with his wife and children. Gardaí were aware that he held bank accounts containing huge sums of cash but there was nothing they could do about it. In a search of his home in the late 1980s detectives found a bank book for an account in Amsterdam which was held in his wife's name. They also discovered evidence that he was dealing in oil shares. O'Callaghan was not an overtly intimidating or violent hood. 'He had no interest in fighting or bullying and was quiet and unassuming,' recalled a local detective. 'But no one in the underworld would mess with him because Tommy had plenty of serious muscle to call on if he had a problem.' The muscle included Tommy Savage and two former members of the Provisional IRA.

The fifth member of the syndicate was Jeremiah 'Judd' Scanlan from Wilton in Cork. In 1986, the 36-year-old was jailed for three years at Uxbridge Magistrates Court in London, on a charge of conspiracy to smuggle heroin. When he was released in 1988, he went back to Cork and assisted in the construction of the crime empire.

The Munster Mafia's closest associates outside Cork were INLA hoods Tommy Savage and Mickey Weldon, and George 'the Penguin' Mitchell. Savage and the Munster Mafia had been involved in organizing the cannabis shipment which was intercepted in Rosslare Harbour in 1990. It was one of the first major set-backs for the syndicate.

Investigating Gardaí discovered that McCarthy used the cover of the rugby international to collect the hash, which had been sent as air freight from Schipol Airport in Amsterdam to Paris. The smooth-talking ex-cleric invited Mary Vesey to travel with him on the ferry from Rosslare to Cherbourg and on the drive to Paris. To lessen his chances of arrest, Father Hash then spun a yarn that he had to fly home to Cork on urgent business. He asked her to drive the car back and arranged to meet her in the Talbot Hotel in Wexford. But McCarthy heard a radio news report about the drug seizure as he was travelling to Wexford and promptly went on the run to Spain.

Mary Vesey meanwhile gave Gardaí a full statement about how the charming theologian had hoodwinked her into a world of trouble. After several months in hiding, McCarthy's conscience finally got to him and he returned to Ireland to confess his 'sin'. The DPP acknowledged that Mary Vesey was innocent of any involvement and the charges against her were dropped. In 1992 Father Hash pleaded guilty and was jailed for five years.

The Rosslare seizure had attracted much unwelcome Garda attention on the Munster Mafia and they kept their heads down until the dust settled. Losing shipments was an occupational hazard and they had plenty of cash reserves built up from the many importations which hadn't been seized. At the time, the Gardaí simply didn't have the resources necessary to target such a sophisticated group in a prolonged surveillance operation – and had to bide their time.

The main opposition to the Munster Mafia's business in Cork was a family-based criminal organization led by notorious brothers Seanie and Kieran O'Flynn. The O'Flynns and their four other brothers – Donal 'Duckie', Bobby, Christy and Noel – had a ferocious reputation for violence and were the most feared gangsters in the city. From the Togher area, most of the family had been involved in serious crime for many years, including robbery, assaults and extortion. The O'Flynn gang had a core of about 25 members, many of whom were related by blood or marriage. They had carved out a large slice of the drug trade in Cork and were among the first gangs to bring in large quantities of ecstasy. The gang's army of dealers plied their trade openly in several pubs and clubs in the city centre. And if the proprietors didn't like it they were threatened, beaten or had their premises burned down. Unlike their main competitors, the O'Flynns never attempted to disguise what they were – brutal thugs.

The family introduced the gun to the streets of the city to keep control of the drug trade. Stories of the mob's viciousness are still told in Cork's underworld. On one occasion Kieran O'Flynn walked into a city pub armed with a sword and ran it through a man sitting at the counter. 'That's what you get for messin' with me,' O'Flynn told his stricken victim. As he casually walked out of the pub, with the blood still dripping off the sword, O'Flynn warned the other shocked patrons, 'and none of you saw anything either.' Another man, who made the mistake of taking up with the former girlfriend of a senior gang member, was abducted. He was taken to Cork Airport in the boot of a car, stripped naked and savagely beaten. The gang was also responsible for scores of other attacks and shootings in the city. Their brutality ensured that no one ever did see anything. The O'Flynns were only too willing to show the local police that they were not afraid of them either.

One experienced detective, who spent years investigating the family, described how they operated: 'They were very dangerous men who weren't very bright. They expressed themselves through violence and had no problem shooting or maiming anyone who crossed them. A few of them had been in the Army and they were physically big men which helped their image greatly. We knew of several incidents where they walked into pubs and attacked people but such was their reputation for extreme violence that we could never get witnesses or victims to come forward. They took over a number of pubs and clubs to sell drugs but the owners were too terrified to stop them. You could say they were to Cork what the Dunnes were to Dublin – only a lot worse.'

Seanie O'Flynn regularly boasted to cops that his family had kept heroin out of the city. On one occasion he even told officers at Togher Garda Station that he was going to set up a branch of Concerned Parents Against Drugs (CPAD).

The O'Flynns' brother-in-law, Michael Crinnion, stood out as the most violent member of the entire mob. He was married to their sister Collette, with whom he had four young children. Born in 1960 and also from Togher, Crinnion had been a violent, dangerous thug all his life. In the early 1980s he received a lengthy jail sentence for attacking a man with a hatchet on Shandon Street, and in 1988 got three years for armed robbery. 'When he was younger he would go around with a group of other boys and just beat people up if he didn't like the look of them. When he got in with the O'Flynns he thought he was untouchable,' said one former associate interviewed for this book. Crinnion was the gang's top enforcer and hit man – two jobs he carried out with great enthusiasm.

In 1990, Crinnion and the O'Flynns began flexing their muscles against the opposition. While the gang avoided direct conflict with the leading members of the Munster Mafia, they began targeting hoods further down the drug-dealing food chain. Individuals who didn't buy their drugs from the O'Flynns and who tried to deal on their patch, were threatened, beaten and shot. Tommy O'Callaghan and his associates, who had a much bigger operation, watched with increasing anger as the violent gangsters grew more arrogant and dangerous.

In late 1990 the O'Flynn mob went too far – and brought Cork to the brink of an all-out gang war. Crinnion, together with Seanie and Kieran O'Flynn, abducted a mid-ranking dealer whom they tortured, before stealing a large shipment of drugs and money. The dealer, who worked directly for another major player in the city, John Dorgan, was told that if he wanted to stay alive it would be in his interests to work for the O'Flynns instead. Dorgan was a close associate of Tommy O'Callaghan and Judd Scanlan. The Munster Mafia decided that something had to be done about the O'Flynns and called in Tommy Savage to help them wipe out the problem. By early January 1991, both sides began to limber up for a violent confrontation.

The O'Flynn brothers would later claim to Gardaí that they made approaches to Dorgan and his associates to sort out their differences but were rebuffed. On 11 January they claimed that a group of masked men, including Tommy Savage and John Dorgan, had attacked Kieran O'Flynn's home in Thorndale Estate. The following day Dorgan made contact with the O'Flynns to discuss peace. He suggested that he meet with Seanie later that evening. But Dorgan and his associates were not interested in peace. They planned to shoot O'Flynn and any more of his brothers and henchmen who turned up. Tommy Savage had already arrived in the city in the company of another Dublin hood to carry out the plan.

That evening the O'Flynns accidentally discovered that Savage had arrived in Cork. They were terrified of the Zombie and knew what his presence meant. Seanie O'Flynn and his older brother Duckie decided to make the first move. They heard that Dorgan and his gang were drinking in the Arcadia pub on Douglas Street. They summoned their troops and 12 gang members gathered in another local pub, including all the O'Flynn brothers, Crinnion and their associates James Daly and Michael 'Dublin Mick' Leonard. At least three of them were carrying firearms. The mob drove off in three cars to the wrong pub – the Arcadian. Realizing their mistake, they then headed to the pub on Douglas Street.

At 10.45 p.m. the group arrived at the door of the Arcadia, which was full of Saturday night drinkers. Dorgan was in the pub with a number of his associates, including Dave Healy. The dealer who had been abducted and robbed by the O'Flynns had left a short time earlier. Duckie, Seanie, James Daly and Michael Leonard went in first. Christy O'Flynn would later claim that Dave Healy pulled a gun and confronted his brother Seanie. Healy was overpowered by Seanie O'Flynn and the gun fell to the floor. In the ensuing melee, Dorgan was grabbed and dragged towards the door. Duckie O'Flynn caused panic when he fired blanks from a revolver and customers dived to the ground. At the same time Noel O'Flynn produced a sawn-off shotgun and fired shots into the bar from the door.

Christy O'Flynn later told detectives what happened next. 'Sean and Daly pulled Dorgan to the door and told me to hold him there. I kicked the shit out of him. Duckie fired two shots out of the dummy gun. Noelie went ape shit with the sawn-off, firing all over the place. He emptied it and re-loaded,' he claimed.

In the confusion John Dorgan escaped through a back door and the O'Flynns fled through the front. They broke up and ran in all directions. The would-be killers had missed their target but had managed to shoot two of their own men. James Daly was hit in the eye by a shotgun blast and it couldn't be saved. Christy O'Flynn was hit in the shoulder but wasn't seriously wounded. 'All the men with me had guns. Duckie had his own revolver, it's a beauty. I took four guns away from the scene, Duckie's, two dummies [guns] and the sawn-off. I took the guns home and wrapped them and buried them,' he said in his statement. He claimed it was only then that he discovered he was injured.

Tommy Savage and his Dublin pal arrived in a taxi driven by one of O'Callaghan's men, minutes after the shooting. Garda cars were beginning to arrive at the scene and shocked customers had spilled onto the street. When the INLA thug spotted the commotion, he ordered the cab to drive off.

Detectives were astonished that no one had been killed or seriously injured. One of the original investigators recalled: 'This was nothing short of an act of madness and it was a miracle that it didn't turn into a massacre. Dorgan could certainly count himself as being very, very lucky that night. This was the kind of incident that would become so familiar in Limerick ten years later.' The timing of the attack proved to be fortuitous for everyone concerned. If the O'Flynns had arrived 20 minutes later the Arcadia Bar would have been the scene of a bloodbath.

Paddy McSweeney, a leading member of the Munster Mafia (© Padraig O'Reilly).

(*Left*) John McCarthy ('Father Hash'), a convicted drug-dealer and member of the Munster Mafia (© Padraig O'Reilly).

(*Below left*) Jeremiah 'Judd' Scanlan, a member of the Munster Mafia. Found dead in his home in Cork (© Padraig O'Reilly).

(*Below*) Alan Buckley, the antiques dealer who worked as an organizer with the Munster Mafia and George 'the Penguin' Mitchell (© Padraig O'Reilly).

John 'the Manager' Noonan, who organized a huge £150 million hash shipment for the Munster Mafia, George Mitchell and a British crime syndicate in 1995.

John McGrail, a convicted armed robber and member of the Penguin's gang.

Derek 'Maradona' Dunne, the League of Ireland footballer and heroin-dealer, shot dead in Amsterdam in 2000.

Peter Bolger, a convicted fraudster and the Penguin's bagman (© Padraig O'Reilly).

State Solicitor Barry Galvin (*left*) and Chief Superintendent Tony Quilter pictured in Cork, 2009 (© Padraig O'Reilly).

Kevin Carty, the former Chief Superintendent and Assistant Commissioner who targeted the Munster Mafia and the Penguin's organization.

Austin McNally, the former Chief Superintendent who targeted the Penguin's organization.

Detective Sergeant Pat Walsh, who was one of the top undercover operators in the Gardaí.

(*Above*) Former Commissioner Pat Byrne, who was appointed a few weeks after the murder of Veronica Guerin in 1996.

(*Above right*) John O'Mahoney, Assistant Commissioner of the Gardaí and former head of the Criminal Assets Bureau (© Padraig O'Reilly).

(*Right*) Retired Garda Commissioner and inaugural head of the CAB, Fachtna Murphy (© Padraig O'Reilly).

William 'Jock' Corbally, who was tortured
to death by PJ 'the Psycho' Judge and his
associates in 1996.

Declan 'Decie' Griffin, a drug-dealer and
police informant who helped set Jock
Corbally up for murder. Later shot dead in a
Dublin pub (© Padraig O'Reilly).

Mark Dwyer, a drug-dealer who was
involved in the murder of Jock Corbally.

'Cotton Eye' Joe Delaney, a drug-dealer and
associate of PJ Judge who tortured and
murdered Mark Dwyer in December 1996.

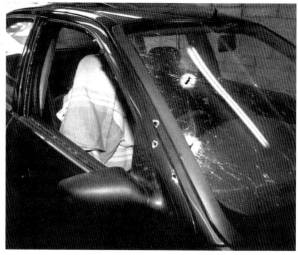

(*Left*) Detective Jerry McCabe, who was shot dead three weeks before the assassination of Veronica Guerin.

(*Above*) Jerry McCabe's squad car.

(*Above*) Kevin Walsh from Limerick, the leader of the IRA gang responsible for shooting Detective Jerry McCabe to death (© Padraig O'Reilly).

(*Above right*) Dicky O'Neill, the Provo boss who is still wanted for the killing of Jerry McCabe.

(*Right*) Gerry Roche, the IRA man still wanted in connection with the murder of Jerry McCabe. Roche, who was also a former INLA member, provided explosives to Martin Cahill to blow up State forensic scientist Dr James Donovan.

(*Above*) Eddie Ryan, whose murder ultimately kicked off gang war in Limerick in 2000.

(*Right*) Roy Collins, RIP. Shot at Roxboro shopping centre, Limerick, on 9 April 2009.

(*Below*) Steve Collins with a picture of his murdered son, Roy (© Padraig O'Reilly).

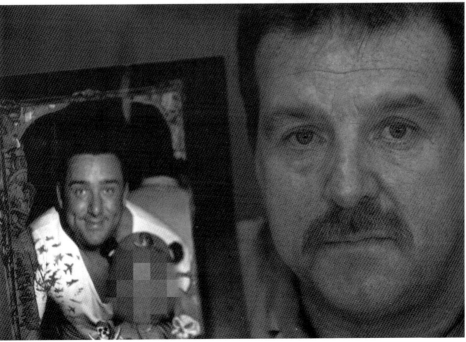

Kieran Keane, who murdered Eddie Ryan and was himself executed by the McCarthy/Dundons in 2003.

(*Above*) Gerard Dundon, searched by cops outside his home in Limerick City (© Padraig O'Reilly).

(*Right*) John Dundon.

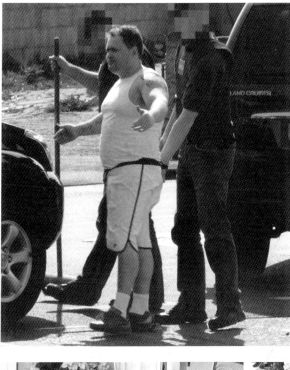

Wayne Dundon, searched by cops outside his home in Limerick City (© Padraig O'Reilly).

(*Left*) Members of the Regional Support Unit during a raid at Gerard Dundon's house on Hyde Road, Limerick City (© Padraig O'Reilly).

(*Below left*) Christy Keane pictured while doing time in Portlaoise Prison.

(*Below*) Brian Collopy, Limerick (© Padraig O'Reilly).

(*Above*) Martin Foley ('the Viper', *left*) and the late Derek Hutch.

(*Right*) Brian O'Keefe, the Crumlin drug-dealer who shot Martin Foley in 1995.

(*Below*) Shane Coates (*left*) and Stephen Sugg, the notorious Westies.

Bernard 'Verb' Sugg, a member of the Westies.

(*Left*) Pascal Boland, murdered by the Westies.

(*Above*) Todd O'Loughlin, the retired Detective Inspector who investigated the Veronica Guerin murder, the Westies and the emergence of the new gangs (© Padraig O'Reilly).

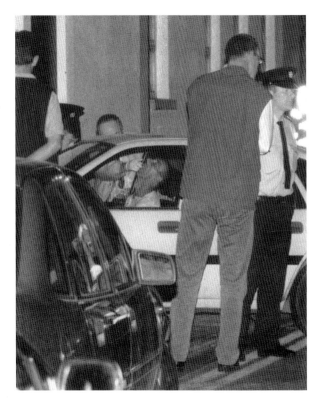

(*Above*) Martin 'Marlo' Hyland.

(*Right*) Michael Brady, murdered on the orders of Marlo Hyland and PJ Judge in 1996 (© Padraig O'Reilly).

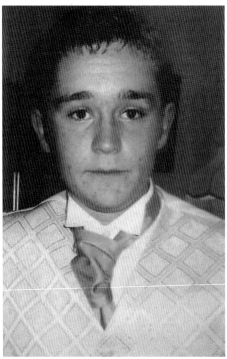

Anthony Campbell, the innocent apprentice plumber killed in the assassination of Martin 'Marlo' Hyland.

Baiba Saulite, who was murdered by Martin 'Marlo' Hyland's gang.

Lebanese criminal Hassan Hassan at Dublin Airport, flying to Beirut after his release from Portlaoise Prison on 20 March 2010 (© Padraig O'Reilly).

Eamon 'the Don' Dunne, the gang member who organized the murder of his boss Marlo Hyland and who was himself executed by his own men in 2010.

(*Right*) Close friend of the Don, Brian O'Reilly (*left*), who survived a gun attack in 2010, with Dessie O'Hare at a gangland funeral (© Padraig O'Reilly).

(*Below*) Christy Gilroy, the hit man and heroin addict who carried out a double murder for the Don. Gilroy was also murdered on the Don's orders.

(*Below right*) John Daly, the notorious Finglas gangster who phoned the *Liveline* programme from his prison cell. Murdered by the Don's men.

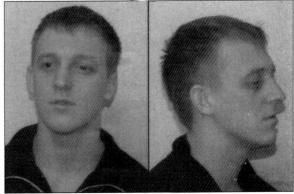

(*Right*) 'Fat' Freddie Thompson (© Padraig O'Reilly).

(*Below*) Brian Rattigan, who murdered former associate Declan Gavin in 2000. The murder sparked the infamous Crumlin/Drimnagh blood feud which claimed over a dozen lives in less than ten years (© Padraig O'Reilly).

(*Below right*) Mark Desmond, the Ballyfermot drug-dealer at the centre of the canal murders investigation in 2010.

Murdered gangland pals Aidan Byrne and Paddy Doyle.

Christy Kinahan being
confronted by the author in
Antwerp, Belgium, in 2009
(© Padraig O'Reilly).

(*Above left*) John 'the Colonel' Cunningham, Christy
Kinahan's partner-in-crime.

(*Above*) Kevin Lynch at the wedding of Christy Kinahan Jr
(© Padraig O'Reilly).

(*Left*) Jason Martin, the English criminal whose murder in
Ballyfermot caused a new gang war between former
friends.

(*Right*) Derek 'Dee Dee' O'Driscoll, the drug-dealer whose gang was involved in the double murder of brothers Kenneth and Paul Corbally.

(*Below*) Brothers Kenneth (*left*) and Paul Corbally from Ballyfermot, who were both murdered in a feud in 2010, pictured here with their father, Paddy Corbally, at the funeral of another gangster (© Padraig O'Reilly).

(*Below right*) Jasvinder Singh Kamoo, Christy Kinahan's business associate in Spain (© Padraig O'Reilly).

Peter 'Fatso' Mitchell pictured in Spain in 2008, where he had been in hiding and running a major drug-trafficking operation since the murder of Veronica Guerin.

Gardaí arrested Seanie O'Flynn, Michael Crinnion and James Daly as they ran away from the pub. The three men were extremely aggressive and threatened the arresting officers. Despite his serious injury Daly, who was bleeding heavily from the left eye, told the cops to 'fuck off' and tried to punch one of them. As they were being taken away in a squad car Seanie warned his associates: 'Sing dumb and say nothing. We done nothing.' Later when he was being questioned, O'Flynn claimed that Tommy Savage and another named associate had fired the shots in the bar. He also accused McSweeney and O'Callaghan of organizing it.

At first the police were inclined to believe O'Flynn's version of events, especially when they discovered that Savage was in Cork. The following morning they located the INLA man and his Dublin accomplice, and discovered that John Dorgan and his wife were staying in the same B&B. Dorgan was carrying £10,000 in cash, which detectives believed was the payment for the hit. The four were arrested and taken in for questioning. Savage refused to leave his cell for the duration of his 48 hours in custody. The O'Flynn and Savage groups were later released without charge.

A few days later the O'Flynns decided to further convince the police that they hadn't been involved in the Arcadia incident. They fired shots into the home of Kieran O'Flynn and smashed up his car, to make it look like another attack by the Dorgan/O'Callaghan side. But the ruse didn't work. A week later detectives arrested Christy O'Flynn, who made a full admission about what had really happened.

Duckie, Kieran, Bobby and Noel O'Flynn were arrested, along with Michael Leonard. Noel O'Flynn and Leonard later admitted their involvement while the others said nothing. Duckie O'Flynn managed to escape from the police station. Meanwhile Noel, Christy O'Flynn and Leonard were charged with possession of firearms with intent to endanger life. They were also charged with 'unlawfully and maliciously shooting' at James Daly with the intention of doing grievous bodily harm. The State, however, was eventually forced to drop the charges because Daly was not prepared to make a complaint or give evidence in court.

Gardaí finally caught up with Duckie O'Flynn when he was arrested and charged with stabbing another local drug-dealer, John Brett. On 20 October 1991, Brett, from Desmond Square, Cork, was drinking with

Noel O'Flynn in The Three Ones pub on Barrack Street. Eye-witnesses later claimed that Duckie O'Flynn stabbed Brett with a four-inch kitchen knife. Brett fell to the ground clutching his intestines, which were hanging out of his stomach. Noel O'Flynn, who was Brett's friend, struck Duckie as he left the pub. Brett was critically injured and was in intensive care for almost two months. Despite his injuries, Brett was abusive and unco-operative when detectives interviewed him. Noel O'Flynn refused to make any statement to the police. 'You know the score. Jesus, my friend and my brother are involved. I am saying nothing,' he told detectives. Gardaí arrested Duckie when they tracked him to a safe house he was renting in Baltimore, County Cork, on 13 December. He was later charged with the attempted murder of John Brett and causing grievous bodily harm. Duckie was also charged with possession of a firearm at the Arcadia Bar with intent to endanger life, and injuring James Daly. He was further charged with escaping from lawful custody.

When detectives asked Duckie why he had done a runner he replied: 'If you leave the door of a bird cage open the bird will fly away. I had been questioned about the same thing for a day and a half and my stomach was killing me. I was after a dose of ecstasy and it was like as if someone put their hand up your hole and was pulling your guts out.' O'Flynn then told Gardaí that if he was released he would 'clean the place up of ecstasy' and warned: 'This place is going to get worse than Dublin.' He also offered to give them illegal guns in return for his freedom. 'I could get you two pieces. One is a big hand job from America. It would blow a hole in the wall there,' he boasted. The detectives told him they weren't interested.

The charges were subsequently dropped against Duckie O'Flynn for both the Arcadia shooting and the attack on Brett. John Brett refused to make an official complaint or be a witness for the prosecution. He made a full recovery and went back to work. In November 1999 he was caught with over €500,000 worth of ecstasy in Glanmire and was subsequently jailed for 11 years. In May 2007 his younger brother, David 'Boogie' Brett, was executed by former associates near the village of Ballydesmond. Boogie had also been involved in the drug trade.

Meanwhile Tommy Savage and Mickey Weldon ran into troubles of their own and were forced to move their operation to Amsterdam. In December 1991 their associate, Patrick 'Teasy Weasy' McDonald, was

shot dead by a lone gunman as he fixed the hair of an elderly female customer in his salon in Marino, North Dublin. The armed robber was
shot six times. Weldon and Savage were two of the top suspects, as
they'd had a major falling out with McDonald in the months before the
murder. Associates of Gerry Hutch, 'the Monk', who worked with the
INLA men, had also been involved in the plot. But Savage and Weldon
left the country before they could be arrested. The Zombie later moaned
that he was forced to 'emigrate' because the Gardaí and the media had
let it be known that he was their prime suspect in the case. He claimed
that an IRA hit team from South Armagh had agreed to assassinate him
in revenge for McDonald's murder.

In the seven-year period between 1988 and 1995, eight cannabis shipments, with a combined street value of £200 million (over €375 million
today) were seized by the Gardaí, Customs and the Irish Navy. Six of
the seizures were made along the Cork and Kerry coastline. But successive governments still denied that Ireland was being used as a gateway
for drug-smugglers. Everyone involved in law enforcement knew the
seizures were only the tip of the iceberg.

In February 1991, the Munster Mafia were planning another major
transaction. They struck a deal to buy a shipment of 700 kilos of cannabis direct from the Moroccan producers. They invested over £800,000
(over €1.6 million today) in the deal and it stood to make them at least
£1 million in profit. They recruited a local antiques dealer, Christopher
'Golly' O'Connell, to front the operation. The 50-year-old from The
Mews, in posh Montenotte, was a chancer who didn't mind how he
made his money. O'Connell was perfect for the job because no one suspected he was involved in crime. A detective who knew him recalled:
'Golly was an arrogant bluffer who was always ducking and diving.
Even though he was often seen in the company of Judd Scanlan, Buckley and McSweeney he was thought of as a bit of a rogue who would
talk to anyone. There was no suspicion about what he was really up to.'

The gang decided to charter a yacht and collect the hashish off the
Moroccan coast. It would be the first of several such operations. The
shipment was to be brought back to Ireland and landed in one of the
hundreds of isolated coves along the Cork coastline. In February,
O'Connell hired a skipper and a deck hand for a trip to collect 'gold

coins'. He then rented the *Karma of the East* from its owner in Dartmouth, England. He paid £16,000 in cash to hire the boat for six weeks.

In June, O'Connell and his crew flew to England to pick up the yacht, and the crew set sail for the Algarve while O'Connell flew ahead to meet the gang's supplier. But the group's distinctive Cork accents were to ultimately prove fatal for the Munster Mafia. A local policeman who regularly holidayed in Cork was curious when he heard the accents in Dartmouth. He made a few discreet enquiries, discovered who had chartered the yacht and relayed the information to his colleagues in Ireland. In Cork the previous sightings of Golly in the company of the drug-traffickers suddenly took on a new significance. The vessel's progress was tracked through its GPS but there was still no way of knowing what exactly it was up to.

From the beginning the yacht had engine problems. They were forced to stop off on the northern Spanish coast for a number of days while repair work was carried out. The boat set sail again and on 15 July O'Connell and his crew left the Portuguese coast. They headed for Gibraltar, where they rendezvoused with a Moroccan boat and transferred the 700 kilos of hash in 28 bales of what the crew thought were gold coins and antiques. When the cargo was stowed the *Karma of the East* set sail for Cork. The voyage back was a nightmare. The engine developed more mechanical problems as the crew wrestled with rough seas.

The engine finally blew up in flames just as the Cork coastline came into view in the early hours of 23 July. O'Connell was reluctant to call for help and scanned the coastline for hours, as if expecting someone to be waiting for them. When no one appeared the skipper sent a 'Mayday' message to the Marine Rescue Co-ordination Centre (MRCC). A lifeboat was dispatched to tow them into Courtmacsherry.

Fate again conspired against O'Connell. The MRCC informed RTÉ radio that they were co-ordinating the rescue of a yacht that had suffered fire damage off the Cork coast. When a member of the Customs Drug Surveillance Unit (CDSU) heard the report, he immediately went to investigate with a colleague. The unit had been recently established to collate intelligence on the activities of known drug-dealers; however, it only had a handful of members and was grossly under-resourced. The CDSU had been looking out for the yacht and arrived as the vessel was being pulled into the harbour. They searched the yacht and found the drugs. The Munster Mafia had taken a major financial hit – and Golly O'Connell was facing serious charges for drug-smuggling.

The syndicate recovered and continued to thrive. For every shipment seized, at least ten more were getting through. The growing demand for narcotics ensured that they were constantly working on more imaginative smuggling methods. But they and the rest of the country's criminal mobs were about to find themselves crossing swords with another formidable Cork man – the State Solicitor for the city, Barry Galvin.

The Criminal Justice System had never seen the likes of Barry Galvin before. He is one of the undisputed heroes in the story of Gangland. Galvin was the only professional working on the frontline of law enforcement who was prepared to risk his reputation, and his safety, to demand that action be taken to tackle the growing criminal menace. He relished challenging the consensus but he was an unlikely rebel. He was a fourth-generation solicitor of Cork's respected family law firm Barry C. Galvin and Son. His grandfather was a recipient of the Law Society gold medal when he qualified as a solicitor, and Barry Galvin came top of his class in the 1965 bar exams in King's Inns and was awarded the prestigious Brooke Prize. As a young barrister, he specialized in the fields of corporate banking and taxation law. He also worked in criminal defence.

From his appointment as State Solicitor for Cork City in 1983 Galvin was responsible for the prosecution of all criminal cases. His reputation for hard work and his razor-sharp legal brain won the admiration of his peers and Gardaí. The indefatigable lawyer was driven by a passion for law and order, which he believed should be there to protect the ordinary citizen from criminals. But Galvin found himself becoming increasingly frustrated with the Criminal Justice System. It had failed to keep pace with the activities of organized crime, to the detriment of the public. As he reviewed Garda investigation files in his role as public prosecutor, the evidence of the changing trends in crime was there in black and white. Gardaí were seizing a wider variety of drugs, and in much larger quantities than ever before. The level of violence involved in crimes like burglary and the wanton destruction of property were both escalating. And the spectre of gangland violence had already arrived on the streets of his city.

Through his close working relationship with local Gardaí and Customs, Galvin realized how they were hamstrung in their efforts to take on the Godfathers. He recalled: 'I had developed a deep concern that the criminals and drug-traffickers were gaining significant ground and nothing was being done about it. They could flaunt their wealth in the knowledge that no one would touch them. The culture of organized crime has a very corrosive effect on the wider society and I could see how it was undermining whole communities. But we had laws there which could be utilised against them but there just wasn't the will to use them.'

Galvin took a personal interest in the activities of Tommy O'Callaghan, Judd Scanlan, Paddy McSweeney and the O'Flynns. In the late 1980s he successfully opposed the transfer of a pub licence to a bar on Shandon Street. O'Callaghan had purchased the bar for £145,000 through a front company called Capricorn Taverns. Some years later, Galvin successfully obtained a court order to shut down the Screaming Monkey pub in the city. He said it was a front for the O'Flynns, whom he described as a major Cork drug gang. Garda witnesses named Bobby and Christy O'Flynn as two of the pub's secret backers. Galvin successfully closed a number of other pubs in Cork in the same way.

Galvin also argued that the existing tax laws could be used to at least go after the criminals' wealth. It was vital to show the Godfathers who had avoided being caught that they were not untouchable. In the Finance Act of 1983, provision had been made for the Revenue Commissioners to tax earnings from criminal activity, but the State still appeared to be afraid to use the law – except for Galvin. Following the Arcadia pub shooting, he convened an ad hoc inter-agency group to examine the activities of local hoodlums. He invited officers from the local Garda Drug Squad and Customs to his office at the South Mall, Cork.

The group drew up a list of the top ten drug-traffickers in the region. At the top of the list were the members of the Munster Mafia. Over time, the various officers collated information in a detailed dossier that included employment records, criminal records, intelligence on known investments, property and business dealings, lists of known associates, the cars they drove, the holidays they took and the homes they lived in.

When it was completed Galvin sent it to the Revenue Commissioners in Dublin. He included an extensive covering report, suggesting how the existing tax codes could be used to make life uncomfortable for the mobsters. He got no response.

Despite the frustrating setback, Galvin was determined to make life difficult for one member of the crime syndicate. He decided there was enough evidence to pursue a criminal prosecution against Tommy O'Callaghan, for failure to make tax returns contrary to sections of the 1983 Finance Act. The gang boss was shocked when he was convicted and jailed for six months. O'Callaghan appealed the conviction to the High Court but lost. However, he subsequently appealed to the Supreme Court and won his case.

The State Solicitor was also concerned at how Europe's criminal elite saw Ireland as an ideal bolt-hole from justice. Major international drug barons, like Dutch trafficker Jan Hendrik Ijpelaar and Englishman David Huck, presided over their empires from the safety of their luxury homes in counties Clare and Kerry. Intelligence sources were also aware that Ireland was a gateway for some of Europe's biggest gangs. They were using isolated Irish inlets to smuggle huge quantities of drugs, intended for transportation onwards to the UK and the Continent. Galvin wrote dozens of detailed and well-researched reports for the various departments, outlining what needed to be done. No one in authority wanted to know and the campaigning Cork man was seen as a nuisance.

In the face of such a level of denial, and fuelled by his crusading zeal, Galvin decided to share the unpalatable truth with the Irish public. In 1992 he put his neck on the line when he appeared on the *Late Late Show*. For the first time since Saor Eire started robbing banks in 1967, someone from the cutting edge was prepared to shine a light on the true extent of organized crime in Ireland. Galvin revealed how wealthy villains, both local and foreign, were able to enjoy their ill-gotten gains and that nothing was being done about it. He described the West Cork coastline as the headquarters of international drug-trafficking into Europe and how the only two customs officers assigned to the region had no boat, radar or radios. He was seriously critical of the inaction of successive governments. The public was astounded by the amounts of money Galvin claimed the mobs were making. Most significantly, he called for the establishment of a single agency, combining the skills of

Customs, Revenue and the Gardaí, similar to the Drug Enforcement Agency (DEA) in the US. Galvin's media campaign put organized crime firmly on the national agenda – and incurred the collective wrath of the mobs and the Fianna Fáil Government.

The revelations were seriously embarrassing for the administration. Instead of confronting the issues raised, the then Minister for Justice, Padraig Flynn, attempted to discredit Galvin. He claimed in the Dáil that Galvin had been 'questioned' and his allegations were found to have been exaggerated. In his sneering manner, Flynn conceded there was a drug problem, but stated it wasn't of the scale 'suggested by the State Solicitor for Cork'. It was further proof of how the State's complacent attitude had allowed gangland to thrive over the previous two decades.

'I was quite amazed at the reaction I got from Mr Flynn. It was an effort to suppress what I had to say and belie it as untruthful,' Galvin recalled later in a rare interview. 'Instead of dealing with the problem of organized crime they [Government] just tried to make it go away but it wasn't going to go away. That was misleading the Dáil because he [Flynn] knew there was a serious problem because the reports that I had on file were available to him as Minister for Justice.'

Over the next few years, Galvin was vindicated, as the Gardaí and Navy made a string of huge drug seizures around the coastline. One of them involved two tons of hashish on the *Brime*, a yacht owned by David Huck. The haul was intercepted by Gardaí and the Irish Navy off the Kerry coast in July 1993. The Moroccan cannabis was destined for England. The crew of four men – from England, Holland, Belgium and Ireland – were convicted and jailed. Huck was also subsequently caught by the British Navy with another shipment. One of the largest seizures made was a £10 million hash haul that belonged to the Munster Mafia.

On 9 July 1994, a yacht called the *Nicoletta* arrived off the Galway coast with a ton of Moroccan cannabis on board. Undercover Gardaí watched as four men collected bales of hash from the yacht in a dinghy and brought them ashore. The men, criminals from Cork and Dublin, were loading the haul into a camper-van when they were surrounded by armed police. One of the four men arrested was John Dorgan's associate Dave Healy. The other three were Patrick Kelleher from Shandon in Cork and Ronnie Byrne and John McKeown from Dublin. Byrne, from the inner-city and McKeown, from Finglas, were well-known drug-traffickers. Both men had originally been armed robbers and McKeown was an associate of PJ Judge. The joint operation was backed financially by Tommy O'Callaghan, John Dorgan and Patrick McSweeney. Two months earlier, over Stg£250,000 had been withdrawn by members of the Munster Mafia from local banks and sent abroad as part-payment for the load. The *Nicoletta* had been chartered in La Baule in France and set sail for the Moroccan coast on 22 May. The syndicate had originally agreed to buy three tons for Stg£3 million. But when the Moroccans met the yacht, they had just one ton on board. Rather than wait for the remainder of the shipment, the crew set sail for Ireland, where an international surveillance operation ensured that the Irish Navy and the Gardaí were waiting for them. The four men were subsequently convicted and jailed for up to ten years each. The seizure was further proof that Barry Galvin had been correct all along.

Meanwhile, the O'Flynns had also suffered a number of major setbacks – although it didn't stop them throwing their weight around. In 1994 the Cork Drug Squad caught Kieran O'Flynn with 53 kilos of hashish in a speed boat at Hop Island in Cork Harbour. O'Flynn had collected the drugs, which were dropped over the side of a container ship from Rotterdam as it approached Cork docks. He was arrested and charged. Due to the work of Barry Galvin and the Gardaí, O'Flynn was refused bail and was subsequently jailed for seven years. In the same year Christy O'Flynn was jailed when he pleaded guilty to shooting at another man with intent to do him grievous bodily harm in September 1992. And in 1995, Seanie O'Flynn was caught with over 100 kilos of hash by Spanish police in the Costa del Sol. While the investigation was continuing, the Godfather was held in a Spanish prison.

Back in Cork the enforced absence of three important members of the family business presented unique opportunities for the Munster Mafia. A new generation of young, hardened criminals emerged to claim a stake in the drug trade. One of them was a violent young thug called Michael 'Danser' Ahern, from Churchfield Green on Cork's north-side. Ahern was a protégé of Tommy O'Callaghan. Born in 1967, Danser had been a champion under-16 boxer and could 'sort out' other criminals who got in his way.

Ahern was the leader of a tough new gang with big ambitions. When

John Gilligan set up his huge drug-dealing empire, Ahern's mob were major customers. Danser was a close friend of Brian Meehan, Paul Ward and Peter Mitchell. Through O'Callaghan, his gang also had associations with the crime organizations run by the Penguin and Tommy Savage. Ahern had plenty of reason to be cocky. With the three O'Flynn brothers out of the way, he saw his chance to expand.

Ahern's mob began pushing into territory controlled by the O'Flynns on the north-side of the city. This led to confrontations between the 'soldiers' on both sides, involving fist-fights and stabbings. It wasn't long before they resorted to firearms, leading to one of the first major gang wars in the history of organized crime.

On 4 November 1993, Paul 'Mossy' O'Sullivan, a close associate of Ahern, was drinking in the Unicorn Bar on Great William O'Brien Street. Around 10.45 p.m. two men called his name at the door. When he walked out to investigate, he met two men who were wearing motorbike helmets. One of them produced a handgun and shot O'Sullivan twice, hitting him in the neck and head. The victim was critically injured and a Garda spokesman later revealed that the hit men clearly intended killing him. O'Sullivan was confined to a wheelchair as a result of his injuries. Michael Crinnion and members of the O'Flynn family were later arrested and questioned about the attack but there was insufficient evidence to charge anyone. Ahern and his gang pulled back from O'Flynn territory – but not for long.

In January 1995, the uneasy peace was shattered when the O'Flynns made a move into Ahern's drug-dealing territory in the sprawling estates in Churchfield and Gurranabraher. Ten of Ahern's dealers were taken aside by a mob led by Crinnion and threatened. The enforcer said that they would be shot if they didn't switch their allegiances. Ahern decided that it was time to finish the job that John Dorgan and Tommy O'Callaghan had started in 1991. The O'Flynns, particularly Duckie, Bobby and their brother-in-law Crinnion, would have to be wiped out.

Ahern turned to his friends in the Gilligan gang for help. Brian Meehan and Paul Ward were happy to oblige. The gang had a large arsenal of automatic weapons and Meehan was anxious to try them out on some real people. On 11 February 1995 they launched the first strike. That night three men, wearing balaclavas and overalls, burst into the Steeple Bar on Shandon Street. Crinnion, Bobby and Duckie O'Flynn had been drinking there all evening but had left 15 minutes earlier. Ahern and his accomplices called out their names and when they discovered that they were gone, ordered the patrons to get on the floor. They sprayed the walls and ceiling with bullets. No one was injured but the young drug-dealers succeeded in sending a message to the O'Flynns – it was a declaration of war. In another incident a lone gunman fired a shot at Crinnion as a warning, and he also received death threats. The gang sent him a bullet in the post, but the enforcer laughed it off and let it be known that he wasn't afraid.

In retaliation the O'Flynn gang abducted one of Ahern's associates on 28 February. They took him at gunpoint to Ballinhassig outside the city, where he was shot in the arm. He managed to get away before he was recaptured and finished off.

The stakes were about to get even higher. Ahern and his mob decided it was time to murder Michael Crinnion. In March, Gardaí foiled a potential attack when they stopped two members of Ahern's gang who were following the enforcer. A month later the gang were more successful. On the night of Saturday 8 April, Crinnion was working as a bouncer at the An Clannad Bar on Barrack Street, a short distance from a local Garda station. He regularly worked there and Duckie and Bobby O'Flynn were inside drinking. Crinnion was talking to the pub owner when a man walked by. As he passed Crinnion, the hit man suddenly turned and fired five shots into the enforcer, before running off. The gangland hard man collapsed and died in the pub doorway.

On the day and night of the murder, Danser Ahern and his closest associate ensured they had a cast-iron alibi by staying in a hotel in Dublin. Gardaí later received reliable information that led them to believe that Brian Meehan was the gunman and that a number of other members of the Gilligan gang were in Cork that night. No one was ever charged with the killing.

Michael Crinnion's murder attracted considerable media attention on the crime family and the underworld scene in Cork. The killing was to herald a steady increase in gangland executions around the country, as the 1990s would see some of the worst violence yet in the story of organized crime. At his funeral, Fr Brendan Whooley berated the press for the 'lack of mercy and compassion' shown in their reports about Crinnion's brutal career as a gangster. He warned journalists to 'judge not, lest you be judged'. A half hour later, as the funeral cortège was leaving the church, Duckie O'Flynn and a mob attacked and seriously injured an RTÉ cameraman who was covering the event. When Fr Whooley, still dressed in his ceremonial robes, tried to intervene, the gang roughly pushed him aside.

Over the following days the *Cork Examiner* and its sister paper, the *Evening Echo*, ran a campaign exposing the activities of the O'Flynns. Duckie O'Flynn and one of his associates, Martin O'Donovan, threatened to burn down Togher Post Office if it continued to sell the newspapers. They also threatened staff in a second store.

Gardaí launched an investigation into the incidents and into the assault on the cameraman. O'Flynn and O'Donovan were both charged. The case was handled personally by Barry Galvin. Duckie O'Flynn was subsequently jailed for two years for the attack on the RTÉ man. Duckie and O'Donovan were also convicted and jailed for threatening the shop-owners.

The murder of Crinnion and the imprisonment of several more members of the O'Flynn family left the gang weak and in disarray. Shortly afterwards Seanie O'Flynn was jailed for three years by a court in Malaga. But the O'Flynns were not the only Cork criminals who were having difficulties with the law.

In March 1997 the newly formed Cork Divisional Drug Unit, headed by then Detective Superintendent Tony Quilter, had another major success against the Munster Mafia. They caught Judd Scanlan in the process of swapping £20,000 worth of ecstasy for six kilos of hash. Quilter's squad couldn't believe their luck. One of Cork's Mr Bigs had decided to be hands-on in what was a relatively small deal for the mob. Quilter, who later became the head of the Garda National Drug Unit (and recently promoted to Assistant Commissioner) was the bane of local drug-traffickers. He'd led the investigation which resulted in the capture of Kieran O'Flynn and was also involved in targeting other members of the family, who tried to intimidate the cop but failed. Scanlan was convicted and jailed for 22 years on the drugs charges in 1999. It was one of the stiffest sentences ever handed down to a drug-dealer. Six years into his sentence Scanlan appealed his case on a point of law and was granted bail while a retrial was pending. In 2007 he was found dead at his home, after dying during a binge of booze and drugs.

In the meantime the Divisional Drug Unit had scored a string of major successes against the Munster mobs. One seven-month undercover investigation, codenamed 'Operation Blackwater', was a combined initiative between Quilter's unit, the GNDU and the National Surveillance Unit. It resulted in the seizure of millions of pounds' worth of cocaine, ecstasy and cannabis. In one seizure alone Gardaí intercepted £500,000 worth of ecstasy and another £5 million worth of hashish, in a shipment organized by Danser Ahern and his mob. As a result Ahern moved his operating base to Portugal to stay out of harm's way.

The Munster Mafia's old enemy wasn't having much luck either. When Seanie O'Flynn was released in April 1998, he set about reorganizing the family business. He moved to the city of Utrecht in Holland and began dealing with a major Dutch ecstasy supplier. Back in Cork, the Divisional Drug Unit began liaising with their Dutch colleagues in a bid to catch the dangerous gangster again. As a result of the cooperation between the two police forces, a trap was set for O'Flynn by undercover Dutch cops. They had been tapping his phones and keeping him under surveillance for weeks when they struck gold. They were aware that he had done a deal for 25,000 ecstasy tablets, which were to be smuggled back to Cork. O'Flynn agreed to pay £45,000 for the haul, which had a street value of £250,000. Seanie's potential profit from the deal was at least £100,000 – and this was just one of several deals he had successfully organized. At 5 a.m. on 15 August 1998, the police watched as O'Flynn met his Dutch contact and handed over the cash. The officers made their move when they saw Seanie putting the tablets in the boot of his car. He was charged and put in custody.

Seanie O'Flynn's first trial appearance on the drugs charge was adjourned when he went berserk in court. He was enraged by the sight of an RTÉ camera-crew who had been given permission to record the proceedings. Seanie began screaming and grabbed court documents to shield his face. 'I'm not taking part while the camera is around,' he shouted at the judges. O'Flynn refused to recognize the court and fired his lawyers as he was led back to the holding cells.

When his trial resumed, O'Flynn claimed that he had not been involved in trafficking but had only agreed to transport the drugs. On New Year's Eve 1998, he was convicted on the drugs charge and given a lenient two-year sentence. With a third taken off the sentence for good behaviour and the four months he had already been in custody, O'Flynn was facing only a year behind bars. He couldn't believe his luck. The presiding judge said he took into account the fact that Seanie's privacy had been violated by the presence of the TV cameras and that he had no previous convictions in Holland. When the judge finished delivering the sentence O'Flynn smiled and thanked him. When asked if he wanted to appeal the sentence, the Cork gangster shook his head and replied: 'No, no, definitely not.'

The Dutch prosecution service appealed the sentence, however, on the grounds that the jail term was too short. In July 1999, the Amsterdam Court of Appeal ruled that he should serve three years. The judges said that they were satisfied that O'Flynn was a drug-trafficker. One of Cork's most notorious Godfathers had to spend a further eight months behind bars, but if he'd been caught for the same offence in Ireland he would have been facing at least eight years.

When he was released from prison in 2000, O'Flynn moved to Spain and was a lot more careful about how he conducted business. But there were more problems in store for the crime family. In Cork, his brother Kieran had established his own drug-distribution network which, according to local sources, had caused a bitter falling out with Seanie in Spain. But Kieran's operation would not last for long.

At 11.15 p.m. on the night of 7 June 2001, Kieran O'Flynn was watching a movie called *The Hitman* when there was a loud knock on the front door of his home at Thorndale Estate, in Togher. As the 40-year-old was about to open the door, a gunman fired two shots through the glass, hitting the drug-dealer in the throat and chest. As the drug-dealer fell back into the hallway, the hit man stepped inside and finished him off with two more shots. O'Flynn choked to death on his own blood, as his partner and children looked on in horror.

Seanie O'Flynn didn't show up for his younger brother's funeral. It was a quiet affair, reflecting the fact that the family had lost their power in the gangland jungle. In 2010, the dissident republican group the Real IRA claimed responsibility for the murder. It also declared it had carried out four other murders in Cork and Dublin which had been classified as gangland executions. The group claimed it had carried out murders to protect communities from the ravages of drugs. But the truth was the total opposite. The Real IRA, like the INLA, is nothing more than a criminal organization. It murdered O'Flynn because he refused to give them a cut of the action, and claimed the kill to scare other drug-dealers into paying protection money. No one was ever convicted of Kieran O'Flynn's murder, which brought an end to the family's dominance of the local drug trade. Duckie and Christy O'Flynn both died separately from what were described as natural causes.

Seanie O'Flynn continues to live in Spain, but his one-time enemy, Danser Ahern, also came to a gruesome end, in Portugal. From his base in the Algarve, Ahern had established a huge multi-million-Euro business, shipping high-quality cocaine to gangs in Dublin and Cork. In 2005 the GNDU targeted the gang and made a number of major cocaine seizures in Dublin, including a cocaine-mixing factory, and a number of people were charged. The busts caused a rift in the gang and Ahern was blamed. In September 2005, he was snatched near his home in Lagos outside Albufeira. He was beaten, stabbed and shot four times in the head by his partners. Portuguese police found the Cork villain's body stuffed into a freezer. His killers were planning to cut up the corpse to get rid of it. Four Irishmen, three of whom were from Cork, were acquitted of Ahern's murder but convicted of perverting the course of justice.

In the meantime the Munster Mafia have continued to prosper. Tommy O'Callaghan and John Dorgan moved their operations to southern Spain; at the time of writing, Dorgan was facing charges for shooting another Irish criminal in the Costa del Sol. At the time of writing Paddy McSweeney it still contesting the Criminal Assets Bureau's huge tax demand. He has successfully avoided any more conflict with the law. Alan Buckley also still lives in Cork and claims to be 'retired'.

18.   The Watershed

The sudden, violent demise of underworld fixer Paddy Shanahan in 1994 caused a lot of headaches. He was laundering money through his building firm for various Godfathers and they now had a problem. One of them was Gerry Hutch, who decided to make up his losses with another major cash injection. On 24 January 1995, the Monk master-minded the daring robbery of £2.8 million from the Brinks-Allied security company's cash-holding depot in North Dublin. The meticu-lously planned heist was the result of months of preparation which began two days after Shanahan was whacked. It was the biggest cash robbery in the history of the State – with Hutch breaking his own record from exactly eight years earlier.

Garda intelligence later reported that the Brinks team included Hutch's long-standing associates and friends Geoffrey Ennis, Gerry Lee, Willy Scully, Paul Boyle and Noel Murphy. The gang, who were work-ing on inside information, struck just after 5.30 p.m. when the last cash-in-transit van of the day returned to the depot in Clonshaugh. The security van had been left at the depot gates by its Army and Garda escort. As the troops and police drove away, a flare was fired into the air to signal that the coast was clear. In the days before the robbery, the gang had loosened the perimeter fences around the depot. They also bridged ditches which ran through the large area of waste-ground that bordered the complex from the rear.

The first jeep smashed through the weakened fence just as the last security van drove into the loading bay and the roller-shutter doors were being lowered. The jeep rammed the shutters, pushing them in and upwards and leaving a gap on either side for the raiders to get in. Three armed gang members ran in under the door and fired shots into the air, to threaten the startled staff unloading the cash van. They then began grabbing the cash bags and carrying them to a second jeep that had reversed up to the fence between the warehouse and the cash depot. The gang were finished in less than ten minutes. They jumped into the jeep and drove, in darkness, out through the hole in the fence, across the makeshift bridge and through the adjoining fields.

Later that night Hutch's life-long friend Geoffrey Ennis was arrested near his home on the North Strand. A search of his car revealed a number of traffic cones, wet and muddy overalls and boots. He was held for 48 hours and released without charge. In the follow-up investigation Gardaí also discovered that the gang had stolen Paddy Shanahan's Pajero jeep for the raid. It was as if the Monk saw it as a fitting tribute to his murdered pal.

Within days, most of the gang members, including Hutch, had brought their families on a luxury holiday to Florida. The heat of the sun was a welcome alternative from the sort of heat they were attracting in Ireland. Inevitably the Brinks-Allied job attracted intense media attention – and created a new criminal celebrity to replace the General. The media revealed that the suspected ringleader was a faceless gangster with the bizarre nickname 'the Monk'. Gerry Hutch instantly became a household name.

A year after the heist Hutch gave his only newspaper interview, to journalist Veronica Guerin. Although he flatly denied any involvement in the heist, he told the journalist: 'The Brinks was a brilliant job. The best of luck to whoever done it.' Guerin asked Hutch where he got his money. 'I don't think it's your business where I get me money from. The guards know where I got it and they know it's legal,' he replied. Hutch also explained his insistence on loyalty among friends and associates which had kept him on the right side of a prison fence. 'My philosophy in life is simple enough. No betrayal. That means you don't talk about others; you don't grass and you never let people down.'

There was intense embarrassment for the authorities in the wake of the Brinks-Allied robbery when it was revealed that Gardaí had issued internal bulletins, warning that the Monk was planning a big job. There had been a major alert in November 1994, when a member of the gang was spotted watching a security van at the North Side Shopping Centre in Coolock. The Monk and his associates had been placed under surveillance. At the time it was suspected the gang were planning a repeat performance of the Marino Mart job by hitting a cash-in-transit van. Surveillance teams, backed up by the Emergency Response Unit (ERU) and the Serious Crime Squad, had watched the suspects for almost two months. Just before Christmas the operation was scaled down because it seemed the gangsters had abandoned their plans.

In the farce that followed the only person to face trial in connection with the Brinks job was *Irish Independent* journalist Liz Allen, who broke the story about the Garda warnings. She was charged under the Official Secrets Act for publishing the bulletins. The journalist and her newspaper were convicted and fined £380 between them.

On 29 January, Veronica Guerin added to the public outcry when she exposed the fact that Hutch had availed himself of a tax amnesty a few years earlier. Although she had only been working as a journalist for two years, Veronica was already well known as a result of her campaigning newspaper work.

Shortly before 7 p.m. the following evening there was a knock on the front door of her home. Her husband and son were out at the time and she was getting ready to go to a *Sunday Independent* staff party. When she answered the door, a man wearing a motorcycle helmet pushed her inside, knocking her to the ground. He produced a handgun and pointed it at Veronica's head. The thug then lowered the weapon and shot her in the thigh, narrowly missing a major artery. Veronica was hospitalized and underwent surgery. She made a full recovery and courageously vowed to continue her work.

The incident should have been a warning to the authorities that the underworld was moving to a sinister new level. Instead, malicious rumours were spread by criminals and a few Gardaí and journalists that Veronica had set up the shooting herself. Five months earlier a shot had been fired at the journalist's home. It was seen as a warning that she was getting too close for comfort but the rumour-mongers also cast doubt over that incident. The reality was that the journalist was lucky to escape with her life on 30 January. She was given armed police protection for a time but asked the Garda authorities to take it off because she felt it was interfering with her work as a crime reporter.

Inevitably the Monk was the prime suspect for the attack, but investigating Gardaí soon eliminated him from their enquiries. It later emerged that John Traynor had organized both attacks. Even though he was one of the journalist's main underworld sources, the duplicitous thug wanted to show that he had the 'bottle' to shoot the reporter because she had annoyed him. He later bragged that the incident boosted his reputation

in the eyes of other gangsters, especially John Gilligan. The Coach purposely timed the attack to take place so that the Monk would be the
obvious suspect. Traynor was arrested and questioned about the incident, but there was no evidence linking him with the crime.

John Gilligan, Traynor and his mob grew more confident and dangerous by the day. They were becoming richer beyond their wildest dreams
and were not shy about showing off their new-found wealth. They
showed no fear of the law and, for a time at least, it appeared that they
were untouchable. Garda units throughout Dublin were making reports
to HQ about the lifestyle and property acquisitions of the gang members. It was obvious that the gangsters were rolling in money from the
drug trade but there was no focused effort to investigate them.

There was plenty of evidence that the diminutive thug was becoming increasingly arrogant – and wealthy. In December 1994 Gilligan
threatened to have a senior investigator from Her Majesty's Customs
shot after officers in Holyhead seized a parcel containing £76,000 in
cash. UK Customs suspected it was the proceeds of crime. The cash was
being brought to Belgium by a truck driver as part of a drug deal.

Gilligan rang from Dublin and angrily demanded the return of the
money. He claimed he could prove it was from gambling and that it was
intended for investment purposes. The case was passed to Roger Wilson
of the Customs National Investigation Service in Manchester. By then
the police and customs on both sides of the Irish Sea were aware that
Gilligan was involved in drug-trafficking. He had been secretly filmed
by surveillance officers meeting with criminals in Brighton. Gilligan
was not arrested on that occasion because he had not been the main target of the undercover investigation. Roger Wilson decided that the
money should be confiscated under UK drug-trafficking legislation.

When Gilligan heard this he flew into a rage. 'He's [Wilson] backed
me into a corner . . . it's not a problem for me to get someone to shoot
him . . . I'm not goin' down that road, I just want me money back. But
if someone messes with my family I'll have them fucking shot,' Gilligan
snarled down the phone at a Customs official. The threat against the
officer was taken seriously and his superiors subsequently placed him in
a special protection programme.

Gilligan fought the case through the courts and the cash was eventually returned to him by order of Holyhead Magistrates Court. A week after the Holyhead seizure, the Dublin District Court ordered Gardaí to return £47,000 they had taken from Brian Meehan. Gilligan told the court that Meehan was minding the cash for him and that it was the proceeds of his gambling. The State was unable to prove that the money was from drug-dealing.

At the same time construction had commenced on the magnificent indoor equestrian arena at Jessbrook. In less than two years the Gilligans invested over £1.5 million into the project, which included a luxurious family home next door. Everyone was paid with wads of cash. The mob boss also bought houses and flash cars for his children with his drug money.

Gardaí monitoring Gilligan's meteoric rise were increasingly frustrated by an apparent lack of will on the part of management to mount a major investigation into his activities. They had also filed reports to the Revenue and the Department of Social Welfare in the hope that they would investigate abuses of the system by members of his family. His daughter Treacy was receiving lone parent's and rent allowance, while his son Darren was on the dole, even though he had one bank account containing £80,000.

The Department of Social Welfare launched an inquiry into Treacy Gilligan, based on the information collected by the Gardaí. When she was quizzed about a new car she claimed it was a present from her father. The officials asked for proof of this and warned that her social welfare money would be cut off if she did not produce the evidence. When Gilligan heard this he was furious. He made several threatening phone calls to the social welfare officer dealing with his daughter's case. The investigator passed on the Treacy Gilligan file to head office. A note in her social welfare file recorded how Gilligan, described as a 'very dangerous man', had made 'unspecified threats'. A further memo by department officials in the file recorded their decision to 'drop the subject about the car and continue paying her lone parent's allowance'.

The Revenue Commissioners, who were also prompted by Garda reports, wrote to Gilligan asking him to furnish a tax return. The corrupt Godfather wrote the words 'FUCK OFF' on the back of the letter and returned it.

The Gilligans did not hear from the Revenue or the Department of Social Welfare again. The dangerous Godfather had spectacularly exposed the State's inability to tackle the proceeds of crime. But Gilligan was about to force the State to finally take decisive action against Gangland. The sequence of events which would result in the fight back began when Veronica Guerin took an interest in the good fortune of John Gilligan.

For several months she had pestered John Traynor to set up an interview for her with Gilligan. The Coach warned that his partner was a very dangerous man and advised her to back off. However, she was determined to put her questions to him in person. On the morning of 14 September, Guerin decided to visit Gilligan at Jessbrook. He was still wearing his silk dressing-gown when he answered the door. 'Yeah?' he snarled at Veronica.

'Mr Gilligan?' she asked.

'That's right,' he snapped back.

Veronica explained who she was and said she wanted to ask him some questions about his wealth and the equestrian centre. Gilligan flew into a blood-curdling rage. He lunged at the journalist, punching her about the head and face with his fists. 'If you write anything about me I'll fucking kill you, your husband, your fucking son, your family, everybody belonging to you, even your fucking neighbours,' the psychopath screamed at her.

Veronica later told Gardaí that Gilligan seemed to be physically carrying her towards her car and pushed her onto the bonnet, while continuously hitting her in the head and body. She thought he was going to kill her. When he let go, Veronica slid, battered and dazed, onto the ground beside her car. Trembling with fear, she struggled to get to her feet. 'Get to fuck out of here, get off my fucking property,' Gilligan continued to shout. As she opened the car door Gilligan grabbed her again and shoved her violently into the driver's seat. He continued spitting obscenities and threats, as she fumbled with her car keys in the panic to get away. Gilligan reached into the car and grabbed her again by the neck. 'Have you a fucking mike, where's the fucking wire?' He tore open Veronica's cotton shirt and ripped her jacket. 'I'll kill you and your whole fucking family if you write anything about me,' he hissed, slamming the car door shut. 'Now get to fuck out of here.' Veronica drove away at speed, leaving Gilligan standing fuming in front of his mansion.

Later Gilligan went to see Traynor. He was in a rage and said that he was going to have 'that interfering bitch done, once and for all'. The following day Gilligan rang the journalist. In a calm, menacing tone he warned her: 'If you do one thing on me, or write about me, I am going to kidnap your son and ride him. I am going to shoot you. Do you understand what I am sayin'? I am going to kidnap your fucking son and ride him, and I am going to fucking shoot you. I will kill you.'

Veronica made an official complaint to the police and Gilligan was later charged with assault and causing criminal damage to the journalist's clothing. Gilligan used Traynor to offer the journalist money if she'd drop the charges, but she refused. Based on Gilligan's previous record and the nature of the attack, he was facing at least six months in prison. The Godfather and his henchmen decided that wasn't going to happen – Veronica Guerin needed to die. Tony Hickey, who led the investigation into the murder of Veronica Guerin, said the motive was clear-cut. 'Gilligan had a history throughout his criminal career of intimidating witnesses and he threatened Veronica with dire consequences if she pressed charges against him,' the retired Assistant Commissioner recalled. 'If he was out of the picture and in prison for twelve months then his international contacts would dry up. That was the reason for her murder. It was pure greed.'

From 1995 onwards there was a marked increase in the number of gangland murders taking place on the streets – none of which were being solved. Gilligan and his murderous mob believed the murder of the journalist would just be another unsolved case. Brian Meehan had already killed Michael Crinnion in Cork and then, on 25 November 1995, there were three murders within 24 hours, in what became known as Bloody Friday. In the early hours of the morning Eddie McCabe, a small-time drug-dealer, stopped his car along a road in Tallaght. A single mum called Catherine Brennan had taken a lift with him to the local 24-hour shop. When McCabe got out of his car a gunman appeared and shot him in the head and chest, killing him instantly. Then the killer turned his attention to the innocent woman in the passenger-seat. He didn't want any witnesses so he shot her in the face. The chief suspect was a close associate of Shavo Hogan and Martin 'the Viper' Foley.

As Gardaí began to investigate the first double gangland murder in the country, another hit man was getting ready to kill. Later that night ticket tout and fraudster Christy Delaney, a former associate of Gilligan's, was shot dead at his home in Finglas. Gardaí believed that the motive for the murder was connected to Delaney's business dealings with Tommy Savage. He had been involved in collecting and laundering drug money for the INLA thug.

On 5 December there was a third dramatic gangland shooting. A hit man tried to murder Martin Foley as he left a girlfriend's flat in Fatima Mansions. But this shooting wasn't the result of a row about drugs. Foley and another drug-dealer from Crumlin, Brian O'Keefe, were both vying for the affections of the same woman. O'Keefe emerged from the shadows and shot Foley twice. The gunman couldn't finish off his love rival because Foley kept twisting and spinning around on the ground. When Gardaí arrived on the scene Foley, who was seriously injured, said that the IRA had shot him. But when he discovered that he was going to survive Foley refused to even tell the police his name. Despite injuries to his spleen, the gangster made a remarkable recovery and was back on his feet in weeks. It was the Viper's second close shave, but it wouldn't be his last.

After he'd recovered, Foley and Shavo Hogan started putting pressure on John Traynor for money they reckoned they were owed from the proceeds of the sale of some of the Beit paintings to the UVF. The Viper was told to fuck off, but Traynor decided to do something about his old associate. In the meantime Foley was accused of spreading rumours that the Gilligan gang were involved in heroin dealing. Criminals are notorious gossips and scandalmongers. In the Dublin underworld Foley is considered to be one of the worst. 'An auld woman with a moustache – and an ugly auld woman at that', was how one villain described him. When Gilligan's gang heard about the rumours they decided to finish the job Brian O'Keefe had started.

Foley and Hogan were buying their drugs from their neighbours, Brian Meehan and Paul Ward. On 1 February 1996, Meehan arranged to meet Foley on the pretext of collecting a payment. But a short distance from Foley's home on Cashel Avenue, Crumlin, Meehan and Ward ambushed him. They were armed with an Agram 2000 machine-gun and a .45 automatic pistol which had been shipped from Holland. They blocked Foley's car in and jumped out, opening fire. The hail of bullets peppered the veteran hoodlum's car, as he reversed up the road while they ran after him. The Viper abandoned his car and made a run for it, with Meehan in pursuit carrying the two weapons while Ward went back to collect the getaway car. Foley tried to take refuge in a house but Meehan ran in after him. Meehan opened fire again, this time hitting Foley in the back as he ran upstairs. Other bullets went through a bathroom door. Foley leaped through a window in a back bedroom, landed on an extension roof outside and jumped into the garden of the house next door. Meehan climbed onto the roof and fired more shots as the Viper raced through several gardens in his desperate bid to escape. Foley burst through the back door of another house and bolted it. He ran through the house, locked the front door and phoned for police and an ambulance as he lay cowering on the floor.

Foley had cheated death for the second time. He was hospitalized for two weeks and again made a remarkable recovery. Foley knew who had shot him and why, but he hadn't the 'bottle' to take revenge. His keen survival instinct told him that there was little point taking on Gilligan's powerful gang. Martin Foley would survive another two gun attacks in which he was shot and left for dead both times. His body is peppered with at least 22 bullet wounds. He also lost the top of a finger. As a result he's earned legendary status in gangland history as the mobster they couldn't kill.

Four weeks later Meehan and Peter Mitchell fired a number of warning shots at one of PJ Judge's dealers who was encroaching on their turf in the inner-city. As a result Judge went looking for Meehan to kill him. But Gardaí prevented an escalation of that feud when they stepped in and arrested everyone involved. The gangsters decided to wait and fight another day.

On 1 April 1996, Johnny Reddin, a drug-dealer and underworld heavy, was having a drink in the Blue Lion pub on Parnell Street, the scene of several gangland shootings. Reddin was a close associate of Paul Ward and sold drugs for the Gilligan gang. At the time he was facing a charge relating to the death of a teenager, Sean McNeil, who was killed in a north city night-club. As Reddin sipped from his pint, a hit man walked up to him and produced a pistol. 'Here, Johnny, take it out of that,' he said, and then shot him once in the head. Reddin's was to be the fifteenth unsolved gangland murder in Dublin in less than four years. Gardaí later confirmed that they received reliable information that the shooter was Dutchie Holland. The hit had been organized as a 'favour' for Sean McNeil's associates, who had sworn to revenge his murder. At the time Paul Ward was said to be 'very angry' with his gangster pals over the murder.

Two days after the Reddin murder, Brian Meehan was arrested by Gardaí in the early hours of the morning. He was brought to the Bridewell Garda Station for a drug search. While the violent mobster was being strip-searched, he began masturbating in front of an officer and asked him: 'Do you like men with big cocks?' He turned around, grabbing his buttocks and exposed his anus: 'Maybe you fancy me arse instead.' – which is how Meehan earned himself the fitting sobriquet, 'the Tosser'.

During the search, the cops found over £600 in cash, and seized it for forensic examination. Meehan sneered at the officers: 'Youse fuckers need it more than I do. Give it to the Police Benevolent Fund. Youse are a bunch of fucking idiots working and paying tax. I earn more in a week than you earn in a month.' He was charged with causing a breach of the peace and indecent behaviour. Meehan couldn't care less.

A few weeks later, on 25 April 1996, Meehan, Mitchell and Ward sprung a notorious armed robber called Thomas 'Bomber' Clarke as he was being driven to court in a prison van. Gilligan had been asked to help the dangerous thug escape by another criminal associate and was happy to oblige. The gang drove a stolen BMW in front of the prison van on the Naas Road, at the junction with Boot Road. The prison warders were threatened at gunpoint, as Clarke jumped out of the van through a window. Gilligan had organized for Clarke to be smuggled out of the country to Holland in a truck. Johnny Wildhagen provided a safe house. To impress his Dutch business-partners, Gilligan offered Clarke's services as a hit man. Bomber Clarke was subsequently caught while watching the home of one of the gang's rivals in Amsterdam. With their power growing every day, the gang believed they were untouchable and had no hesitation proceeding with their plans to murder Veronica Guerin.

The journalist had become the focus of Gilligan's dangerous attention. His trial for the assault was due to be remanded at the next hearing of the District Court in Kilcock. The gang knew that Guerin was due to appear for speeding offences in Naas Court the following day. Gilligan decided his henchmen would attack her on the way back to Dublin. Dutchie Holland agreed to be the hit man and Meehan would drive the bike. Peter Mitchell and one of the gang's most important bagmen, Russell Warren, would watch her movements and report them back to the hit team. Warren and his family ran a cash-counting centre at their home in Tallaght. A shiny new .357 Magnum was oiled and loaded for Dutchie.

On 7 June 1996, a few weeks before the gang intended to carry out their plan, Detective Garda Jerry McCabe and his partner Ben O'Sullivan were providing an armed escort for a post office lorry. It was delivering £81,000 to the post office in Adare, County Limerick. At 6.55 a.m. the truck stopped at the post office and the two Special Branch officers pulled up six feet behind. A four-man IRA gang immediately drove up behind them, at speed, in a stolen jeep and rammed the squad car. A second jeep pulled alongside. Masked gunmen jumped out and stood on either side of the detectives' car, while two more hooded raiders stood in front. The two detectives never had a chance. The leader of the gang, Kevin Walsh from Patrickswell, fired three bursts of lethal armour-piercing rounds into the car with his AK47. Jerry McCabe was killed instantly and Ben O'Sullivan was critically injured. The gang didn't touch the money in the truck and left the scene in one of the jeeps. McCabe was the thirteenth member of the force to be murdered in the line of duty since Dick Fallon was gunned down in 1970.

The news of the shooting of the Gardaí was greeted with widespread shock and revulsion. Within an hour of the attack, investigators were convinced that it was the work of the IRA. The robbery had the hall-marks of Kevin Walsh's Munster unit, which had been responsible for armed robberies in the mid-west and south-west for several years. Sub-sequent ballistic tests on the bullets found at the scene showed that the murder weapon had also been used in the robbery of a post office van in Kilmallock two years earlier.

Whenever the republicans were involved in an embarrassing act of terrorism they tried to deny it. Sinn Féin was due to sit down to con-tinue the peace talks process three days later. That afternoon the Provos issued a statement: 'None of our units were in any way involved in this morning's incident in Adare. There was absolutely no IRA involve-ment.' The Fine Gael Coalition Government believed the Provos at first, although the Garda top brass were telling them otherwise. Garda intelligence sources confirmed that the Provos had carried out the attack. The Garda Commissioner of the day, Pat Culligan, issued an unambiguous statement: 'I and members of An Garda Síochána have no doubt whatsoever that it was carried out by members of the IRA.'

The Provos were eventually forced to admit that their members had been involved in the atrocity but then tried to claim that the shooting was not sanctioned. Sinn Féin leader Gerry Adams, who was also a senior figure on the IRA Army Council, played down the organization's involvement. He tried to wriggle out of the publicity disaster by blaming a breakdown in the command structure. 'In fairness to them what they did was carry out this act having been authorized by someone within the IRA,' Adams claimed. He said the attack had not been authorized by the Army Council but 'authorized at a lower level, by an authorized person'. Martin McGuiness, Sinn Féin's deputy leader and a member of the Army Council, refused to condemn the horrendous act – even though he was involved in the peace-process talks.

The republicans even spun a yarn that the murder weapon had been fired accidentally. The Gardaí who investigated the case do not believe this. Kevin Walsh was an experienced gunman who had fired his weapon in anger many times before. He wasn't the kind of terrorist to make such mistakes. His gang members, Jeremiah Sheehy, Pearse McAuley and Michael O'Neill, were initially charged with murder, attempted murder and firearms offences. In March 1998 Kevin Walsh, who had been in hiding, was finally caught in a house in County Cavan. When the ERU swooped, he was armed with an AK47 rifle and a handgun. At the time there was speculation that Walsh had been 'allowed' to continue to be at large because he was involved in the peace-process negotiations on behalf of the IRA.

The four terrorists subsequently pleaded guilty to the lesser charge of manslaughter in the Special Criminal Court. The State accepted the plea after a number of witnesses admitted that their lives had been threatened if they testified. McAuley and Walsh each got 14 years, Sheehy got 12 and O'Neill was sentenced to 11 years. Sinn Féin, which had initially denied and then denounced the crime, vigorously campaigned to have the men released under the Good Friday Agreement, portraying the cop killers as 'patriots'. The Government held firm and the gunmen served their full sentences.

Fifteen years after the incident in Adare, three members of the IRA are still wanted by the Gardaí in connection with it. They include the man who was OC of the IRA's Southern Command at the time, Richard 'Dickie' O'Neill, who lived in Tallaght. O'Neill was 'stood down' by the IRA Army Council after the Adare fiasco. He has been living in Spain ever since, where he is known to associate with dissident republicans and international drug-traffickers. The second wanted man is Paul Damery from Cork, whose fingerprints were found on the incendiary devices recovered from the Adare gang's getaway jeep. The third suspect, Gerry Roche, was the former INLA bomb-maker, who supplied the explosives to the General for the bomb attack on State forensic scientist Dr James Donovan in 1982.

Roche's career path had been interesting since he helped Martin Cahill. The violent INLA terrorist was involved in the blood feuds that tore the criminal organization apart in the late 1980s. He was close to both Tommy Savage and Michael Weldon and was one of the organization's 'liquidators'. He was supposedly thrown out of the INLA and moved to live in Shannon, County Clare, where he joined the IRA Munster Brigade. In 1990 Roche and two other Provos were arrested by Belgian police in Antwerp while plotting to attack British Army bases in Germany. In the raid police recovered three AK47 rifles, two automatic rifles, a revolver and a pistol. Roche admitted to being the leader of the group and took responsibility for the cache of firearms. On 30 April 1991, he was convicted of conspiracy to attack the British bases, possession of firearms and false documentation. Upon his release from prison, Roche had immediately returned to Ireland and became active again with the Munster Brigade. Roche's involvement was yet more proof of the dangerous nexus between the republicans and the organized crime gangs.

The McCabe murder was good news for John Gilligan. To him it seemed like every cop in the country was working on the case. He decided that meant they would be distracted from fully investigating the Guerin hit – the time was right for murder.

On 25 June 1996, the assault case against Gilligan was adjourned for two weeks at Kilcock District Court, in County Kildare. Veronica had attended the brief hearing with her husband, Graham, and a friend. That evening Gilligan flew to Holland with his teenage mistress, Carol

Rooney. He told his girlfriend: 'After tomorrow all my problems will be over.'

The following afternoon, Veronica Guerin was shot dead as she drove back to Dublin after appearing for the speeding offence at Naas Court. On her return journey to Dublin, Veronica was constantly on her mobile phone and didn't notice the motorbike behind her. When she pulled up at traffic lights, at the same junction of the Naas Road and Boot Road where Gilligan's mob had sprung Bomber Clarke, the bike pulled alongside. Dutchie Holland stepped off and fired five shots into the journalist with the powerful Magnum handgun. The courageous journalist died instantly. The bangs of the murder weapon were for ever recorded in the voice message she was leaving for a contact, as she was shot.

Gilligan personally supervised the murder operation on his mobile phone from a hotel room in Amsterdam. Carol Rooney witnessed everything and later recalled what Gilligan said to Meehan after the job was done: 'Ah well that's that. She wasn't going to get away with it. I wonder what criminals she will be writing about and investigating in heaven.' She told Gardaí how Gilligan received full reports directly from Meehan and Holland. When the diminutive thug phoned Dutchie later that day he said: 'Did you hear the good news? I hear you put a smile on her face.' Rooney also told how Gilligan was terrified of the lone raider: 'He was terrified of Holland because he said he could put a bullet in your head if the price was right.' Gilligan threatened to do the same thing to Rooney and her family if she ever opened her mouth. He also told his terrified girlfriend that Veronica had cancer and 'was going to die anyway', as if that was some sort of warped justification for the atrocity. The journalist had been in perfect health.

If Gilligan thought his problems were over he was sadly mistaken. The hit would prove to be the most monumental miscalculation in the history of organized crime in Ireland.

The journalist's murder caused an unprecedented outpouring of public anger and revulsion. Coming so soon after the Garda McCabe murder, it also sent a shudder of fear through the Establishment. Politicians, judges, prosecutors, civil servants, media, anyone who could interfere with the workings of organized crime were justified in believing they could be the next target.

Tony Hickey remembers the shock his colleagues felt at the murder. 'Despite the fact that there had been an attack on Veronica's house and she had been shot I don't think that anybody would visualize a situation prior to the 26th of June that anyone would have thought of assassinating her.'

Within 24 hours of the atrocity, people began placing flowers at the gates of the Dáil in Kildare Street. Soon there was a virtual wall of flowers, symbolizing the sentiment of a nation reeling from shock at what felt like a criminal coup. Thousands of notes and prayers pinned to the bouquets expressed sorrow, demanded action and asked God to mind the woman who overnight had become a heroine in the eyes of the Irish people. A brave young mum who had stood up to the cowardly Godfathers had been wiped out in the most brutal fashion.

The politicians inside the railings of Leinster House did not need a ton of flowers to realize they had to act decisively. Decades of neglect and inaction had created a monster that now threatened the security of the Republic. Organized crime had issued a spine-chilling threat and society demanded vengeance.

Over the period of a month, the toughest package of anti-crime legislation in the history of the State was enacted by a united parliament. The most significant new law was the one giving power to a revolutionary new multi-agency unit called the Criminal Assets Bureau (CAB). The CAB included Gardaí and officers from Customs, Social Welfare and Revenue. They were given authority to seize the assets and money of the criminal Godfathers. The Bureau could go wherever the money trail brought them. They could search the offices of solicitors and demand bank records. It would prove to be one of the most successful law enforcement agencies in the world. Four years after he'd highlighted the problem on the *Late Late Show*, Barry Galvin was the first man the Government called to help establish the new Bureau and fine-tune the necessary legislation.

Within weeks of Veronica Guerin's murder, Pat Byrne was appointed as Commissioner of the Gardaí. Byrne, a talented officer who had trained with the FBI and Scotland Yard, had spent most of his career in anti-terrorist operations and national security. A few months earlier he'd impressed the Cabinet when he gave them a detailed briefing on the state of drug-trafficking and organized crime in the country. Byrne was a modern, forward-looking cop who believed in using a more sophisticated approach to taking on the crime gangs. He promoted Tony Hickey to the rank of Assistant Commissioner and put him in charge of the Guerin murder investigation. The force's most experienced financial and fraud investigator, Chief Superintendent Fachtna Murphy, was appointed as the head of the CAB. Felix McKenna, the man who'd helped secure Gilligan's residence in Portlaoise Prison in 1990, became his second-in-command and Barry Galvin became the Bureau's legal officer. The criminal underworld was about to be turned upside down.

The investigation into the murder of Veronica Guerin involved the biggest search and arrest operation ever mounted by the Gardaí. It was based in Lucan Garda Station and the squad of detectives became known as the Lucan Investigation Team. Their approach was robust and aggressive. In the months following the murder every criminal and terrorist got a visit from the team, irrespective of where he stood in the gangland hierarchy. Over 330 individuals were arrested, 1,500 were interviewed without arrest and 3,500 statements were taken. A large quantity of drugs, guns and cash were also seized. The investigation unearthed a huge amount of information and evidence. For the first time the Gardaí got a full picture of the true extent of organized crime. It was an example of what could be achieved when law enforcement resources were fully focused. Information gleaned also helped detectives to solve scores of hitherto unsolved crimes.

In the eyes of a dying breed of so-called ordinary decent criminals, the murder was an egregious breach of unspoken protocols. During the investigation, the Gardaí received an unprecedented level of co-operation. The criminals wanted to see Gilligan and his ruthless thugs get their comeuppance just as much as the law-abiding community. But they were not solely motivated by a sense of outrage – the consequences of the crime were very bad for business. With so much intense police activity, whole drug-distribution networks were closed down overnight. Greedy gangsters, who were waiting for the dust to settle so they could go back to 'work', were getting nervous as there appeared to be no sign of the Gardaí winding down. To make matters even worse, the criminals were reading about the powerful new agency that could take their money and property from them. And it was all Gilligan's fault. One gangster, who was particularly agitated by the arrival of the Untouchables, as the CAB officers became known, declared at the time: 'Gilligan or one of those fuckers will have to be whacked for this. They've fucked everything up.'

The sense of panic in the underworld was so intense that several crime bosses emptied their bank accounts and left the country to get out of the way before the CAB hit. One of the fleeing gangsters was the Penguin. George Mitchell even suggested Gilligan's mob should murder a Garda to divert the heat. He advised his old pal that a third high-profile murder investigation – alongside the Guerin and McCabe cases – would stretch the cops beyond their limits. But the Garda offensive was so strong that Gilligan didn't have a chance to carry out the evil strategy. Nevertheless, Hickey and his team were ordered to be extra vigilant and officers, armed with Uzi submachine-guns, were deployed at night to guard the investigation incident room. The actual station house was also refurbished to accommodate bomb- and fire-proof safes, to store evidence in the case. Hickey summarized what his officers were up against during one of scores of court appearances connected with the case: 'We know from intelligence that the people concerned [the Gilligan gang] have the resources, the money and the firearms and will resort to anything, to maintain this wall of silence which they believe is necessary to protect themselves.'

One notorious criminal who decided to relocate after the murder was Gilligan's old pal, kidnapper John Cunningham. In September 1996, Cunningham had two years left to serve of his sentence for the Jennifer Guinness kidnapping and had been moved to Shelton Abbey Open Prison in County Wicklow. He'd been granted temporary release to attend the wedding of his adopted daughter Caroline. But two weeks before the bash, an off-duty prison governor spotted Cunningham and another former member of the General's gang, Eamon Daly, out drinking in a pub with the prison officer who was supposed to be guarding them. As a result Cunningham lost his privileges, including temporary release, and was due to be sent back to Limerick Prison. The Colonel decided to do a runner instead. Gilligan organized a safe house for him and then helped to smuggle Cunningham out of the country, using the same route that had worked so well for Bomber Clarke.

Cunningham was warmly welcomed by his former gangland pals in Holland. A big party was thrown in his honour at one of the city's plush restaurants. Many of his old friends, including Gilligan, had become extremely wealthy men while Cunningham was inside. Gangland had undergone dramatic changes during those ten years. The Colonel was regaled with stories about how easy it was to make money in the drug business. He was given money, a nice place to live and told that if he wanted to get involved in the rackets there was plenty of 'work' available.

At first Cunningham dealt with Gilligan's Dutch contacts and helped to organize drug shipments for the gang. But following Gilligan's subsequent arrest he formed a partnership with another expat, a Dublin hoodlum called Christy Kinahan. Together they would build a vast criminal empire.

Meanwhile the Lucan Investigation Team was making significant progress. In October they made the breakthrough which brought down the Gilligan gang. Following a series of arrests three members of the organization agreed to become witnesses for the State.

Detective Inspector Todd O'Loughlin was a central player in the historic criminal investigation. 'One of the first things we noticed was the extent of the operation and the size of the pyramid that Gilligan had created. In a two-year period we conservatively estimated that his organization had smuggled in cannabis worth over £200 million on the streets. We had never seen a gang making such profits before and it opened our eyes to the true extent of organized crime,' he recalled. 'It took 400 arrests before we finally got a full picture of the size of this pyramid. The people who served time with him in Portlaoise wouldn't talk and they remained loyal right to the end. But because of the size of the operation he also recruited people who were not hardcore criminals like Charlie Bowden, Russell Warren and John Dunne. When they were taken into custody they had remorse, which none of the other guys had, and through this then we were able to obtain details of the entire organization, and this was how we dismantled it from within.'

Charlie Bowden, Russell Warren and the Sea Bridge shipping manager John Dunne became the first official supergrasses in Irish organized crime. In the fast-moving situation Tony Hickey and Pat Byrne found themselves in completely uncharted waters. They established an ad hoc witness protection programme and the DPP had to agree to grant the three criminals immunity from prosecution. At the same time Gilligan was arrested in London's Heathrow Airport with over £300,000 in cash which he had collected from Michael Cunningham, the Colonel's brother. Brian Meehan was convicted of murder and Gilligan got 20 years for drug-trafficking. Paul Ward, who was originally convicted of the murder, was subsequently acquitted on appeal, and Dutchie Holland was also jailed for drug-dealing.

Gilligan's use of intimidation and fear helped him to escape the murder rap. His former mistress Carol Rooney and the Dutch criminal Martin Baltus were both too scared to testify against him. Several other associates were also convicted and jailed for drug and gun offences. The CAB seized property and cash belonging to all the gang members, including houses and apartments owned by Meehan, Ward, Mitchell, Holland and Traynor. By 2011 John Gilligan was still fighting a seemingly endless legal battle with the Bureau, to stop them selling off Jessbrook.

The Criminal Assets Bureau caused turmoil in the underworld. Murphy, McKenna and Galvin sat down with the Gardaí in the Bureau and began compiling a long list of their principal targets. Apart from Gilligan, the list included the Monk, the Munster Mafia and several of the foreign villains Barry Galvin had talked about on the *Late Late Show*. They pursued drug-dealers, smugglers, terrorists, pimps and money-launderers. They seized houses, cars and cash. Hundreds of hidden bank accounts, in Ireland and across Europe, were traced and frozen. The CAB's very first seizure of money was from Derek 'Maradona' Dunne, who flew home from Amsterdam in October 1996 to withdraw £57,000 from his bank account.

The Bureau also forced one of the world's biggest drug-traffickers, Mickey Green, to flee his Irish bolt-hole from justice. Dubbed 'the Pimpernel', the former London bank robber, who was wanted by police all over the world, had quietly arrived in Ireland in the early 1990s after escaping the FBI in the US. The CAB seized and then sold his luxury mansion near Kilcock, County Kildare.

Tax demands began falling onto doormats in the homes of gangsters all over the country. The investigation centred on Gerry Hutch, his gang and his mentor Matt Kelly was extended to take in at least a dozen other associates. Between them they were forced to pay over €10 million in taxes and penalties based on their criminal activities. In a ten-year period, the CAB recovered over €100 million from organized crime.

The Bureau's investigations were ground-breaking. In their probes into George Mitchell's finances they discovered a link between the gang's bagman, convicted fraudster Peter Bolger and former Government minister Michael Keating. As a result the high-flying politician was publicly disgraced and forced to pay a large tax bill. The most spectacular success was the conviction and imprisonment of Raphael 'Ray' Burke, who was Minister for Justice when John Gilligan was doing time in Portlaoise Prison. Burke was part of a corrupt clique of Fianna Fáil politicians, led by the former Taoiseach Charles Haughey. Ironically Haughey was the man credited with assisting in setting up the smuggling ring that first provided weapons for organized crime gangs back in 1968. The story had come full circle.

George Mitchell, Gilligan and other criminals pooled their money and mounted a number of major High Court challenges to have the 'draconian' powers of the CAB revoked. In March 1997, John Gilligan made his first attempt to have the Bureau abolished when his Irish legal team mounted a challenge to the constitutionality of the Proceeds of Crime Act which had set up the Criminal Assets Bureau. It was the first major test of the new legislation and the Bureau's survival depended on the outcome.

During the four-day hearing David Langwallner SC, Gilligan's counsel, claimed that the powers allowing Gardaí to confiscate and dispose of an individual's assets meant: 'We are on the slippery slope towards the creation of a police state.' He stated that the Proceeds of Crime Act 'masqueraded as a civil statute when it was a criminal law which circumvented the criminal process'. He described as 'Kafkaesque' the fact that the word of a Chief Superintendent or Revenue Official could have an individual's assets frozen, put in receivership and disposed of, on the basis of assumed criminality, without charge, trial or conviction. He likened the Proceeds of Crime Act to emergency legislation, where the courts were deemed to be inadequate to protect the public and preserve public order. But Ireland, he claimed, was not in a state of emergency and had one of the lowest crime rates in the world.

Detective Superintendent Felix McKenna (who would later become the CAB's second chief) told the court that one of the effects of the

Proceeds of Crime Act over the previous eight months had been to
'force criminals above ground'. Before the Act, a lot of money had also
been taken out of bank accounts and moved abroad. 'Over the last six
to seven months, one major criminal gang has put millions of pounds
into apartment blocks and licensed premises, principally in Dublin,'
McKenna revealed.

Deputy Commissioner Noel Conroy testified that people would
become frustrated and disillusioned with the criminal justice system and
be less likely to come forward as witnesses or informants, if major criminals were not stopped. Conroy said that the Bureau was a success and
revealed 'major criminals are being forced to work on the shop floor' of
their activities since the Proceeds of Crime Act came into force. He
emphasized that this meant they were running the gauntlet of being
charged with criminal offences.

Underlining the changed times, Conroy was the first senior member
of Garda management to publicly give a frank assessment of how organized crime had evolved in Ireland. In the past, the top brass had no place
for such candour. He told how criminals had switched from armed robbery and used that money to get involved in supplying drugs on a grand
scale, using runners or couriers, so they could remove themselves completely from the operation. 'The Godfathers could command respect
and fear within the criminal community,' he said, 'so that the runners
would not inform on them and they had become wealthy.' Conroy said
the Proceeds of Crime Act had resulted in major criminal figures
attempting to leave the jurisdiction with their cash and trying to dispose
of properties.

Ms Justice Catherine McGuinness delivered her seminal judgment on
the first anniversary of Veronica Guerin's murder. The judge ruled that
the Proceeds of Crime Act was constitutional. She said the question was
whether the Act, within the framework of the Constitution, was a pro-
portionate response to the threat posed to society by the operations of
the major criminals, described in evidence by Felix McKenna and Noel
Conroy. She said it appeared that, as a matter of proportionality, the
legislature was justified in enacting the Act and restricting certain rights
through the operation of it.

She said the two Garda officers 'painted a picture of an entirely new
type of professional criminal who organised, rather than committed,

crime and thereby rendered himself virtually immune to the ordinary procedures of criminal investigation and prosecution'. The judge stated: 'Such persons are able to operate a reign of terror so as effectively to prevent the passing on of information to the Gardaí. At the same time, their obvious wealth and power cause them to be respected by lesser criminals or would-be criminals.'

The judgment represented a decisive victory against the underworld. It showed the Godfathers that there was a new, unified determination to take them on.

The Penguin had already decided to take his own form of action and put out a contract on Barry Galvin. He was aware that Galvin was one of the driving forces behind the Bureau. The fact that he was not a cop made Mitchell consider that he would be vulnerable. And he wasn't the only criminal with the idea. English drug-trafficker John Morrissey, a business acquaintance of Mitchell, had moved to live in Kinsale, County Cork in 1995. He was a major international crime figure who had been linked to a string of gangland murders in Europe and the UK. Morrissey spent €600,000 opening an upmarket restaurant in the town, where he was known as 'Johnny Cash' – because he always paid in cash. Among his new friends was the local antiques dealer and drug-trafficker Alan Buckley.

Barry Galvin ensured that Morrissey didn't get a warm welcome and the CAB hit him with an initial tax bill of over €100,000. In December 1997, the gang boss was forced to leave his beloved adopted home when the Bureau seized whatever assets and cash of his they could locate. Garda intelligence sources and their UK colleagues received information that Morrissey was plotting revenge. He planned to fly a hit team into Cork to murder Galvin. Mitchell's men had agreed to supply the weapons. But the plan was foiled when a massive security operation was put in place and armed bodyguards were assigned to the crusading legal officer. Gardaí and their UK counterparts ensured that the plan never got off the ground. Commissioner Byrne took the unprecedented step of issuing Galvin with a Garda revolver for extra protection.

The murder of Veronica Guerin and the demise of the Gilligan gang was a watershed in the history of organized crime. And for a short time at least, the underworld appeared to be on the back foot.

19. The Penguin

George 'the Penguin' Mitchell was released from prison in October 1991 and immediately set about establishing his own drug-dealing empire. Mitchell hated his time in prison and, according to former associates, 'went to bits' inside. The experience taught him to be much more cautious in how he conducted business in the future. In criminal terms, the former biscuit delivery man was a complete workaholic, with a finger in every pie. Within a few years he had become one of the biggest drug-traffickers in Europe, with contacts in the Russian Mafia and the Colombian drug cartels. Mitchell was an extremely devious and clever mobster. He was also as dangerous as he was smart and had no problem resorting to violence and murder to sort out his problems.

The Penguin surrounded himself with the most potent collection of villains yet seen since the heyday of Martin Cahill's gang. The group of hardened mobsters were involved in every type of serious crime, including drugs, armed robbery, extortion, hijacking, handling stolen goods and gun-running. In addition to his brother Paddy, George's inner-circle included his long-time friend from Ballyfermot, Johnny Doran. The armed robber had been released from prison in 1989 after serving eight years for his part in the Stillorgan heist. In December 1990, the leader of the same team, Frank Ward, was also released from prison. Doran, who became Mitchell's right-hand man in the new drug venture, brought Ward into the mob. Meanwhile, Ward made ends meet by carrying out a string of armed robberies around Ireland. Other members of the gang included INLA man Danny Hamill, Gerry Hopkins and Stephen Kearney from Ballyfermot. Thirty-year-old John McGrail from St Theresa's Gardens, a convicted armed robber, was one of the gang's main organizers. The mob was also joined by Mickey Boyle, the Bray kidnapper, when he got out of prison in 1993. The dangerous head-case became the Penguin's hit man.

Mitchell began to regularly commute between Dublin, London and Amsterdam to do deals with other gangs. He also dealt in firearms, which were smuggled into Ireland and the UK by the most important member of the Penguin's organization, Liam Judge from Allenwood, County Kildare. Judge was a long-distance truck driver who had an excellent knowledge of the transport business and routes across continental Europe. One former friend recalled how the trucker had no idea about drugs when he first got involved with Mitchell. 'He was a gent really; a real character and a serial womanizer. Judgey knew fuck all about gear [drugs] in the beginning. I remember once that there was a bag of speed [amphetamine] sitting on the table and he put a spoon of it in his tea thinking it was sugar. He was out of his head for days.'

Judge organized the transport of drugs in container trucks from the Continent to warehouses he rented around Dublin and the Midlands. In one elaborate scam, Judge and Mitchell imported huge quantities of ecstasy inside second-hand car tyres which were delivered to Judge's yard in Allenwood. Despite his suspicious nature, Mitchell trusted his transport manager and placed him at the heart of the organization.

But there was a side to Judge the Penguin knew nothing about – the trucker was also a police informant. He had been recruited following an arrest for drunk-driving in 1993 and would prove to be one of the most important touts in gangland. Judge lived a precarious existence as a double-agent but seemed to like the buzz. At one stage he operated a lay-by chuck-wagon for truckers on the Johnstown Road in County Kildare. It was a popular meeting place for drivers seeking illegal work and for drug-traffickers who needed transport. No one knew that the wagon had been equipped with bugging equipment by Judge's Garda handlers. Intelligence gleaned from the talkative truckers and traffickers led to several arrests and no one ever suspected where the information came from.

It wasn't long before Gardaí began taking notice of the Penguin's activities. In October 1993, Mitchell and Stephen Kearney travelled to the Costa del Sol to organize a cannabis deal with an English gang. The plan was to swap a truck-load of French wine for the hash which would then be driven by Kearney to the UK. Mitchell flew back to Dublin alone. When Kearney returned on the ferry from the UK a month later, Gardaí seized £60,000 in cash which they found hidden in the spare wheel of his car. Cops also seized £80,000 when they searched a car driven by another gang associate who had also returned from the UK. The cops suspected the money was part-payment for drugs. An unsuccessful claim was later made in the Dublin High Court for the return of the money. It was under a Police Property Application by a convicted London fraudster called Kenneth Chester Whitehead. On appeal, the Supreme Court upheld the High Court decision that it did not believe Whitehead was the true owner of the cash. In the days before the Criminal Assets Bureau, the courts would have been left with no option but to return the money if a more credible claimant had come forward.

In early 1994, the Gardaí came as close as they would ever get to the heart of George Mitchell's organization when he rented a yard and large lock-up building in Mount Brown in Kilmainham, West Dublin. The premises were perfect for what he had in mind. The lock-up was situated on a small lane, surrounded by a high wall and steel gate. Drug shipments, arms deals, armed robberies and hijackings were organized by the Penguin's mob from the yard. The lock-up was used to store stolen goods and vehicles. Cash and valuables taken in various heists were also handed over to Mitchell there, who invested the loot in cannabis, ecstasy and firearms. The mob soon had access to an awesome arsenal of firepower. One Serious Crime Squad officer recalled: 'It was a very efficient operation and the yard in Mount Brown was run like a central depot for a large legitimate business. There were about fifteen in the gang and they were up to everything.'

The existence of the Penguin's crime depot first came to police attention during a routine investigation by the Drug Squad when they tailed a suspected drug-dealer there. It was decided to keep a discreet eye on the yard to see what was going on.

The discovery of the yard coincided with the appointment of Detective Chief Superintendent Kevin Carty as the new head of the Central Detective Unit. Carty, who had spent most of his earlier career as a Special Branch officer, was one of the force's most talented officers, with an impressive reputation as a resourceful investigator. On one occasion he was awarded a Scott Medal for bravery when he disarmed and arrested a wanted IRA man. Carty was unarmed and off-duty at the time. He was an astute strategist who believed in taking a proactive, enlightened approach to criminal investigations. The new CDU boss disagreed with a policing policy which was driven by budgets and a reluctance to mount long-term, costly operations. Carty believed that to catch a criminal you had to invest time and resources to get the job done. He pursued a policy of recruiting informants in the underworld and using the latest sophisticated surveillance techniques.

Within days of his arrival in the summer of 1994, Carty and his new second-in-command, Det. Supt Austin McNally, convened a conference for detectives to assess the preliminary surveillance on the yard. It was obvious that it was a meeting place for George Mitchell, Johnny Doran, Frank Ward, John McGrail, Mickey Boyle, Danny Hamill and several other major-league villains, who had been spotted regularly visiting the yard. Members of the Drug Squad, Serious Crime Squad, National Surveillance Unit (NSU) and the Emergency Response Unit (ERU) were mobilized to take on the Penguin's mob. Carty decided there was only one way to find out what the villains were up to – covert surveillance, using microphones and cameras. Late one night a team of surveillance experts, led by Detective Sergeant Pat Walsh, secretly gained access to the yard. Walsh was the resourceful and unconventional undercover investigator who'd recruited Liam Judge as an informant. Known as 'Feshty' to his colleagues, he was a legendary character among the ranks of Ireland's thief-takers. Over a period of almost twenty years his work as a 'spook' led to the seizure of hundreds of millions of pounds worth of drugs and the conviction of dozens of underworld players.

The surveillance soon began to produce remarkable results. One SCS member recalled: 'It was amazing. Not a day would go by without some crime being planned there. It was like shooting fish in a barrel. They were talking about all kinds of criminal activity. It was clear that they considered the yard a completely safe haven.'

As the operation continued into September, the SCS was gleaning an awesome amount of top-grade intelligence. The main problem for the investigation squad was how to deal with each crime without making it obvious that the yard had been compromised. If the gang abandoned it then the investigation would be over.

A month after the murder of Martin Cahill, the Gardaí had their first major break-through when Mitchell imported a cache of deadly machine-guns and automatic pistols for the IRA. The weapons – 9mm Heckler and Koch, MP5 machine-guns and Glock pistols – were smuggled into the country with a load of drugs in the back of a container truck organized by Liam Judge. It was the Penguin's way of keeping the terrorists off his back. Carty's team recovered two MP5s and five Glock pistols in a search of bogland near Clane, County Kildare. They also found a large amount of ammunition and drugs. In another search, two Armalite military assault rifles were found. It confirmed one chilling piece of information overheard through the hidden microphones – the gang members were prepared to shoot their way out of trouble if they were confronted by the police.

The Penguin's newest recruit, Frank Ward, had been using the yard to store guns and stolen getaway cars. He was already back on the list of the Serious Crime Squad's most wanted criminals. In December 1992 officers had raided an apartment used by Ward in upmarket Dublin 4. During the search they found a number of disguises, including wigs and false beards. They also discovered detailed notes of surveillance carried out on a bank official in County Meath, as well as on the movements and transport used by the distinguished Senior Counsel Adrian Hardiman (now a Supreme Court judge). Gardaí suspected that Ward and his associates were planning to abduct the two men. There was insufficient evidence with which to charge Ward, but the police arrested the robber and let him know that they were on to his scam. The plot was immediately aborted.

Ward recruited his 26-year-old nephew, David Lynch, into the gang. Lynch was also from Sligo and was every bit as violent as his uncle. Lynch, who had served time with Ward in Portlaoise Prison, was released from jail in 1994 after a five-year stretch for armed robbery. He wasted no time getting back to business. On 8 April 1994, Ward and Lynch robbed the Bank of Ireland in Nenagh, County Tipperary. They later crashed their getaway car, hijacked a Telecom Eireann van at gunpoint and escaped. Over the following months Ward and his nephew did at least four similar jobs together. But their days were numbered.

The officers listening in on the yard heard that Ward and Lynch were planning another robbery. During the covert operation, Carty's men had also planted tracking devices on a number of the stolen cars. On 23 October, a major operation was mobilized when the electronic tracking system alerted the cops that one of the cars was on the move. Officers followed as Ward parked the car, fitted with false plates, in the car park of the Children's Hospital in Crumlin. Members of the NSU stayed in the area and waited for his next move. The officers in charge of the operation were aware that this was a potentially dangerous situation.

They were aware of Ward's extremely volatile personality and knew he would have no compunction shooting Gardaí if they intercepted him. Carty's team also didn't know what bank or town he intended to hit. They were anxious to avoid a confrontation similar to the one with the Athy Gang four years earlier.

The following morning a large team of detectives shadowed Ward as he left the hospital car park. He took a meandering journey, through country back roads, heading west. The surveillance and back-up teams stayed out of sight because Ward was always on the look-out for the police. An Air Corps' Cessna spotter aircraft, equipped with tracking equipment, was scrambled to monitor his progress. Eventually Ward made his way to Longford Town, where he met Lynch off the Dublin train. Lynch was carrying a .357 Magnum and a sawn-off shotgun in a hold-all bag. They put on bullet-proof vests, drove down the town and parked outside the Ulster Bank on Main Street. Seconds later they burst through the front door, threatening to shoot customers and staff. In less than a minute they took £10,000 in cash. They ran to the getaway car and sped out of town, towards Mullingar.

The local Garda station was alerted to the raid and officers arrived at the bank within a minute. The surveillance and SCS teams heard the call on their radios and headed in the direction of the tracker signal. Ward took to the back roads but was being tracked all the way by the spotter-plane. The pilot relayed the raiders' progress to the SCS and the other units closing in on the ground, while an ERU team set up an ambush. When Ward spotted the road block he tried to reverse away but crashed. At the same moment an ERU officer threw a stun-grenade under the getaway car to prevent the robbers opening fire. The two men were arrested following a violent struggle. Officers later discovered that the raiders were wearing bandages on their fingers and palms to avoid leaving prints behind them. They also wore wigs, false moustaches and make-up to obscure any chance of identifying them on the security video. Ward and Lynch were charged with the robbery, possession of firearms and an earlier heist.

Despite Garda objections, Ward was subsequently released on bail. But the SCS learned that Mitchell had agreed to help him flee the country. The notorious robber had obtained a legitimate passport, under a different name. They re-arrested Ward and his bail was revoked. In 1996 he pleaded guilty to two counts of armed robbery and was jailed for 11 years. Lynch was also convicted and sent to prison for eight years.

A month later, on 28 November 1994, Mitchell's trusted sidekick, Johnny Doran, and 24-year-old David Lindsay from Baldoyle, North Dublin collected 50 kilos of hash from Liam Judge in Kildare. Lindsay was one of the new breed of young gangsters and he had greatly impressed the Godfather. As the two villains drove back to the yard, along the M50 motorway, they were intercepted by the SCS who tried to pull them over. Doran drove off at speed and the police gave chase. In his bid to get away Doran rammed one of the squad cars but lost control. A second squad car collided with the rear of his car and sent it spinning into a fence. Doran and Lindsay were arrested by the same team who'd nabbed Ward the previous month and charged with drug-trafficking offences. But the Penguin was anxious that his protégé didn't take the rap and convinced Doran to put his hands up and accept responsibility. Doran was subsequently jailed for 12 years.

On two occasions other members of the gang came tantalizingly close to being caught red-handed. In one nail-biting episode, John McGrail, Danny Hamill and other gangsters were shadowed on their way to ambush a security van in Blackrock. A flat-bed truck had been stolen and brought back to the lock-up, where the gangsters had welded a large, sharp, metal girder to it, to smash open the doors of the security van. The Gardaí had watched the crew carry out surveillance on the movements of the security van over a number of weeks. On the morning of the job the gang set off with the truck and a number of getaway cars, one of them carrying weapons. As the gang drove towards Blackrock, a large force of detectives shadowed their every move. But the stolen truck was recognized by a friend of its owner. The man had phoned the Gardaí and started tailing the truck in his van. The conscientious citizen then blocked in the truck, while waiting for uniformed Gardaí to arrive. McGrail and his hoods immediately jumped out and ran away, to the absolute horror of the watching cops. There was nothing they could do and the sting operation was aborted.

The police made a number of other significant arrests but their main target, the Penguin, proved to be an elusive adversary. Mitchell decided to vacate the lock-up shortly afterwards, as he knew there was a chance that the recovery of the truck could lead police back to the yard. The gangsters had no idea how close they had come to a long stay in Portlaoise Prison.

By the mid-1990s Mitchell was one of the biggest suppliers of ecstasy to the Irish market. He bought the drugs in Holland, where they were made in huge, underground factories. When Mitchell visited one of these plants he decided that it would be much more profitable if he cut out the middleman and set up an Irish manufacturing operation. As Mitchell's pals were being arrested for drug-offences and armed robbery he began putting his plan together with the Munster Mafia. Mitchell and Alan Buckley used another former Catholic priest, who was also a senior member of the IRA and a major crime figure, to buy a tablet-making machine for them in Liverpool for £1,000. The machine was then shipped into Ireland and stored in County Kildare. It had the capacity to make 62 tablets a minute. That minute's production was worth £620 based on the average street price at that time. In full production the little factory had the capacity to churn out over £37,000 worth of the drug an hour – £300,000 per day or £2 million each week. It was a licence to print money.

Buckley approached Dubliner Terence Fitzsimmons to organize the day-to-day running of the operation. The Cork antiques dealer supplied him with money to rent various premises and buy chemicals. He also introduced Fitzsimmons to English chemist Brian Cooper, who would mix the chemicals for the tablets. In turn Fitzsimmons recruited 36-year-old Raymond Jones from Blanchardstown, whose job as a spray-painter and panel-beater meant that he was familiar with chemicals and the companies that supplied them. Using a false name, Jones then rented a warehouse in an industrial estate in Mulhuddart, West Dublin for £240 per month. Buckley gave Jones a list of the chemicals needed. To avoid arousing suspicion Jones convinced legitimate companies that he was involved in the manufacture of a steroid for Spanish bulls. He claimed the steroid reduced the amount of pain the bull felt and enabled it to fight longer.

When the chemicals were delivered they were moved to Wentworth House in Lucan, where Cooper made MDMA, the base chemical compound used in ecstasy. Buckley and Mitchell picked the remote location because of the chemical mix's noxious odours. If the highly volatile chemicals were not mixed correctly they were also liable to explode. The MDMA was then to be transported to a rented farm shed at Spricklestown, near Ashbourne. Buckley promised Laurence Skelly, the owner of the farmhouse, a bonus of £5,000 when the first 9,000 tablets were made.

Mitchell and Buckley had no idea that they were under the eye of the newly formed Garda National Drug Unit (GNDU) and its chief, Kevin Carty. At the time Garda management had begun the process of finally modernizing the various detective units in the force. The old CDU had been reorganized as the National Bureau of Criminal Investigation (NBCI), which included the Serious Crime Squad, and the Fraud Squad became the Garda Bureau of Fraud Investigation. The NBCI was placed under the command of Tony Hickey, who was then a cheif superintendent. The new units were much larger. New drug squads were also being mobilized and trained in every Garda division and district in the country.

Carty and Det. Supt McNally had learned of the Penguin's plot to establish the first E factory in the country from Liam Judge and the surveillance operation at Mitchell's yard. In March 1995 an investigation, codenamed 'Operation Barbie', was launched. Over the following months the GNDU and SCS monitored the preparations from a discreet distance. The main objective of Operation Barbie was to catch Mitchell and Buckley on the production line. They observed the two crooks visiting the farm on a number of occasions to review the preparations. The Penguin was anxious to get things up and running but full production would take another three months. In the meantime he had some pressing problems to deal with.

George Mitchell's main business associate in the UK underworld was one Peter Daley, the leader of a powerful South London gang. Daley's organization was locked in a bloody feud with the Brindles, another notorious South London crime family. It was one of the worst gang wars seen in London since the days of the Richardsons and the Krays in the 1960s. The war broke out in August 1990 when armed associates of the Brindles walked into the Queen Elizabeth pub in Walworth, which was owned by John Daley. They demanded protection money and threatened Daley by placing a gun in his mouth. The following month Daley's gang struck back. Ahmet 'Turkish Abbi' Abdullah was a member of a third feared South London crime family, the Arifs. The Arifs were major drug-traffickers, associates of Peter Daley and sworn enemies of the Brindles. Thirty-year-old Turkish Abbi, a convicted killer, walked into a drinking club and shot Brindle henchman Stephen Dalligan seven times. Dalligan survived the attack.

The war escalated in March 1991 when Turkish Abbi was shot dead by two gunmen in a South London betting-shop. Twenty-seven-year-old market trader Tony Brindle and his brother Patrick were charged with the murder. While they were out on bail their younger brother David visited Daley's pub and began throwing his weight around. He was severely beaten by James Moody, one of Daley's enforcers. The 52-year-old mobster was a former member of the Kray gang. The Brindles threatened to have Daley and Moody murdered.

A few weeks later, in August, David Brindle was shot dead in The Bell pub in Walworth when two hit men burst in and sprayed the place with machine-gun fire. One of the killers shouted: 'This one is for Abbi.' Another innocent drinker, a grandfather, was also killed in the attack and five others were injured.

In May 1992 the trial of the Brindle brothers made British legal history. Jurors and witnesses were screened from the public gallery and the dock. The jurors were also given armed police protection for the duration of the trial. One witness who managed to make it to the stand told the judge that he could not give his evidence because he feared for his life. The Brindles were acquitted.

Over a year later, in June 1993, a man walked into the Royal Hotel pub in Hackney where James Moody was holding court, and ordered himself a pint. He took a long gulp, produced a handgun and shot James Moody four times in the head. Then in August 1994 another contract killer murdered two innocent men in a devastating blunder. The victims had been mistaken for Peter Daley and one of his henchmen. As the murder rate escalated the Daley gang decided they had to take more drastic action – and turned to George Mitchell for help.

Initially Daley's mob asked Mitchell to provide a hit team to help them wipe out three members of the Brindle gang. In spring 1995 the Penguin called a meeting with Mickey Boyle and a number of other gang members, to discuss the request. The targets were to be George and Patrick Brindle and at least one of their closest associates. Surveillance had already been carried out by Daley's hoods and it was reckoned that Tony Brindle was too secure for a hit. Mickey Boyle volunteered to organize the murder operation and later travelled to London, to assess the 'job'.

In the meantime Mitchell had also come to the assistance of his Cork partners-in-crime – the Munster Mafia. The Cork mob were afraid that Golly O'Connell was considering turning State witness against them in the Courtmacsherry drug case and asked Mitchell to send him a message. On Saturday 22 April, O'Connell parked his car in a restaurant on the Naas Road in Dublin. He was approached by three masked men and shot in the back of the leg.

That June, Boyle proved his credentials as a hit man when Mitchell sent him to murder Fran Preston, who had no links to crime. Preston had fallen foul of the Penguin's protégé David Lindsay, after he had an affair with a girlfriend of Lindsay. Preston was gunned down at his home in Baldoyle, North Dublin by Boyle. It was the second time that the Penguin had gone to such extremes to protect Lindsay. Mitchell and Lindsay were among the suspects later questioned about the murder, but no one was ever charged.

At the same time Mitchell found himself on a potential collision course with the Monk and his mob. Soccer star Derek 'Maradona' Dunne lived with Mitchell's only daughter, Rachel, with whom he had a daughter. The 28-year-old footballer's exploits with St Patrick's Athletic made him a hero to thousands of kids. But Dunne was also one of the biggest heroin-dealers in the north inner-city. He was a member of a group of young criminals from the area who'd made a conscious decision to become drug-dealers. Maradona had no problem selling his drugs to the same kids who admired him. One of Dunne's business partners was another local sporting hero, Thomas 'the Boxer' Mullen. The drug-dealers, who were not addicts themselves, had witnessed at first-hand the devastation the heroin scourge had caused throughout their neighbourhoods – but that didn't upset the likes of Dunne or Mullen. In May, Dunne had beaten up Gerry Hutch's nephew following a row. Immediately after the fight, Dunne and Rachel Mitchell were forced to move out of their home as the result of an arson attack.

Mitchell made it clear to the Hutches that he would not tolerate his daughter and grandchild being caught up in the crossfire. He also let it be known that he was prepared to protect Dunne. Dublin's underworld teetered on the brink of war for a number of weeks. There was speculation that Mitchell had brought in hit men from the UK to deal with any problems. He also had a large group of loyal hoods around him who weren't afraid of the Monk. By the summer of 1995 there had been a steady increase in the number of gangland shootings and murders. There was no scarcity of new weapons available – or the men to use them. Eventually the standoff subsided when it was agreed that Dunne would not return to the north inner-city. After that Mitchell and Hutch, who had both invested money in Paddy Shanahan's construction business, made up their differences and the Penguin could focus his attention on his ecstasy factory again.

Operation Barbie had moved into a critical stage when the Maradona row erupted. By the end of June the secret factory was ready to go into production. Gardaí believed that Buckley and Mitchell were so anxious to see it up and running they would turn up to see the first batch being made. But the team were forced to make their move on the night of 30 June 1995, when Brian Cooper suddenly decided to leave the country. The chemist was angry that he had not been paid £7,000 which Fitzsimmons owed him for work already done. He decided to make up the shortfall by taking enough MDMA mix to manufacture £157,000 worth of tablets when he got back to the UK. Cooper was busted as he boarded a ferry. The following morning Jones and Skelly were arrested as they made the first batch of 9,000 tablets, worth £90,000. Fitzsimmons was later arrested at his home in Castleblayney, County Monaghan. Detectives searched the other premises used by the gang and recovered enough MDMA to make £2 million worth of the drug. Cooper's sudden decision to leave had effectively saved the Penguin. It was another close shave.

Alan Buckley was subsequently arrested and questioned but there was insufficient evidence with which to charge him. The other arrested men informally identified Mitchell and Buckley but refused to testify against them in court because they were terrified. Buckley had told Fitzsimmons that the gang had been secretly watching his wife and children, just in case he didn't do what he was told. 'He said my job was to get the chemicals for the gang and if I didn't I was going to be shot,' Fitzsimmons later claimed to detectives. In June 1997, Jones and Fitzsimmons were both jailed for ten years, with the final seven years suspended. Cooper was also jailed for five years, while Skelly got a five-year suspended sentence. All of them pleaded guilty. In direct reference to Mitchell, a senior GNDU officer told one of the hearings that he was 'quite capable of having people shot'. One person who would agree with that comment was London villain Tony Brindle.

Mitchell's plan to wipe out the Brindles had, however, been compromised from the start – by his hit man Mickey Boyle. Within weeks of his release from prison in 1993, Boyle began terrorizing the wealthy residents of North Wicklow again. He was responsible for at least 16 armed robberies and attempted abductions, in less than two years of his release. In each case the families of businessmen were held at gunpoint in their homes, while ransoms were paid.

In 1993 Boyle tried to organize a protection racket aimed at wealthy landlords and businesspeople, using the guise of being a subversive group. Detectives quickly identified Mickey Boyle as the prime suspect behind the crime spree but he proved a difficult target. He used the forests and mountain tracks in North Wicklow to give his watchers the slip. Boyle had a warren of hides scattered throughout the area, which were impossible to detect. One Garda recalled: 'He operated like some kind of Rambo.'

When the Serious Crime Squad arrested Boyle in February 1995, following a hijacking, detectives were stunned when he agreed to co-operate with their investigation. The unpredictable gangster offered to work as an informant – and help them to catch George Mitchell. The officers were suspicious of Boyle but decided to wait and see what happened.

In a series of meetings, Mickey Boyle gave his Garda contacts general information about Mitchell and his associates. At the same time, however, he continued to target the families of businessmen in Wicklow, using the same methods he had used in the 1980s.

In May, Boyle told his handlers about the meeting with George Mitchell to discuss the Brindle murder plot and outlined the plan for the proposed hits. He gave the detectives the name of the gangland armourer being used and the location of the safe house, where guns and other hardware were being stored. When the cops advised Boyle not to get involved he was amazed that they cared about what happened outside Ireland.

London's South-East Regional Crime Squad (SERCS) confirmed that there was some truth in the information about the proposed Brindle hit. A major surveillance operation, codenamed 'Partake', was mobilized on both sides of the Irish Sea; the objectives were to foil the Brindle assassinations and to arrest Boyle and the other members of the Penguin's gang.

Over the following eight weeks, Boyle made a number of trips to London. He was secretly watched by the SERCS as he stalked members of the Brindle family. By the end of August 1995, Mitchell and the Daleys had decided to just hit Tony Brindle. Armed police watched as Boyle staked out Brindle's home at Christopher Close, in Rotherhithe. Scotland Yard's specialist firearms squad, SO19, moved into the area to prepare for the showdown.

Boyle proved to be very patient. On 20 September his target finally appeared and the hit man was waiting in a parked van. At 10.42 a.m. Brindle emerged from his house and walked to his parked car, and the SO19 squad braced themselves for action. As the London gangster reached his car, Boyle fired three shots at him from inside the van, hitting Brindle in the chest and thighs. As Brindle staggered back to his house, Boyle jumped out of the van and went to finish him off. At the same moment two police marksmen fired a total of 14 shots at Boyle, hitting him five times. The Penguin's hit man was critically injured and spent over two months in intensive care. When he recovered, Boyle was charged with attempted murder and two counts of possession of firearms with intent to endanger life. Brindle, who made a full recovery, refused to co-operate with the police investigation and accused them of allowing him to be shot.

Mickey Boyle was convicted and sentenced to three life sentences following a three-month trial in 1997. Armed police officers ringed the court and jurors were placed under protection. Boyle had put up an extraordinary defence, claiming that he had been a member of both the IRA and the INLA, while at the same time being a police informant. The hit man also put the boot into his old friend George Mitchell, who, he claimed, had coerced him into the shooting. 'Mitchell told me that if I sorted out the Brindles that he would be able to re-establish himself in London and that we would all be better off,' said Boyle.

The increasing heat as a result of the various arrests and the Brindle assassination bid in London had turned the media spotlight on George Mitchell. In June 1995 this writer published a major exposé of his activities in the *Sunday World* newspaper and shared his nickname with the Irish public, assigned because of the way the overweight Godfather walked with a waddle. Although Mitchell wasn't named, the newspaper ran his picture, with the eyes blacked out, and detailed his involvement in organized crime. The story centred on the ongoing Maradona dispute. The Penguin became a household name.

A month after Mickey Boyle's arrest in London, Mitchell was back in the news. This time Gardaí publicly named him in court as a major player in the drug trade in the city, when they objected to the renewal of a night-club licence. A senior officer told the District Court that Mitchell was a 'noted drug-pusher' whose men had threatened security staff at the Waterfront night-club at gunpoint. Inspector Thomas Murphy revealed: 'The purpose of the visit [of the gunmen] was to intimidate the bouncers and to allow Mitchell's lieutenants to operate with impunity on the premises. Mitchell sent in his lieutenants with firearms to remind them who was the boss.' The case gave the media the chance to legally name Mitchell and show his picture. Life was becoming decidedly difficult for the crime lord.

But the workaholic Penguin was too busy putting together one of the biggest drug shipments in European history to worry too much about being named in court. By the mid-1990s, Mitchell was part of a major international consortium involving Irish, English, Dutch, American and Canadian drug-traffickers. The plan was to smuggle 13 tons of cannabis for the Irish and UK markets. It was to be shipped directly from Pakistan for an estimated investment of over £10 million. The syndicate expected to more than double their money on the deal.

Mitchell was playing with some of the heaviest hitters in the world. The Dutch gang was one of that country's biggest crime organizations. It was known as 'the Octopus', because its tentacles spread throughout the world. Two major criminal gangs, based in Canada and America respectively, were also involved. The Canadian organization was led by international player Normand Drapeau. The American partners were Gary Matsuzaki and his sidekick, Brian Auchard. Matsuzaki was born in New Zealand but lived in the US, where he had Mafia connections in New York, Los Angeles and Montreal. He was a business associate of Drapeau. They were among the top targets of the American Drug Enforcement Agency (DEA).

The Irish end of the deal involved Mitchell and members of the Munster Mafia. The job of organizing the collection of the drugs was down to John Noonan, a former truck driver from Finglas in north-west Dublin. He was known as 'the Manager' because of his logistical skills. The self-proclaimed smuggler was also nicknamed 'the Sicilian' because of his dark skin and slicked-back, black hair.

Unfortunately for the syndicate, the international law enforcement community had learned of the plot. The story of what became known as the 'Urlingford bust' is one of the most daring undercover operations ever carried out by the Irish police. The international investigation involved police and customs on three continents. The Irish operation was codenamed 'Way Fair' and was spear-headed by Kevin Carty and his GNDU team. On 16 October 1995, Gardaí confirmed that the deal was on when they secretly monitored a meeting in Cork City between John Noonan, Alan Buckley, Gary Matsuzaki and Brian Auchard. The GNDU and their international colleagues managed to infiltrate the gang, and the man Noonan hired to land the haul was a Garda agent.

On the night of 7 November a trawler, crewed by armed undercover Gardaí, set off from Castletownbere, West Cork, to rendezvous with the mother-ship, the *Master Star*, inside Irish territorial waters. The 13 tons for the Irish mob was the last drop-off from an original load of 500 tons. The rest of the cargo had been off-loaded along the way. The Navy kept the ship under surveillance as the huge haul of hash was unloaded, while loud rock music boomed from the *Master Star* and men, armed with assault rifles, roamed its decks. The hash haul was then brought back to Castletownbere by Carty's men and loaded onto a container truck supplied by Noonan.

Later that day undercover Detective Sergeant Pat Walsh drove the load to Urlingford, County Kilkenny, where he parked the 40-foot trailer along the Dublin Road. The plan was for Noonan and other gang members to arrive in another truck and take the hash away. However, the operation fell apart when news of the action in Castletownbere leaked out and Noonan failed to turn up. He was arrested in Dublin carrying £233,000 in cash. He would later boast in a newspaper interview that he wasn't busted with the Urlingford shipment because the police lifted him prematurely. Matsuzaki and Auchard had left the country before the drugs arrived. No one was charged in connection with the shipment.

The GNDU were left with no choice but to move in and claim the biggest drug seizure in the history of the State. There was considerable public controversy when it emerged three months later that the under-cover Gardaí had been in control of the drug shipment. But the brave and highly risky operation illustrated to the underworld that the Gardaí had developed much more sophisticated methods of investigation. In 1997 the GNDU finally caught John Noonan, as he collected a large haul of ecstasy. He was subsequently jailed for eight years. While the Urlingford seizure was a major financial blow to the Penguin and his partners, George Mitchell had managed to escape the net – yet again.

By the late 1990s the Penguin had become a powerful and extremely wealthy gangster. His personal wealth was estimated to be in the region of £10 million. Mitchell had so many irons in the fire, and so many dif-ferent criminals working with him, that the cops could only latch onto a handful of his myriad scams. But Ireland was becoming too difficult a place for the ambitious Godfather to do business without being hassled by the police. Always the pragmatic villain, Mitchell was the first major crime figure to leave Ireland as a result of the murder of Veronica Guerin in June 1996. He got out before the unprecedented backlash by the State and the newly established Criminal Assets Bureau. Mitchell decided to move his family to live permanently in Amsterdam, where he continued to build his international empire. Maradona Dunne also moved to Hol-land, after he was acquitted by a Liverpool court of conspiring to ship heroin into Ireland in 1996.

Mitchell continued to supply drugs to the Irish and UK markets. In October 1996, the GNDU were tipped-off by the US DEA that a freighter called the *Tia* had set sail from Suriname in South America bound for Ireland with a cargo of timber. Hidden in the cargo was 3 tons of high-quality cocaine. Mitchell, Alan Buckley and 'Father Hash' John McCarthy planned to land it on the Cork coastline. The deal, with a staggering street value of £250 million, was negotiated through a Colombian cartel, on behalf of Mitchell's international partners. When the *Tia* arrived in Irish waters in November the Irish Navy were waiting for it. When the freighter anchored off Castletownbere, the Navy and Gardaí stormed aboard – and found nothing. But naval divers discovered hidden compartments for stowing drugs under the ship's hull and the

DPP decided to charge the skipper and the ship's cook with conspiracy to import cocaine. The cook pleaded guilty to the charges while the skipper was found not guilty on the instructions of the trial judge. Fr Hash was arrested and questioned but never charged.

A year later Mitchell was implicated in a plot by the Russian Mafia to ship a load of heroin, worth millions, to Shannon Airport from Moscow. Intelligence was also uncovered by Dutch police that he had successfully established an ecstasy factory in the Gambia in West Africa.

Mitchell continued to stay one step ahead of the law – until March 1998, when he was caught red-handed stealing £4 million worth of computer parts. The components, which were being transported from the Hewlett Packard factory in County Kildare to a Dutch customer, were being tracked by Irish, English, Belgian and Dutch police forces. 'Operation Wedgewood' had been set up a year earlier to smash a multi-million-pound trade in stolen computer parts which Mitchell had organized from Holland. Detectives couldn't believe their luck when they surrounded a disused warehouse near Schipol Airport in Amsterdam. The Penguin was caught sitting behind the wheel of a forklift, in the process of unloading the goods. The gangster, who usually stayed a safe distance from the merchandise, had been forced to intervene after his associates failed to intercept the truck as it drove through England.

At his trial in August 1998, Mitchell was described as the ringleader in the operation. The Penguin claimed he was a businessman trying to make an honest living. When he was challenged about his prison record, the Godfather said: 'In prison I furthered my education, doing business studies and accountancy, but when I came out I was over the borderline of forty and couldn't find work easily. I arrived to start a new life in Holland. I was working every day up to my arrest.'

In September 1998, George Mitchell was jailed by a Dutch court for two and a half years and served one year. When he was released, the Penguin was a lot more careful. But gangland violence came back to haunt him a year later when his son-in-law Maradona Dunne was shot dead in 2000. Maradona was blasted to death in front of his wife Rachel, when members of a Dutch gang called to their home demanding payment for ecstasy.

By the mid-Noughties, Mitchell was high up in Europol's list of top ten most wanted Godfathers.

20. The Peacemaker

On New Year's Eve, 1993 a Limerick traveller family gathered together to mourn the death of their brother, whom they'd buried earlier that day. Patrick 'Pa' McCarthy had been stabbed to death when he called to the home of the city's most notorious Godfather. The group of ten adults huddled around a small fire in the cramped caravan, drinking cider. There were also two young children with them. Around 10.30 p.m. two of the mourners left the crowded caravan, which was parked at the Cooperage Canal Bank. They were challenged by masked men who stepped from the shadows. The couple were warned to keep their mouths shut and go while they still had a chance. Then two hit men, armed with a shotgun and an automatic pistol, stood in the door of the caravan and opened fire on the group inside. They clearly intended causing a massacre. This was the moment gangland violence arrived to stay on the streets of Limerick.

As the emergency crews and police arrived, they found a scene of bloody chaos. One of the brothers, Michael McCarthy, had a gaping gunshot wound in his neck and was bleeding to death. He died on the way to hospital. His brother Joe was hit in the back and leg and his sister Nora in the hip. Their cousin Noreen also suffered a leg wound. Miraculously the two young children were uninjured.

The outrage was the first major news item of 1994 and was greeted with shock and revulsion across Ireland. But less than a decade later the savagery had become a depressingly regular occurrence in Limerick, the amount of gun crime making it one of the most violent cities in Europe.

Gerry Mahon was one of the detectives who investigated the incident. He spent his entire Garda career, which spanned almost forty years, working on the streets of Limerick. From the time he joined in 1971, Mahon worked his way up through the ranks from uniformed beat-cop to become the city's Chief Superintendent. He witnessed how Limerick's crime mobs dragged the population into a gangland hell of murder and mayhem. The attempted massacre was his first taste of the madness that would soon follow. 'It was a shock to the whole system and a wake-up call. This was the first time that a criminal gang had stooped to such a level of sheer violence and brutality. That incident in 1993 announced the arrival of gangland in its most brutal form in Limerick. It was a taste of what we would be facing on a regular basis a few years down the road,' recalled the former chief, who retired in 2009. 'The clear intent was to wipe out the McCarthy family so there would be no witnesses to testify against the suspect for the death of Pa McCarthy. The only reason that they weren't all killed that night was that the ammunition used by the gunmen was defective and they had to stop firing after seven shots.'

The murders of Pa and Michael McCarthy and the near massacre of their family confirmed the fearsome reputation of the city's first major crime gang – the Keanes.

Christy Keane and his younger brother Kieran were the first members of the local criminal underworld to discover the value of the drug trade in the early 1990s, and they became the undisputed Godfathers of the city. Within a few years they controlled the largest drug-distribution network in the Mid-West region, supplying cocaine, ecstasy and cannabis. Like their counterparts in Dublin and Cork, they set up a network of drug-dealers and also got involved in money-laundering, trading in illegal firearms, counterfeit money, protection rackets, prostitution, smuggled goods and stolen vehicles. They had links with the O'Flynns in Cork, John Gilligan and the INLA. By the late 1990s the money was coming in so fast that the gang had a number of counting-centres throughout the region. At one stage, Christy Keane had to resort to using a wheelie-bin to store his cash. The war broke out when their rivals decided to take the money and power from them.

The Keanes grew up in St Mary's Park, a rundown Corporation estate in the shadow of King John's Castle, just north of the city centre. Also known as the Island Field, it would become their exclusive domain where Christy Keane was king. It was a perfect base for an organized crime network. Physically there was only one way in and out of the Island and strangers were quickly spotted. It was an extremely difficult area for Gardaí to keep under surveillance. The Keanes had started life as hard workers who ran a successful coal business. According to local people they inherited their mother's work ethic and they could have been hugely successful, legitimate businessmen. Instead, Christy Keane decided to play both sides of the fence, working hard and robbing at the same time. By the time he was 20 years old Keane had a string of convictions, mostly for larceny and burglary.

Christy Keane's most trusted lieutenant and enforcer was a psychotic thug called Eddie Ryan, from Hogan Avenue in Kileely across the River Shannon from the Island Field. Ryan had a long criminal record for theft and violence, dating back to when he was 12. He was a dangerous individual who took pleasure inflicting pain. In 1977, at the age of 17, he stabbed another man to death during a row on a city-centre street and was jailed for five years. In 1984, he found himself back behind bars for armed robbery. By the time Ryan returned to the streets the Keanes were moving into drugs. Together they built a formidable criminal empire. Ryan, who had close connections with republican terrorists, also worked as a freelance hit man. He dealt with unpaid debts and suspected police informants. 'When Eddie Ryan called to your door looking for something you gave it to him or else he'd give you something you didn't want. He was a ferociously violent bastard and everyone was scared of him,' one former associate recalled.

The incident which ultimately led to the shooting on the canal bank was the death of Pa's partner, Kathleen O'Shea, in February 1993. She was killed when she stumbled into the path of an oncoming van driven by Daniel Treacy, Christy Keane's nephew. A Garda investigation later concluded that it had been a tragic accident. Pa McCarthy, who had a history of violence, was heart-broken and threatened to kill Treacy. In a bid to compensate him, the Keanes and the Treacys paid for his wife's funeral. After that Pa McCarthy began putting the squeeze on the Keanes for money. For a while they paid him but finally refused to pay any more. McCarthy then moved with his children to Cork.

McCarthy returned to Limerick that year for Christmas and went on a non-stop drinking binge. On the night of 28 December, McCarthy drove to St Mary's Park with his brothers, Willie and Joe, and a friend, David Ryan. All four were drunk and McCarthy was in an aggressive mood. He called to Christy Keane's home at St Ita's Street, where he met Keane's other nephew, Owen Treacy, the van driver's brother. Twenty-two-year-old Owen was a member of Keane's drug gang and close to his uncles Christy and Kieran. McCarthy began making threats and demanding money. Christy Keane joined Owen Treacy at the door and a scuffle ensued, during which Pa McCarthy was stabbed in the chest. He died in the back of his van, as his brother Joe drove him to hospital. Joe and Willie McCarthy and David Ryan later told detectives that they witnessed Christy Keane stabbing Pa. A few hours later Gardaí arrested the Godfather and his nephew for questioning about the murder. The two men were later released while Gardaí compiled a file on the case for the DPP. It was then that the decision was made to get rid of the witnesses.

Gardaí didn't have to look far for suspects on 1 January 1994. Later that day, Eddie Ryan and his wife, Mary, Christy and Kieran Keane and another gang member, Declan 'Darby' Sheehy, were arrested in connection with the cold-blooded outrage. There wasn't enough evidence with which to prosecute a case but detectives were satisfied that Eddie Ryan and the Keane brothers had been involved.

On 4 January Christy Keane was formally charged with the murder of Pa McCarthy. The following morning the funeral of Michael McCarthy took place. The priest who officiated at the Mass described the murders of the brothers as 'senseless and mindless'. He told mourners: 'Violence begets violence, leading inevitably to more suffering and more grief and more loss of lives.' Less than ten years later, the priest's prediction had become a paradigm for life in the city's seedy underworld.

In March 1995, Christy Keane was acquitted of the murder of Pa McCarthy when the remaining witnesses proved to be unreliable. His mob continued to thrive and prosper.

The genesis of gangland in Limerick can be traced back to the sprawling working-class suburbs which were built in the 1960s and 1970s to alleviate the misery of the people living in its grim, poverty-stricken tenements. But the new estates, like those in Dublin, caused more problems than they actually solved. Former local TD Des O'Malley tried to convince the Corporation that they were making a mistake.

'From the late '60s the housing policy in Limerick Corporation changed when the Department of Local Government insisted local authorities build more houses altogether on the outskirts of cities rather than within the cities. And the first very big development of that kind in Limerick was in Southill where 2,000 or so houses were built in the late '60s. It wasn't a success; that was the beginning of the breakdown of the old social and community structure in Limerick,' said O'Malley. 'Houses were built without back up facilities of any kind, there were no churches, no schools, no shops, no pubs, nothing and I think very quickly people started to amuse themselves by engaging in violence and vandalism and that gradually degenerated into much worse. What I think was particularly blameworthy was that even though it was clear by the mid-1970s that Southill hadn't been a success, the Corporation went ahead and built a similar estate at Moyross on the other side of the city. I remember pleading with the city manager at the time not to do it because we were going to replicate the problems that we had in South-ill. Limerick is still suffering from the results of those decisions. By the early '90s large areas of these estates were burnt out and derelict. They had become breeding grounds for crime.'

Former Chief Superintendent Gerry Mahon had a similar recollec-tion. 'When I arrived as a young Garda at the end of 1971, the city was much smaller than it is now and there was very little serious crime until the mid to late 1970s. The big problem was the IRA and the INLA who were very active in the region and they robbed practically every bank in the county,' he recalled. 'The first thing that struck you when you went into a home in these estates was unemployment, an absent parent and poor conditions – bad clothing, no heating, no food in the fridge. There was no school, no looking for a job. They lived in another world really, without any support from society.'

The new estates in Southill became a hub for anti-social behaviour and vandalism. The tension and hopelessness of the situation led to feuding between families, which often spilled over into violence and even murder. Inter-family feuding has been a peculiar feature of certain parts of Limerick for generations. Knife crime became a particular prob-lem. The situation got so bad that the Corporation turned to a notorious local criminal, Michael 'Mikey' Kelly, to help them solve it. The deci-sion would have far-reaching consequences for the development of organized crime in Limerick.

Mikey Kelly and his family were among the first residents to move into the new houses in Southill. Kelly was a close friend and long-time

criminal associate of Eddie Ryan, with whom he carried out armed robberies. Like Ryan, Kelly was a violent thug with a string of convictions
for serious crime, including wounding, robbery, demanding money
with menaces, possession of firearms and shooting at a person with
intent to maim and endanger life. His last recorded conviction was in
July 1986. In 1982 Mikey Kelly was the prime suspect in the murder of
another local criminal called Ronnie Coleman. Coleman was associated
with two other families who were feuding with the Kellys. One night
Coleman smashed a pint glass into Kelly's face in a city pub. On 12
October that year Mikey got his revenge, when he stabbed Coleman
several times in the chest. Kelly was charged with the murder but was
acquitted. At the time an associate of Kelly's was also feuding with the
McCarthy brothers from St Mary's Park (no relation to the McCarthys
above). Their sister was married to Eddie Ryan's brother, John. Two
months after the Coleman murder, Sammy and Tommy McCarthy
were stabbed to death during a pub row in Limerick. The incident
earned Limerick the unflattering media tag line, 'Stab City'.

Mikey Kelly was a clever manipulator of the media and successfully
portrayed himself as an ordinary decent criminal who had retired and
wanted to give something back to society. Kelly loved to tell the story
of how he underwent a transformation of biblical proportions when Fr
Joe Young visited him in his prison cell in the mid-1980s. Kelly, who
was serving a sentence for armed robbery, had beaten up a number of
prison warders and there was a stand-off at his cell. Fr Young arrived to
mediate and asked him if he was all right. Kelly claimed that he told the
priest to 'fuck off', whereupon Young replied: 'No. You fuck off.' And
that, according to Mikey Kelly, was all it took to convert one of the
country's most violent thugs into a born-again 'crime-free' citizen.
When he got out of prison, Kelly exploited his new status, living on the
coattails of Fr Young who was a curate in Southill. Kelly claimed that
his only ambition in life was to repay society for the wrongs he had
done.

In 1988, he helped to supervise the Garda Activity Programme in
Southill. It was a local community project organized by the Gardaí at
Roxboro Road Station. The aim was to break down the barriers between
the police and the local youth. Kelly suddenly found a way of building
a respectable façade. His photograph appeared in the local newspapers

attending various meetings with senior police officers, and he began rubbing shoulders with members of the Establishment in Limerick. Mikey's story about his road-to-Damascus conversion was soon paying dividends.

Kelly was an attractive character for the media because he was probably the only criminal ever to speak so frankly about his exploits. It all added to his respectable image and led to a flattering documentary about his life, *The Hard Man*, which was broadcast on RTÉ in 1995. In it he bragged about his past as a 'vicious, dangerous criminal' who was addicted to booze and violence. The truth was that he was still a nasty, drunken brute who subjected his wife to constant beatings.

Mikey took full advantage of his new-found respectability and set up a company, M and A Security, in 1991. The poacher turned gamekeeper inveigled lucrative contracts from businesses and the Corporation. Break-ins and vandalism were reduced when there was a Kelly sign over the door. It was a perfect, hugely profitable protection racket. Des O'Malley still believes that it was a dreadful mistake. 'What really worried me about the situation was that it was an indication by public authority in this country that you could and should deal with criminals in the course of public administration and I felt that we'd all live to regret that. I rang the authorities to protest but the response was that Kelly was effective. But everyone knew that his [Kelly's] modus operandi was breaking people's legs. It served to give a foothold to the type of criminality that we have today.'

By making Kelly 'respectable' the Corporation had sent out a toxic signal – in Limerick crime pays. The reality was that the gangster was a parasite. He used his new-found status as a protector of the people to collect money each week from the ordinary hard-pressed citizens of Southill. Kelly's apparent acceptance by the Establishment made it seem like he could do what he wanted. This is a view shared by local TD and current Minister for Finance, Michael Noonan. 'Mikey Kelly was running a protection racket and agents of the State were hiring him and paying him to continue with the protection,' said Noonan, who has represented Limerick in the Dáil for over thirty years. 'Kelly never put in security guards. All he did was put up the sign and sent the word out. The State should never have been involved in that because it validated crime.'

But the cosy relationship between Kelly and the Gardaí turned sour when they began to investigate his operation. In 1993 an associate of Kelly's bought a pub in the city which became a popular haunt for the criminal fraternity. But in 1994 Garda Brendan Sheehan from Roxboro Station began to regularly inspect the premises, to ensure it adhered to the licensing laws. But Kelly's associate didn't take kindly to the 'invasion' and made complaints to Sheehan's superiors. On one occasion he arrived in Roxboro Station at 2 a.m., demanding to know why the Garda had insisted that the pub shut its doors at closing time. Despite this Sheehan continued to do his job and raided the pub for after-hours drinking. At one stage Garda Sheehan reported that he had been followed home by a known criminal with links to Mikey Kelly from Roxboro Station one morning, when he finished his shift at 6 a.m.

The confrontation took a more sinister turn when another associate of Kelly's, a small-time gangster called James O'Gorman from Cork, claimed to Gardaí that there was a plot to murder Sheehan. O'Gorman said that a number of firearms had been brought in from England for the hit. The threats were taken seriously and, when a gun was found during a search of the home of one of Kelly's associates, Garda Sheehan was transferred from Limerick to Ennis.

Following the incident Mikey Kelly held a press conference to protest his innocence. A video was also played for the media which showed O'Gorman retracting his earlier claims and making counter-allegations that the Gardaí had put him up to it. Mikey Kelly had clearly organized the video session as he could be seen sitting across the room from O'Gorman. During the press conference Mikey Kelly bawled his eyes out and accused the police of victimization and not accepting that he was a reformed man. It was a performance that Christy 'Bronco' Dunne would have been impressed with – although tears were not his thing.

What Mikey didn't tell the press was that his associate had visited O'Gorman's brother Paul in Manchester, and had left him on a life-support machine. Subsequent criminal charges against the man were dropped, after Mikey visited Paul O'Gorman's girlfriend and reminded her that she had vulnerable children. Paul O'Gorman later signed an affidavit stating that he had not been attacked.

But the media began looking behind Kelly's façade of respectability and asked some awkward questions. A special *Primetime* investigation was broadcast in September 1995, in which the O'Gormans told their story. Mikey denied that he had done anything wrong and threatened to sue RTÉ, but never proceeded with the case.

Two months later he was back in the sights of the local Gardaí. This time Kelly was paid to force a man to leave Limerick, following a custody row over a child. The victim was abducted by two of Kelly's henchmen, Pat Nash and Alan Wallace, when he refused to go quietly. They slashed his face with a knife and pistol-whipped him. But the man went to the police and both Nash and Wallace were arrested and charged. They were later convicted and jailed. Tony Reynolds, the man who had hired Kelly in the first place, was given a suspended sentence and ordered to pay the victim £12,000 in compensation. Mikey Kelly was also arrested, but the DPP decided there was insufficient evidence with which to charge him.

Irrespective of the *Primetime* programme, the local media continued to lap up everything Mikey had to say, and he gave them plenty of juicy copy. The self-styled Godfather used a mixture of lies, malicious allegations and legal actions to protect himself. And behind the scenes people were intimidated and beaten. One associate went missing – Gardaí believe Kelly had him murdered and buried in the foundations of a house. When anyone dared to question Kelly's scams and lies he ran to the media, claiming a 'vendetta against the peacemaking Kelly family'. For the benefit of the emerging crime gangs in the city, he stepped up his campaign to undermine the police. He even announced in the local newspapers and on radio that he was setting up a private police force in Southill because the Gardaí were not doing their jobs. At the time Kelly claimed his 'patrols' had logged over 4,700 calls for police assistance which weren't answered. But following an independent investigation it was found there was no evidence that the calls had been made.

Mikey's signature approach was to make outrageous allegations to the local media against local politicians, businesspeople and police officers who crossed him or his family. There would be no evidence to back up his claims, which he would drop once the seed of doubt was sown. In one case, he presented an anonymous boy to a number of journalists with a chilling story about how he and other boys had been paid for sex by a number of well-known local politicians. Kelly promised the nation that the case would be brought before the courts because the boys concerned were under his 'protection'. He then called for the resignations of two politicians. But the case disappeared and so did the youngster, amid claims that it was all made up by Kelly to gain power, gangland-style, in the council chambers. Despite this, his charade paid off and he was elected to the city council in 1999. He topped the poll, becoming an alderman. From then on he always referred to himself as Alderman Michael Kelly. Kelly's next ambition was to seek election to the Dáil. Organized crime had won a major victory in Limerick.

At the end of the decade, the four sons of traveller Kenneth Dundon returned to Limerick after spending much of their lives in England. Dundon had married Anne McCarthy from Prospect, a working-class ghetto on the southern side of the city, and had moved to London. Dundon was an extremely violent man and a role model to his kids. Wayne, Dessie, Gerard and John Dundon were violent savages like their father – and the last people Limerick needed.

Wayne Dundon was a particularly dangerous thug who loved inflicting pain and fear. He once beat his mother so badly that she was hospitalized for three weeks. When he was 18 years old he was jailed for a series of robberies from elderly people in London. During one burglary he savagely beat up a wheelchair-bound pensioner.

When they returned, the brothers teamed up with their equally violent cousins, the McCarthys, including Larry Junior, James and Anthony. This was the genesis of the McCarthy/Dundon gang, Murder Inc. As a group they were notorious for double- and even treble-crossing associates and fellow gang members. Loyalty was alien to these thugs and their treachery was so notorious that they were called 'the piranhas' behind their backs.

The following is a description of the McCarthy/Dundons from a serving Garda in Limerick who knew them best. 'They are the most devious and dangerous bastards that we ever encountered in Limerick or anywhere else in Ireland. They were called the piranhas because they would eat each other if they were hungry enough. They run with the hares and hunt with the hounds. Killing or maiming comes like second nature to all of them and they have absolutely no fear of the law. They are so dangerous that they would be shaking your hand one minute and then shoot [you] in the back, as soon as you turn away from them. They don't care about doing time or being shot and injured, although they would prefer to avoid both if they could. They accept danger as part of everyday life, like it is an occupational hazard.'

As soon as they arrived back in Limerick, the Dundons and their cousins began causing mayhem. They got involved in the drug trade but steered clear of conflict with the Keanes – for the time being at least. The McCarthy/Dundons became embroiled in a series of bitter and extremely complex feuds with other criminal families, including the Caseys and the McNamaras. At one stage the McCarthy/Dundons began feuding with the Caseys. But they later settled their differences and Wayne Dundon married one of the Caseys. The two sides then joined forces and went after the McNamaras. It led to a string of shootings, assaults and abductions, as up to four extended families got involved. Houses and cars belonging to each side were burned out and shots were fired through front windows.

Members of other families, including associates of Mikey Kelly's, also got involved in the feud. One associate was charged with shooting one of the Caseys in the face with a humane killer. Casey suffered a circular wound to his cheek and the bones in his upper jaw, nose and eye socket were shattered. He was lucky to be alive.

The local Gardaí were determined to bring the situation under control. An inspector in Roxboro, Jim Browne, set up an operation to put an end to the feuding. Browne would later find himself on the frontline in the war against the Limerick gangs. Over time the Gardaí charged several of the combatants with serious offences, including criminal damage, assaults and possession of firearms. Such were the myriad charges that the victim in one case could also be the accused in another. As a result of police objections to bail, most of the accused thugs were locked up while awaiting trial, which restored a degree of calm to the city. But then Alderman Mikey Kelly stepped in to make matters much worse.

To much public fanfare, Kelly established his own version of a 'peace process', which he tried to equate with the Northern Ireland situation. But his real motivation for the peace talks was to get his associates off a number of charges, including a shooting. Kelly 'brokered' the peace deals between the various protagonists and victims, in a bid to undermine the Garda investigations. As a result, all the victims who had given statements to the police in the various criminal cases shook hands and

withdrew their evidence. Kelly organized a number of carefully choreographed press conferences for the local media, where the former
enemies posed for pictures and shook hands. The result of the so-called
peace deals was that none of the injured parties was prepared to give
evidence in court and the charges were struck out.

Mikey's strategy worked well. When the various cases came before
Limerick Circuit Criminal Court, the warring witnesses withdrew their
statements with the result that dozens of charges were dropped. The
victims in some of the cases had been the attackers in others.

By thwarting the criminal justice process Kelly had assisted in the
development of the McCarthy/Dundon gang. If the Gardaí had succeeded in putting the main players behind bars, it is argued that the
subsequent gang wars could have been avoided. This is the view of the
former Fianna Fáil Defence Minister, Willie O'Dea, TD for Limerick:
'Kelly interfered in the Gardaí's business and ensured that certain people
could operate freely and become proficient in crime. These people
formed the basis of the membership of the future gangs. There is no
doubt that Mikey Kelly was a very significant figure in the evolution of
organized crime in this city.'

Kelly kept up his campaign against the Gardaí. Whenever a member
of the family or an associate was stopped or arrested, Mikey organized
protest vigils outside Roxboro Garda Station. He also called the local
media to ensure maximum publicity. His vendetta came to a head in the
autumn of 2001 when he was charged with beating his wife, Majella.
She later withdrew the charges; however, at the time she told this writer
how she had endured twenty years of beatings at the hands of her
'peacemaker' husband. Majella Kelly said that her life would have been
in danger if she didn't later recant her statement, and she admitted that
she told lies to the court when she dropped the charges. But a few
months afterwards Majella Kelly was forced by her husband to make
outrageous allegations against the officer in charge of her case, Inspector
Jim Browne, who had become Mikey's nemesis. She brought a malicious private prosecution against the officer, claiming sexual assault.
Kelly was doing everything in his power to destroy the one man who
was seen as a serious threat to organized crime in the city.

'It was probably better than actually killing the man, making such
an allegation,' one of Browne's colleagues remarked at the time. But

Majella Kelly's claims were dramatically dismissed in Limerick District Court by Judge Peter Smithwick after the tape of her interview with this writer was played. Judge Smithwick said: 'This is an evil conspiracy of the Kelly family to denigrate members of the Gardaí, particularly Inspector Browne, who is innocent of the charges against him.' The judge said he believed Kelly had coerced his terrified wife into taking the action.

The vexatious case turned the public against Kelly and it finished his political career. In the general election he got a mere 700 votes and later resigned his seat on the city council. The Southill 'peacemaker' was investigated by the Criminal Assets Bureau and was subsequently convicted and jailed for eight months for tax offences. His security business was also closed down.

In May 2004 Kelly, who had moved back to live with his mother in Southill after splitting from his wife, was found unconscious in his bed with a gunshot wound to the head. He never regained consciousness and died in hospital a month later. It is still not known if he shot himself or was killed by someone else.

By the time of his demise Limerick was already firmly in the grip of war.

21.   The Vacuum

PJ Judge presented himself to the world as a gentle, soft-spoken man, with good taste in clothes. He was an unremarkable-looking individual who could have passed himself off as an average 'Joe public'. But the façade of respectability disguised a cold-blooded monster whose name was synonymous with terror. He held the distinction of being one of the most savage thugs to feature in the history of gangland. Long before the likes of the McCarthy/Dundons appeared on the streets, Judge had earned the nickname 'the Psycho'. No criminal was ever given such a fitting sobriquet.

A retired detective, who witnessed Judge's career from the cradle to the grave, described him: 'I have known practically every major criminal in Dublin for over thirty years and I have never met one like Judge. There was a behavioural kink in the bastard. He was the worst, most evil fuck I ever came across. He committed two of the most brutal murders I have investigated and he even tried to kill Guards.' A criminal who once worked with Judge agreed with the worldly-wise cop. 'He scared the shit out of everyone. There was something about that fucker that just wasn't right. He talked like butter wouldn't melt in his mouth but could cut your heart out and smile into your face at the same time. Most criminals kill because it's just part of the business but Judge loved it.'

When PJ Judge was released from prison in 1989, like so many of his cronies he decided to take advantage of the new career path – the drug trade. Within a few years he controlled a huge drug distribution network across Dublin, through fear and extreme violence. He was introduced to the drug trade by his neighbour John McKeown, who controlled many of the cannabis rackets in the north and west of the city. The Psycho invested the robbery cash he had hidden in 'off-side' bank accounts to buy a number of small consignments of hash. He gradually expanded and the money came rolling in. Then he branched out into heroin, ecstasy and amphetamines.

Two years later Judge was one of the biggest operators in the Dublin underworld. He controlled 'patches' right across the south, west and north of the city. He had extensive contacts with other drug gangs in Limerick and Cork. The nearest the Gardaí came to catching Judge with his drugs was in August 1991, when he was spotted by detectives near the Grand Canal. Judge made a run for it when he saw the cops, throwing a jacket into the canal. It was later found to contain amphetamine tablets worth over £10,000. He was charged and released on bail. A file on the case was sent to the Director of Public Prosecutions, who decided it would be difficult to connect Judge with the jacket containing the drugs.

After his lucky escape, Judge continued expanding his business. From the beginning he decided that he would not allow anyone to rip him off or not pay up on time. He let it be known that anyone who messed with him would be in for a severe beating or a bullet. Judge organized his network of dealers like a military operation, with strict rules. If they were drug-abusers then they indulged their habit on their own time. There was also a stringent 'no credit' policy. Judge believed that allowing junkies to owe him money would lead to others 'taking liberties'. If any of his pushers lost money or drugs, then Judge punished them by doubling the value of what was lost. If it wasn't paid the errant pusher was tortured or shot. When a pusher was not working hard enough he was sacked from Judge's 'golden circle'. Then the word would be put out and the pusher would be blanked by everyone in the business. It was not unusual for the Psycho to have his pushers out moving drugs around the city at three or four in the morning, as he drove around checking up on them. He was guaranteed total loyalty and secrecy from his people for two reasons: they were absolutely terrified of the man, and they made plenty of easy money.

The fact that Judge was also bisexual added to the complexity of his character. It was well known in underworld circles that he took sexual advantage of some of his younger, more vulnerable male drug-dealers. But no one ever dared say anything about it to his face. He also had a string of girlfriends, some of whom were known prostitutes. Judge sadistically beat his male and female lovers quite severely, for no apparent reason. On one occasion he gave a girlfriend such a beating that she ran into the Bridewell Garda Station for protection. Judge burst in after her, demanding that the terrified woman leave with him. The police told him to get out or he would be charged with assault and breach of the peace. The girlfriend, however, was too scared to prefer charges and later relocated, to avoid bumping into her psychotic boyfriend again.

The Psycho didn't stop at inflicting pain, he was also a murderer. Michael Godfrey was a small-time crook who had the misfortune of becoming Judge's partner-in-crime. Godfrey, who was born in Dublin in 1938, had returned to Ireland in 1985 after spending several years in England. He set himself up as an insurance broker but went bust five years later. He had been involved in a large-scale compensation scam, organized by Martin Cahill's associate, inner-city hoodlum Stephen 'Rossi' Walsh. Walsh's gang made fraudulent claims against public utilities and insurance companies, based on 'accidents' they arranged around Dublin. Over a three-year period, the Irish insurance industry estimated that Walsh was behind dozens of staged accidents where compensation and legal fees worth £2 million had been paid out. He used a core group of 23 individuals and Godfrey's knowledge of the insurance business was a big help. In 1992 Walsh's luck finally ran out when he blew up a pub on Dublin's north-side. The thug was found lying in the smouldering ruins of the premises by firemen. He was charged with arson and subsequently jailed for 14 years. Many years later the underworld hard man was also exposed as a habitual paedophile. In 2010 he was convicted for the rape and sexual abuse of two children.

Godfrey was introduced to Judge in 1989. The pair were first involved in a money-counterfeiting scam together, until Godfrey was caught in the UK in 1991 and jailed for 30 months. When he returned to Ireland, he set up a front company in an industrial unit in Glasnevin. The plan was to import large quantities of cannabis for Judge, who was anxious to cut out the middlemen in the business. In February 1993 they travelled to Belgium where they agreed to buy 30 kilos of hash from a Dutch dealer for £30,000. It was to be a pilot operation and, if it went well, they would place regular orders. When the first consignment arrived on 12 March, Judge refused to take it because it was not the cannabis he'd sampled in Holland. The Psycho was in a chilling temper and ordered Godfrey to get the money back. Instead Godfrey sold the hash to John Gilligan's lieutenant, Peter 'Fatso' Mitchell, for almost double its price. Judge heard about the deal and flew into a rage. He accused

Godfrey of ripping him off and demanded all the cash from the transaction. The conman's perceived disloyalty had sealed his fate.

On the night of 31 March 1993, Judge first went looking for Mitchell, armed with an automatic pistol. He couldn't find him and shot one of Fatso's associates in the leg instead. The man was hospitalized but refused to co-operate with detectives investigating the case. Judge was subsequently arrested for questioning but refused to talk. He was released without charge.

Three days later, Judge sent two associates to abduct Godfrey from his flat. They took him to Scribblestown Lane, a cul-de-sac situated on waste ground on the outer fringes of Finglas, North Dublin. When the car arrived Godfrey was taken into a field where Judge was waiting. The Psycho caught his victim by the throat and beat him. He hurled abuse at Godfrey who pleaded for mercy. Judge ordered one of his thugs to shoot him in the head with a .32 pistol. The man fired a shot at Godfrey, injuring him. The conman was still alive and pleading for mercy. Judge grabbed the gun from his accomplice, cocked it and finished his partner off with another bullet in the back of the head. The Psycho then calmly walked away, got into his car and drove off. Gardaí investigating the murder knew that he was the killer but didn't have the evidence with which to charge him. His accomplices were prepared to do jail-time rather than incur the Psycho's wrath.

Judge began supplying the new gangs of young drug-dealers, who were emerging across the city by the mid-1990s. For many of them, it was a badge of honour to be working for the notorious gang boss – and no one would dare take them on. One of his protégés was a tough young robber called Martin 'Marlo' Hyland from Cabra. Hyland had a predictable criminal career, progressing from car theft and burglaries to armed robbery and then the drug trade. Officially it began in 1986 at the age of 17, when he was convicted for a number of minor offences. Six months earlier, his sister Julie had been murdered by her drunken husband, Michael Brady. Brady beat and raped his wife, before strangling her. The murder had a profound effect on young Marlo, who was close to his older sister. After that he steadily got involved in more serious crime. Marlo and his pals terrorized their neighbourhood, snatching cash from insurance agents and rent collectors on their rounds in Cabra. They also robbed trains and trucks as they travelled through the area.

Hyland was a joyrider and was also considered a good handler of a motorbike. He used his 'skill' during armed hold-ups in building societies and banks around Dublin. He was banned from driving several times, although he had never actually passed a driving test. He continued to drive illegally and was caught so many times that he was eventually banned for life. A former friend described Marlo: 'He was a great character as far as I was concerned, a real rebel who was up for anything. Martin was a good talker and very charming. He was always in control of things. I suppose he got that from when he was growing up. He was very mouthy sometimes and didn't know when to keep his trap shut.'

In 1987, Hyland was jailed for a variety of offences, including robbery, malicious damage and dangerous driving. When he came out of prison in the early 1990s, he began dabbling in drugs. Initially Marlo bought his supplies from Noel Mullen, a former associate of the General who was a customer of the Gilligan gang. Hyland also began to deal in heroin, ecstasy and cocaine. The young gangster despised the police and in 1995 was involved in a campaign of intimidation against officers attached to Cabra Station. But Hyland's move into the big league began when he started working with PJ Judge. At the time Judge was in a relationship with Marlo's sister Ellen. Marlo and his cronies learned a lot from their sinister mentor and Hyland made many contacts who would be valuable to him in the future.

A gang of young drug-dealers from Ballyfermot were also part of PJ Judge's network. The leading members of the gang were Derek 'Dee Dee' O'Driscoll, Seanie Comerford, Mark Desmond, Paul Meehan and brothers Paul and Kenneth Corbally. They started their criminal careers as joyriders and became known as the M50 gang because they indulged in high-speed nocturnal jousts with the police on the new motorway which had opened in 1992. Within a short space of time the names of these thugs would become synonymous with the new, violent gang culture.

On Halloween night 1995, Gallanstown, a grim estate on the outskirts of Ballyfermot, exploded in an orgy of destruction. The estate had become a major centre for gangs of drug-dealers and joyriders. During the riots 16 stolen cars were used to ram police vehicles and hundreds of petrol-bombs were thrown. Such rioting had rarely been seen on the streets of the Republic, even at the height of the Troubles. On the surface it appeared to be a spontaneous explosion of pent-up frustrations, by a generation of kids with no hope or prospects. But the truth was rather different. The Gallanstown riot was carefully planned and choreographed by the M50 gang. On the night of the riot they sat in a pub in Ballyfermot, listening to scanners tuned to the police radio frequencies and directing operations on mobile phones. The gang wanted to show the police how upset they were about the recent seizure of over £100,000 worth of heroin.

It took a force of over seventy Gardaí to take back control of Gallanstown that night, after an intensive four-hour battle. Hundreds of petrol-bombs had been prepared in advance and stolen cars were hidden off-side weeks beforehand, for what the hoods referred to as 'the games'. Planks had been collected and nails hammered through them, to puncture the tyres of the police vehicles. The planks were painted black to make them practically invisible. The plan was to lure the police into a trap and pelt them with petrol-bombs.

Amazingly the casualties were light that night. However, a young child was badly burned when a petrol-bomb being thrown by his father prematurely ignited. But the rioting mob would not allow an ambulance in to take the injured child to hospital. The Gardaí were forced to baton-charge their way into the house, so that the paramedics could do their jobs.

Less than a year after the riots it was discovered that Judge's henchman, Dee Dee O'Driscoll, and the Gilligan gang were both paying a corrupt cop called John O'Neill for inside information. The disgraced cop, who was based at Tallaght Station, was exposed by the Lucan Investigation Team and subsequently jailed.

Aside from the M50 crew, Judge's associates included Mark Dwyer, also from Cabra, and Declan Griffin from Coolock, North Dublin. Griffin, born in 1970, cut his teeth as a young robber and drug-dealer with Dave 'Myler' Brogan. By 1995 he was heavily involved in the importation of heroin and ecstasy with Judge. Decie Griffin was also a duplicitous character, not unlike John Traynor, who played both sides of the tracks to protect his own interests. Dwyer, who was three years younger than Griffin, had been involved in crime since his early teens. A small man, he shared Judge's passion for violence.

Judge recruited Griffin and Dwyer for the murder of his former neighbour and friend William Jock Corbally. It was one of the most gruesome and depraved crimes ever perpetrated in gangland. Superstitious criminals still recall how it brought a 'curse' on all those involved.

Jock Corbally was from Ballygall Parade, around the corner from Judge's home on Ballygall Crescent. He was four years older than the Psycho. They had been good friends in their younger years and had carried out robberies together. But the relationship turned sour when Judge was arrested and charged with an armed robbery at Ballyfermot Post Office. Judge had been arrested after the robbery in a van which Corbally told Gardaí he had loaned to the Psycho to move furniture. Judge was subsequently convicted and jailed. He had borne a dangerous grudge against Jock ever since. Judge was also jealous of Corbally, who was a charming character. But the likable rogue simply didn't possess either the ruthlessness or the acumen to be a successful gangster. When Judge was released from prison in 1989, Jock was starting a two-year stretch for possession of drugs.

On his release, Corbally returned to Finglas, where his enemy now controlled the local drug trade. Judge had even recruited Corbally's two teenage sons, William Junior and Graham, into his operation. In October 1990, Judge gave them £800 worth of hashish to sell for him. The teenagers, however, only managed to sell £200 worth and smoked the rest themselves. The Psycho took pleasure giving William Junior a serious beating, and warned him of dire consequences if the money wasn't paid up. Their father was furious when he heard this. He didn't want his sons getting mixed up with Judge. Jock met his nemesis and promised to get the balance of the money back. Judge, however, decided that he now wanted £1,500, instead of the original £600 owed. It was interest on the drugs he'd originally given the two kids. Corbally told Judge he didn't have that kind of money.

In April 1991 the situation came to a head when Jock was attacked by Judge near Ballygall Crescent. Corbally got the upper-hand when he hit Judge across the head with an iron bar. The Psycho had to get 20 stitches. Judge was humiliated and swore bloody vengeance. He ordered Jock and his two sons to leave the country or else face the music. Jock refused to go and signed his own death warrant.

In late 1992 Jock won a reprieve from his problems, when he was jailed for five years for stealing a truckload of beef. In the meantime the Psycho's business thrived. But he never forgot his vendetta and continued to threaten the lives of Jock's two sons.

In January 1996, Judge got the opportunity he had been waiting for. Declan Griffin was looking for a courier to smuggle heroin for him. Griffin had been arrested a month earlier in Dublin Airport, after arriving on a flight from Amsterdam with 3 kilos of heroin and 3,000 ecstasy tablets. Jock, who was always strapped for cash, was happy to take the job. Griffin paid him £1,000 to bring a kilo of heroin over from Holland. What Corbally didn't know was that Judge had also invested in the shipment.

When Corbally returned to Dublin, he decided to pull a stroke on Griffin. He arranged for an associate to hide the heroin near Sutton Dart Station. Jock's hare-brained plan was to tip off the Gardaí – but only after he'd taken a quarter of the kilo for himself. When the heroin was seized on 19 January, Griffin was furious. Details of the seizure were all over the media the next day and the hood knew he'd been ripped off. Judge decided that the time was now right for his long-awaited retribution, and he instructed Griffin to lure Jock into a trap.

On 28 February 1996, Griffin called Jock with the offer of £1,000 for another run to Holland. He asked the hapless courier to help him dig up the money for the drugs as it was hidden in a field. They arranged to meet in Chapelizod, West Dublin. Jock's family and friends later recalled that he was 'very excited' that evening that he was going to make another 'earner'. Griffin picked up Corbally and brought him to a field at the back of the Green Isle Hotel near Baldonnel. Judge, Mark Dwyer and a former member of the INLA, who acted as a bagman for the gang, were waiting. As soon as Griffin drove into the field they opened the passenger door. To Jock Corbally's horror, PJ Judge's face suddenly emerged from the darkness. 'Jock, we want to have word with you,' the Psycho said with a menacing grin.

Jock tried to beat them off but they dragged him out into the field. They beat Corbally with an iron bar, a baseball bat and a pick-axe handle, as he screamed in agony and begged for mercy. But the more he screamed the more frenzied Judge became. 'Do you remember the time we fought before?' the Psycho snarled, as he laid into his victim. Judge accused Jock of being a 'rat', shouting: 'Mountjoy is full of fellows because of you.' He turned Corbally on his back and smashed in his pearly-white teeth – Jock's pride and joy.

After a while Judge and Dwyer took a break because they were so exhausted. Jock was lying on his stomach whimpering. His body could take no more and he fell silent. Judge, Dwyer and the third man dumped Jock into the boot of a second car.

The Psycho drove off in the direction of County Kildare, where he buried his former friend in a grave he had dug earlier that day. According to sources in the underworld, Judge finished off Jock by cutting his throat. He then dumped lime on top of the body, before filling in the grave. To this day it is unknown if Corbally was alive or dead when he was buried. His grave has never been located, despite several search operations involving Gardaí and hundreds of soldiers.

An hour after the incident Mark Dwyer returned to his flat in Phibsboro. An eye-witness who later spoke to Gardaí said Dwyer's clothes were covered in blood and dirt. The Psycho's sidekick was in a 'buzz'. 'I'm after whacking Jock Corbally. We killed Corbally with an iron bar and a knife and I am waiting for a phone call to say he is buried,' Dwyer excitedly told the witness. Judge phoned him shortly afterwards. Dwyer was heard asking: 'Is that baby tucked up in bed?' Judge is said to have replied: 'The baby is tucked in and sound asleep.'

It didn't take long for rumours of the demise of Jock Corbally to trickle out through the gangland grapevine. When he was officially reported missing by his family, the Gardaí launched a major investigation which lasted for several months. Decie Griffin typically tried to play both sides. He gave Gardaí information about the incident, while playing down his own role. A number of other individuals who had spoken with Dwyer also secretly reported what they knew to the Gardaí. But such was the Psycho's reputation that no one would stand up in court against him. In May 1996, this writer published an extensive investigative story on the disappearance of Jock Corbally in the *Sunday World* newspaper. Although Judge wasn't named, everyone in the underworld knew the identity of the Psycho.

The exposure drove Judge berserk and he called a meeting of all his henchmen to discuss what to do about it. He was determined to find out who was 'touting' on him. He plotted to have this writer abducted, tortured to discover the source and then murdered.

At the same time, the Gardaí were taking a much closer interest in Judge. Several shipments of his drugs were intercepted and money was seized from his bagmen. But he won a reprieve of sorts when Veronica Guerin was murdered. For a time the full resources of all the specialist police units were focused on the Gilligan gang. As soon as they were available again, Assistant Commissioner Tony Hickey intended to go after Judge.

Despite the unprecedented reaction to the journalist's murder, however, Judge was still determined to carry out his plans for this writer. Gardaí mounted an operation to prevent the attack taking place. But Judge soon had more blood on his hands.

In June 1996, Michael Brady, Marlo Hyland's murderous brother-in-law, was released from prison and went back to work as a labourer on building sites around Dublin. According to Brady's friends and work-mates, he had emerged from prison a changed man. He was described as a 'gentle giant' who worked hard and had given up alcohol for good. When Marlo learned of Brady's release, he decided to finally avenge his sister's murder. PJ Judge was happy to help out.

On the evening of Thursday 5 September, Brady returned to his apartment off Sarsfield Quay in the north inner-city, after playing a soccer match. Around 9.30 p.m., he pulled up at the electronic gates to the car park. As he was waiting for them to open, a motorbike pulled up alongside his car. The pillion passenger got off and ran over to the driver's door. The hit man fired four shots, hitting Brady in the head and chest. He died instantly and became the thirteenth gangland murder victim in two years.

The following morning's newspapers carried front page pictures of Brady's lifeless body behind the wheel of his car. His mouth was open and his head leaned back on the head rest. The powerful and shocking picture became an iconic image of Ireland's growing gangland culture.

Marlo was spotted with Judge and one of his trusted lieutenants in the Royal Oak bar in Finglas the next day. They were laughing and in a celebratory mood. Hyland and Judge were overheard congratulating the lieutenant on a 'job well done'. Hyland, Judge and a number of other associates were subsequently arrested and questioned about the murder, but there was no evidence to link them with the crime and it remained officially unsolved.

In the months that followed, Judge became increasingly paranoid and dangerous. The Gardaí were making major inroads into his operation and the continued publicity about Jock Corbally's murder was turning him into a pariah. One of the victims of the crackdown was Marlo Hyland. Cops seized a large shipment of hash for which Hyland still owed Judge £130,000. This put Marlo in a difficult situation. He knew how dangerous and volatile Judge could be, especially when he was owed money by his closest associates.

At the same time the Provos, who had a strong presence in Finglas and Cabra, also began making enquiries into the Corbally murder. The dead man and his family were well liked in the area and there was a lot of sympathy for Jock's heart-broken mother, Maureen Corbally, a gentle, God-fearing woman. But the Provos, who controlled the Concerned Parents movement, were secretly being paid off by Judge and Hyland. After an initial run-in with the terrorists in the early 1990s, the two hoods had done a deal and were left untouched, even when a major campaign was launched by the CPAD in Finglas and Cabra that year.

The Psycho, however, was becoming a liability. Garda attention on the area was disrupting the IRA's criminal rackets. Investigations by this writer were also beginning to get at the truth of their duplicitous relationship. Garda intelligence sources, including well-placed informants in the Sinn Féin/IRA camp, revealed that a number of prominent republicans met with Marlo Hyland to discuss the situation. They suggested that he get rid of the Psycho and take over the operation. They were pushing an open door. Hyland and some of his most trusted associates had come to the same conclusion. Judge's days as a feared crime lord were numbered.

On the evening of 7 December 1996, Judge went for drinks at the Royal Oak pub in Finglas. He was with Ellen Hyland and was joined by Marlo and another associate. They were the only people who knew where the gangster was going to be that night. As Judge was preparing to leave, Marlo slipped away to make a call from the pub's coin box. He didn't use his mobile phone because it could be traced. Judge and Ellen Hyland left at 12.30 a.m. and got into his car. As Judge started the engine, a lone figure appeared from the shadows and fired two shots, hitting the Psycho in the back of the head. He slumped over the driver's seat, dead. Marlo ran from the pub to check that his sister was safe. Although deeply shocked, she had escaped injury.

Very few mourned the death of PJ Judge but his murder attracted considerable attention. Marlo and many of his associates were conspicuous by their absence from their boss's funeral. Sinn Féin and the IRA were happy to be the chief suspects. The 'patriotic' republicans had rid society of another parasite. But they had also installed a more amenable Godfather to take his place.

Three days after Judge's funeral, Mark Dwyer suffered a chillingly similar fate to Jock Corbally. The Psycho's sidekick was horrifically tortured for hours by drug-dealer Joe 'Cotton Eye' Delaney and then shot in the head. The 51-year-old Delaney was a business partner of both Judge and Dwyer. A few months earlier a large consignment of ecstasy which Delaney had paid for in Holland was 'stolen' when it arrived in Dublin. The drug-dealer was a dangerously unhinged individual whose obsessive, paranoid behaviour was exacerbated through constant cocaine abuse. He began to suspect that Mark Dwyer had been responsible for the rip-off. At the time, PJ Judge had already confided in Delaney that he was planning to kill Dwyer, because he suspected him of talking to the media about the Jock Corbally incident.

In the early hours of Saturday 14 December, Delaney's son Scott, a close friend of Dwyer's, and a number of other hoods abducted Mark and brought him to the drug-dealer's home near Naas, County Kildare. Over the next three hours, Cotton Eye tortured and beat Dwyer in a bid to force him to reveal where the stolen drugs were hidden. Eyewitnesses later described a horrific scene, worthy of a Quentin Tarantino movie. Delaney used a jemmy nail bar, an iron bar, a pick-axe handle and a number of knives on his victim. Dwyer was repeatedly stabbed in the arms and a shotgun was pressed so hard into his chest that the track of the barrels could be clearly seen on his skin. Joe Delaney put on a CD by M People and turned up the volume to drown out Dwyer's screams of pain. When the torture session was over, Delaney was none the wiser about what had happened to his precious drugs, but he decided to finish Dwyer off anyway.

Delaney's men took the bloodied bundle that was Mark Dwyer out of the house and dumped him into the boot of a car. They drove to

Scribblestown Lane, which would become a popular place for gangland executions and a dumping ground for bodies. Dwyer was thrown on to his knees and sat there hunched over, still tied and bound. A sawn-off shotgun was placed against the back of his skull and a single shot ended his agony. Cotton Eye presided over the execution. He then had his son Scott tied up, and left him lying semi-conscious beside his former friend. Delaney wanted it to look like vigilantes were responsible for the outrage. But after a major Garda investigation Joe Delaney was charged and stood trial. A number of witnesses, including his son Scott, testified in the case. In 1999, Cotton Eye was jailed for life. It was the first gangland murder ever to be successfully prosecuted before the courts.

In another sequel to the Jock Corbally story, an underworld enforcer called Anthony 'Chester' Beatty was shot dead in 1997 because he was suspected of taking part in the Dwyer murder. A criminal associate of Rossi Walsh, Martin Comerford, was charged with the murder. The day before his trial was due to start Comerford gave his friend, Paul McCarthy, a shotgun. He asked McCarthy to shoot him in the leg. At the last second, as McCarthy was about to pull the trigger, Comerford pulled the gun up to his chest and took the full blast from the gun. It was suicide by proxy. Despite the tragic circumstances of the case McCarthy was later convicted and jailed for life for the murder of his friend.

The final chapter of the Jock Corbally curse came when Declan Griffin also found himself at the business end of a hit man's gun. On 5 April 2003, he was shot dead in a pub in Inchicore by a notorious gangland assassin called Shay Wildes. Griffin had met the killer to discuss a hit he wanted to organize. The drug-dealer, who was wearing a bullet-proof vast, sat down at a table and handed Wildes an envelope containing €5,000 in cash. The hit man put the money in his pocket and then shot Griffin in the head. Wildes had received a better offer – to whack his client. Fear and intimidation later ensured that the hit man was acquitted of the execution because witnesses were too scared to testify.

By the end of the 1990s, the new generation of criminals was entering an underworld that had been in existence for thirty years. Organized crime had become an integral component of contemporary Irish life. In the process life had become a lot cheaper. The public were no longer easily shocked by the activities of serious criminals. At the same time Ireland's economy was on the up and was about to give birth to the Celtic Tiger. With it came a boom in the drug trade.

In Gangland the departure of Godfathers like Judge and Gilligan had left a very large vacuum that had to be filled. With vast profits to be made, the void was quickly filled by gangs of volatile young men who were emerging from the sprawling working-class estates in cities around the country. The thugs created an atmosphere of intimidation and fear as they used their neighbourhoods as hubs for organizing business. If anyone tried to stand up to them or was suspected of calling the police, their homes were burned down. The corrosive influence of the hoods on communities extended to the younger kids who were drawn in by what they perceived as the glamorous gangster lifestyle.

The most notorious example of the new breed of thugs to emerge was two close friends, Shane Coates and Stephen Sugg from Blanchardstown, West Dublin. Together they became one of the most feared and violent partnerships in gangland – better known as the Westies. Coates' reputation for extreme violence was so powerful that he was dubbed the 'New Psycho' in acknowledgement of his status as PJ Judge's replacement.

Assistant Commissioner Tony Quilter, the former head of the Garda National Drug Unit, explained their arrival on the scene. 'Post the Gilligan gang there was a flight of the more experienced drug-traffickers to Europe. That was where they could prosper; that was where they had the contacts and where they needed to be in terms of organizing distribution, logistics and finance,' he said. 'It left a vacuum here in Ireland and into that vacuum came other smaller groups, keen to make a name for themselves but ruthless in their approach. These gangs were typified by the Westies. They were in-your-face criminals who had scant regard for law and order, who perpetrated misery and violence throughout their community.'

Coates and Sugg, who were both born in the early 1970s, had been best friends since their early teens. They began their careers as joyriders and worked their way up to more serious crimes. From the beginning former neighbours, criminal associates and police recall how the pair had a natural predisposition to violence. Even as teenagers they had fearsome reputations when they got involved in a number of feuds in which guns were used. In 1990 Coates was shot in the stomach and seriously injured. As a result of the attack he was forced to wear a colostomy bag.

One officer who knew the youthful terrors recalled: 'You could see then that they were both very close and Sugg was greatly influenced by Coates. They had very little fear of anyone and they were very violent.' Coates and Sugg both notched up extensive criminal records for car theft, robbery and violence, and served a number of jail sentences. Coates was the dominant partner in the criminal enterprise. 'Coates led Sugg around by the nose. Without Coates, Sugg was nothing,' recalled a former associate.

In the same month that Veronica Guerin was murdered, they were both sentenced to five and a half years each for attempted robbery, possession of firearms, ammunition and car theft. In January 1997, a judge reviewed the sentences and decided to give the aspiring mobsters a chance to mend their ways, by suspending the final three years. However, as a strict condition of their release, the court ordered the pair to enter a bond not to associate with each other on the outside. It was a clear recognition that together they were a toxic partnership. Probation reports handed in to the court suggested that both men stood a better chance of going straight if they were separated. But the dangerous duo had no intention of either quitting crime or breaking up. The following July their friendship cost them their liberty when their sentences were re-activated, after police produced evidence that they had broken the court order. In December 1998 the court lifted the ban on their association and the Westies were free men again.

From the time of their first release from prison, Coates and Sugg began establishing their drug empire. The deadly duo used the same two devices as PJ Judge to establish their business – extreme violence and fear. The Westies established contacts with heroin suppliers in Birmingham and used brutal force to take control of the drug scene. Dealers and pushers who were not working for them were severely beaten and threatened with death if they didn't become employees. Addicts were warned that if they didn't deal with the Westies then they would be dealing with no one. One addict later recalled: 'If you wanted gear [heroin] then you got it from them. If you dealt with anyone else or pushed gear for another dealer, then you were looking at a stint in

intensive care.' Several heroin-dealers either moved out of Blanchardstown or began working for the Westies.

Coates and Sugg assembled a large gang of young criminals and
addicts to run their drug-dealing operation on the streets. Some worked
at cutting up the heroin, breaking it down and bagging it into street
deals, while others acted as couriers and sellers. Sellers in turn sold
batches of deals on to street-pushers. The gang also did business with
other young drug gangs across Dublin. Gangs in the area who were
involved in the distribution of cannabis or ecstasy were forced to pay a
'tax' to the Westies if they wanted to continue walking, breathing and
dealing. One gang member recalled: 'They're mental. They beat you
and they'd kill you. They've no fear of anybody. They think they're
bullet-proof.' By the end of the decade, the Westies had amassed a fortune and had an estimated yearly turnover of over £1 million. The
operation was well organized, well equipped and very efficient.

The Westies copper-fastened their reputations when heroin-dealer
Pascal Boland decided to set up his own operation on their patch. A former associate of PJ Judge, the 43-year-old father-of-one had been mixed
up in the trade for many years and had been jailed for seven years in the
1980s for dealing heroin. When he received an initial warning from the
gangsters, the veteran laughed at them: 'You're fuckin' nobodies, now
fuck off with yerselves.'

On the evening of 27 January 1999, Sugg and Coates were waiting for
Boland when he arrived at his home at Ashcroft Court in Mulhuddart.
Coates confronted Boland and repeated his earlier warnings. When
Boland laughed in his face, Coates pulled out a gun and shot him seven
times. Coates then ran to a stolen getaway car driven by Sugg.

In October 1999 Detective Inspector Todd O'Loughlin was one of
the senior officers attached to a special team drawn from the Western
Garda division to investigate the Westies.

'Basically they were joyriders, tearaways and small-time criminals
prior to the demise of the Gilligan gang. But they saw the opportunity
of filling the vacuum and creating an empire for themselves in West
Dublin,' he revealed. 'I have no doubt that they wanted to enslave the
community out there in West Dublin. They realized that we had taken
down the Gilligan group from within and they ensured, by acts of gro-
tesque violence, that this was not going to happen to them.'

O'Loughlin's squad compiled a list of 40 serious attacks the Westies had carried out in just over a year. The gang had used guns, baseball bats, knives, broken bottles, batons, iron bars, jump leads and vice grips on their victims. A drug-addict and mother who owed them money had lighted cigarettes held to her breast, and another addict was thrown off one of the tower-blocks in Ballymun. But there had been many more incidents that the police didn't know about. Victims were approached and asked if they wished to press charges. No one was prepared to make a complaint. The Westies had successfully insulated their operation with a wall of silence.

O'Loughlin commented: 'They used different methods of torture. I recall instances where they used jump leads to electrocute people. They used vice grips on people's fingers and genitalia. They used baseball bats to beat people and of course they began shooting and murdering rivals and associates that they didn't trust. One guy was beaten with iron bars first and then he was held down and his face was sliced up and it took over sixty stitches and several blood transfusions to put him together again.'

The Westies moved to live in Spain in the summer of 2003 because they were getting too much heat from the Gardaí. At the same time their former associates, brothers Mark and Andrew Glennon, moved in to take over their patch when they murdered Sugg's younger brother, Bernard 'Verb' Sugg, in August 2003. The Westies were planning to return to Dublin to settle the score, but they never got the chance. Their reign of terror came to an abrupt end when they were lured to a warehouse in Alicante in January 2004. The Westies' fatal mistake was that they thought they could throw their weight around in Alicante like they had done in Blanchardstown. As they walked into the warehouse, two other Irish criminals shot them dead and then buried their bodies under the concrete floor. Sugg's and Coates' remains were eventually found in the summer of 2006 after an informant told the police about the hit.

By the time the Westies were exhumed, the mindless, brutal violence they were synonymous with had become the norm throughout Gangland. The new millennium would be an era of unprecedented violence.

PART FOUR

The Noughties

22.   Gang Wars

In the history of organized crime in Ireland, the first decade of the new millennium will be remembered as an era of unprecedented mayhem, bloodshed and murder. Since 2000 narcotics have been at the heart of all organized criminal activity in Ireland. At the height of the economic boom, the Irish drug trade was estimated to be worth in the region of €1 billion. It led to a proliferation of armed mobs competing for a slice of the action – and a dramatic increase in violence. A virulent species of ruthless, gun-toting, juvenile thugs emerged, for whom life became as cheap as the price of a heroin fix. The volatile mobsters showed that there were no longer any boundaries beyond which they would not go, particularly in Dublin and Limerick.

There was no official declaration that hostilities had begun, but Gangland quickly descended into a state of all-out war. Murder was now the only option for resolving 'business' problems in the corporate world of the drug-trafficker. In 1993 there were three gang-related executions in Ireland. Ten years later, in 2003, that figure had risen to 20. Hit men improved their accuracy, going on trips to Eastern Europe and the USA to train in the use of firearms. At home, thugs as young as 18 and 19 equipped themselves with the most sophisticated hardware available – the Glock-automatic being the preferred weapon of choice.

The most disturbing aspect of the new underworld was that the cocaine-crazed hoodlums no longer seemed to care who they killed. So far this century the death toll has reached almost 200. The list of victims included several innocent people who were in the wrong place at the wrong time or had stood up to the hoods. The callous murders of people like Roy Collins, Shane Geoghegan, Joseph Rafferty, Donna Cleary and Anthony Campbell illustrated the depths to which criminals, bereft of humanity, were prepared to sink. Hundreds of other people – both innocent and not so innocent – were also injured and maimed in the madness.

The first decade of the century was marked by a string of blood feuds in Dublin and Limerick which turned several thugs into household names. Martin 'Marlo' Hyland, Eamon 'the Don' Dunne, Wayne Dundon, Freddie Thompson and Brian Rattigan became synonymous with the barbarism. At any one time, Gardaí had a list of at least forty gangsters who were classified as potential targets of the warring sides.

Gangland's new generation even reintroduced the bomb to Irish streets, in a bid to wipe out their opposition. In the new millennium the services of the Irish Army Bomb Squad have been more in demand than at the height of the Troubles. The savagery earned Ireland the dubious reputation of being one of the most violent societies in Western Europe. In 2006 there were more gangland murders in Dublin than there were in London, a city with a population thirteen times larger.

The wild excesses of the Celtic Tiger generation fed the crisis. As salaries soared, lifestyles changed and bad habits were acquired. If heroin was synonymous with the doom and gloom of the 1980s, cocaine was the poison of choice for the good times of the Noughties. By the middle of the decade, more Irish people per capita were snorting the Colombian marching-powder than anywhere else in Europe. In the process the profits from drug-trafficking rocketed. With so much money at stake, greed turned young hoods into merciless monsters. The level of violence became the barometer to gauge the amount of drug activity on the streets.

But Gangland's expanding population could no longer use the excuse that social deprivation and a lack of opportunities had caused their involvement in crime. Unlike the Cahills and the Dunnes, the vast majority of the new brat pack did not grow up hungry. In the early years of the new decade there was practically full employment, with good wages on offer even for the unskilled. Crime was a career choice. Inner-city community activist Eddie Naughton knew the kids who became mobsters in the Noughties. 'What happened was that there was a generation coming up who knew there was phenomenal money in drug-dealing. These kids weren't interested in work because there were easier ways of making money,' he revealed.

Retired English doctor and psychiatrist Dr Tony Daniels, who worked with inmates in the UK prison system, has argued that liberal social agendas in the West have contributed greatly to the creation of a criminal underclass. The liberal philosophy of loving the criminal, not the crime has given young thugs an excuse for their behaviour – it's all society's fault. Daniels has little time for politically correct explanations about why young men become involved in serious crime: 'The idea that criminals lack self-esteem is preposterous. The problem is not that they lack self-esteem, the problem is that they have far too much of it. They haven't been humiliated nearly enough and haven't been told how stupid they are. People fight turf wars and by doing so they become king of the castle and they feel big and important and actually, you can see it in their swagger.'

The violent Westies in Blanchardstown, West Dublin were the pathfinders, epitomizing the evolving gang culture. They provided the first clear indication of the changing psyche of the average Irish criminal. In an interview for the RTÉ TV series, *Bad Fellas*, Assistant Commissioner John O'Mahoney commented: 'I would describe the modern-day criminal as unpredictable and paranoid; he is totally protective of his turf and he will go to any lengths to protect his business.'

Retired Detective Inspector Todd O'Loughlin had extensive experience of the life expectancy of a successful Godfather. 'The reality is that none of these gangs last any longer than three to four years before the leaders are murdered and someone else takes over. PJ Judge was murdered and replaced by Marlo Hyland. He in turn was disposed of by Eamon Dunne. Now he too is dead. It is a tragically predictable cycle,' he said.

'People get involved in organized crime because there is big money to be made. Some people get in at the small end and suddenly it grows and they find themselves high up in the pyramid. These drug pyramids are effectively pyramids of death. They find that they are facing the possibility of being murdered because they have lost a drug shipment or haven't paid for one or are under suspicion that they are talking to somebody,' O'Loughlin continued. 'Because CAB has been so effective, money is now being stashed in attics, in woods and other places. And inevitably money goes missing and this is a death sentence for the individual who has control of that money. This is one of the main reasons for most of the gangland murders I investigated.'

John McGroarty, former chief of the Drug Squad, agreed: 'In modern times drugs underlie so much of the murder and mayhem that it is hard to find a [gangland] murder that isn't attributable to drugs and internecine gang rivalries. They fall out, double-cross one another and steal each other's shipments of drugs. The problem for a gang leader is to stay alive and as soon as he perceives somebody as being a threat to his operation or his life, well then something very definite and permanent is going to be done about it.'

Dr Liz Campbell of Aberdeen University studied Ireland's new culture of gangland violence. Her paper, 'Responding to Gun Crime in Ireland', was published in the *British Journal of Criminology* in 2010. Dr Campbell stated: 'Proportionately speaking Ireland has five times as many gun killings than in comparable countries like England, Scotland and Wales and there are legitimate concerns, particularly in relation to Limerick.' In 2008, for example, she found that 38.2 per cent of murders and manslaughters committed in the Republic involved firearms; in the same year, gun killings in England and Wales accounted for just 6.8 per cent of the total. The respected academic argued, however, that tougher laws and harsher sentences were not a solution – and represented 'an unduly narrow perspective'. Dr Campbell suggested that tough sanctions clearly didn't deter the killers. Education and more police on the streets of urban black-spots was one of the solutions she offered. She commented: 'It [gangland crime] is an intersection of urban deprivation, the drugs trade and also an expression of masculinity on the part of the individuals involved. This is certainly a male crime.'

In 1999, there were ten gangland murders in Ireland, which was the highest number yet recorded since the emergence of organized crime. By the end of 2010 the average annual death toll had doubled to 20 as more and more criminals expressed their masculinity – and set a trend which has plagued the streets of Irish cities and towns ever since.

On Sunday 9 January 2000, a couple strolling on the banks of the Grand Canal near Aylmer Bridge at Kearneystown in County Kildare made a gruesome discovery. The walkers were first drawn to a human hand, pointing up from the dark, freezing water. On closer examination they realized that there was a naked body of a man lying face-up in the still canal. With chilling symbolism, the body's right arm had a tattoo of the Grim Reaper that had been partially eaten away by animals. It seemed like the corpse of the murdered young man had beckoned from his watery grave. When firemen pulled the body from the water they discovered a gaping gunshot wound to the right cheek. The area was immediately sealed off by Gardaí and Crime Scene Investigators were brought in.

The following morning a Garda diver, who was searching for a murder weapon in the canal, located the fully clothed body of a second man. He was lying face-down, in just over a metre of water, a short distance from where the first body had been found. His face had been blown off. He also had a second gunshot wound to the chest.

Reports of the gruesome crime dominated news coverage in Ireland and also featured internationally. Only once in gangland history had there been a double execution before 2000 – when drug-dealer Eddie McCabe and his innocent companion, Catherine Brennan, were ambushed in Tallaght, West Dublin in 1995 (see Chapter 18). But there would be many more in the following years. The double murder served to symbolize Gangland's vision of the future.

The naked body was that of 19-year-old Patrick 'Whacker' Murray, a small-time hash-dealer from Ballyfermot, who was last seen alive on 29 December. The other murder victim was 21-year-old Darren Carey from Kilmainham, who was involved in the heroin trade in West Dublin. He was last seen on 30 December. His injuries were so horrific that he had to be positively identified by his moustache, hair and eyebrows.

State Pathologist Professor Marie Cassidy found that both men had been executed with a shotgun blast to the head. The blast had fractured Patrick Murray's right cheekbone. Shotgun pellets had sliced through the brain tissue and become embedded on the inside of the skull. The large amount of soot around the entry wound indicated that the gun was held close to his head when fired. Death had been instantaneous. The body was then dumped in the cold water, helping to preserve it. There were no other injuries on the body to indicate that Murray had been beaten or restrained before his murder. Nor did he have any defensive injuries.

Darren Carey had also been shot, twice at close range – in the chest and head – with a shotgun. Prof. Cassidy felt that Carey had first been shot in the head, with the blast aimed through the bridge of the nose. A large exit wound shattered the base of the skull. The second shot had been aimed at the left side of the chest. Forensic experts found traces of blood and bone tissue on the opposite bank to where the body was found. DNA analysis later confirmed that the tissue belonged to Carey. It confirmed that he had been murdered on the canal bank, while Murray was killed somewhere else.

The investigation of the Grand Canal murders was the largest underworld manhunt since the murder of journalist Veronica Guerin, less than four years earlier. The level of public revulsion and shock at the crimes ensured that it got top priority. The young desperados had crossed the Rubicon and had set a chilling precedent.

The officer in charge of the investigation was Assistant Commissioner Tony Hickey. All enquiries led back to the heroin trade, lifting the lid on the sordid underbelly of drug rackets in twenty-first-century Ireland. It was a world filled with desolate young addicts who had to endure constant violence and terror at the hands of the dealers who enslaved them. The finger of suspicion for the outrage fell on Mark Desmond, a brutal 24-year-old thug from Ballyfermot. A member of the M50 gang, Desmond got the nickname 'the Guinea Pig' after he volunteered to undertake clinical drug tests for money. It was the only time he ever attempted to earn an honest crust. After the double murders of Carey and Murray the media gave him a new nickname – 'the Canal Butcher'.

Born in 1975, Mark Desmond had been involved in violent crime since his early teens. He was every bit as sinister and violent as the Westies. Desmond, along with heroin-dealers Derek 'Dee Dee' O'Driscoll and Seanie Comerford, had been one of the masterminds behind the notorious 1995 Gallanstown riots. Desmond sold heroin for O'Driscoll and also acted as the M50 gang's enforcer, dispensing pain and terror. As part of PJ Judge's network in Finglas, Desmond in particular showed that he was just as dangerous as the Psycho. When he was 16, Mark threatened other drug-pushers with a shotgun and stole their 'gear'. He was also responsible for a string of shootings and stabbings. After Judge's murder, Desmond and his pals were among those who swooped to fill the vacuum it created.

The M50 mob built up an extensive heroin-dealing operation. They also supplied a growing demand in provincial towns in the Midlands. Since the late 1990s, heroin abuse had spread and was no longer confined to the cities. Athlone, County Westmeath was one of the first towns to be hit by the plague.

The Canal Butcher inherited his predilection for violence from his father, 'Dinny Boy' Desmond, who was a heavy for hire and had been involved in protection rackets since the 1960s. Dinny Boy sorted all arguments, even petty disputes, with his fists. The drunken bully terrorized his wife and children and they suffered the brunt of his fists when he was drunk or just in a bad mood. Despite the beatings, Mark Desmond idolized his father; his other role model was Martin Cahill, a close friend of Desmond's father. The Guinea Pig aspired to become Gangland's new General.

Desmond stood out from other up-and-coming young hoods. He had a fascination for guns and enjoyed inflicting pain, including on members of his own family. As a child he was a talented boxer, with a promising career in the sport until he dropped out. Instead he used his 'talents', and his father's reputation, to push his weight around and beat up anyone who annoyed him. When he left school at the age of 13, Mark Desmond could barely read and write. During the Garda investigation into the Grand Canal murders, Desmond's brother summed up Mark's personality: 'I have nothing to do with my brother; he is a header, a loner, a fucking psycho,' he told cops. Desmond's younger sister described Mark as a 'mad bastard' with a violent temper. She explained how once, when he was in a 'bad mood', he had smashed up the home of their mother, Elizabeth. His girlfriend, with whom he had a son in 1999, also told police about the horrendous physical and verbal abuse she had suffered from her lover. On one occasion he put a shotgun to her head and threatened to kill her.

The Guinea Pig grew up with utter contempt for the police and let them know it at every possible opportunity. He regularly threatened to kill officers who crossed him and often followed individual Gardaí to their homes, in an attempt to intimidate them. One detective who knew him well recalled: 'From the time he was a kid he was showing seriously violent tendencies. He really was a very nasty character who bullied and terrorized his neighbourhood. Everyone was afraid of him. We knew of several incidents in which he had beaten or sliced people up over petty disputes. He had shot at people; he tried to burn their houses. Desmond preyed on young drug addicts, who he used as slaves in his heroin business. They lived in constant terror of the man which is why it was impossible for us to get anyone to give evidence against him in court.

He was psychotic and he left us in no doubt that he could easily shoot one of us.'

If he was questioned about a crime Desmond would do everything to distract – and frequently repulse – officers. One detective recalled his typical behaviour: 'He would be totally unpredictable, a real bastard to deal with, just like Martin Cahill. Desmond would throw himself on the ground and begin screaming and taking off his clothes. He would pick his nose and then eat it in front of you. He would offer to share it with his interrogators in the hope that someone might get sick. He would fart and belch and spit. Then he progressed to rubbing his own shit across his face. He was a complete animal.'

The Guinea Pig had a natural talent for the savage new methods being used to run the drug trade. He controlled much of the heroin being sold on a patch that included Lower Ballyfermot and St Michael's Estate in Inchicore. St Michael's Estate was a Corporation flat complex that had become rundown and neglected. It was a popular centre for the wholesale dealing of heroin, making life utterly miserable for the residents who were trying to give their kids a decent upbringing. Heroin addicts from all over Dublin descended on the complex every day to buy their 'gear'. One young drug addict who worked for Desmond told police that he was collecting up to €2,500 a day for his boss.

Desmond waged a campaign of terror on his patch. He controlled a large group of hopeless drug addicts who were totally dependent on him for their daily fix. Many of them were as young as 15 and they became his glorified slaves. A number of them, both male and female, would later claim to Gardaí that, in addition to horrific beatings from Desmond, they had been sexually assaulted and raped. The girlfriend of one of Desmond's dealers described how the Guinea Pig seemed to get a 'rush' whenever he witnessed her being beaten by her boyfriend. If anyone stepped out of line they were severely beaten, stabbed or shot. The same treatment was meted out to anyone with the temerity to encroach on his patch. In a two-year period leading up to the murders of Murray and Carey, Desmond had been responsible for an astonishing catalogue of violent incidents.

The one-man crime wave shot and seriously injured at least five people who had crossed him. Drug-pusher Mark McLoughlin incurred the wrath of the Guinea Pig when he started selling 'gear' on Desmond's turf. In January 1995 McLoughlin was abducted and taken into the Dublin Mountains. Desmond stripped him naked and tied him to a tree. Then he whipped McLoughlin with copper wire, before leaving him naked and injured on a mountain road in the freezing night air. McLoughlin survived the incident and made a complaint to police. Desmond was charged with abduction and assault but the charges were dropped when the victim was forced to flee the country. In another incident Desmond smashed a broken bottle into the face of a teenager who'd ripped him off for about €2,000. The boy's father gave Desmond a beating. In retaliation, the Guinea Pig poured petrol over a horse owned by the man and set the animal ablaze.

Despite several attempts to bring him before the courts, Desmond's campaign of terror ensured that witnesses and victims were too afraid to press charges against him. He was also very hard to catch in the act of handling drugs or guns. He was paranoid about informants and he beat and tortured anyone whom he so much as suspected of 'ratting'. Like his hero the General, he was also obsessive about not leaving finger-prints or other forensic evidence on his drugs or guns. Desmond also regularly covered his face.

The event which ultimately led to the Grand Canal murders took place on 3 December 1999. Patrick Murray and another Ballyfermot youth, 18-year-old Gary Kelly, were arrested in Dublin Airport carrying a kilo of heroin between them, worth over €200,000. The drug mules were bringing the 'gear' back from Amsterdam for Desmond when customs officers pulled them over for a search. The Guinea Pig's gang had decided to buy their heroin directly from Holland. There they could buy it cheaper and cut out the middlemen, like Dee Dee O'Driscoll. One of Desmond's partners was Darren Carey, who, coincidentally, was living with the daughter of veteran heroin drug-trafficker Martin Kenny, the one-time associate of the Dunnes.

Desmond and Carey had flown to Holland to establish a contact for the drugs. Then they recruited the two hapless mules to do the run for them. Murray, who was not an addict, had been selling small amounts of hash for Desmond and Carey. But his stash had been stolen and Murray owed the monster almost €4,000. Desmond said he would halve the bill if the mule brought the heroin back from Amsterdam. Murray and Kelly made their fatal mistake when they decided to take a direct flight from Schipol Airport to Dublin. Desmond had instructed them to travel by boat, via the UK. When the bedraggled pair stepped off the plane, they were instantly tagged by Customs. The teenagers were searched and arrested by Gardaí. They were charged under the Misuse of Drugs Act.

When he heard the news of the bust, Desmond flew into a blood-curdling rage. The violent drug lord questioned his two couriers about what they had said while in police custody. The two mules admitted that the detectives had been particularly interested in Desmond, but they went to great lengths to convince him that they had given nothing away and were prepared to do time for the drugs. The Guinea Pig informed Murray that he now owed him €38,000 as punishment for losing the drug haul. Desmond also warned Kelly: 'Keep your mouth shut, do your time and you'll be okay. I don't take prisoners.'

In the days leading up to Christmas it appeared that Desmond had decided not to take any further action against his couriers. On Christmas night he illustrated his festive spirit at a family party, when he stabbed and seriously injured his cousin Jonathan Desmond – no charges were pressed.

A few days later, however, the Guinea Pig contacted Carey and told him to set up a meeting with Murray to 'sort out' the drug-bust issue. Desmond had got paranoid that Murray might agree to become a witness for the State. On 29 December the nervous drug mule went to meet Desmond. Murray was never seen alive again.

Investigators would later discover that Murray was murdered a short time after he went to meet Desmond. They were satisfied that the murder had taken place somewhere other than the canal and had probably been witnessed by Carey, who then panicked. There was phone evidence that Carey made several attempts to contact Desmond the following day. That evening Carey travelled with Desmond and another gang member, Noel 'Fat Boy' Foy, a nephew of the General's brother-in-law, to dump Murray's body. When the naked body was dumped in the canal, Carey was shot in the face and then the chest. Before he was murdered Murray had told Desmond that Carey had been ripping him off. The paranoid Canal Butcher was also fearful that Carey, who was upset by the murder, would go to the police.

The Garda investigation into the double murder unearthed a horror story that even shocked some of the most hardened detectives on the job. A number of witnesses, including Jonathan Desmond, gave Gardaí full statements about the double killing. Mark's cousin also showed detectives where Desmond had hidden two stolen shotguns and a rifle, under a garden shed in Ballyfermot. A member of the public had also found another shotgun hidden in a hedge in Clondalkin. Forensic tests later showed that the weapon, a Churchill double-barrelled shotgun, had been used in the murders. Forensic examination linked the Churchill and the other weapons and cartridges to those used in the murders. The guns had been stolen by drug addicts from Athlone, County Westmeath. The junkies took the weapons during burglaries throughout the Midlands and bartered them with Desmond for heroin.

In the meantime the Canal Butcher had fled to England, where he was being kept under surveillance by the police. In March 2000 he returned to Ireland and was arrested on an outstanding warrant for a three-month jail sentence for road traffic offences. While Desmond was inside, the Gardaí built their case against him.

Detectives found that with Desmond out of circulation people were more willing to talk. Over fifty people were arrested and hundreds of statements taken. Hundreds of phone records were analysed and traced and hours of surveillance work were logged. Informants were also quizzed. Investigators got so much information that they also opened files on a string of other crimes committed by Desmond, including rapes, sexual assaults, stabbings and shootings. However none of the cases went ahead, because the victims retracted their statements out of fear.

In June 2000 Desmond was charged with the double murders and possession of firearms with intent to endanger life, and was twice refused bail. But just four days before the trial was due to commence in November 2002, at the Central Criminal Court, the State's main witness, Rachel Stephens, pulled out. Desmond was infatuated with Stephens and had confessed to her about the murders. Stephens told Gardaí that she was too terrified to testify, even though she was in the Witness Protection Programme, saying: 'Mark Desmond could have me killed the way he killed those young fellows.' She did, however, agree to give evidence relating to the three outstanding firearms charges.

On 18 November, Desmond was formally arraigned on the firearms charges before the Central Criminal Court. He replied: 'Not guilty, stitched up by the police and State.' He then sacked his legal team and asked for an adjournment to find a new one. This was a familiar tactic used by John Gilligan and other villains in an attempt to frustrate the legal process. But Mr Justice Paul Carney refused Desmond's request and said it had all the 'hallmarks of somebody who is playing ducks and drakes' with the court. 'You have taken it upon yourself to sack your legal team one year after being returned for trial,' he told the accused.

Desmond decided to defend himself when the trial began the following morning, in front of Mr Justice Liam McKechnie. It was the biggest gangland trial since John Gilligan's conviction for drug-trafficking in 2001. There was heavy security, with armed members of the ERU guarding the courtroom to prevent Desmond escaping – or being shot. Measures were put in place to protect jurors and to prevent any attempts to intimidate them.

Desmond never wasted an opportunity to harass and intimidate the witnesses. Both Rachel Stephens and Jonathan Desmond gave evidence about the firearms. Jonathan Desmond, who was also in the Witness Protection Programme, was flanked by two ERU officers as he was cross-examined by his cousin Mark. The sense of tension in the courtroom was palpable throughout. During the first week, Dee Dee O'Driscoll and some of his henchmen stood at the back of the court every day. The Canal Butcher even menacingly announced to the witnesses that O'Driscoll was 'now in court overseeing the proceedings'.

On 11 December 2002, the jury unanimously found Desmond guilty on the firearms charges. As the verdict was read out, relatives of the victims clapped and cheered. There were shouts of 'you murderer' and 'I hope Darren comes back and haunts you'. Others, including the mothers of the two murdered men, openly wept. Desmond was sentenced to eight years. He taunted the relations of Murray and Carey and told them, 'I'll do it [his sentence] on me back.'

The Guinea Pig served his sentence on E1 wing in Portlaoise Prison, alongside some of Ireland's most feared criminal Godfathers. But even there he continued to be involved in violence. In October 2004, he was moved to the basement of the prison after he stabbed another inmate. Two months later his legal team appealed his conviction in the Court of Criminal Appeal. They argued that Desmond did not have access to proper legal representation because he had conducted his own defence.

As a result, they contended, Desmond had introduced issues that should not have been brought to the attention of the jury, including telling the jury that he was a suspect for the double murders. In the normal course of a trial, other crimes unconnected with those being prosecuted would be excluded from the jury. The court overturned the conviction, stating that the refusal by Mr Justice Carney to grant Desmond an adjournment in November 2002 had prevented him from obtaining a fair trial, in accordance with the law, and was contrary to the principles of natural and constitutional justice. Mark Desmond was freed from prison in January 2005.

Since his release the dangerous hoodlum has continued to be involved in organized crime and has survived at least one gun attack. The Canal Butcher also became embroiled in a number of gangland feuds and many of his associates were murdered. Based on the life expectancy of the average Godfather, Mark Desmond is a man living on borrowed time. At the time of writing Gardaí suspect him of involvement in the disappearance of James Kenny McDonagh, who was last seen alive on 27 October 2010.

Ireland's second double gangland murder was a shocking opening to the new millennium. But over ten years later, such mindless violence has become the norm in the underworld. While detectives were still investigating the Grand Canal murders, in Limerick the first shots were about to be fired in what would become the worst gang war in Irish criminal history.

23. A City under Siege

By 2000 in Limerick the cracks had begun to appear in the relationship between Eddie Ryan and the Keanes. The first sign of tension between the bloodied collaborators emerged when Ryan set up his own drug-distribution network. The situation then deteriorated as the Keanes' former enforcer was sucked into a long-running feud between the McCarthys, his brother John's in-laws, and the Keanes' closest allies, the Collopy family.

Tribal feuds were not new in Limerick. They were a constant feature of life in the working-class ghettos. Vendettas were passed down like a family heirloom from generation to generation, resulting in dozens of senseless murders. Two of the reasons that they seem to be peculiar to Limerick is a siege mentality and a predilection for extreme violence among some of the fighting clans, which, local historians have claimed, are a genetic inheritance. The bloodlines of some of the participants in the ongoing violence could be traced to members of the British Army and the notorious Black and Tans. The familial roots of others of the warring clans could also be linked to the most violent elements of the travelling community.

The spark which lit the fuse was an apparently innocuous squabble over damage to a car owned by Pa McCarthy, John Ryan's brother-in-law (no relation of the Pa McCarthy murdered in 1993). It would ultimately lead to a frenzy of unprecedented blood-letting and savagery that lasted for most of the decade. The violence was driven by blind, murderous hate, as two sadistic groups tried to wipe each other off the face of the earth. At the root of the blood lust was a manoeuvre to take control of the multi-million-Euro drug trade in the Mid-West region. The feuding gave a new meaning to the motto engraved on Limerick's coat of arms – 'AN ANCIENT CITY WELL STUDIED IN THE ART OF WAR'.

The McCarthys blamed one of Jack Collopy's children for the damage to the car. Recriminations eventually led to an incident in a pub when one of the McCarthys attacked and injured Jack Collopy's wife.

Later that night, John Ryan and one of his in-laws escalated the violence by assaulting Jack Collopy at his home. Ryan stabbed Collopy in the gut and beat him around the head, leaving him critically injured. Jack Collopy spent two weeks on a life-support machine and had to learn how to walk again.

In October 1997 Pa McCarthy was shot and injured as he drove a car past the Collopys' house in St Mary's Park. The bullets narrowly missed three young children sitting in the back seat. McCarthy later identified three members of the Collopy family, who were charged in relation to the incident. The three men were acquitted following a trial at Limerick Circuit Criminal Court in 1999.

At first Eddie Ryan and the Keanes had agreed to remain neutral in the row. But, as Ryan's drug business prospered, the mood changed and the Keanes began putting pressure on him for drug money he owed them. In another incident one of the Collopy children was involved in a brawl with John Ryan's daughter. Following that incident John and Eddie Ryan fired shots at the Collopys' home.

As Eddie Ryan got more involved in the feud, the Keanes formed up behind the Collopys. Rumours and gossip further fuelled the growing enmity between the two sides. By the summer of 2000 the bitterness had reached boiling point, as the children from both sides also became involved. In one incident a row broke out between John Ryan's daughter Samantha and Natalie Keane, Christy Keane's daughter. Both fathers agreed that the only way to resolve the dispute was for an arranged fight between the two girls. Natalie Keane gave up after 30 minutes of combat. The 19-year-old had had a piece of her ear bitten off and the victory went to the Ryans.

On 25 October there was another row, this time between John Ryan's daughter and a niece of Christy and Kieran Keane at St Mary's Secondary School in Corbally. The following day the girl's mother, Anne Keane, the wife of Christy's brother Anthony, was attacked by John Ryan's two daughters, Samantha and Debbie. Anne Keane was kicked, beaten and slashed in the face with a Stanley blade. The girls were subsequently charged with assault but the case never got to court.

Later that evening a number of shots were fired through the front window of John Ryan's home at the Lee Estate – in the heart of Keane territory. He called his brother Eddie, who armed himself with a sawn-off shotgun. The brothers then went to pay a visit to Christy Keane and his nephew, Owen Treacy. As the Ryans arrived, Owen Treacy fired several shots at them, hitting the car and shattering the rear window. Eddie Ryan returned fire as they sped away.

What had started as a relatively petty row had escalated into armed conflict. Eddie Ryan was determined to spill Keane blood. On Friday 10 November 2000, Christy Keane was waiting to collect his son from school. Eddie Ryan had decided it was the perfect ambush point and was lying in wait with a 9mm automatic pistol under his jacket. When Keane spotted Ryan walking towards him, Christy opened his window to talk to his former partner. But Ryan wasn't in a talking mood and pointed the gun at Keane's head. The weapon jammed as he squeezed the trigger. Ryan tried to shoot again but Keane drove off at speed down the pavement, sending children and parents scrambling out of the way.

There was no longer any chance of reconciliation. The war that would bring Limerick to the brink of anarchy had begun.

Later that evening Eddie Ryan fled Limerick to stay with his girl-friend in Northern Ireland. He returned the following Sunday afternoon for the funeral of his brother-in-law. It was a big mistake.

As a mark of respect Ryan decided not to wear his bullet-proof vest to the removal ceremony in St John's Cathedral. Afterwards he went to The Moose Bar with his son, Kieran. The feared gangster arrived just before 9 p.m. As Ryan ordered a round of drinks, Kieran Keane got a phone call, informing him that his target had been spotted in the pub.

At precisely 9.53 p.m. Kieran Keane and 19-year-old Philip Collopy walked into The Moose Bar, armed with two handguns. Keane shouted at Eddie Ryan: 'You bastard, come out ya bastard.' Keane and Collopy remained standing in the doorway as they fired 14 rounds at their former friend. Two innocent women who were sitting close by were seriously injured in the hail of indiscriminate bullets. The attack was over in seconds. As the gunmen ran to a getaway car, they fired seven more shots at the front of the pub. Kieran Keane was delighted with his night's work. He cheered in the back of the getaway car. 'Eddie is dead, Eddie Ryan is dead; he's gone.'

Eddie Ryan was hit eleven times: two rounds hit him in the right shoulder, seven in the back and one each in the hip and left arm. Some of the specially designed bullets which hit him were used by the German police to shoot out car tyres. He collapsed in his seat. A customer ran over and asked where he had been hit. 'Everywhere,' gasped the underworld hard man. He slid from his chair onto the floor and died.

Eddie Ryan's son Kieran had been lucky. He was in the toilet when the shooting started. If he'd been with his father, the hit men would have killed him too – and considered it a bonus.

The Ryan murder was described by a Garda spokesman as one of the most callous and indiscriminate gangland attacks ever in Limerick. But within a few years such outrageous incidents would be commonplace.

Kieran Keane, Philip Collopy and Owen Treacy were arrested for questioning about the attack three weeks later. The getaway driver, Paul Coffey, admitted his role in the plot and told the police what had happened that night. But the police could only put Keane and Collopy away if Coffey agreed to be a witness for the State. The Keanes ensured that the driver kept his mouth shut and Coffey was the only gang member convicted in relation to the Ryan murder.

The murder of Eddie Ryan sparked a major upsurge in violence. Over the next few months there were at least thirty petrol-bomb and gun attacks on John Ryan's house alone. And for each attack there was retaliation. There was also a series of shootings and stabbings. Then the warring sides graduated to bombing campaigns. In one incident a booby-trap device was found under the car of a gangster associated with the Ryans. Gardaí suspected that the INLA had made the device for the Keanes. It was discovered when it failed to explode and fell off the car. Gardaí could see that it was only a matter of time before there were more murders. The victims had lucky escapes in many of the attacks. In one incident in May 2001, Owen Treacy's father Philip, a baker, suffered serious burns when two petrol-bombs were thrown through the front window of his home in County Clare. Extra armed patrols were deployed to the main flash point in St Mary's Park. At the same time Gardaí arrested and charged several people in connection with the various strikes.

Three months later, Gardaí had a lucky break when Christy Keane got careless. He was stopped walking across a field with a coal sack on his shoulder. When searched there was hashish with a street value of €240,000 inside. In May 2002 Christy Keane was found guilty by a jury at Limerick Circuit Criminal Court and was jailed for ten years. His brother Kieran took over the reins of their drug empire and ensured that the feuding continued. But even darker forces were now lurking in the shadows.

The McCarthy/Dundons – Murder Inc. – had patiently waited like vultures for the right time to make their move. Their plan to secure domination of the Limerick drug trade was fairly straightforward. The malevolent mob intended wiping out all their opposition. There would be no room for compromise or negotiation. They had built up their own drug-dealing operation while the feuding families were distracted, and had forged extensive contacts in Manchester and London. They also bought drugs from the Keane/Collopys and even supplied them with firearms. It was all part of a campaign that would be one of the most extraordinary double-crosses in gangland history.

In secret the leader of the McCarthy/Dundons, Larry McCarthy Junior, had formed an alliance with Eddie Ryan's close associate, Sean 'Cowboy' Hanley. Ryan had gone into business with Hanley when he first made his break from the Keanes. Through Hanley, the McCarthy/Dundons also teamed up with former publican James 'Chaser' O'Brien, who was a major drug-trafficker. O'Brien's partner-in-crime was millionaire gangster Anthony Kelly from Kilrush, County Clare.

Evidence of the new partnership was exposed in March 2002, when Gardaí arrested 16-year-old Gerard Dundon. He'd just collected €500,000 worth of drugs from a Limerick grandmother who worked for O'Brien. The follow-up investigation resulted in the seizure of large amounts of cocaine, ecstasy, cannabis and heroin. A ledger Gardaí found showed that the gang had moved drugs worth over €1 million in the previous eight months. Dundon got a suspended sentence in recognition of his tender age.

With Christy Keane safely locked up, the McCarthy/Dundons began to flex their muscles. Around the same time that the Godfather was starting his jail sentence, members of Murder Inc. travelled to Florida and spent a week practising their marksmanship at a gun school. Then in November 2002 the Piranhas set the tone for their reign of terror – and showed that they would murder anyone who crossed them. Two of the gang's hit men, Gary Campion and James Martin Cahill, murdered night-club bouncer Brian Fitzgerald. Fitzgerald's 'crime' was that he had 'the cheek' to stand up to the sadistic mobsters when he stopped their dealers selling drugs in Doc's night-club. The bouncer made an official complaint to the Gardaí when Larry McCarthy Junior threatened his life. McCarthy had been charged with the offence – signing Fitzgerald's death warrant. A month later Murder Inc. members shot dead another innocent man, used-car dealer Sean Poland. He had sold a car to one of the gangsters and the McCarthy/Dundons decided they wanted the cash back. After shooting him, they ransacked his house and walked away with €1,000.

Despite intense heat from the police and a public outcry over the two murders, the McCarthy/Dundons were still getting ready for their offensive. They approached Kieran Keane and offered to abduct Eddie Ryan's sons for an agreed fee of €60,000. Keane liked the idea. The feud between his gang and the Ryans had been intensifying. He knew that Eddie's sons would not rest until they had avenged their father's murder. Keane reckoned that the €60,000 would be money well spent. But Kieran Keane had no way of knowing that he was walking into an elaborate trap. The McCarthy/Dundons and their partners had agreed a clandestine pact with the Ryans. By getting rid of the core of the Keane/Collopy gang, Murder Inc. and their partners could become one of the biggest criminal gangs in Ireland.

On the night of 23 January 2003, Eddie Junior and Kieran Ryan were supposedly abducted off the street and taken away in a van. Over the following six days, Limerick became a powder-keg as everyone expected the Ryans to turn up dead. Potential combatants openly wore bullet-proof vests and houses were either shot at or petrol-bombed. But while hundreds of police and troops searched for their bodies, the two thugs were hiding in Tipperary – waiting for the rest of the plan to be executed.

On 29 January Keane and his nephew Owen Treacy went to meet Dessie Dundon at a house on the outskirts of the city. They had been convinced that the gang were holding the Ryans there for them. Kieran Keane wanted to see his enemies die, or possibly to pull the trigger himself.

In the sitting-room of the house they met Dessie Dundon and Anthony 'Noddy' McCarthy, who sprung the trap. McCarthy suddenly produced a .38 revolver and ordered the two men to get down on the floor. The gang grabbed the €60,000 and Keane and Treacy were tied up. Their captors ordered them to arrange a meeting with Philip and Brian Collopy. The mob hoped to murder the four most important members of the opposition in one strike. But, even after being beaten and tortured, the two captives refused to give in to the demand.

The Murder Inc. killers decided to cut their losses – they could catch up with the others at a later date. Keane and Treacy were bundled into a van and taken to a country road outside Limerick. Keane was pushed onto the road and stabbed six times in the side of the head. The gangland killer was then executed with a gunshot in the back of the head. Owen Treacy was stabbed 17 times in the throat, neck, ear and chest. One of his attackers, David 'Frog Eyes' Stanners, stared into his victim's face and hissed: 'This is the last face you are going to see.' Treacy pretended to be dead and the gang left.

Although seriously injured, Treacy raised the alarm and was rushed to hospital. Leaving him alive would prove to be a catastrophic mistake for the mob. Treacy later identified his kidnappers and his uncle's killers. As a result Frog Eyes Stanners, Christopher 'Smokey' Costelloe, James McCarthy, Dessie Dundon, Noddy McCarthy and Keith Galvin were convicted and jailed for life.

The gangland schism led to a state of war between the two sides. It claimed the lives of twenty people over the next seven years and many more were maimed in the bloodshed. The feuding sides sent teenagers as young as 15 out with machine-guns to settle scores. At one stage the McCarthy/Dundons, who claimed responsibility for most of the bloodshed, paid €100,000 for an armour-plated jeep.

The Keane/Collopys spilled the first blood after the death of Kieran Keane. They had been patiently waiting for a chance to hit John Ryan and in July 2003 he dropped his guard. As he was helping a friend lay a patio a gunman shot him three times. Ryan died a short time later in hospital.

As the feud intensified, victims were horribly mutilated before being killed. One of them was 23-year-old Michael Campbell McNamara, a member of the Keane/Collopy gang. In October 2003 he was lured to his death by three members of the McCarthy/Dundon mob. McNamara was systematically tortured and forced to call Brian Collopy to lure him into a trap. But Collopy's instincts saved his life when he didn't turn up. When McNamara's body was found the next day, it was discovered that he had been stabbed at least ten times, in the back and chest. He was then blasted in the head with a shotgun. A second shot was fired into his pelvis and buttocks, causing horrific injuries.

Among the most sickening acts of terrorism committed by Murder Inc. were crimes against the people of Limerick. In November 2008 one of the gang's hit men shot dead Shane Geoghegan, a totally innocent man. Gardaí believed that the rugby player had been mistaken for a drug-dealer the Piranhas wanted to kill. That was followed with the cold-blooded murder of businessman Roy Collins on Holy Thursday, 2009. Roy was shot dead on the orders of Wayne Dundon. Dundon, who was in prison, had also ordered the botched hit the previous November. The gunman was an impressionable thug, 24-year-old James Dillon, who was arrested within an hour of the murder. Dillon was jailed for life in 2010 but was too terrified to name the people who'd sent him to commit the crime.

Roy's murder was another act of revenge against the Collins family, who had bravely stood up in court and testified against the evil mobster. In 2004 Roy's adopted brother, Ryan Lee, had refused Dundon's 14-year-old sister, Annabel, entry into the Collins family pub. The thug whom the travellers nicknamed 'the Ditch Rat' was infuriated, and made threats against the 18-year-old barman before leaving. He'd returned a short time later armed with a gun, and shot and seriously injured Ryan as he stood serving drinks behind the counter. Wayne Dundon was subsequently arrested and charged with making threats to kill Ryan Lee. Despite attempts to intimidate the family, Ryan and his father, Steve Collins, gave their evidence in court. Dundon was initially jailed for ten years, but the sentence was later reduced by the Court of Criminal Appeal to seven years. Dundon had vowed to get revenge. He'd ordered his associates to burn down the family's pub, and it later transpired that he'd sent instructions to pay a hit man to murder Steve Collins in November 2008. The businessman's name was found on a piece of paper, under the name of the drug-dealer Shane Geoghegan was mistaken for.

Dundon's move against Roy Collins was to remind everyone in Limerick that he has a long memory. Steve Collins and his family still receive 24-hour police protection, to prevent another attack.

The murder of Roy Collins was a watershed in the history of organized crime in Limerick. In an unprecedented public display, over 5,000 people joined the Collins family in a protest march through the city in May 2009. The ordinary decent citizens were sending a clear message to the mobs – we have had enough. As a direct result of the outrage the then Minister for Justice brought in tough anti-gang legislation in July 2009. The laws gave police the powers to plant surveillance equipment in the property and cars of targeted suspects. It also made it an offence to direct an organized crime gang or to be a member of one.

The local Gardaí had also been scoring major successes in their war against the gangs. Since the feud first broke out, over 500 individuals had been convicted for serious crimes connected to it, including murder, attempted murder, assaults and stabbings. The Limerick police consistently have the highest detection rate for gangland murders in Ireland. Other gang members were jailed for possession of drugs, guns and bombs. Between 2005 and 2010 there were almost 400 incidents in which firearms were discharged in the city. In the same period 220 people were convicted for firearms offences alone.

When Wayne Dundon was released from prison in 2010 he returned to a completely changed gangland environment. A specialist surveillance unit had been brought in from Dublin to harass and follow the gang members wherever they went. A new Armed Response Unit was also established in the city, to pile the pressure on the hoods.

By 2011 the tough response from the Gardaí was paying off. Most of the major players in both Murder Inc. and the Keane/Collopy factions were either serving long sentences or awaiting trial. The number of incidents where firearms were discharged had dwindled from 103 in 2007 to 19 in 2010. In 2011 that figure had fallen even further.

Gardaí in the city say that it would be premature to declare that the war is over. As long as some of the protagonists are alive they will ensure that the hatred is passed on to the younger generation. At the time of writing, however, serious cracks have been emerging in the once unbreakable alliance between the members of Murder Inc. Associates are before the courts, charged with threatening to murder each other. In the meantime, other criminal families have seized their opportunity to fill the vacuum.

Peace in Limerick will always be a fragile thing.

24. The Dapper Don

In the early hours of 25 May 2010, Spanish police swooped on one of the biggest organized crime syndicates in Europe. The target of the major international investigation had tentacles which spread across the world. At the same time as the Spanish made their move, law enforcement agencies in Ireland, the UK, Belgium and Brazil also carried out searches and made arrests as part of the carefully co-ordinated operation. Seven hundred police were involved in the swoops and 32 people were arrested. In Spain the authorities described it as the most extensive investigation they had ever conducted against a criminal consortium.

The syndicate controlled a large slice of the drug trade across Europe and in the process had accumulated awesome wealth. It had an estimated balance sheet of €1 billion from drug-trafficking, arms-dealing and money-laundering. The investigation had also uncovered evidence of a global property portfolio worth in excess of €800 million. Through a complex network of front companies, corrupt financiers, lawyers and brokers, the multi-national organization invested in real estate and businesses in Ireland, Spain, Belgium, Portugal, Dubai, South Africa, China, Antigua and Barbuda, Namibia, Brazil, the UK and Cyprus. In Brazil the group owned six leisure complexes and a string of residential properties worth €500 million, with another €150 million invested in Spain alone. The environmentally conscious mob also put their money into waste-disposal companies and renewable energies. They invested in food, cement and commodity markets. In Ireland they owned a dry-cleaner's and a ticket sales business. The money-laundering web used a network of 31 companies in different countries through which the dirty money was channelled. The group owned their own transport companies and a string of warehouses dotted across Europe, the UK and Ireland to store the drugs, which were usually disguised as domestic goods.

But this global criminal empire did not involve either the Colombian drug cartels or the Mafia. This was an exclusively Irish operation.

A Spanish government minister later dubbed the syndicate 'the Irish Mafia'.

The Godfather at the top of the complex pyramid was veteran gangster Christy Kinahan, aka 'the Dapper Don'. His principal partner was his long-time pal John Cunningham, 'the Colonel'. Fifty-three-year-old Kinahan and 59-year-old Cunningham had come a long way since they started off as petty thieves on the streets of Dublin. And unlike many of the Godfathers who had emerged in Ireland since the 1990s, the wily mobsters had avoided a hit man's bullet.

The life stories of the ageing gangsters mirrored that of organized crime in Ireland over the previous four decades. Kinahan and Cunningham were among the first generation of young hoods who established the Republic of Gangland's independence. They worked their way up the ladder from petty crime, fraud, armed robbery and kidnapping, to international drug-trafficking and gun-running. The magnificent villas where the veteran hoods were arrested near San Pedro, outside Marbella on the Costa del Sol, underlined how well they had done for themselves. Kinahan's home was valued at around €5 million. The two luxury residences were in stark contrast to the conditions the gangsters had grown up in – the Colonel in the working-class sprawl of Ballyfermot and Kinahan in the bleak Oliver Bond flat complex, in inner-city Dublin.

The swoops were the culmination of a two-year international investigation which had been prompted by the Garda National Drug Unit in 2008. With the apt codename 'Operation Shovel', it had succeeded in digging up the true extent of the syndicate's activities by following the money trail. From the Costa del Crime, Kinahan and Cunningham dealt in huge, multi-ton loads of cocaine, hash and heroin. Spanish police also revealed that they were investigating a number of gangland murders linked to the mob. In Ireland one man was arrested and several business premises were searched by officers from the GNDU and the Criminal Assets Bureau. In the UK the Serious Organised Crime Agency (SOCA) arrested 11 more suspects, while another 20 arrests took place in Spain. The Dapper Don's two sons, 32-year-old Daniel and 29-year-old Christy Junior, were also among those taken into custody. Daniel Kinahan was in charge of his father's drug business, while Christy Junior handled the money.

Kinahan was the overall Godfather, and brains, behind the entire operation. The multilingual underworld sophisticate dealt directly with the Mafias in Russia, Sicily and Israel, as well as with the main drug producers – the Moroccan, Turkish and Colombian cartels. In ten years it was estimated that Kinahan had accumulated a personal fortune of €100 million.

From his Mediterranean retreat, the Dapper Don also had a controlling influence on organized crime in Ireland. He was the top player in an exclusive and very secretive society of veteran villains. Kinahan and his faceless associates, all of whom are gangsters in their fifties, were – and still are – the overlords of Gangland. One member of the group, a convicted criminal, maintains a public image of non-involvement in the drug trade. His participation is a closely guarded secret, as he pulls the strings through his relatives. Another player in the exclusive cartel is a powerful and respected businessman who has been in the background of organized crime for the past four decades. Such is the power of these individuals that they make the life-and-death decisions which determine the fate of many Irish gang leaders. Through Kinahan, this hierarchy commands the respect and loyalty of several of the country's most ruthless young gangs. If they want someone dead, then the Dapper Don only has to give his protégés the nod.

In 2010 Kinahan was rated as being among the top five suppliers of hashish, cocaine, heroin and ecstasy to the UK market. He also featured in Europol's list of the top ten criminal Godfathers in Europe. With his old friend George 'the Penguin' Mitchell on the same list, the Irish were punching well above their weight in the international mob scene.

In the story of organized crime there are many remarkable characters who stand out from the rest of the gangland rabble – mostly for the level of violence and fear they are capable of inflicting. But Christy Kinahan was probably the most unusual of the lot. Born in inner-city Dublin in 1957, he was handsome, suave and well-spoken. He earned the nickname 'the Dapper Don' because of his expensive taste in designer clothes. His Dublin brogue was soon replaced by a cultured European accent. He was considered to be something of a gangland sophisticate who used various stretches in prison to obtain two university degrees. Kinahan also learned several languages, including Spanish,

Dutch, French and Arabic. Described as highly intelligent, he was a born entrepreneur who could just as easily have been a successful businessman in the legitimate world.

Kinahan started off his criminal career with a handful of convictions for burglary, receiving stolen goods and using forged cheques. As the Dunne family lost their grip on the heroin trade, he was one of the people who moved in to fill the vacuum. When John Cunningham was caught for the Jennifer Guinness kidnapping in April 1986, his future partner-in-crime was already making a name for himself in the drug trade. Kinahan was in business at the time with an Algerian trafficker called Rebah Serier. A strict Muslim, 30-year-old Serier was also becoming a major player on the international crime scene. Together they controlled one of the largest heroin distribution operations in Dublin.

But the partnership ran into trouble in September 1986 when the Drug Squad swooped, following a rare surveillance operation. They had been watching Kinahan's luxury apartment at Crescent House in Fairview, North Dublin, which was the central hub of his operation. The posh gangster had taken a step up in the world since he'd left his wife and two young sons for another woman. His boys were left to grow up in the much less salubrious surroundings of the Oliver Bond flats complex.

When officers burst into the apartment they caught Kinahan and Serier red-handed, with £117,000 worth (€300,000 today) of heroin. The officers who busted the Dapper Don included former members of the defunct Mockey Squad – Michael O'Sullivan, Jim McGowan and Noirin O'Sullivan. When they searched the apartment they found Linguaphone® tapes which Kinahan was using to learn Arabic and French. He also owned an impressive library of academic books. The two hoods were arrested and charged with drug offences.

In March 1987 Kinahan pleaded guilty and was jailed for six years. At his hearing it was claimed that he was a heroin addict. However, it has emerged that this was untrue and Kinahan was trying to win sympathy from the court. Serier was given four and a half years. He was described as a man of mystery and Gardaí were unable to uncover background information on his life before he reached Ireland. The Algerian's defence counsel alleged Kinahan had sucked Serier into the drug trade.

Many years later, a member of the Drug Squad confirmed that both men were much bigger players than the Gardaí had realized. In the 1980s there was little contact between European police forces in relation to ordinary crime. The officer admitted: 'We didn't realize at the time just how big Kinahan was in the drug trade. Our focus was here in Ireland and when we caught him it was a major success. But in the prevailing culture we didn't look beyond our borders to get a bigger picture. We weren't interested in what was going on outside as long as we got a conviction. Serier also became a very significant player in Europe later on.'

After his release from prison in 1991, Kinahan went back to crime. In June 1993 he was arrested in possession of £16,000 worth of travellers cheques which had been stolen in a bank robbery carried out by Thomas 'Bomber' Clarke. When he was questioned, Kinahan responded: 'Out in the garden beside the stone wall there was an old man who said nothing at all. He sat in the garden and said nothing at all.' When the puzzled cops asked him what he meant, Kinahan replied: 'Nothing at all.'

The Dapper Don later accused drug addict Raymond Sallinger of tipping off the police about the travellers cheques. After that Sallinger moved to London where he remained for several years. In January 2003, shortly after Sallinger moved back to Dublin, he was shot dead as he sat drinking in a pub in the Liberties. The prime suspects were members of a young crime gang from the north inner-city led by Gary Hutch, the Monk's nephew, who were close to Daniel Kinahan. The Dapper Don has a long memory.

While out on bail, Christy Kinahan fled to Holland and began building a new drugs business. The partnership between Kinahan and John Cunningham began shortly after the Colonel absconded to Holland from prison in September 1996. The men had built up a relationship when they were inside.

A month later, the Lucan Investigation Team shut down John Gilligan's drug-trafficking operation. Gilligan was arrested and charged with money-laundering offences by the British police and held on remand in Belmarsh Prison. On the day the diminutive thug was busted, he had just collected a case full of cash from the Colonel's brother, Michael Cunningham, at Heathrow Airport. Kinahan and John Cunningham took over where Gilligan left off.

In the meantime the Dapper Don had experienced more trouble with the law enforcement community. He was arrested by Dutch police while in possession of ecstasy, cocaine and firearms and was jailed for four years in Amsterdam's Bijlmerbajes Prison. Kinahan, however, served less than a year and was soon back in business with the Colonel. The pair also teamed up with Dutch drug-dealer and gun-runner Johannes 'Joopie' Altepost, who'd met Kinahan in prison. Shaven-headed Altepost had a reputation for serious violence and had extensive contacts with gun-dealing gangs in the former Yugoslavia. The new syndicate began supplying large quantities of drugs and firearms to gangs in Ireland and the UK. Kinahan had built up extensive contacts in the UK over the years and carried a British passport. The syndicate's business soon dwarfed Gilligan's operation.

In November 1997, the GNDU got an indication of the extent of the gang's activities when they seized over 300 kilos of hashish in a house in Tallaght, West Dublin. The drugs had been shipped into Ireland hidden in potted plants. The haul had a street value of £3 million (over €5.4 million). Five men were arrested and charged in connection with the seizure but were subsequently released over a legal technicality. The GNDU later discovered that Kinahan and Cunningham had supplied over a ton of cannabis in the previous month. The seizure coincided with the death of Kinahan's father. When Christy slipped back into the country for the funeral, he was arrested on foot of the outstanding arrest warrant from 1993. In March 1998, he pleaded guilty and was jailed for four years in Portlaoise Prison. With Kinahan behind bars, Cunningham took control of the business.

In the following three-year period it was conservatively estimated that Cunningham shipped drugs worth in excess of €150 million and an unknown quantity of arms and ammunition into Ireland. In the two years between 1998 and 2000, Amsterdam café owner Peter Lingg, one of Cunningham's 'managers', exchanged over €10 million worth of Irish and English currency into Dutch guilders at one Bureau de Change in the city. The money was payment for drug shipments. The syndicate was supplying gangs in Dublin, Limerick, Belfast, London, Manchester and Liverpool. Cunningham's old pals in the General's gang were among his customers. His friend Eamon Daly, who was released from prison in 1997, became one of Cunningham's biggest customers in Dublin. The syndicate was also supplying Martin 'the Viper' Foley and his then sidekick Clive Bolger, and Seamus 'Shavo' Hogan.

In December 1998 the Gardaí seized a huge consignment of cannabis and firearms which had been dispatched to Ireland by Cunningham. The drugs and guns were discovered concealed in eight pallets of pitta bread, transported to Ireland by truck. The load contained 780 kilos of cannabis; 15 lethal Intratec or 'Tec-9' 9mm automatic machine-pistols, capable of firing hundreds of rounds per minute; 10 9mm automatic pistols; silencers for each of the 'Tec-9s'; and spare magazines and ammunition. It was the largest cache of illegal weapons ever intercepted with a drug haul by the Irish police. Technical experts later found that all the weapons had been manufactured in Eastern Europe. The discovery prompted a major international investigation involving Irish and Dutch police. It was to have serious consequences for John Cunningham.

Westlodge Freight, the transport company used to collect the drugs and guns, was owned by Kieran Smyth, from Dundalk, County Louth. Even though he had no criminal record, Smyth was a central cog in a vast international smuggling operation, based along the border with Northern Ireland. Smyth provided a logistics service to criminal and republican gangs, smuggling drugs, tobacco, oil and guns. He also acted as a money-launderer for his various clients, using an illegal bank which masqueraded as a Bureau de Change at the Dromad border crossing in County Louth. A CAB investigation later discovered that Smyth personally made an estimated £12 million (€21 million) in less than two years, which he laundered through the illegal bank.

In an operation codenamed 'Plover', the GNDU tracked the pallets of pitta bread back to Peter Lingg in Amsterdam. In September 1999, the Amsterdam Serious Crime Squad launched an investigation into Lingg. The police quickly established that he was involved in a major conspiracy and he was placed under 24-hour surveillance. His phones were also being tapped. In early November the undercover squad tailed Lingg to a meeting in a car park with a mysterious Irishman. They photographed him and sent the pictures to Dublin. The unknown man was quickly identified as John Cunningham.

The Gardaí informed their Dutch colleagues and underlined the Colonel's importance. In Holland the undercover surveillance teams began watching Cunningham and bugged his phones. It was obvious that Cunningham was a very busy man, organizing deals by phone and in person. The operation continued for the next four months. The team discovered that the firearms came from Joopie Altepost's Eastern European contacts. The powder used in the manufacture of ecstasy tablets was bought from a gang in the south of Holland. Cunningham then brought the powder to a number of flats which were equipped with tablet-making machines. The tablets were vacuum-packed and placed in foil-lined boxes. Each tablet cost the Colonel about £1. When he sold one to his Irish and UK clients, he quadrupled his initial investment.

Cannabis and cocaine were also sourced from a number of gangs in Amsterdam. In a typical transaction Cunningham would collect cash from truck drivers coming from Ireland and England. He would then put together the various orders and arrange for their delivery to Ireland, hidden either in pallets of foodstuffs or in holdall bags which were handed to Kieran Smyth's most trusted drivers. Dutch military intelligence was called in to decipher Cunningham's code system. He used it for telephone numbers, delivery times, amounts of money and quantities of drugs.

The tap on Cunningham's phones produced top-grade intelligence which enabled the GNDU to identify most of his Irish associates, including Eamon Daly, Martin Foley and Clive Bolger. Cunningham's partner in Dublin was 30-year-old Chris Casserly from Coolock, North Dublin, who was also a close associate of Christy Kinahan. Between November 1999 and March 2000 the eavesdropping led to a string of successful seizures in the Republic, Northern Ireland, Belgium and France. The busts were carefully orchestrated so that the mob would not work out how they were being caught. Between the four jurisdictions, police seized a total of 156 kilos of amphetamines, over 400,000 ecstasy tablets, £100,000 in cash and a number of automatic weapons. The different shipments were being sent to Casserly, Foley, Bolger and Daly. In the process seven of their couriers and associates were arrested and subsequently convicted.

Operation Plover had a devastating impact on the drug-dealers. After each bust the Dutch and Irish cops listened in as the villains discussed what was going wrong. In February 2000 the police also overheard conversations between Kinahan and Cunningham. Kinahan was speaking on a mobile phone from his cell in Portlaoise Prison. In one call Kinahan, using code, asked the Colonel to organize the delivery of five kilos of cocaine to an associate of his son Daniel in Dublin.

On Friday 10 March 2000, the Dutch cops swooped on the Colonel and his associates, as he was in the process of filling an order for weapons and drugs on behalf of a UK gang. When Cunningham was searched, he was carrying an automatic pistol in his belt. In one of his safe houses, the cops found an awesome arsenal of weapons. The cache included two Intratec machine-pistols, one submachine-gun; one Steyr military assault rifle; nine handguns and magazines, along with silencers and hundreds of thousands of rounds of ammunition. In another of his hideouts they found a sophisticated machine for vacuum-packing ecstasy pills.

In Cunningham's home at Weteringbrug outside Amsterdam, the cops found 50 kilos of amphetamine powder, 100,000 ecstasy tablets, 2 handguns and ammunition. At the same time another squad stopped a van that the Colonel had met earlier. In it they found 4 handguns, 1,000 kilos of cannabis and 30 kilos of ecstasy. The total value of the drugs seized was over £9 million (over €15.4 million). Peter Lingg, Joopie Altepost and three others were also arrested.

Three days later, Gardaí searched 13 addresses across Dublin and arrested 7 members of Casserly's drug network. Five of those arrested were subsequently charged with drug-trafficking and money-laundering offences. The four men and one woman, none of whom had been known to Gardaí, were convicted and jailed for terms ranging from 18 months to 6 years. Detectives found a ledger that one of Casserly's managers had used to keep track of the drugs. It showed that in a four-month period, Cunningham had shipped two and a half tons of hash and 80,000 ecstasy tablets to Casserly. The street value was just over €31 million.

During questioning the bookkeeper admitted that in the previous 14 months the gang had been distributing an average of 150 kilos of hash every week. It was conservatively calculated that in that period alone, the Irish end of the Cunningham/Kinahan business empire had been worth €100 million. Chris Casserly and another accomplice, named later in High Court documents as Sam O'Sullivan from South County Dublin, fled Ireland before they could be arrested. Casserly moved to Spain and continued to work for the syndicate.

The success of Operation Plover led to bitter recriminations among

Cunningham's clients. Foley and Bolger had an angry falling out with Casserly and began threatening to have him shot. Kinahan sent instructions from prison that the Viper, who was despised by most criminals, should be silenced instead. In September 2000, Foley was ambushed as he left a swimming pool in Dublin. A hit man fired several shots at the mobster but only managed to hit him in the ankle and graze his skull with another bullet. The drug-dealer had survived his third attempted assassination in five years. As he waited for an ambulance to arrive, Foley moaned: 'I'm fuckin' sick of this! This is gettin' fuckin' ridiculous.'

In February 2001, John Cunningham was jailed for nine years on charges of drug-trafficking and gun-running. But the sentence, which was unusually harsh by Dutch standards, was later reduced to seven in the appeal courts. His bagman Peter Lingg was jailed for five years, and Joopie Altepost got four. Two Englishmen and another Dutch national, who were arrested in the operation, were also convicted on drug charges.

A week before Cunningham's trial, his transport manager, Kieran Smyth, was abducted from his home. Smyth was tortured before being shot twice in the head, at close range, with a shotgun. His body was dumped at a roadside near Ashbourne, County Meath three days later. At the time of his murder the CAB had stepped up their enquiries into his business. One of Smyth's many clients decided that they couldn't risk the money-launderer doing a deal with the State. The Provos were the prime suspects for the execution.

Cunningham was released from prison in Holland in November 2004 – and was immediately extradited to Ireland where he served the remainder of his sentence for the Guinness kidnapping. He was freed in 2006 and went to live with his family in the Costa del Sol.

The syndicate's thriving drug operation did not suffer from the Colonel's absence. In March 2001, a month after Cunningham's conviction, Christy Kinahan had been released from Portlaoise Prison. The Dapper Don could have been back on the streets several months earlier, but when he was offered temporary release for good behaviour, the ambitious drug-trafficker politely declined. He opted to stay inside while he completed an environmental science degree through the Open University.

Kinahan had little difficulty getting back into the narcotics trade. He had maintained his international contacts thanks to his son Daniel and his new business partner, Chris Casserly. Casserly, who lived in a luxury villa on a mountainside in Sitges, near Barcelona, handled the logistics for various drug-smuggling routes from Spain into Ireland, the UK and Holland. The Dapper Don began living between homes he purchased in Holland, England and Spain. In a short time he was attracting the attentions of law enforcement agencies across Europe.

The true extent of the Dapper Don's criminal activities could only be gauged by the number and size of his drug shipments which were intercepted by police. Unlike most other offences, the available data on the true monetary value of the drug economy is solely dependent on the quantities of drugs seized and intelligence gathered by law enforcement agencies. Internationally it is accepted that law enforcement agencies only seize 10 per cent of the total amount of narcotics in circulation at any one time. But this is a best-case scenario and purely aspirational.

The economic principle of supply and demand is also a factor in the effect, if any, the seizures have on the overall drug trade. If a shipment is confiscated it causes a shortage of a particular type of narcotic and the price increases. If the price stays the same then it shows that supply has not been adversely affected. In the event that prices fall it is because there is a glut on the market.

Fifteen months after Kinahan's release the GNDU got their first indication of how big he had become. In the summer of 2002, the then GNDU boss, Det. Chief Supt Ted Murphy, launched 'Operation Zombie'. It specifically targeted Kinahan and his partner Chris Casserly and the investigation involved police forces in Spain, Holland, Belgium and the UK. Intelligence sources revealed that the Dapper Don was smuggling multi-ton loads of cannabis, concealed in boxes of tiles. They were being transported by truck from Alicante in Spain, directly to England and Ireland. On 16 August 2002, the GNDU made their move after the syndicate delivered a 1.5-ton shipment of hash to associates of Casserly in North Dublin. In the search of a van and a number of houses detectives seized a ton of hash, along with €100,000 worth of cocaine. They also recovered three firearms, including a machine-gun. A member of the gang was arrested and charged.

Then three days later, a surveillance team tailed another member of the Kinahan gang to the Slade Valley Equestrian Club near Rathcoole,

County Dublin. When the club was searched another 500 kilos of hash and three automatic weapons with silencers were found buried in the grounds. The total street value of the haul was estimated to be between €15 and €20 million. It represented a net loss of the €2 million Kinahan and his associates had invested. As a result of Operation Zombie, four people were arrested, including Philip Sherkle, a close associate of both Kinahan and his son Daniel. A file was sent to the DPP but no charges were preferred against Sherkle. Raymond Molloy, the manager of the equestrian centre, took responsibility for the drugs and guns. Molloy subsequently disappeared and is presumed dead.

The setback was merely a temporary hiccup for Kinahan. A year after the Rathcoole drug bust, English police in Surrey launched 'Operation Embargo' in an attempt to catch the Dapper Don. As a result one of his close associates was arrested with one million ecstasy tablets which had been smuggled in from Holland. Kinahan escaped before police could arrest him. In December 2003, the British National Crime Squad received reliable intelligence that the well-educated drug baron had supplied a half ton of cocaine to the notorious Adams crime family in London. By that time Kinahan was a 'flagged target' by police and customs agencies throughout Europe.

A month later, in January 2004, the international drug-dealer was the target of a new investigation, this time by the UK Customs. Code-named 'Operation Bite', it was set up to target a transport company being used by the Kinahan syndicate for smuggling tobacco and drugs. While the undercover investigation was going on, Daniel Kinahan also found himself under the watchful eye of the British police. He was implicated in a race-fixing scandal involving champion jockey Kieran Fallon. It was claimed that the drug syndicate had been involved in a 'bet to lose' racket in which jockeys were paid to 'hold-up' horses in various races around the UK. Philip Sherkle, Fallon and four other men were charged with conspiracy to defraud. A year later the men were acquitted following what the English press dubbed the 'trial of the century'.

While the race-fixing investigation was ongoing, the Operation Bite team seized a ton of cannabis which the syndicate had shipped in from Spain in pallets of tiles. But according to Customs intelligence officers, the effect of the seizure on the market was 'negligible'. It later emerged that Kinahan and Casserly had successfully imported another 15 tons before the route had been compromised. Eight days later, the authorities struck again and this time recovered 1.5 tons of cannabis. A total of nine well-known local drug-traffickers were arrested and subsequently convicted.

In October 2004, the Kinahan syndicate was suspected of the gangland murder of drug-trafficker Boudewijn Kerbusch, who was shot dead in Oss, Holland. Kerbusch had been recruited to smuggle drugs into Ireland hidden in a truck transporting seafood and smoked fish. The syndicate blamed Kerbusch for the seizure of 700 kilos of cannabis by UK police.

Despite the police operations Kinahan's empire continued to prosper and expand. The Dapper Don took control of the syndicate's money-laundering activities with his son Christy Junior and left the running of the business to his son Daniel. In August 2007 Christy Kinahan Junior was married at a no-expense-spared wedding bash at a luxury hotel in County Wicklow. The guest list was a 'who's who' of international organized crime and included the Dapper Don's most trusted business associates. At the reception, Christy Kinahan looked like a man who hadn't a care in the world. Business was booming.

In February 2008, the GNDU seized a 1.5-ton shipment of cannabis which was being transported in a container truck in County Kildare. Intelligence sources discovered that between October 2007 and January 2008, the Kinahan group had already sent at least six similar loads. The drugs were hidden in foodstuffs sent from a bogus company in Spain to another fake company the syndicate had set up in Dublin. The gang was also involved in smuggling large quantities of cocaine, heroin and weapons. In addition they dealt in various chemicals used for bulking up cocaine. One shipment of arms to 'Fat' Freddie Thompson's gang in Dublin included military-spec rocket-launchers. Luckily for some unknown victim, the Organised Crime Unit intercepted the weapons.

But the drug shipments and the movements of cash were only the ones that the various law enforcement agencies were aware of. Sources in the underworld revealed that, at any one time, the organization could have several tons of hashish and cocaine stored in warehouses in southern Spain.

Another major international investigation was launched against the

Dapper Don a few months later. This time the Belgian Federal Police were taking him on. They probed Kinahan's involvement in a number of property deals, a real estate company and the purchase of a former casino in the heart of Antwerp. They investigated his portfolio, which included a mansion in the city's most upmarket neighbourhood, known as 'billionaire's row', where the Dapper Don lived with one of his many girlfriends. With the assistance of several European police forces, the detectives uncovered evidence of how Kinahan had bought his Belgian property by channelling funds through a complex web of offshore companies in Hong Kong, Panama, Cyprus and the Republic of Vanuatu in the South Pacific. The enquiries also exposed an extraordinary web of corruption, involving organized crime gangs, a soccer team and members of the Belgian police. Two senior officers attached to the robbery squad of the Antwerp police were secretly watched meeting with Kinahan and other local gangsters.

In May 2008, Kinahan was arrested and put in custody while the Belgian police continued their money-laundering investigation. At the same time three properties were frozen and a number of bank accounts blocked. While he was out of the picture, Kinahan's sons and John Cunningham assumed control of the operation.

A year later, Kinahan was released from custody but was ordered to remain in Belgium. In September 2009 the Antwerp Correctional Court convicted the gang boss on ten counts of money-laundering. The presiding judge, Luc Potargent, described how the sophisticated mobster had done everything in his power to undermine the judicial process. He also accused the Godfather of refusing to clarify where the money came from, who its real owner was, and the true nature of his relationship with the string of offshore companies. Kinahan took advantage of the Belgian justice system and was granted bail when he lodged an appeal against the conviction. In any event he would only have had to spend a few months inside. Under Belgian law a convict only has to serve one-third of certain sentences – and Kinahan had already been in prison for a year.

In the meantime Kinahan was allowed to return to Spain, where he quickly resumed his position at the helm of his empire. The Dapper Don's organized crime syndicate was made up of a core of 12 senior members including his sons, John Cunningham, Indian businessman

Jasvinder Singh Kamoo and Kevin Lynch, a convicted armed robber from Ballyfermot. Described as a 'very sinister' thug with connections to the IRA, Lynch had become a confidant of Kinahan while they were both doing time in Portlaoise. Other key figures in the network were Gary Hutch and a Dublin-based businessman who owned a number of launderettes in the city. An accountant from Estepona in southern Spain and her English boyfriend were involved in looking after the group's very healthy finances.

The Dapper Don and his associates had become globe-trotting businessmen in their quest to launder their cash. In 2009 alone investigators discovered that the syndicate had transferred over €16 million from 22 bank accounts. Money was sent to the UK, Spain and Holland to pay for drugs. The profits from the deals were then moved to countries all over the world. John Cunningham and one of the gang's bagmen from Dublin visited Brazil to transfer another €15 million, as part of a major property deal. In October 2009, Daniel Kinahan travelled to Dubai, in the company of two associates from England and Morocco, to supervise the movement of cash to banks there. In November, Christy Kinahan travelled to China for the purpose of setting up a meat export business with the Chinese Mafia. It was suspected that the real purpose of the deal was to launder money through bogus companies in China, while drugs were trafficked from there to the West. Kinahan also began trading in various commodities markets.

In the same month Daniel Kinahan and a member of Gary Hutch's Dublin mob visited South Africa to do business with an international drug gang based in Cape Town. The gang's English money-launderer was known to have transferred Stg£10 million to a bank in Zurich that same month. The money was then transferred to an offshore account in Antigua and Barbuda. The gang's agents in cities such as Liverpool, Dublin, Amsterdam and Antwerp were also transferring huge amounts of cash through Western Union, using bogus names and documentation.

Like a major multi-national company, the mob invested heavily in state-of-the-art technology. Kinahan and his close circle had learned from the mistakes of the past and tended to keep their phone conversations to under a minute. When the Dapper Don arrived back in Spain from Belgium, he invested money in satellite phones which could not be intercepted by police. The organization had access to a helicopter, which was used to move money, drugs and people. They even paid €200,000 for a sea-going speed boat.

The sheer size and capacity of the syndicate's criminal empire was truly astonishing. It was an extremely efficient and sophisticated operation. Irish criminals had come a very long way since Larry Dunne imported his first shipment of heroin.

But there was trouble brewing for the Dapper Don. A massive international investigation had been launched in 2008 which was spearheaded by the Spanish national police force, the Guardia Civil. The 'Irish Mafia' had grown so powerful that it could no longer be ignored. The Kinahan syndicate had turned the Costa del Sol into a hub for Irish organized crime. The investigation was partially prompted by a string of gangland shootings and murders involving Kinahan's mob. In February 2008 notorious gangland hit man Paddy Doyle, from the north inner-city, was shot dead, just outside Puerto Banus. He had become a liability to his former associates. Another member of the mob had also shot and injured one of their Moroccan associates. In April 2010 the Kinahan syndicate was responsible for the high-profile murder of notorious crime boss Eamon Dunne, aka 'the Don' (see Chapter 26).

A month later the international police investigation finally moved against Kinahan and his organization. When Kinahan and his inner circle were arrested, they were brought before the courts in a blaze of publicity, escorted by heavily armed cops. In most European jurisdictions, including Spain, suspects can be arrested and held without charge as part of an ongoing criminal investigation. The Spanish authorities revealed that they were investigating serious crimes including murder, drug- and gun-trafficking and money-laundering. International arrest warrants were also issued by Spanish magistrates for Kinahan's Dublin bagman Mathew Dunne, and for Fat Freddie Thompson and Gary Hutch.

Kinahan spent six months in prison before he was released on bail. In 2011 the Belgian authorities sought his extradition to serve the remainder of his money-laundering sentence after his appeal there was turned down. In August 2011 a Spanish court granted the request and the Dapper Don was returned to Belgium. When he finishes his sentence he will be returned to Spain. Meanwhile the rest of the gang members were released on bail and ordered to surrender their passports. Cunningham, who claimed to a judge that he was just a tourist, was one of the first to be set free.

At the time of writing, the investigation into the Kinahan/Cunningham syndicate was still ongoing. According to police sources it may take a number of years before the complex web of international intrigue has been unravelled.

Despite his absence, the Dapper Don's organization regrouped. The final chapter in the story of the former inner-city drug-pusher has not yet been written.

25. Marlo's Story

The violent life and death of Martin 'Marlo' Hyland can be summed up in the words of the seventeenth-century political philosopher Thomas Hobbes: 'The life of man is nasty, brutish and short.' The script for Hyland's life could have come from a gangster movie or even a Shakespearean tragedy. His story is a paradigm of the stereotypical modern-day Godfather. A young hood starts off in life as a petty crook and makes it to the place where every aspiring criminal wants to be – the head of the 'family'.

In Gangland the laws of the jungle dictate the order of things. Power is maintained through fear and violence. In this predatory world potential challengers wait in the shadows for any sign of weakness or vulnerability on the part of the Godfather. Then power is taken – at the point of a gun. A sudden, violent death is an inevitable occupational hazard for the modern mob boss. In order to protect his business, he must be prepared to murder anyone, even former friends, whom he suspects of posing a threat. At the same time there is the ever-present danger of being busted by the police.

Applying these laws is how Marlo Hyland embarked on his journey to become Public Enemy Number One. He got rid of his boss and mentor, the Psycho, PJ Judge and built a powerful criminal organization. But his time at the top was 'nasty, brutish and short'. Hyland's days were numbered when he became weak and his organization began to implode, after sustained attack from the police. And like the wounded leader of a pride of lions, he was replaced when a younger, ambitious opponent moved in for the kill.

During his reign Marlo ushered in a new approach to organized crime. He tried to create one big, nationwide crime corporation, by bringing various gangs and terrorist groups together. It was a plan worthy of the Sicilian or American Mafia of old. Hyland planned an underworld where there would be an 'understanding' between the various mobs. Territory would be agreed by mutual consent and negotiation;

resources would be pooled for the profit of all the corporate members, such as cash pools for drug shipments and hit men to deal with problems. In Marlo's new gangland order everyone, as they say in Sicily, could 'draw from the well'.

Marlo worked hard to manoeuvre himself into a position of power and influence. Hyland liked being in control of the action and secretly pulled the strings in several gangland feuds. He was good at networking and nurtured the image of a strong man who could get things done. He inspired loyalty among his closest associates, some of whom were prepared to do anything he asked. Within a few years of Judge's violent end, Hyland controlled a large gang of up to twenty of the most violent criminals to emerge in the Noughties. All of them were staunchly loyal to their boss. The group included thugs John Daly, Paddy Doyle, Johnny Mangan, Willie Hynes and Eamon Dunne. Marlo also established strong links with gangs throughout the country, including the notorious McCarthy/Dundons in Limerick.

By the Noughties Marlo's main drug-supplier was the Kinahan syndicate. He also worked closely with another major player in the drug-dealing rackets, Troy Jordan, who was based in County Kildare. Originally from Tallaght, West Dublin, Jordan was involved with the INLA and John Gilligan. He came to prominence as a result of the gangland upheaval that followed the Veronica Guerin murder. He was the target of several major Garda investigations which resulted in large drug seizures. But, like Marlo, Jordan remained a safe distance away from the merchandise.

Hyland also enjoyed a long-standing partnership with well-known members of Sinn Féin/IRA who were on his payroll, including the senior figures who'd 'advised' him to get rid of PJ Judge. Hyland supplied guns and getaway cars for Provo murders and heists which they didn't want connected to the Movement. He was also involved in a multi-million-Euro VAT fraud with his Provo pals. So-called C2 fraud was a popular source of income to increase the Sinn Féin/IRA war-chest.

A Criminal Assets Bureau investigation into Hyland's financial affairs exposed his close business relationship with John Noonan, the Sinn Féin and IRA member who'd helped start the Concerned Parents Against Drugs (CPAD) organization. The hypocritical republican gangster, who had gone to the brink of war with the General twenty years earlier, had been laundering his money through bank accounts controlled by Marlo. Noonan became a major CAB target and was hit with a tax bill for over €2 million. He told investigators that the money he put through the drug-dealer's accounts belonged to Sinn Féin and the IRA.

Hyland also used the prison system to network. He acted as a benefactor to villains on the inside whom he considered to be of future worth to him. Marlo regularly visited Patrick 'Dutchie' Holland and INLA mass-murderer Dessie O'Hare. Prison records showed that Hyland visited Dutchie at least 13 times in two years. The generous Godfather regularly lodged money into the accounts of individual prisoners so that they could buy goods from the prison tuck shop – and drugs from other lags. Hyland kept €50 from the profits of every kilo of drugs he sold to give to the wives and girlfriends of associates who were doing time. Like John Gilligan, Marlo worked hard at being popular.

Hyland began to feature as a target for the GNDU shortly after the Psycho's murder. In October 1997, one of his associates, Noel Mullen, was caught with £400,000 worth of hash he was moving for his boss. As a result he was jailed for five years. Less than a year later, in April 1998, the GNDU chalked up another significant victory against Marlo when they seized £2 million worth of hashish. As a result his loyal henchman Willie Hynes was jailed for six and a half years. But the seizures had little effect on Marlo's operation. They only accounted for a fraction of the number of shipments he was organizing.

By the new millennium, Hyland controlled a huge wholesale drug business, importing cocaine, cannabis and heroin. At one stage he was importing up to several hundred kilos of cannabis every few weeks alone. He was making a tidy profit in the process, selling it at a wholesale price of €1,100 per kilo. In addition, he was bringing in weapons for his gang and to sell to other villains.

Marlo's gang were also involved in the systematic theft of high-performance cars, which were stolen to order and sold to a gang specializing in high-spec motors. The leader of that mob was a Lebanese-born thug, Hassan Hassan, who shipped the cars for sale in the Middle East. Marlo also supplied getaway cars to other gangs. In March 1999 cars stolen by Hyland's gang were used in two shooting incidents. The IRA used one in a gun attack on a drug addict called Alan Byrne. Byrne was a witness for the State against members of the CPAD and Sinn Féin who had been charged with beating his friend, Josie Dwyer, to death. Byrne survived the gun attack and later testified in court. The second car was used in the gangland murder of 34-year-old drug-dealer Tom O'Reilly in Rathfarnham.

Detective Inspector Brian Sherry had overall responsibility for all criminal investigation in West Dublin. Marlo had been his number one target for several years. He recalled: 'Marlo was a very interesting, but not a very pleasant character to deal with. There is no doubt that he was the first criminal who tried to involve everyone in his enterprise. He was a facilitator who brought the different gangs under the one umbrella, in one network, a bit like the Mafia. He was involved in everything that was happening. It was a very dangerous situation to have one man in such a powerful position. He was pulling all the strings. Before his death Marlo's name was coming up in investigations all over the place. At one stage it seemed like nothing happened in this town without some involvement from him. In the end he became too big for his boots.'

By 2004, Marlo was firmly established as the Mr Big of the largest criminal network in the country. The mob was also involved in armed robberies and protection rackets. Marlo acted as a consultant for other criminal groups, planning robberies and drug deals, for which he charged a fee or received a slice of the profits.

Between 2002 and 2004, Hyland's gang began targeting security vans delivering cash to ATM machines in Dublin and surrounding counties. With the help of corrupt employees, the mob had identified a major weakness in the delivery system. Between October 2003 and July 2004, the aptly dubbed 'Hole in the Wall' gang got away with an estimated €3 million. Hyland and his associates were soaring to the top of the Gardaí's 'most wanted' list.

Inevitably the Godfather used an ever-increasing spiral of violence to maintain control of his organization. His gang had been linked to the murder in November 2001 of Finglas hard man Gerard 'Concrete' Fitzgerald. A year earlier, Fitzgerald had ordered the murder of his own nephew, Francis Fitzgerald, who had been a member of Marlo's mob. And in 2005 Hyland ordered the gruesome execution of 26-year-old drug-dealer Andrew 'Chicore' Dillon from Finglas.

Dillon had been a member of the Westies gang before he moved over to Hyland's mob and he took part in several of the security van heists. In 2004, Dillon was accused of stealing drugs belonging to veteran Finglas drug-trafficker John McKeown, an associate of Hyland. Dillon had sold the drugs and put the money he made from the deal in the bank. When McKeown demanded payment, the hapless thief couldn't get his hands on the money – the CAB had frozen the account. Dillon was forced to flee to the UK after McKeown had tried to murder him.

Hyland decided to lure the gangland fugitive back to Ireland – and make an example of him. 'Marlo sent him word that he could come back and that everything would be all right,' recalled Brian Sherry. 'We knew that everything would not be all right and tried to advise him to stay where he was. But Dillon was really a harmless idiot who got in over his head. He wanted to believe everything was sorted because he couldn't survive on his own in England. It was a big mistake.'

Hyland welcomed the errant villain when he returned in May 2005. He purposely lulled Dillon into a false sense of security. Three months later, on 17 August, Dillon met Eamon Dunne and two other thugs. Dunne told him they were going to collect a getaway car for a heist. The gang then drove to a lane off Ashbourne Road, north-west Dublin, where they shot Dillon three times in the face and head. Dillon's body was then dumped in a ditch. Eamon Dunne had proved his credentials as a cold-blooded killer. Over the next five years he would be responsible for at least 13 more murders.

Eamon 'the Don' Dunne was born in February 1976 and grew up in Blackhorse Grove in Cabra. He came from a respectable family and was not driven into a life of crime as a result of deprivation. He was described as being highly intelligent, achieved good results in his Leaving Certificate and was better educated than most of his associates. After school he worked for a short time in a meat factory but soon gave it up for a more lucrative criminal career. Dunne was one of the up-and-coming hoods who were greatly impressed with the glamorous lifestyle of the Godfather in the area – Marlo Hyland. He and a group of other teenage villains joined Hyland's drug-dealing pyramid. Over time Dunne became one of Marlo's most trusted associates.

Dunne's first serious run-in with the law came in June 2002 when a Garda unit pulled his car over for a drug search. By then local cops were aware that he was part of Hyland's mob and he was regularly stopped. That day Garda Paul Keane struck lucky when he found €13,000 worth of cocaine and ecstasy in the car. An airgun was also recovered. Dunne was charged with ten charges relating to the sale and supply of drugs and possession of the illegal firearm. When the gangster was released on bail he went back to work.

Five months later, on 6 November 2002, Dunne was dispatched to 'sort out' a problem with a 19-year-old drug-pusher who owed Marlo money. The young psychopath abducted the pusher and gave him a severe beating, breaking one of his arms in the process. He was then bound, gagged and dumped in the boot of Dunne's car. Fortunately for the victim the officer who'd arrested Dunne in June spotted his car parked at Glasnevin Avenue around 8 p.m. Garda Paul Keane decided to check it out for a second time. When the eagle-eyed officer and his colleagues asked Dunne to open the boot they found his terrified victim inside. But Dunne showed that he had the brass-neck to be a major player – when the cops asked him why a man was tied up and gagged in the boot of his car, Dunne laughed and said it was part of a birthday prank. The officers didn't believe him and he was arrested. Police believed that Dunne had intended to execute his captive. The victim was rushed to hospital and treated for his injuries.

Dunne was later charged with false imprisonment and assault. The Don was now facing two sets of serious criminal charges and a long stretch behind bars. The false imprisonment charge was dropped when the victim withdrew his statement and left the country. On 24 February 2004, Dunne pleaded guilty to the drug charges. However, two months later he decided to change his plea to not guilty, claiming that he didn't understand the charges that he had originally pleaded to. He then set in motion a series of appeals to the High Court and Supreme Court, which guaranteed his freedom. By the time of his death in 2010, the Supreme Court appeal had still not been heard.

Chicore Dillon was one of the 19 people, including two sets of brothers, who fell foul of hit men in 2005. It was the highest number of gangland murders on record in a single year, since organized crime first emerged in Ireland. In addition, two armed robbers, 33-year-old Colm 'Collie' Griffin and 24-year-old Eric Hopkins, were also shot dead by the

Emergency Response Unit during an attempted post office heist in Lusk, County Dublin.

All but four of the gangland murders in 2005 were the result of blood feuds across Dublin. One of the worst became known as the Crumlin/Drimnagh feud. The seeds of the conflict could be traced to a bitter split in a gang of young drug-dealers from the neighbouring working-class areas – the traditional homeland of organized crime. In 2001 Brian Rattigan stabbed his former friend Declan Gavin to death outside a fast-food joint in Crumlin. Rattigan and his pals had accused Gavin of being a police informant after he was caught with a large haul of ecstasy. The murder led to war, with Rattigan leading one side of the feud and Fat Freddie Thompson the other. Both men were sadistic killers. Thompson was a close associate of Christy Kinahan's sons, Daniel and Christy Junior.

Over the following nine years the Crumlin/Drimnagh feud claimed the lives of 16 gang members. Dozens of criminals and innocent people were also injured in the madness. There were scores of shooting incidents and arson attacks, as well as grenade and bomb attacks.

Behind the scenes, Marlo Hyland facilitated the ongoing war. It was in his interests that the Crumlin/Drimnagh bloodbath continued. He reasoned that the murder spree would soak up police resources and keep specialist units busy on Dublin's south-side – and far away from his patch on the north-side. As part of the same strategy he quickly intervened to stop a simmering feud between two rival gangs in Coolock. If it had kicked off then the area would have been swamped by extra detective units – and that would have been bad for business.

The bloodiest episode in the Crumlin/Drimnagh gang war occurred during a 48-hour period which began on Sunday 13 November 2005. Around 9.40 p.m. two members of Thompson's gang, 25-year-old Darren Geoghegan and 30-year-old Gavin Byrne, were shot dead by two hit men at Carrickwood Estate in Firhouse, South Dublin. They'd been lured into a trap to meet an associate of Thompson's, 25-year-old Paddy Doyle. Investigating Gardaí believed that the murders were ordered by Thompson, who feared that the two men were posing a threat to his leadership.

Paddy Doyle, who was from the inner-city, was a member of the gang led by Gary Hutch, which had close ties with the Kinahan organization. Doyle was also a close associate of Marlo Hyland.

The following Tuesday, 15 November, Paddy Doyle was in action again. This time his victim was Noel Roche, a member of the Rattigan gang. The 27-year-old was shot dead as he travelled in a car through Clontarf, on Dublin's north-side. His younger brother John had been whacked eight months earlier, as part of the same feud.

Doyle was also the prime suspect in the murders of two other Rattigan gang members, Terry Dunleavy and, six months later, Joe Rattigan (Brian Rattigan's brother) in 2002. The Roche hit brought to six the number of murders Doyle had been directly connected to. His accomplice in the Noel Roche hit was 19-year-old Craig White, from the north inner-city and a member of Marlo's extended gang. White was subsequently convicted of Noel Roche's murder and sentenced to life. Doyle fled the country and moved to live in Spain. He continued to work for Marlo's mob, in conjunction with the Kinahan organization. It later emerged that Hyland had provided the murder weapon, a Glock automatic, and the getaway car used in the Roche hit.

The bloodshed in November 2005 had again placed the gangland crisis at the top of political and police agendas. As a result, Garda Commissioner Noel Conroy announced the establishment of the Organised Crime Unit (OCU), which would specifically target big criminal gangs. It was not good news for Marlo. But the police had already set an operation in place to smash his criminal empire.

A few weeks after the murder of Andrew Dillon in August 2005, the National Bureau of Criminal Investigation (NBCI) launched a top-secret investigation, targeting Marlo Hyland, codenamed 'Operation Oak'. The Godfather had become a source of major concern at the highest levels of the Garda Síochána. They were aware of his attempts to form powerful alliances and create a glorified Crime Inc., across the country. Hyland was facilitating a veritable crime wave and becoming so big that he could soon be completely out of control. Marlo was to the new millennium what Martin Cahill was to the 1980s and John Gilligan to the 1990s.

On 9 September 2005, a secret Crime and Security memo was circulated to the chiefs of all the specialist units. The document summarized the need for radical action. It read: 'Ongoing intelligence at this branch confirms that Martin Hyland continues to be heavily-involved in serious crime. Hyland is recognised as the leading figure in a criminal gang based primarily in West Dublin. However, Hyland is linked to a substantial number of the crime gangs operating throughout the DMR [Dublin Metropolitan Region] and beyond. Hyland contin-ually endeavours to establish links to the most violent criminals in this jurisdiction. His gang are involved in murder, armed robberies, pro-curement of firearms, drug distribution and major fraud. In recent times Hyland has become closely linked to both Dessie O'Hare and Patrick "Dutchie" Holland.'

The newly formed OCU, which was attached to the NBCI, was mobilized to spearhead Operation Oak. The young, enthusiastic cops were ordered to get close-up and very personal with Marlo and his men. Other units, such as the CAB and the National Surveillance Unit, were also deployed to build up a comprehensive picture of the gang's opera-tions. The mob's phones were tapped and informants were recruited within the overall group. The investigation would have devastating consequences for the gang.

The first strike in the offensive came eight days after the Noel Roche murder, when €300,000 worth of cocaine was seized in Limerick on 23 November. Three members of the McCarthy/Dundon gang were arrested after collecting the drugs from Marlo's people in Dublin. A week later, two of Marlo's associates were nabbed while transporting a ton of hashish on the Swords Road, on Dublin's north-side. That was quickly followed by a raid on one of the gang's cocaine-mixing factories in Skerries, North County Dublin. Detectives seized €210,000 worth of cocaine and enough mixing agent to more than double the drug's value. Two of Marlo's associates were arrested and charged with the find. The following day, in Stamullen, County Meath, over €200,000 in cash was seized from a 36-year-old gang member. He was arrested under money-laundering legislation. Detectives later found a specially constructed hide under a garden shed that the bagman used to store cash for Marlo.

On 4 February 2006, Marlo's trusted sidekick Johnny Mangan, and another gang member, were caught with over €340,000 worth of hash-ish. Two days later Operation Oak struck again. This time police seized cocaine worth almost €500,000. On 17 February, the undercover Gardaí busted another cocaine-processing operation and seized €200,000 worth of the drug.

The sudden surge in police swoops caused panic in Hyland's organization. By the end of April 2006 drugs worth €9 million had been seized, and ten gang members had been charged with drug offences and attempted robbery. Files on eight other mob members were being prepared for the Director of Public Prosecutions, relating to possession of drugs, money-laundering and handling stolen goods. On a daily basis gang members were being stopped and searched by the Garda squads involved in Operation Oak. The CAB also began raiding their homes, and the offices of their solicitors and accountants, in search of the gang's money and assets. Hyland, Eamon Dunne and the other thugs tried to intimidate members of the OCU but it had little effect.

With his empire under sustained attack, Hyland was growing more paranoid and volatile by the day. Drug shipments were still getting through the Garda net, but the losses were soaking up profits. Cash flow became a major problem and he still had to pay his suppliers in Spain and Holland. Christy Kinahan was his biggest creditor. Marlo knew that, if he couldn't pay up, he would find himself in the sights of a hit man's gun. The vulnerable Godfather was desperate to surround himself with formidable allies, reckoning they would provide a comfort zone around him. When Dutchie Holland and Dessie O'Hare were both released from prison in April 2006, Hyland gave the two killers money and provided them with accommodation.

Marlo had the equally pressing problem of finding out why the cops were suddenly being so successful. He launched an investigation to find the Garda mole he believed was in the midst of his mob. The paranoid mobster's chief suspect was his former associate, 42-year-old Paddy Harte. Harte had made the fatal mistake of setting up a drug-distribution network in opposition to the Godfather. Hyland convinced two of his closest lieutenants, one of whom was Harte's friend, that the former associate was a tout. He offered them €50,000 to kill him. On 29 May 2006, Harte was shot three times in the head when he returned home after taking his children to school. But the murder did not stop the inexorable Garda offensive, as the drug seizures and arrests continued.

By the time Operation Oak came to a conclusion it had led to the seizure of over €20 million worth of heroin, cocaine and cannabis and an arsenal of 16 firearms and ammunition. A number of stolen vehicles and over €200,000 in cash were also recovered from the mob. By autumn 2006, a total of 41 people in Marlo's organization had been arrested, including Willie Hynes and Johnny Mangan. Mangan had been caught twice in a matter of months with large drug shipments and was facing years behind bars. A total of 26 gang members were facing serious criminal charges for drug-trafficking, attempted robbery and possession of firearms. Operation Oak had also prevented at least three gangland murders and thwarted a number of attempted robberies. In policing terms it had been a spectacular success. For Hyland it was a disaster.

Marlo's once-powerful empire was crumbling around him. As the situation deteriorated he became more isolated. Members of the gang facing serious charges blamed him for their predicament. There were murmurings of resentment over the Harte murder from those closest to Marlo. The Godfather had reneged on his contract with the two hit men and hadn't paid them for the execution. Gang members were becoming as dangerously paranoid about a rat in the camp as their boss. And the finger of suspicion was moving in the direction of Marlo himself. After all, he had organized the operations that had been compromised.

There was even evidence that Hyland turned to God in a bid to halt his descent into hell. He carried a bundle of prayers, miraculous medals and a scapular in his pocket. Marlo was desperate for friends and he was prepared to go to extraordinary lengths to curry favour. In November 2006 he was contacted by John Dundon of the McCarthy/Dundon gang, who was still serving four years for threatening to kill Owen Treacy. Dundon wanted Hyland to organize one of the most shocking murders in gangland history. The target was a 26-year-old Latvian, a mother-of-two called Baiba Saulite.

Dundon was sharing a cell with Baiba's estranged Lebanese husband, Hassan Hassan, an associate of Hyland, who was serving a four-year sentence for running the stolen car ring. Hassan had already tried to solicit criminals on the outside to kill his wife and her lawyer, John Hennessy. Hennessy had represented Baiba in a bitter courtroom battle for custody of the Hassan children. Hassan had abducted his two sons and sent them to the Middle East but was forced to bring them back by the Irish courts and he was subsequently charged with kidnapping. In February 2006 there had been an arson attack on Hennessy's home in

Swords and he'd managed to get out of the house with his partner just in time. Gardaí said it was a case of attempted murder. In October Baiba had been forced to move into hiding in Swords, after her car was petrol-bombed outside her home. In the same month Gardaí learned that the McCarthy/Dundons had provided a gun and silencer to a Moroccan asylum-seeker to murder Hennessy. The hit was foiled when the Moroccan was arrested on a separate matter.

Investigating Gardaí later learned that Hassan made two further attempts to have both Baiba and her solicitor murdered. When the two potential killers refused the job, the Lebanese thug turned again to Dundon, who phoned Marlo. If anyone could organize the hit, the Godfather could. Marlo agreed to do it because he was anxious to ingratiate himself with Murder Inc. Hyland recruited Paddy Doyle, who flew back from Spain, Eamon Dunne and three other young mob members. None of them had any qualms about murdering an innocent woman.

In the meantime Baiba and Hennessy were placed under surveillance by Hassan's associates. On Tuesday 14 November, a Garda patrol spotted Marlo and Dessie O'Hare meeting in a hotel in Swords. It was never established if this encounter was connected to the murder plot.

On Sunday 19 November, a pizza delivery arrived at Baiba's door. She hadn't ordered one. At the same time Hassan received a phone call in prison, informing him that his wife was at home. Dundon then called the hit team in Cabra to give them the go-ahead. Marlo's men had been given a picture of Baiba, along with a map and directions. Shortly before 9.45 p.m., Baiba was having a cigarette with a friend at the front door when a man wearing a scarf and baseball hat suddenly ran up to her. The young thug from Cabra pulled a handgun from his jacket and shot Baiba four times at close range – killing her instantly. Within minutes of being called to the scene the Gardaí took Hennessy out of Dublin, under armed guard.

Not since the murder of Veronica Guerin had a killing so enraged and shocked the entire nation. Baiba's murder struck a chord with the public. There was also outrage that a solicitor had been targeted for simply doing his job. It was proof that the crime bosses had again become so powerful that they didn't care who they butchered. Completely innocent people were being deliberately gunned down, on what seemed like a regular basis. In the previous March another young mother, Donna Cleary, had been shot dead when Dwayne Foster, a drugged-up thug from Finglas, indiscriminately opened fire with an automatic weapon at a house party. In June another innocent victim, 23-year-old Keith Fitzsimmons, was gunned down in a case of mistaken identity by a drug gang. In Limerick, the McCarthy/Dundons had been responsible for the murders of three innocent men.

Within days of the outrage, detectives had established that Marlo and his gang were involved. Gardaí raided Hassan's prison cell and he was later arrested and questioned about the vile crime. They discovered that Hyland had contacted Troy Jordan and asked him for a Magnum revolver. When Jordan heard about Baiba's execution he was furious with Hyland. He told the crime boss that if he'd known about it he would not have handed the gun over. Hyland claimed that he also didn't know and blamed the McCarthy/Dundons. No criminal wanted to be associated with the murder.

A sense of nervousness hit Gangland as villains everywhere braced themselves for a backlash, similar to that which had followed Veronica Guerin's murder. But before the week had ended Marlo's name was being connected with even more bloodshed. Four days after Baiba's murder, 26-year-old Paul Reay was gunned down in Drogheda, County Louth. He was facing charges after being caught in one of Marlo's cocaine factories. Reay was shot four times as he was about to go to court for a remand hearing. He'd decided not to wear his customary bullet-proof vest that morning. He died a short time later.

Hyland was anxious not to be publicly connected with Baiba's killing, but everyone knew he was involved. The crime added to the mounting pressure on the Godfather. In the weeks after the Saulite murder, Hyland was taking a lot of cocaine and was described by associates as a human wreck. His situation mirrored that of Tony Montana, from Oliver Stone's movie *Scarface*. Being in Marlo's mob was no longer seen as a badge of honour. Even his most loyal henchmen had stand-up rows with their boss over the collective heat he had brought down on them. Several gang members, including Dunne, began to distance themselves from him. As the gang began to implode, friends turned into foes.

The beginning of the end came when Hyland had a serious falling out with an associate called Michael 'Roly' Cronin. Cronin was a convicted heroin-dealer who was classified by Gardaí as a major player. The 33-year-old had been running with Marlo and members of John Gilligan's gang since his release from prison in 2004. Hyland owed Cronin money for drugs and was unable to pay up because of the huge losses he was suffering. One of Hyland's henchmen tried to shoot Cronin but he escaped uninjured. Cronin was determined that it wouldn't happen again.

Eamon Dunne decided he had played the part of the loyal lieutenant for long enough. As his boss became a liability Dunne saw his opportunity to stage a coup and joined forces with Cronin. Dunne approached Marlo's loyal henchmen who'd carried out the Paddy Harte hit. They were still waiting for the €50,000 Hyland had promised them; they were also facing serious drug charges and long jail sentences. Dunne had little difficulty convincing them that the Godfather had to be terminated.

Gardaí picked up intelligence that Hyland was a marked man and warned him that his life was in danger. The suspicious gangster had become very nervous about his personal security and moved to live with his niece, Elaine Hyland, and her family at Scribblestown Lane in Finglas. Eamon Dunne and his co-conspirators decided to hit Hyland at the house.

On 12 December, Marlo woke up with a headache. He asked his niece for painkillers and went back to sleep. Around 8.54 a.m. plumber David Murphy and his 20-year-old trainee, Anthony Campbell, arrived to repair a number of radiators. Campbell had only been working with Murphy a few weeks and was happy to be making some extra money before Christmas. Elaine Hyland left the house to bring one of her children to school. Around the same time Murphy went to pick up some parts, leaving Anthony working alone.

Marlo's henchmen had been watching the house and reckoned that it was empty when they saw Elaine Hyland and the plumber leaving. The hit men used a key to get inside. When they discovered Anthony Campbell in the front room, one of the killers held him at gunpoint. The other hit man crept upstairs to Marlo's bedroom. He fired two shots from an automatic pistol into the back of the gangster's head, as he lay face down in the bed. He fired four more rounds into Marlo's back for good measure. When the killer returned to the terrified young plumber he decided he didn't want to leave a witness. The hit man raised his gun and fired a single shot at Anthony Campbell, who put his hands up to protect himself. The bullet passed through his arm and hit him in the side of the head. Anthony fell to the ground beside the radiator he had been repairing. Gangland had claimed another completely innocent victim.

Six minutes after they first entered the house, the two killers left in a black Volkswagen Passat that had been stolen in County Kildare ten days earlier. They drove in the direction of Tolka Road. Eamon Dunne, who had been patrolling the area keeping watch for the police, followed in a second car. He picked up the hit men on Glasilawn Lane in east Finglas after they'd set fire to the getaway car. Dunne drove them away and disposed of the murder weapon.

The murder of Anthony Campbell sparked fresh public outrage and revulsion. The fact that it came so soon after Baiba Saulite's death added to the gravity of the situation. There was a real sense that organized crime was out of control. And the blood-letting didn't stop there. Another three men were gunned down in the last two remaining weeks of 2006. Two of the victims had been murdered as part of yet another feud, this time in the north inner-city, which had been sparked when drug-dealer Christy Griffin was exposed as a paedophile. The murders pushed the gangland death toll to 24, making 2006 the bloodiest year ever in the history of organized crime.

Over the following months over 1,000 people were interviewed and 600 statements were taken as part of the investigation into Marlo's murder. The investigation team worked in tandem with their colleagues on the Saulite murder. Detectives had soon compiled a detailed picture of both crimes and who was involved. A number of individuals gave Gardaí important information which could only be acted on if the informants were prepared to stand up in court. But no one would testify against Gangland's new overlord – Eamon Dunne – and his killers.

Early in the investigation detectives were tipped off that the stolen car used in the double murder had been parked at the basement garage of the Linnbhla Apartments, in Ballymun, North Dublin. The car had been parked there from the end of November until 12 December. When Gardaí examined the basement they discovered that it had been used as a secret depot for Marlo's gang. They located two stolen cars, both fitted with false plates, which had been taken in North Dublin the month before the murders. Gardaí also discovered a van which had been registered to a fictitious company. The vehicle had been specially adapted to transport large quantities of drugs. The search also opened a direct link with the ongoing investigation into Baiba Saulite's murder. One of the recovered cars had been stolen from the same address – and at the same time – as the one used by Baiba's killers. A loaded Israeli assault rifle was discovered in the boot of another car, the number plate of which was found in the garage.

Detectives then discovered that Eamon Dunne and a close associate, Brian O'Reilly from Ballymun, were registered directors of Shelneart Security, the company hired to 'protect' the apartment block a year earlier. A finger-print uplifted from one of the stolen cars also matched one of Marlo's former associates. Gardaí later froze the Shelneart bank account, which they believed was being used to launder drug money.

Eamon Dunne, O'Reilly and several members of Marlo's gang were subsequently arrested and questioned about the double murder of Hyland and Campbell and about Baiba's murder. However, no one was ever charged with either crime. Gardaí in Swords submitted a file to the DPP recommending that Hassan be charged with conspiracy to murder his wife. However, the DPP decided not to proceed with the charges. Hassan Hassan was released from prison in March 2010 and immediately left the country, under the watchful eye of the Gardaí.

The vacuum Hyland left behind was quickly filled. Marlo is still remembered in Gangland as the boss who got out of his depth. 'He was a great bloke, very good to people loyal to him but he just got too big and brought down too much heat on everyone else and that's not on. The lads who took his place are cuter and they are a lot more ruthless,' one former friend remarked.

Eamon 'the Don' Dunne was already earning notoriety as the underworld's most bloodthirsty crime boss.

26.   The Don's Downfall

Eamon Dunne kept his head down in the months following his successful coup and prepared the ground work for a new order in Gangland. As
Gardaí unravelled the truth behind the most significant underworld
assassination since that of Martin Cahill, they expected more bloodshed
as gang members sought either revenge or vied for supremacy. But most
of Marlo's once loyal henchmen had no stomach for retribution and
simply switched their allegiances to the Don. Several of Hyland's former associates who had been caught in Operation Oak were also exiting
the stage – for long prison sentences. In addition, Dunne had the all-
important support of Christy Kinahan and his powerful syndicate.
Veteran villain Eamon Kelly also emerged as Dunne's mentor and
adviser. They were regularly spotted holding clandestine meetings
around Dublin. Another powerful figure in the background who
approved of the new arrangement was Kelly's former protégé, Gerry
'the Monk' Hutch. Those who didn't like the new regime were either
pushed aside or given no option but to co-operate. In Gangland, loyalty
is dictated by profit, not personality.

In the immediate aftermath of the murder there was speculation that
Dessie O'Hare and Dutchie Holland might avenge their former benefactor. But the cruel truth was that Marlo's demise had been a necessary
sacrifice to protect the interests of the wider gangland community.
Dutchie was a pragmatist and moved to England after Hyland's murder,
where he 'worked' as a hit man for hire. In May 2007 he was charged
with conspiring to commit a kidnapping and was subsequently jailed
for eight years. The 70-year-old contract killer defied the laws of the
gangland jungle in 2009, when he died peacefully in his sleep in Parkhurst
Prison.

O'Hare, who claimed to have found God, had no moral qualms about
joining forces with his friend's killer. After all, the Border Fox had
plenty of experience when it came to butchering former comrades.
Dessie O'Hare was also a close associate of Eamon Kelly. The INLA

and Kelly's other protégé, Declan 'Whacker' Duffy, were equally comfortable with the new order.

In August 2007 evidence of Dunne's working relationship with the
INLA was discovered by the anti-terrorist Special Detective Unit
(SDU). Following a tip-off, the SDU and ERU raided a house in Cush-
lawn Drive, Tallaght. Inside they found Dunne and Declan Duffy in the
process of torturing a drug-dealer. Dunne, Duffy and seven other hoods
were arrested and questioned, but they were never charged. Their victim was too terrified to make a complaint against them. Duffy and the
INLA had also become embroiled in the Crumlin/Drimnagh feud,
which resulted in a further escalation of the violence. Garda intelligence
learned that Duffy had accepted a €100,000 contract to murder 'Fat'
Freddie Thompson.

The Don stayed out of the feud and instead completely restructured
his gang's drug-trafficking business. This was soon reflected in a quanti-
tative reduction in seizures. From the start of his reign Eamon Dunne
ruled with an iron fist. His policy was to deal swiftly and severely with
any potential challengers. As a result he became one of the most blood-
soaked Godfathers in the history of organized crime in Ireland.

The first gangster to make the mistake of moving against Eamon Dunne
was John Daly, a former key member of Marlo's gang. Daly was a volatile, loud-mouthed bully, who was also a psychotic killer. In May 2007,
he became a household name when he phoned the *Liveline* radio programme to attack this writer. He caused upheaval throughout the prison
system when it was discovered that he'd contacted the show on a mobile
phone from his prison cell in Portlaoise. As a result of the public furore
there was a universal clamp-down on phones in prisons, which seriously
disrupted the operations of gangsters like John Gilligan.

Daly spent the remaining four months of his sentence for armed robbery in isolation in Cork Prison. As his release date in August 2007
approached, Daly began making plans for his freedom. He had already
contacted a number of Hyland's associates, looking for money that he
said the Godfather had promised him upon his release. When he was
ignored, Daly began issuing death threats.

As soon as he arrived back in Finglas, he began to throw his weight
around. The Gardaí warned him that there were at least three or more

contracts out on his head. He told them to 'fuck off'. Daly also made it known that he would not be bending the knee for anyone, and especially not the Don. He was going to set up his own gang and made no secret of the fact that he intended to shoot Dunne. But Daly was too arrogant to realize that there was a new order in the gangland jungle where he was once a feared predator. He was also isolated as many of his equally psychotic pals had already died. In underworld folklore it was claimed that Daly and his 'Filthy Fifty' gang cronies had been the subject of a gypsy's curse, after they'd murdered a young man some years earlier: two committed suicide, two others died of natural causes, another accidentally blew his head off; and others were murdered.

In the early hours of 22 October 2007, Daly became the thirteenth victim of the gang to fall under the 'curse'. He was getting out of a taxi at his home in Finglas when a lone gunman shot him five times, at close range. Eamon Dunne was a firm believer in striking first. The murder of Daly served to reinforce the Don's fearsome reputation.

But ten days later, Dunne ran into trouble. He was one of seven men arrested as they were about to ambush a security van containing almost €1 million in cash in Celbridge, County Kildare. A major Garda undercover operation had been put in place when they learned of the plot. Dunne was charged two days later with conspiracy to commit robbery and was remanded in custody. Strenuous objections to bail meant that he spent Christmas and the New Year in prison. On 15 January 2008, he was finally granted bail. The Don was confident that he was going to beat the rap. He commenced High Court proceedings to have the charges against him thrown out, on the grounds that his detention was unlawful.

Dunne also fought for his continued dominance of Gangland. On 17 July 2008, Finglas criminal 34-year-old Trevor Walsh, a close friend of John Daly, was released from prison. The Don saw Walsh as another potential threat. He decided to strike before the former prisoner had a chance to take revenge for Daly's murder. On the night of Walsh's release a gunman shot him four times as he walked home from the pub at Kippure Park in Finglas. A month later, on 23 August, two gunmen walked into the Jolly Toper pub in Finglas, where drug-dealer Paul 'Farmer' Martin was drinking with mourners after a funeral. Thirty-nine-year-old Martin was a convicted armed robber who was also suspected of the gangland murder of taxi driver James 'Gonty' Dillon in 1999. Farmer was a close friend of both Marlo Hyland and John Daly, and had openly challenged the Don's authority when he refused to stop selling drugs on Dunne's patch. Dunne also feared that Martin was plotting to have him murdered. When Farmer spotted the gunmen, he made a dash for the door. One of them opened fire, hitting him in the back. As he lay on the ground, the same gunman finished Martin off, with four more shots in the head.

Meanwhile the alliance between Michael Cronin and Dunne hadn't lasted very long. A bitter dispute flared between the two drug-dealers and they vowed to kill each other. Cronin escaped two gun attacks in 2008 and then went looking for the Don, armed with a grenade. But he threw the bomb away when he spotted a Garda surveillance team. The Don then hired Christy Gilroy, a 35-year-old drug addict from the inner-city, to sort out his difficulties with Cronin. Gilroy, who was facing armed robbery charges, had been hiring himself out as a contract killer. The drug addict had been buying drugs from Cronin and had no difficulty luring him into a trap.

On 7 January 2009, Gilroy arranged to meet Cronin and his associate James Maloney in Summerhill, in Dublin's north inner-city. Minutes after getting into the back seat of Cronin's car, Gilroy shot each man twice in the back of the head. The drug addict had just added two more murders to the Don's mounting death toll. As Gilroy fled the scene he panicked, leaving vital evidence behind including the murder weapon, a jacket and a mobile phone. Forensic tests later showed that the gun had also been used in the attempted murder of another Finglas hood, Michael Murray, in the summer of 2008. Murray had accepted a contract from John Daly's associates to assassinate Dunne, but the Don hired Gilroy to strike first. However, Gilroy wasn't successful on that occasion – Murray was wounded in the shoulder and recovered.

Immediately after the double murder, Dunne arranged for Gilroy to go to Puerto Banus, Spain, where he joined Kinahan sidekick Gary Hutch. Gilroy was admitted to a drug treatment clinic in Marbella, which was paid for by the Don.

Less than two weeks later, Dunne's paranoia led to even more bloodshed. This time the victim was one of his closest friends, Finglas criminal Graham McNally. Dunne lured McNally into a trap in a cul-de-sac at

Coldwinters, off the Old Ashbourne Road in Finglas, on 20 January. The thug, who had just returned from a holiday in Thailand, had no reason to suspect anything was wrong. But the Don feared that McNally was secretly plotting against him. A few days after the Cronin and Maloney murders, Gardaí had intercepted two associates of Farmer Martin in Finglas. It was believed that they were on their way to shoot Dunne. The Don suspected that McNally was also in on the plot. As a result, he shot McNally six times in the face and head. Clinical, merciless executions were the hallmarks of Dunne's bloodlust.

The day after the McNally hit this writer made contact with Dunne by phone. The bloodthirsty crime lord was furious about the ongoing media coverage of his activities and at my intrusion into his privacy and grief. When I put questions to him about McNally's murder, he was typically defensive and evasive. He denied any involvement and refused to make any comment at all about the Cronin/Maloney hits.

'I feel that I am now a target over all of this. I feel unsafe. I don't know anything about anyone getting clipped [shot],' Dunne moaned. When asked if he was aware that his name had been linked to the various murders, Dunne angrily replied: 'I didn't murder anyone. What do you mean my name is coming up everywhere as a suspect? I am aware that I am hurt and upset over my friend being killed. I think it is very insensitive of you to be ringing me today after my friend has been killed.

'I am fearful for myself and my family. I don't want my friends or his [McNally's] family to think that I had something to do with it. No one has come to me and said to my face: "I am accusing you." I didn't clip anyone. I did not murder my friend Mr McNally. He was a good personal friend of mine. How did you get my number and where did you get all the information about me?' Dunne ranted down the phone. I explained that I couldn't reveal my sources lest they suffer the same fate as Cronin, Maloney, McNally and all the others.

Dunne was slightly more talkative in relation to the incident involving Farmer Martin's associates. 'I heard that an attempt was supposed to have been made. One guy was released after being caught in a car with a loaded shotgun and the other one was not detained. The police didn't come to me and say there was a threat on my life. I heard McNally was a target as well and the police didn't inform him and he wound up dead. I don't know who shot him. You would know more than I would. Do me a favour and leave me alone for the next few days while I grieve for my friend.'

Dunne agreed to a face-to-face meeting with this writer but he never turned up. A few days later, he went to the courts seeking an injunction to stop the Gardaí leaking stories about him to the media. Dunne, who had a keen interest in studying the law, claimed that there was a conspiracy between the press and the police to damage his 'safety and integrity'. Meanwhile the murders continued.

In February 2009, Christy Gilroy discharged himself from the Spanish detox clinic. Unfortunately for Gilroy, the Don had become increasingly concerned that the hit man would spill the beans if the Gardaí got their hands on him. At the same time detectives had been making frantic efforts to encourage Gilroy to give himself up. His survival depended on who got to him first.

Gilroy was picked up from the clinic by two associates of the Don, who were living in the south of Spain. He was never seen again. Gardaí later received reliable intelligence that Dunne hired a hit man from Ballyfermot called Eric 'Lucky' Wilson to carry out the murder and ensure the body was never found. The 26-year-old was a contract killer who had been hiding in Spain since 2005. He'd skipped bail after he was charged with possession of a cache of firearms, including an AK47 rifle.

Lucky Wilson was also suspected of doing hits on behalf of Marlo Hyland and David Lindsay, the Penguin's former protégé. In 2005 Lindsay had paid Wilson to murder 22-year-old Martin Kenny in Ballyfermot. Kenny was a cousin of Mark 'the Guinea Pig' Desmond. Lucky had also whacked drug-dealer Paul Reay in 2006 for Marlo Hyland. Then in 2008, Wilson killed Paddy Doyle in Spain for the Kinahan syndicate. That was followed in July of the same year with the double execution of his former client, David Lindsay and an associate, Alan Napper. The men were lured to a house in Rostrevor, County Down where they were shot dead. Their bodies were rumoured to have been cut up with a chainsaw. The double murder was ordered by Lindsay's former business partner, Michael 'Micka' Kelly, another dangerous drug-trafficker nicknamed 'the Panda'. Like the Don, this 28-year-old from Kilbarrack, North Dublin, had emerged as a bloodthirsty killer. As well as the deaths of Lindsay and Napper, Kelly organized five other murders. In 2010 his hit man, Wilson, was suspected of causing the disappearance of the Panda's associate Alan Campbell. But both Wilson and Kelly's luck ran out. During a row over a woman in a Spanish bar, Wilson shot dead English gangster Daniel Smith. In 2011 he was jailed for 23 years. And Kelly was shot dead in North Dublin on 15 September 2011.

A month after the disappearance of Christy Gilroy, the Don ordered another assassination. This time Dunne contracted an associate of Wilson's to try to whack Michael Murray again. On 2 March 2009, Murray was shot three times in the head. Then on 12 June, another threat to Dunne's life was erased. The body of 34-year-old criminal, Paul 'Scar Face' Smyth, was found lying in a ditch near Balbriggan in North County Dublin. He had been clinically executed with a bullet in the head. Smyth, who had been a member of Hyland's gang, was Paul 'Farmer' Martin's brother-in-law. He had been approached by associates of both Martin and John Daly to kill the Don, following Murray's death.

Smyth's death brought the number of killings Dunne had either ordered or carried out himself to a total of six in six months. Since 2005, the body count connected with him had reached 12. No criminal in the history of organized crime in Ireland had been personally linked to so many murders. The Don's efforts to control Gangland were measured in blood. Dunne's paranoia and suspicion made everyone around him extremely nervous.

In the wake of the Cronin and Maloney murders, the Organised Crime Unit (OCU) set up a major investigation to target Eamon Dunne in February 2009, codenamed 'Operation Hammer'. It used Operation Oak as a template and officers began putting serious pressure on Dunne and his associates. He was regularly followed, stopped and searched. Dunne and his cronies were arrested and questioned about the various murders and other crimes. The Don objected to the attention and began photographing and filming his tormentors, in a bid to intimidate them. The Criminal Assets Bureau also launched an in-depth trawl of Dunne's finances. In the first eight months of 2009, Operation Hammer resulted in the seizure of over €1.5 million worth of drugs belonging to the Don's syndicate. Fifteen members of the gang were also arrested and charged with serious drug offences. Dunne was beginning to find himself under the same kind of pressure that Marlo had experienced. But it didn't stop his killing spree.

On 11 October 2009, David Thomas died instantly when he was shot twice in the head as he stood smoking outside the Drake Inn pub in Finglas. Gardaí believed that the Don organized the murder as a special favour to a friend. Thomas hadn't been involved in serious crime since he was acquitted of killing a man during a row in another Finglas pub in 2001. But he couldn't avoid the attentions of the most dangerous thug in gangland.

In January 2010, Dunne organized his fifteenth gangland murder in five years. Traveller John Paul Joyce was a major drug-dealer and armed robber who had become involved with the Don's gang. He was released from prison just before Christmas 2009, after doing time for a savage assault in which his victim had been left brain-damaged. Before he was jailed, Joyce had been given the job of disposing of the weapon used to murder Farmer Martin. Instead, Joyce decided to hand it over to the police, in the hope of getting a lighter sentence for the assault charge. But the Don discovered his treachery when detectives showed the weapon to two members of his gang who were questioned about the shootings. Joyce had signed his death warrant.

The drug-dealer was last seen alive when he went to meet an associate of Dunne's, on 7 January 2010. Two days later, Joyce's body was discovered in a ditch near Dublin Airport. Like many of the Don's other victims, the traveller had been dispatched with a bullet in the head. A year earlier, Joyce's younger brother Tommy had also been executed, in a separate gangland feud.

Over the following weeks Eamon Dunne grew even more unpredictable and paranoid. His murder rate had made him Public Enemy Number One. The police continued to pile on the pressure and Dunne soon had other problems.

The spectacular collapse of the Irish economy had not been good for organized crime. Just like in the legitimate business world, the balance sheets of the drug lords were in decline. Gangsters who had invested their ill-gotten-gains in the property markets were also in negative equity. The demand for cocaine had dropped dramatically and there was a shift in the drug market to heroin and home-grown marijuana. At the same time Head Shops were opening in practically every major town in Ireland, selling dangerous, legal highs. The economic downturn had a colossal effect on the underworld.

Criminals began fighting among themselves over unpaid debts, and looked for new business opportunities. Eamon Dunne decided to make up his shortfall by collecting drug debts for other hoods and targeting the Head Shops for protection money. The dangerous thug made the fatal mistake of trying to extort large amounts of cash from a number of veteran villains who were business partners of Christy Kinahan. One major player received a demand for €150,000 from Dunne and was told that the INLA would deal with him if he failed to pay up. The criminal asked for a meeting with the INLA leadership in Belfast to discuss the issue. When he arrived, he was surprised to discover that Dunne was also there. The terrorists told him that the Don had the full support of the organization behind him. The shaken criminal returned to Dublin and met a number of other mobsters to discuss the problem. It was agreed that the Don had become a major liability. Decisive action would have to be taken. In Spain, Christy Kinahan and his associates were also consulted and an agreement was reached. The Don was living on borrowed time.

To make matters worse, Dunne – like Marlo Hyland – had developed a serious cocaine habit which made him even more dangerous and unpredictable. It was known that he was snorting 5g of the drug every day. The coke-fuelled haze accentuated his sex drive, and his aggression. His former associates claimed that he was as addicted to sex as he was violence. Whenever he was stopped and searched, Dunne always had a few Viagra pills in his pocket. The Don had a string of dangerous liaisons with the girlfriends and wives of his associates and other hoods. He was becoming so detached from reality that he didn't seem to care who he was upsetting. It was becoming clear that Dunne had a death wish.

Dunne openly bragged about his various conquests and kept explicit pictures of one gangster's moll on his mobile phone. Another affair that he was rumoured to have had was with a former girlfriend of convicted killer Craig White. White was furious and demanded that his associates on the outside get rid of Dunne. His cronies, in the inner-city gang aligned to Kinahan, assured him that plans for Dunne's demise were already in place. It was now only a matter of when, and not if, the Don would meet the Grim Reaper.

In a macabre twist to the story, it has since been revealed that the malevolent mobster knew that his time was running out. Late in 2009 Dunne organized his own Mafia-style funeral. He booked an undertaker and ordered an aluminium casket from the US, which arrived in Ireland in February 2010. Dunne also picked his own grave, in Dardistown Cemetery, North Dublin. He wanted to be buried head-to-head with his friend and fellow killer Paddy Doyle, who'd been buried in Dardistown after he was murdered in Spain in 2008. Dunne left strict instructions that he was to be laid out in the casket in his parents' home and specified his clothes. He even dictated the dress code for his henchmen and friends — black ties, shirts and suits. Dunne asked that they take turns carrying his casket to the funeral in the local church.

Even in death, the hoodlum seemed afraid of attack or media exposure. His instructed his associates to stand guard over his corpse — to prevent anyone defacing it. Mobile phones were to be banned while the casket was open; to prevent anyone taking a picture and selling it to the newspapers. Dunne even left cash for the post-funeral booze-up in the Swiss Cottage pub, North Dublin.

Detectives believe the actual murder plot was hatched sometime in February 2010. It is known that a number of criminal groups came together, under the direction of Christy Kinahan and his shadowy gangland council. Members of the Dapper Don's gang from the north inner-city got the job of carrying out the shooting. Former members of Marlo Hyland's gang and some of Dunne's associates were also in on the plot. Gangland's hierarchy knew that it would have to be a carefully planned attack, with no room for mistakes. Dunne had a finely honed instinct for other predators, and if he survived, he would unleash hell on his enemies.

On Friday 23 April 2010, Gardaí in Dublin received intelligence that two senior members of Kinahan's mob were in the process of planning a hit in North Dublin. From phone taps, detectives knew that the two thugs had been watching a target for a number of days. But they didn't know the identity of the victim, the time or the location for the proposed assassination. The police hear of planned murder attempts practically every day; most never take place — but this hit was different.

That evening Eamon Dunne attended the fortieth birthday of his friend John Fairbrother in the Faussagh House pub in Cabra. The Don brought his 17-year-old daughter Amy to the party and seemed to be in good spirits. Several of his friends and associates were also there. As usual he was being watched over by two of his henchmen, who acted as bodyguards.

Around 9.30 p.m. a red Volkswagen Passat arrived in the pub car park. Three armed men got out, while a fourth remained behind the wheel. One man stayed outside, while the other two ran into the pub. A number of Dunne's associates made a run for it when they saw the gunmen. One of the hit men made straight for the table where the Don was sitting with his back to the door. The killer fired two rounds directly into the Godfather's face. When Dunne fell to the floor, his executioner fired one more round into his head. The most blood-stained gangster in Ireland was dead. Like Marlo Hyland, Dunne's relatively short life had also been 'nasty, brutish and short'.

As the hit team ran to their getaway car there was panic in the pub. One of the Don's close associates, Mark Buckley, ran from the pub in a state of shock, shouting: 'They got Eamon; they shot Eamon.' The murder was clinical and professional – just like the many assassinations organized by the victim.

Later that night, the prime suspect spoke on his mobile phone to Daniel Kinahan. The Dapper Don's son warned the henchman to assume the call was being tapped by the Gardaí and to say nothing. The hit man, who had recently become a father, left Dublin with his family and stayed down in the country for the rest of the weekend. A week later, he flew to Spain and met the Kinahans in Marbella. A few days later the police in Spain, Belgium, England and Ireland made their move on the Kinahan organization as part of Operation Shovel.

Despite the outpouring of grief and anger from the large number of criminals who turned up, in black, for the Don's funeral, there was no retribution. Dunne's associates, including his partner in the 'security business', Brian O'Reilly, conducted their own investigation to find out who exactly had ordered the hit and then carried it out. Their enquiries ended when two gunmen walked into O'Reilly's local pub in Bettystown, County Meath, and tried to kill him in August 2010. O'Reilly survived the attack, recovered from his injuries – and dropped the investigation.

Elsewhere the murder madness continued. There were another 12 gangland executions in 2010, which brought the underworld death toll for the year to 20. Among the victims were two brothers, Paul and Kenneth Corbally, from Ballyfermot who were gunned down in an attack in June 2010. They had been involved in another ongoing feud, this time with their former partner-in-crime, Derek 'Dee Dee' O'Driscoll. The two sides had declared war after an associate of the Corballys, Manchester criminal Jason Martin, was stabbed to death during a melee between both sides in September 2009.

Four months after the double murder another associate of the Corballys, Robert Ryle, was also whacked. Then in November, the names of two more completely innocent young men were added to the list of the dead. Cousins, 20-year-old Glen Murphy and 23-year-old Mark Noonan, were ambushed by two gunmen at a petrol station in Finglas, North Dublin. They were murdered in a case of mistaken identity, by a hit team involved in a separate gang war in Coolock.

As Ireland nears the end of the first year of the fifth decade of organized crime there is only one certainty – Gangland is here to stay. The underworld and its population have come a long way since a quasi-republican mob called Saor Eire carried out the first professional armed robberies in the State. The first Godfather, Christy 'Bronco' Dunne, who is now in his seventies, must find it hard to recognize the underworld that has evolved since he and his siblings first blazed the trail for others to follow.

Today serious crime and violence have become embedded in Irish culture. All types of illegal narcotics are easily available, in every town and village in the country and gangs have sprung up to control and prosper from the trade.

Since the start of the Noughties, gangland murders have become an almost acceptable reality in our cities and major towns. And as the drug trade continues to flourish throughout Ireland, the violence is guaranteed to continue. The spectre of the hit man now stalks many Irish streets where once there was no problem with serious crime. Adding to the toxic mix are former Provos and the dissident republican gangs, like the INLA and Real IRA. These criminal mobs have become part of the fabric of Gangland since the 1970s and 1980s. The terrorists are no longer distinguishable from what would once have been described as 'crime-ordinary' criminals. The cycle of organized crime is guaranteed to continue.

Ireland has certainly taken a trip down a very different road to the 'straight road' Eamon De Valera once referred to, when he celebrated the Jubilee of the birth of the fledgling Republic. When the nation gathers again to commemorate the centenary of that great event, Gangland will be preparing for its own Jubilee.

Acknowledgements

As always my deepest thanks and gratitude go to the many people whose trust and assistance made this book possible. *Badfellas* is the toughest and largest book I have yet written. It covers such a vast area of time and events, from research built up over 24 years, that it would be impossible to thank all those who have generously helped me along the way. Others, from both sides of Gangland's borders, would prefer to remain anonymous – for obvious reasons. They all know who they are.

Badfellas was inspired by a TV documentary series, *Bad Fellas*, which I wrote and narrated for RTÉ in 2009. I would like to express my deepest gratitude to all those who so kindly, and bravely, told their stories and shared their knowledge and expertise. Some of their contributions are also used in the book to explain the complex history of organized crime.

My deepest thanks go to the series' executive producer at Animo Productions, Adrian Lynch, the producer Mairead Whelan and the series producer/director, Emmy award-winner Gerry Gregg. I also had the honour of working with Mairead and Gerry on the TV series *Dirty Money*, which won a TV *Now* Award for best documentary series in 2008. I would also like to thank former Garda Commissioner Pat Byrne, the series consultant, who helped to pull this hugely complex story together.

My thanks and sincerest best wishes to my former colleagues at the now defunct *Irish News of the World*, who lost their jobs through no fault of their own, because of the criminal activity of others. It was a pleasure to have worked with them during the 16 months I was part of their team.

My thanks also go to my friend and colleague Padraig O'Reilly, who has worked closely with me for the past 24 years. Many of the pictures contained in *Badfellas* were the result of his courageous work. The picture editor for this book, Jon Lee, burned the candle well into the night for many nights as he put together a huge library of pictures. He did a brilliant job.

In particular my thanks as always to my extremely talented, and patient, editor Aoife Barrett of Barrett Editing, who has worked with me on this and three of my most recent books. Aoife's expertise and long hours of hard work helped this book to happen. My thanks to all the staff at my new publisher, Penguin, and to Michael McLoughlin, who insisted I still had another book to write when I thought I didn't. And of course my deepest gratitude to libel expert Kieran Kelly – 'the Consigliere' – of Fanning Kelly and Company for his work on *Badfellas* and most of my other books.

And lastly, as always, my love and gratitude to my long-suffering wife and children, Anne, Jake and Irena, for their endless affection, support and patience.